Praise for Global Jihad and America

In the plethora of studies of Muslim militancy around the world, Professor Taj Hashmi's masterly work stands out. While seeking to deal with "the growing menace of Islamist insurgency," it takes the problematic beyond the binary division of Islamophobia, on one hand, and phobia of the West, on the other. It contextualizes both and questions their given images that are often taken for granted in current discourse. Hashmi takes us back deep into history in order to understand the present objectively and precisely. It is a major departure from all current theories in its depth and originality.

Harbans Mukhia
Former Rector and Professor of History
Jawaharlal Nehru University (JNU), New Delhi

Taj Hashmi's profoundly erudite new book helps to clear the water so callously muddied by Huntington's theory of "the clash of civilizations." His arguments that the inability of the U.S. and its Western allies to understand the complexities and the dynamics of conflict, and consequently its flawed response to so-called "global jihad" has actually made the world much more vulnerable and prone to violence. In a tightly knit well-argued treatise Hashmi concludes that all societies—Islamic and non-Islamic, developed and developing, north or south—faced intensified risks of violence. His conclusion is chilling but cannot be ignored: state-sponsored terrorism and proxy wars—not terrorism by *non-state actors*—pose the biggest threat to the Third World; non-state terrorists pose the biggest security challenge to America. This is a must read for anyone interested in understanding the security threats in the 21st century.

Gowher Rizvi
Professor Emeritus
University of Virginia

A must read, this learned and provocative study argues persuasively that intra-Muslim conflict rather than Muslim–West confrontation will characterize the future. Hashmi's contrast of the tolerant Quran's embrace of all believers with the Mullahs' pernicious interpretation of Shariah to demonize non-Muslims is profoundly illuminating but also deeply disturbing.

Charles B. Salmon, Jr
Ambassador (ret.)
Foreign Policy Advisor
Asia-Pacific Center for Security Studies (APCSS)
Honolulu, Hawaii

This is a most timely contribution by one of the ablest scholars and analysts of Islamic–Western interactions and relationships. He reminds us that before the cataclysmal 9/11 terrorist attacks, the Islamic and Western civilizations were allied against Soviet Communism. Equally, they were at no point in time discrete homogenous cultural–political entities free from serious challenges and fissures within themselves. Taj Hashmi pleads for serious introspection within and dialogue between the two civilizations in search of principles that can promote peace and harmony worldwide.

Ishtiaq Ahmed
Professor Emeritus
Stockholm University

Taj Hashmi's book penetrates the commonly espoused stereotypes and Cassandra-like warnings surrounding America's War on Terror. On important issues he offers insightful perspectives and nuances rarely evident in popular commentary. He discredits the assumption that the driving factor of future violence will be sectarian difference, positing rather that state failures to foster good governance, justice, and human dignity will be its real accelerants. In this elaboration he importantly provides the key to developing effective policy responses.

Colonel David Shanahan (ret.)
US Army
Honolulu, Hawaii

Global Jihad and America

Global Jihad and America

*The Hundred-Year War Beyond
Iraq and Afghanistan*

Taj Hashmi

SAGE   www.sagepublications.com
Los Angeles • London • New Delhi • Singapore • Washington DC

First published in 2014 by

SAGE Publications India Pvt Ltd
B1/I-1 Mohan Cooperative Industrial Area
Mathura Road, New Delhi 110 044, India
www.sagepub.in

SAGE Publications Inc
2455 Teller Road
Thousand Oaks, California 91320, USA

SAGE Publications Ltd
1 Oliver's Yard, 55 City Road
London EC1Y 1SP, United Kingdom

SAGE Publications Asia-Pacific Pte Ltd
3 Church Street
#10-04 Samsung Hub
Singapore 049483

Published by Vivek Mehra for SAGE Publications India Pvt Ltd, Typeset in 10/13 Berkeley by SwaRadha Typesetting, New Delhi, and printed at De-Unique, New Delhi.

Library of Congress Cataloging-in-Publication Data

Hashmi, Taj ul-Islam, 1948–
    Global jihad and America : the hundred-year war beyond Iraq and Afghanistan/
Taj Hashmi.
        p. cm.
    Includes bibliographical references and index.
    1. Terrorism—United States—Prevention. 2. War on Terrorism, 2001–2009.
    3. Islamic Countries—Relations—Western countries. 4. Islamic fundamentalism.
    I. Title.
        HV6432.H384   363.3250973—dc23   2014   2014004948

ISBN: 978-81-321-1378-2 (HB)

The SAGE Team: Rudra Narayan, Shreya Chakraborti, Nand Kumar Jha, and
                Rajinder Kaur

To the victims of all unjust wars and terrorism.
They inspired me the most to speak the truth,
uphold justice, and love peace.

Thank you for choosing a SAGE product! If you have any comment, observation or feedback, I would like to personally hear from you. Please write to me at <u>contactceo@sagepub.in</u>

—Vivek Mehra, Managing Director and CEO,
SAGE Publications India Pvt. Ltd, New Delhi

Bulk Sales

SAGE India offers special discounts for purchase of books in bulk. We also make available special imprints and excerpts from our books on demand.

For orders and enquiries, write to us at

Marketing Department
SAGE Publications India Pvt. Ltd
B1/I-1, Mohan Cooperative Industrial Area
Mathura Road, Post Bag 7
New Delhi 110044, India
E-mail us at <u>marketing@sagepub.in</u>

Get to know more about SAGE, be invited to SAGE events, get on our mailing list. Write today to <u>marketing@sagepub.in</u>

This book is also available as an e-book.

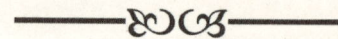

Contents

Contents

Preface and Acknowledgments

No protracted war can fail to endanger the freedom of a democratic country.... If it leads not to despotism by sudden violence, it prepares men for it more gently by their habits. All those who seek to destroy the liberties of a democratic nation ought to know that war is the surest and the shortest means to accomplish it.

Alexis de Tocqueville (*Democracy in America*, 1835)

Since Islam and modern South Asian history and politics—subaltern peasants, working classes, and women—have been the core areas of my research and teaching, I contemplated writing a book on Islamic resurgence and militancy in Pakistan and Bangladesh long before September 2001. However, 9/11 has changed the world; it also has enhanced my interest in the syndrome called Militant Islam. This study reflects the combination of my theoretical and practical knowledge of Islam, Islamism, Islamist militancy, and American Homeland Security issues in relations to the perceived/trumped up Islamist threat to America. My first exposure to the Hawaii-based Asia–Pacific Center for Security Studies (APCSS), in Honolulu, a training academy for military and civil officials in the Asia–Pacific region, 2002, added a new dimension to my approach and understanding of terrorism. I am forever grateful to the APCSS for inviting me to a conference on Religion and Security in South Asia.

Later, my four-year-long stint at the APCSS as a professor of Security Studies (2007–2011) substantially enhanced my understanding of Islamist resurgence and terrorism in global perspective. I benefited most from my interaction with military, police, and diplomat trainees/fellows from 40-odd countries at the APCSS. They enriched my understanding of Islamism, terrorism, and homeland security from their firsthand experience in counterterrorism (CT) and counter-insurgency (COIN) operations, from Australia to Afghanistan and Iraq; Pakistan to Papua New Guinea; and

Fiji, Indonesia, Marshal Islands to Vanuatu. I also learned the intricacies and dynamics of the American Homeland Security by interacting with my colleagues, civilians, and military professors at the APCSS.

However, after I had started working on the unique characteristics of political Islam in Pakistan and Bangladesh in 2009, our younger daughter, Sabrina, asked me while we were on a family holiday in scenic Kawai: "Abbu, why don't you write something focusing on the reasons we have to take off our shoes before boarding a plane?" She wanted me to write something, which not only scholars of international relations and world history would like to read but also business graduates (like herself) would find interesting. Hence, the shift in the approach and content of the book, which now focuses on the loaded concept of global jihad and its ramifications on America's foreign and domestic policies, and vice versa. I have written this book not only for scholars, security practitioners, and policymakers in the West, but also for students, laymen, and the average peace-loving people in the West and the East. I believe Americans, Europeans, Asians, and Muslims will benefit most from this work. It has many new ideas and information for some people, and conversely, some new ideas and information for most people across the board.

Before I explain what this book is all about and why I have written this, I forewarn my readers that this is not another addition to the corpus of the ever-growing literature on global jihad versus War on Terror. I find both the concepts grossly hackneyed, politically motivated, and, hence, prejudicial. The cataclysmic 9/11 unearthed some of the base human instincts, such as cruelty, hate, and hypocrisy, and above all, our proclivity to lie and profligate. I think hundreds of post-9/11 books, essays, and writing in the print and electronic media are mischievously counterproductive, divisive, and harmful to global peace and order. Unfortunately, many of such writers and analysts—crypto-Islamophobes and pseudo-scholars—have already established themselves as Islam and terrorism experts in the West. Ominously, Western policymakers frequently take their advice and act accordingly to counter terrorism through preemptive attacks, and unauthorized invasions of countries. They give the impression that as if terrorism, particularly Islamic terrorism, is the biggest threat to Western civilization!

Unfortunately, the Muslim world is also full of prejudiced, politically motivated, and fanatically anti-American/anti-Western clerics, writers, and analysts. They not only promote and believe in absurd conspiracy theories—such as Jews were behind 9/11 attacks or 9/11 was an insider's job—but they also portray the West as evil, programmed to destroy Islam, and regain their lost colonies in the Muslim world. Many Islamists are out and out fascist in their outlook. They believe and promote the concept of global jihad or total war against all non-Muslims, either to forcibly convert them into Muslims or perform *qital* or mass slaughter of non-Muslims and deviant Muslims. Interestingly, there has been a convergence of opinion between Islam-bashers in the West and Islamists in the East. Both of them believe that Islamists are engaged in a global jihad and the Muslim–West conflict is as inevitable and necessary as the sunrise each morning.

This study raises the question if the ongoing Islam–West conflict has been the main conflict in the wake of the Cold War, and if the world is going through a conflict of cultures, between the Western and Islamic civilizations. If the Muslim world is an amorphous homogeneous entity, ever united, capable, and willing to challenge American and Western interests is another important question. If Islamist parties, such as the Muslim Brotherhood, Ennehda, and Jamaat-i-Islami, can democratize or they are fascistic in accordance with the theory of Islamofascism is an important area of my investigation. Now many scholars, including me, are asking if it is wise to promote Islamist parties only because they want to come to power through elections.

I have critiqued the following premises: (a) if postcolonial Islamist terror and anarchy are legacies of European colonial rule, (b) if the world has already entered the post-terrorist phase of history, whilst terrorism is irrelevant; (c) if terrorism was/is never an existential threat to America or any Western nation; (d) if Islam is a religion of peace and not responsible for Islamist anarchy and terror; (e) if the globalization process has created an uneven playing field for Western and Muslim nations, and thus, somehow responsible for the surge in Islamist militancy; (f) if the American Military-Industrial Complex and the Israel lobby are responsible for the Muslim–West cleavage; (g) if America is an empire and its imperialistic behavior are the biggest threat to world peace; (h) if Islamists are playing the second fiddle to Russia, China, and other contenders in the age-old conflicts of hegemony between America and others.

Before I acknowledge the debt of my friends and colleagues, I must thank my wonderful daughters. Our elder daughter, Shakila, and younger daughter, Sabrina, played an important role in the formulation of some of the core ideas and arguments of this work. I am thankful to them for their constant encouragement and curiosity in the progress and publicity of this work. I thank their equally wonderful mother, my wife, Neelufar. She not only inspired me to work harder but also spared me from almost all household chores during the last three and a half years. Our son-in-law Ralf Rank has always been supportive of my work. I cannot thank them more for making this work possible.

Last but not least, I cannot thank my parents more for inspiring me most. My late father exposed me to liberal Sufi Islam, which promotes tolerance and peaceful coexistence of Muslims and non-Muslims. I learned from him what willpower, moral courage, and integrity are all about, especially from the anecdotes of my grandfather's life. My mother is my first history teacher. She is the one who exposed me to the worlds of music, Sufism, Ramayana, "Ali Baba and Forty Thieves," British imperialism, Mahatma Gandhi, and Subhash Chandra Bose.

I feel indebted and most gratefully acknowledge all my friends and colleagues for helping me in different ways to write this book, especially Luthfur and Humaira Choudhury, Wali Mondal, Enam Chowdhury, Gowher Rizvi, Mustafa Chowdhury, Hasanath Hussain, Sadrul Amin, Hasan Rahim, Hasan Mahmud, Shams Chowdhury, Theodore Wright, Chin Bannerjee, Rahnuma Ahmed, Farida Majid, Sajjad Hussain, Shah Jahan, Sajjad Karim, Abul Kalam Azad, Barkat-e-Khuda, Col. Aziz Ahmad (ret.), Belal Baaquie, Ahrar Ahmad, Ahmed Kamal, Jawed Helali, Manzur Mannan, Mufakhar Bhai, Rashiduzzaman, Harbans Mukhia, Mumtaz Ahmad, Mumtaz Iqbal, Roger D. Long, David Ludden, Peter Bertocci, Joanna Kirkpatrick, Muniruzzaman Miah, Maj. Gen. Muniruzzaman (ret.), LtG Tahir Qazi (ret.), Brig. Zaheer, Babar, Rashid Malik, Ishtiaq Ahmed, Pervaiz Salahuddin, and Brig. Taha Al Jburi; late Enayetullah Khan, late Hari Sharma, late Joe O'Connell, Syed Kamaluddin (Editor, *weekly* Holiday) and Nurul Kabir (Editor, daily *New Age*).

I am thankful to all my colleagues and friends at the APCSS. I am especially thankful to Robert Wirsing, Ambassador Charlie Salmon, Ambassador Lauren Moriarty, LtG Ed Smith (ret.), Brig. Gen. Jim Hirai (ret.), Col Dave Shanahan (ret.), LTC Butch Finley (ret.), and LTC Michael Mollohan (US Army); Captain Carleton Cramer (ret.), Captain James Campbell (ret.), and CDR Mario DeOliveira (US Navy); Ehsan

Ahrari, Rouben Azizian, David Fouse, Steven Kim, Mimie Byrd, Rollie Lal, Virginia Warson, Elizabeth Davies, Tom Peterman, Bill Wieninger, Justin and Kerry Nankivell, Scott Hauger, Shyam Tekwani, Alex Vuving, and Alfred Oehlers.

Last but not least, I am thankful to Rekha Natarajan, Sugata Ghosh, Rudra Narayan, and Shreya Chakraborti of SAGE Publications for publishing my work. I am also thankful to the anonymous readers of my manuscript for recommending its publication.

No one else but I am solely responsible for the drawbacks, limitations, and inadequacies in this work.

Taj Hashmi

1

Introduction

Why are they killing us? We must have done something wrong to some people somewhere.

A 12-Year-Old American Boy (CNN News, September 11, 2001)

In the past decade, Washington has killed, maimed, dislocated, and made widows and orphans millions of Muslims in six countries, all in the name of the "war on terror." Washington's attacks on the countries constitute naked aggression and impact primarily civilian populations and infrastructure and, thereby, constitute war crimes under law. Nazis were executed precisely for what Washington is doing today.

Paul Craig Roberts (Reagan's Assistant Treasury Secretary, September 30, 2011)

Overview

This study questions the assumption if Islamist terrorism or global jihad poses the biggest threat to modern civilization in the East and West. If the Islamic and Western civilizations being incompatible to each other are destined to be at loggerheads for an indefinite period, that is another area of investigation. The cataclysmic mega terrorist attack on America on 9/11, still today is too overwhelming for us to understand, assess, and even mitigate its psychological effect on the collective psyche of Americans. It costs the U.S. economy at least $3 trillion. While the world is gradually entering the post-terrorist phase of history, America is quite low in the Global Terrorism Index (GTI), yet thanks to America's intrusive and hegemonic foreign policy, America is not going to be ever safe from further mega terrorist attacks in the coming decades.

Although state-sponsored terrorism and proxy wars—not terrorism by non-state actors—pose the biggest threat to the Third World, non-state terrorists pose the biggest security challenge to America. However, as the world is going to see the end of unipolarity, where America has been the only superpower since the end of the Cold War, we simply cannot rule out the possibilities of America getting involved in another world war in the coming decades, not necessarily against the Muslim world. Then again, all is not well between the Muslim and Western worlds. And they might eventually cross swords, not because of their cultural differences, but because of conflicting interests and hegemonies. In short, this study is about foretelling the catastrophic effects of the seemingly inevitable conflicts between America (and its allies) and their adversaries in the Muslim world backed by their non-Muslims patrons in the ongoing Hundred-Year War.

Finally, this study does not suggest that the world has already reached the cul-de-sac of its destiny with no point of return. Both America and the Muslim world can play important roles to avert the catastrophe. Meanwhile, the gap between the need of the poor and greed of the rich and powerful (as Gandhi had put it) is widening. And we know, throughout history sections of the rich and powerful brought disasters to human civilization through catastrophic wars and destructions in the name of peace and justice, religion, and freedom. In this backdrop, the most important question today is: Can we avert another disaster while America and its allies proclaim fighting a "war on terror" and their Muslim adversaries assert defending their honor and religion? This study has used historical methods and facts along with the essentials of international relations, politics, and cultural anthropology to explain the phenomenon called Islam versus the West and its ramification in the coming decades.

Who Wants War and Why: The Beneficiaries of 9/11

As to why the erstwhile allies—Muslims and the West—had turned into adversaries soon after the end of the Cold War is an important aspect of the study. It is also an attempt to answer the following questions: (a) whether 9/11 signaled the climax of the conflict, or it ushered in the beginning of a long-drawn conflict, a global jihad or another Hundred-Year War between the Muslim and Western worlds? (b) whether Islam and the West are homogeneous entities, programmed to hate and fight each other? (c) whether Islamist extremism or Western greed and neocolonial hegemonic designs are at the roots of the conflict? and (d) whether a full-blown warfare, not terrorism, is emerging as the real threat to world peace as the world has already entered the post-terrorist phase of history?

It is time we get a convincing answer to the question: How long will we have to take off our shoes before boarding a plane? Someone should explain as to why we hear about the ongoing war on terror (or extremism), on one side and the clarion call for Muslim resistance or even global jihad, on the other. Very similar to many other subjects—individuals, faiths, philosophies, and events—there are two diametrically opposite viewpoints on global jihad or Islamist terrorism/nihilism, and American foreign policy vis-à-vis Islamist terror and anarchy. While most people in the West think they have been the victims of Islamist terror, the overwhelming majority of Muslims and many non-Muslims in the Afro-Asian and Latin American worlds believe the story is the other way round. They believe that even after the end of European colonial rule, the West has been the aggressor and Muslims and people in the Third World have been the victims of neo-imperialist hegemony and exploitation by the West under the leadership of America.

During the Cold War, America and its allies invaded one country after another, and toppled one regime after another—from Argentina to Chile and Haiti, Syria, Lebanon to Iran, Pakistan and Bangladesh, Vietnam to Laos, Cambodia, Indonesia, and Philippines, to name a few—in the name of containing/fighting communism. They did so in the quest of friendly regimes by toppling pro-Soviet or not-so-friendly regimes to serve Western interests. In the process, they killed several million people in scores of countries. The end of the Cold War did not signal the end of America-led invasions of countries, especially in the Muslim world. Among other excuses, America and its allies justify their post-Cold War invasions of Iraq, Afghanistan, Libya, Mali, and Syria (through Saudi-, Islamist- and al Qaeda-backed mercenaries) and threats of impending attacks on Iran in the name of: (a) fighting terrorism and Islamist extremism; (b) destroying

Weapons of Mass Destruction; and (c) restoring democracy and freedom. The U.S.-led invasion of Iraq in 1991—the First Gulf War—signaled the beginning of America's post-Cold War adventures in the Muslim world. Interestingly, while George Bush Sr. glorified the first Gulf War as the forerunner of his New World Order, Saddam Hussein portrayed the war as the Mother of All Battles. We have reasons to believe that the ongoing Hundred-Year War between the Muslim world and America and its allies had already started in 1948 with the first Arab–Israeli war. The post-Cold War Western invasions of countries such as Iraq, Afghanistan, and Libya, and threats of invasions of Syria and Iran have further widened the scope of the Hundred-Year War, which is likely to go beyond 2048. Like previous mega wars, more countries are likely to join the fray. They include Russia, China, North Korea, Pakistan, Egypt, Turkey, Israel, and various non-state actors such as Hezbollah, al Qaeda, and the Lashkar-e-Taiba (LeT).

This study argues that all apparently Islamist movements do not necessarily espouse the revival of the utopian Caliphate of Sunni or Imamate of Shiite Muslims. The overwhelming majority of the leaders of Islamist organizations and movements from Turkey to Tunisia, Algeria to Egypt, Syria, Pakistan, and Indonesia are the traditional *ulama* or Islamic scholars and clerics, but modern-educated middle-class leaders, mainly followed by middle- and lower-middle classes. They do not strive for Islamic orders where religion and responsibility would mold society and politics under the tutelage of autocratic clergy à la post-revolution Iran, but for set of principles where religiosity combined with human rights (liberty, equality, and fraternity) would usher in a post-Islamist democratic order.[1] In short, this is not only a study of the Muslim–West and intra-Muslim conflicts, but is also about the dynamics of post-Islamism in the post-terrorist phase of our history. Both post-Islamism and post-terrorism are derivatives of the end of the Cold War and the phenomenal changes the world has been going through since the early 1990s in the realms of information technology, global economy and global politics, and diplomacy. 9/11 and the consequential global war on terror have not only intensified terrorism and violence at local, national, and global levels, but they have also led to critical thinking among different sections of the global Muslim community. Post-Islamism and post-terrorism are by-products of this pragmatism. The rise of several democratic regimes in the Muslim world, such as Pakistan, Bangladesh, and Indonesia in the

1990s and 2000s, and Muslims' quest for democracy and human rights in Algeria, Tunisia, Libya, Egypt, Yemen, Bahrain, Iran, and elsewhere in the Muslim world (despite their failures and setbacks) suggest that post-Islamism and post-terrorism are no longer the figments of imagination.

Since it is time to argue if the world has already entered the post-terrorist phase of history, it is no longer justified to single out terrorism as the biggest security threat to modern civilization. It is not terrorism but proxy wars, ethno-national conflicts (actually class wars between the haves and have-nots) in the Muslim world, and state-sponsored terror that have been the main destabilizing factors since the end of the Cold War. As the 2012 Report of GTI reveals: (a) while more terrorist attacks are being recorded, the number of fatalities has declined by 25 percent from its peak in 2007; (b) although the second invasion of Iraq led to the fourfold increase in the number of terrorist attack globally, "North America is the least likely region to suffer from terrorism.... The U.S. has had the largest improvement in GTI score from 2002–2011, dropping from 1st to 41st in the index, as the effects of 9/11 dissipated."[2] The 10 most terror-infested countries are Iraq, Pakistan, Afghanistan, India, Yemen, Somalia, Nigeria, Thailand, Russia, and the Philippines. While the U.S. scores the 41st position, Britain is 28th and France 63th in the GTI in December 2012.[3] In view of the 2012 Global Terrorism Index, America-backed French and British invasions of Mali in January 2013 to protect France and Britain from terrorism in North Africa, we have reasons to believe that Islamic terrorism is an excuse for the enduring theft of Africa's vast store of minerals by the West.[4] Since early 2012, the NATO is said to have funded, armed, and simultaneously fighting al Qaeda from Mali to Syria.[5] America's covert support for al Qaeda in Mali to justify French invasion of the country has been unsettling. America's tacit support for Islamist Jabhat al-Nusra—an anti-Assad al Qaeda affiliate in Syria—is equally distressing.

Some well-known terrorist outfits, such as the Irish Republican Army (IRA), Khmer Rouge, Liberation Tigers of Tamil Eelam (LTTE), Revolutional Armed Forces of Colombia—People's Army (FARC), Euskadi Ta Askatasuna or Basque Homeland and Freedom (Basque separatist movement in Spain) (ETA), Babbar Khalsa International (BKI), and United Liberation Front of Assam (ULFA) in India, Harkat-ul-Jihad-al-Islami–Bangladesh (HUJI–B) and Jamaat-ul-Mujahideen (JMB) in Bangladesh, Abu

Sayyaf Group in Southern Mindanao, Philippines (ASG), PFLP (Popular Front for the Liberation of Palestine and Moro Islamic Liberation Front (MILF) in the Philippines, and Fatah and PFLP in Palestine/Israel, have either fizzled out or have adopted peaceful means to press their demands in the recent years. As the death of FARC leader, Alfonso Cano at the hands of Colombian troops in November 2011 almost brought FARC to the point of extinction, similarly, Osama bin Laden's death will destroy al Qaeda eventually. Now al Qaeda is more of a franchise or a movement than simply a terrorist outfit. We need to understand if the world has already reached the post-terrorist phase of history, and is fast entering into the phase of state-sponsored proxy wars and a more devastating phase of global conflicts or another world war. However, the way America is hyping up its surveillance mechanism, which a former Central Intelligence Agency (CIA)/National Security Agency (NSA) employee, Edward Snowden, exposed in June 2013, it appears that millions of Americans are subject to regular government.

This is not an attempt to understand the worldwide phenomenon of Islamist militancy and terrorism by only appraising Muslim societies and communities. We need to know more than *What Went Wrong?* with Islam as one finds in Bernard Lewis's hackneyed study.[6] It is time that we understand what is wrong with the West and other non-Muslim nations across the world. We cannot ignore the mega businesses/multinationals who control and manipulate not only the global market but also the government machinery in the West and in various countries in the Third World. We need to find out if President Eisenhower rightly singled out the Military–Industrial–Congressional Complex as the single-most important factor behind all major wars initiated by the U.S. in the 20th century. In the backdrop of Eisenhower's assessment of why America goes to war, it is essential to study the disastrous consequences of the America-sponsored wars (and almost equally crippling sanctions) against its adversaries, potential enemies, or even against totally innocent nations, who have never harmed the West nor have the capability to do so, such as Vietnam, Laos, Cambodia, Grenada, Iraq, Afghanistan, and Iran, since the beginning of the Cold War. It is time that we find out the truth about the so-called global war on terror, America's Homeland Security, and last but not least, the American/Western justifications for waging wars to protect freedom and democracy. Since we often hear that Islam has emerged as the biggest threat to America's global interests and security, we need an understanding of the Muslim world, and Islamic, and Islamist movements. Are the Muslims going to play the role of fanatic marauders and killers or are they going to be the perpetual victims of Western invasions in the coming years?

It is time to address if there is a way out of what seems to be an inevitable Muslim–West conflict in the coming decades, which is likely to involve some other countries, such as Russia, China, India, Israel, Iran, Pakistan, and North Korea as well. We may agree with historian Niall Ferguson who feels that behind the façade of democratic transition in the Middle East and China's friendliness toward America, peace and tranquility are not forthcoming in the near future:

> The future I fear is the one that comes after most big financial crises: a period of popular anger, political instability, and cross-border conflict. The youth bubble in the Greater Middle East is at its peak. Resource wars are looming as emerging-market demand outstrips supplies of everything from rare earths to fresh water. And China is already a credible threat to our cybersecurity.[7]

It seems the eyes of the storm will be in and around the Middle East and South Asia. While the 9/11 attacks killed around 3,000 people, since 2001, the American and NATO-sponsored invasions of Afghanistan and Iraq alone have killed around half a million civilians, to protect American lives, properties, and democratic values. In view of this, it is time that someone answers the question raised by a 12-year-old boy moments after the second plane had hit the Twin Towers: "Why are they killing us? We must have done something wrong to some people somewhere?" This taboo of a question haunts many. John Kiriakou—a former CIA agent and the whistleblower on torture of prisoners by America—answered the question: "We kill innocent people, that's why others take up arms."[8]

9/11 has left behind unanswered questions and unresolved issues. Apparently, they were terrorist attacks by ideologically motivated people to draw global attention to their cause to establish the supremacy of Islam as an alternative order to Western capitalism. However, we cannot convince ourselves that the desire of establishing the so-called Islamic World Order could at all be a motive behind the attacks. Gallup polls of global Muslims reveal that the *Ummah* (Global Muslim Community) is least interested in an Islamic World Order, let alone supportive of terrorism and anarchy. We need to know who were behind 9/11, but most importantly, we need to know who benefited most from the attacks. We may also raise the question if al Qaeda needs further mega-scale attacks on American soil as terrorists have already achieved their goals by terrorizing, traumatizing, and bleeding America. Analysts have already singled out 9/11 as the most important catalyst in the decline and fall of Pax Americana in the next 50 years. After the America-sponsored invasions of Iraq and Afghanistan, the world has been further polarized between the Muslim and Western worlds. America's keeping the military option wide open has further aggravated the situation, especially in the wake of the America-sponsored selective "regime- change operations" in the Muslim world.

In the backdrop of Western invasions of Iraq, Afghanistan, Libya, Mali, Niger, northwestern Pakistan, and threats of attacks on Iran and Syria, we have reasons to believe that something has gone grossly wrong with Western democracies. Retired American General Wesley Clark confirms that days after 9/11 the Bush Administration decided to invade seven Muslim-majority countries—Iraq, Lebanon, Libya, Somalia, Sudan, and Iran—in five years.[9] Paul Craig Roberts (Reagan's Assistant Secretary for the Treasury) raises the question, if the "war on terror" has been a hoax. He believes that (a) neither America nor the world at large has become a safer place despite the war on terror; (b) the Muslim world in general has become more vulnerable to American invasions than to Islamist takeovers; and (c) no Muslim-majority country has the capability to attack America.[10]

Although Huntington's views on the "Clash of Civilizations" is alarming, we simply cannot turn a blind eye to the widening gulf between the Islamic and Western worlds.[11] Nevertheless, this study is not going to explain the ongoing Muslim–West conflict in terms of a conflict of cultures. We neither subscribe to the "terrorists hate our freedom" type generalization à la George W. Bush, nor do we believe that Western nations in general can sustain fighting another long-drawn world war. However, as this study is going to elucidate, the divergent ideologies, identities, and interests of the Muslim and Western worlds have already been at the roots of the Islamic–West conflict, which is still at the stage of asymmetric warfare. Most importantly, these asymmetric wars and further polarization of countries in the Muslim world on sectarian, ethno-national and other differences have all the potentials to drag several countries into long-drawn regional conflicts. The prospect of further polarization of superpowers and emerging powers, as adversaries to each other, may be the prime development in the coming decades.

The end of the Cold War has intensified global conflicts. Scores of Muslim-majority countries are witnessing pro-democracy, ethno-national, sectarian and separatist movements, terrorism, and insurgencies. West Europe and America are also going through economic crises and uncertainties. Western powers, especially the U.S., France, and Britain, have been on warpath in the Middle East and northwest Africa. These are ominous signs, which do not bode well for world peace. Conflicting ideologies, identities, and interests of the Muslim and Western worlds have prepared the ground for several rounds of face-offs between the two old adversaries representing the Islamic and Judeo–Christian civilizations. Meanwhile, the Muslim world is settling its own old scores on sectarian, territorial, ideological, ethnic, and class lines. Once the major feuds and disputes are over, once the fractured and artificial Muslim-majority countries resolve their ethno-national and sectarian issues, on both intra and interstate levels, Muslims are likely to come closer to each other. Shias and Sunnis, Turks and Arabs, Afghans and Pakistanis have already started talking to each other. The domino effect of the "Arab Spring" is likely to hit the Muslim world by the third decade of this century. Once the pro-Western autocracies in the Muslim world succumb to the pressure of peoples' power and adopt democracy, a showdown between the Muslim and Western worlds cannot be just a figment of the imagination.

In the backdrop of Western cover-ups and the erosion of liberal values and the non-existent "soft power approach" by America, there is nothing to celebrate about winning the war on terror. What the Wilson administration did in 1917 by publicly demonizing Germany as the potential destroyer of American democracy and freedom, by literal portrayal of the Statue of Liberty under German colors is being replicated by America's portrayal of the Islamist threat in the post-9/11 world. The history of American diplomacy and war is full of lies and half-truths. The Truman administration not only blatantly denied any adverse effect of nuclear radiation on civilians at Hiroshima and Nagasaki but it also lied about Japan's "unwillingness" to surrender. "Saving millions of lives" was the justification for Hiroshima and Nagasaki. In August 1964, President Johnson falsely implicated North Vietnam for attacking U.S. ships in

the Gulf of Tonkin, which on August 7, 1964 led to the Gulf of Tonkin
Resolution by the joint-session of the Congress to justify U.S. attacks on
North Vietnam.[12] The subsequent unjust U.S. wars on North Vietnam,
Cambodia, and Laos killed several million civilians in these countries.

The end of the Cold War—roughly coinciding with the beginning
of the globalization process and the I.T. Revolution—paved the way for
another Cold War between the West and its real and imaginary adversaries
in the Muslim world and beyond, China and Russia, for example. In
the wake of the end of the bipolar world, the so-called unipolar world
created new problems between the Western and Islamic worlds. These
conflicts—reflected in ethno-national, sectarian, and class conflicts—are
about conflicts of interests and hegemonies; not Clash of Civilizations.
The end of the Cold War did not bring the promised peace, prosperity,
justice, and freedom for the Muslim world. However, since the Iranian
Revolution of 1979, many Muslims started thinking of staging revolutions
in their own countries. The four Arab–Israeli wars since 1948, the Indian
occupation of Kashmir and Western invasions of Afghanistan and Iraq
embittered Muslims against Jews, Hindus, and Christians. Muslims, as
aggrieved victims, have been going through the following stages of Denial,
Shock, Grief, Compromise, and Acceptance. 9/11 led to Denial, American
retaliation to the attacks Shocked, and further attacks and humiliation
brought Grief. However, most Muslim-majority countries are not willing
to take sides for or against the West.

We need to understand why despite knowing about the lies and
deceptions of their leaders about Saddam Hussein's non-existent "Weapons
of Mass Destruction" soon after the invasion of Iraq in 2003, Americans,
British, and Australians re-elected George W. Bush, Tony Blair, and John
Howard to lead their nations. Is the West in a state of denial and delusion
of grandeur? We need to understand why the U.S. alone has created "at
least 263 organizations" to tackle aspects of its war on terror. By September
2010, America spent more than $275 billion on intelligence alone. Most
importantly, despite spending billions of dollars and losing thousands of
troops, Americans do not have any convincing answer from their leaders
as to why there are no signs of America winning the war on terror in the
foreseeable future.[13] The average American is clueless as to why Muslims in
general were so happy about the shoe throwing at George W. Bush by an
Iraqi journalist Muntadhar al-Zaidi in 2008 in Baghdad. While throwing

his shoes to the President, he shouted, "This is a farewell kiss from the Iraqi people, you dog."[14] Most Americans do not understand why the U.N. General Assembly roared into laughter at the late Venezuelan President Hugo Chavez's reference to Bush as "Devil"[15] in his speech in 2006. They also do not ask why their governments have been singling out tiny Cuba and Venezuela, and of late Iran, as threats to America. Nobody questions why America, in violation of international law, has been arming Taiwan, a "renegade province" against China, and the worst of all, Islamist militants including al Qaeda militants against the secular Assad autocracy in Syria.

An immediate redress to Muslim grievances against Western high-handedness is in order. Sanctions against Iran and Syria and "benign neglect" of Pakistan are not going to do any good to anybody. Just as the Muslim world needs to change and adapt to modernism, America too needs to change and emerge as a "soft" and "smart" power. However, whether the Muslim and Western worlds can really change is the question. In view of the growing belligerence between the two worlds, it seems increasingly unlikely that there will be a convergence of ideas, opinions, and policies between them in the coming decades.

This work is about understanding the prevalent Muslim–West conflict through the prism of cultural relativity or historicism. I believe that human societies are organic, subject to evolutions and transformations. What was acceptable in the West in the medieval and even in the late 20th century is no longer acceptable today. As for example, the military takeover by aggressively religious Oliver Cromwell in Britain and his execution of Charles I in 1649; public execution of "witches" and Protestants in Britain, colonialism and subjugation of people, slavery, racism, the Apartheid in South Africa were normative in the West only in the past. However, by applying the theory of cultural relativity we can better explain events, ideas, and customs in the modern and contemporary Muslim world. Due to the acceptance of certain behavior as normative in a society in the past might still be acceptable today to people elsewhere as they have not gone through the process of reforming their belief systems and political culture. We should try to understand military takeovers in the Muslim world—including the execution of Prime Minister Zulfikar Ali Bhutto by General Zia in 1979—public executions of criminals in Saudi Arabia, subjection of women, and execution of people for committing "blasphemy" in some Muslim-majority countries, only in the light of cultural relativity.

State-sponsored terrorism, torture, and humiliation of enemy combatants and innocent civilians by Western nations are problematic. Guantanamo Bay, water boarding, humiliation, and torture of prisoners by American troops are fresh in the collective memory of the Muslim world. Unabated U.S. bombing of cities and hamlets, and drone-attacks in Afghanistan and Pakistan to target terrorists and insurgents, which mostly killed innocent civilians, had been embarrassing for the average American. The proliferation of small arms or "AK-47 Culture" in parts of the Muslim world since the Afghan "jihad" has further aggravated the situation. However, "Islamic terrorism" is an oxymoron. Violence against innocent people for any cause negates the teachings of Islam. Extra-Islamic factors such as Muslims' quest for justice, good governance, and dignity are the main factors behind "Islamic terrorism." One may agree with Lindner that human beings yearn for recognition and respect; their denial amounts to humiliation. She thinks:

> Humiliation is the strongest force that creates rifts and breaks down relationship among people.... Men such as Osama bin Laden would never have followers if there were no victims of humiliation in many parts of the world.... The rich and powerful West has long been blind to the fact that its superiority may have humiliating effects on those who are less privileged.[16]

We know terrorism is not a primeval cause or the "original sin." Most importantly, terrorism is a "weapon of the weak," poor, disempowered, and exploited people, who apparently are not strong enough to overpower powerful states. However, the cumulative long-term effect of terrorism could be disastrous for nations. 9/11 attacks alone cost America, the richest and most powerful nation on earth, more than $2 trillion by 2004, and by September 2011 it went up to $3.3 trillion. If one takes into account the U.S. budget deficit, which economists attribute to 9/11, by 2011 the deficit reached to $15 trillion.[17] Consequently, American government, security practitioners, and analysts consider terrorism as the biggest threat to the U.S. economy. A few more mega terror attacks on America can virtually destroy global economy and order.

Terrorists, far from being irrational fanatics, are mostly ideologically motivated desperate people resorting to indiscriminate violence against actual or presumed enemies with a political motive to change the system of government or socioeconomic order in a country/region (or the whole world, thanks to the globalization process). In short, terrorists are politically motivated non-state actors, sometimes backed by state machinery to bleed enemy states. Most importantly, terrorism is not an end in itself, but a means toward drawing attention to the cause its promoters are striving for. It conveys a message or warning and draws media attention to the cause its perpetrators espouse. Terrorism, in short, is a symptom, not the disease itself. Its ups and downs could be misleading. However, ominously, terrorism could be the harbinger of mass revolts, insurgencies, and even revolutions, which might lead to long-drawn catastrophic warfare.

It is time that we evaluate 9/11 and all Islamist extremist behavior with an out-of-the-box approach, going beyond the manuals of counterterrorism (CT) or counter-insurgency (COIN). Terrorists convey important messages by drawing our attention to their cause, which they consider legitimate, and even sanctioned by God. Most major terror attacks, preceding and following 9/11, conveyed messages that we either misread or refuse to acknowledge that there are problems that motivate highly educated, rich, and urbane young men and women to kill themselves to kill others. Robert Pape and some other scholars have explained what motivates people to die for killing others.[18]

More often than never, terrorism is least enigmatic and illogical. It could be an end in itself or a means toward an end. Most importantly, terrorists' failure in achieving their long-term goal to coerce their adversaries to concede what they strive for through violence may force them to (a) adopt even more violent means against their enemies (presumed or real) and even against innocent people to draw attention to their cause; (b) give up terrorism altogether; or (c) mobilize mass support among all possible allies to attain their goals through peaceful or violent means. Thus, ominously, the end of bin Laden might signal the end of al Qaeda, but not the end of Islamist anarchic–nihilism. What is very important in this regard is that analysts, experts, and law-enforcers often undermine terrorists' capabilities and potential to gain support among different sections of people, including those who have no common cause or reasons to support a particular terrorist outfit run by people having different ethnic, linguistic, class, or religious identities from theirs. Thus, aggrieved Sunnis, having a common enemy, might lend support to Shiite terror groups, and vice-versa. Most importantly, people having no support for terrorism, might join or support terrorist groups against a common enemy. This explains as to why millions of peace-loving Muslims have had soft corner for bin Laden and his ilk. We often ignore the extraterritorial nature of transnational "jihads." Al Qaeda, Taliban, and their likes not only fight for the "liberation" of Arabia, Afghanistan, Palestine, Iraq, and Kashmir, but they also champion the cause of establishing an alternative global order. Islamists always claim to be the peace-loving champions of justice against injustice and freedom against hegemony. Very similar to Communism, Islam and Islamism promote transnational camaraderie and fraternity among their adherents. Lessons learned in Afghanistan and Pakistan since the 1980s should never be forgotten. Exploiting ethno-national and class conflicts, Islamist extremists have turned yesteryears' "freedom fighters" into transnational rebels, insurgents, and terrorists of today. Islamist terrorism is a combination of fascism, anarchism, and nihilism. It aims at introducing something radically different from traditional Islam albeit in the name of Islam. They do not represent homogenous groups. They are divided on sectarian, ethno-national, and ideological/strategic differences.

As terrorism is about evoking fear in the minds of its victims, consequently, the victim syndrome of the average Americans since 9/11 has replaced hope with fear, trust with mistrust, and tolerance and acceptance with hate and prejudice. In short, the cumulative impact of 9/11 on American politics, economy, culture, and psyche has been overwhelming. In the backdrop of the intensity in attacks against American troops and diplomats in Afghanistan, it seems Americans and American interests are neither safe at home nor abroad. Despite what Obama told the Americans on the 10th anniversary of 9/11: "We took a blow, and emerged stronger;"[19] the facts belie his hyperbole as American economy is in the doldrums, and so, is the state of its insecurity.

I have shown in this work that common race, language, religion, and culture do not necessarily bring people together. The Arab world is a glaring example in this regard. Arabs are loyal to their own nation states, such as Egypt, Syria, or Iraq, and in general do not champion the cause of "Arab Nationalism." However, there is a growing sense of belonging to the *Ummah* among sections of Arab and non-Arab Muslims everywhere.

An understanding of violent Islamist extremism hinges on the understanding of what the postcolonial Third World in general and the Muslim world in particular think of Western hegemony and arrogance.

Evelin Lindner has beautifully explained it through her personal fieldwork experience in Rwanda and Somalia in 1998. She conveys the perceptions of the downtrodden Rwandans and Somalis about the West, in the following manner:

> You from the West, you come here to get a kick out of our problems. You pretend to help or do science, but you just want to have some fun... You pay lip service to human rights and empowerment! You are a hypocrite! We feel deeply humiliated by your arrogant and self-congratulatory help! First you colonize us. Then you leave us with a so-called democratic state that is alien to us. After that you watch us getting dictatorial leaders. Then you give them weapons to kill half of us. Finally you come along to "measure our suffering."[20]

As discussed above, state-sponsored terrorism or proxy war is the new menace to pay attention to. Despite the "uneventful normalcy" in the absence of any major terrorist attack on American soil since 9/11, the September 2011 attacks on U.S. Embassy and NATO troops in Afghanistan were followed by American governments' finger pointing at Pakistan. In the wake of these attacks and on the eve of his retirement on September 22, 2011, Admiral Mike Mullen in his written statement to the Senate Armed Services Committee squarely blamed the Pakistani government, and its military intelligence (ISI) for promoting the Haqqani Network against America and Afghanistan.[21] Senator Lindsay Graham, a member of the Senate Armed Services Committee, went even farther. She felt that America should keep, "all options, including war" open, to stop Pakistan's "hostile acts against the United States."[22] However, as expected, the Pakistani reaction to the American blame game has been anything, but conciliatory. As I have discussed in the text, Pakistan is emerging as one of the eyes of the storm, which is going to engulf many countries and regions in the coming decades.

Clash of Interests and Hegemonies, Not "Clash of Civilizations"

We may impute religious conflicts and terrorism to ethno-national identities and ideological commitments of people. An Imagined Past, shared values and problems, common goals and objectives in the future of mono- or multi-racial groups keep them together. The quest for politico-cultural identities and aspirations for better rights and/or freedom by Imagined Communities are important factors behind religious conflicts and extremism. Marginalized ethno-national groups' expediency, their joining extra-territorial Islamist jihadists, for example, often blur the ethno-national dimension of the respective movements. Southern Mindanao's Moro [Muslim] National Liberation Front's (MNLF) subsumption under the Moro Islamic Liberation Front (MILF) in the Philippines may be cited as an example in this regard. In view of this, we need rereading of Huntington's Clash of Civilizations and question Fukuyama's End of History.

We find Jerry Muller's "Clash of Peoples" theory more acceptable than the one on Clash of Civilizations. Muller argues that ethnic nationalism will drive global politics for generations. He points out as to why Americans do not understand the power of ethno-national identity:

> Projecting their own experience onto the rest of the world, Americans generally belittle the role of ethnic nationalism in politics.... Within two or three generations of immigration, their ethnic identities are attenuated by cultural assimilation and intermarriage.... Americans also find ethno-nationalism discomfiting both intellectually and morally.... Immigrants to the United States usually arrive with a willingness to fit into their new country and reshape their identities accordingly.... The creation of a peaceful regional order of nation-states has usually been the product of a violent process of ethnic separation. In areas where that separation has not yet occurred, politics is apt to remain ugly.[23]

As the discord between modern and traditional Muslims is ideological by nature, so is the conflict between Islam and the West. And ideology is not only about culture and belief systems, but also about power, influence, and identity. While Westernized Muslim elites are unwilling to concede power and privileges to the mullahs, the latter are also unwilling to concede any ground to the former. The Iranian Revolution and the Taliban/al Qaeda experiment in Afghanistan have inspired mullahs and their followers to go the Khomeini or Taliban way. Meanwhile, Western duplicities and open support for Islamists during the Cold War had further emboldened Islamists within and beyond the Muslim world. The U.S. support for mullahs in Iran to topple the elected government of Dr Mossadegh in

1953, and American promotion of the Islamist Muslim Brotherhood (MB) to topple anti-American Nasser in Egypt, are well-known facts. Last but not least, America was directly behind the creation of the mujahedeen in Afghanistan to fight the Soviet Union, and in connivance with the Pakistani military, it was instrumental in the Taliban takeover of Afghanistan in 1996. American duplicity in global politics is not new. As the Pentagon Papers revealed in 1971, America had played an instrumental role in overthrowing and killing President Ngo Dinh Diem of South Vietnam in a coup d'état in 1963, and in deliberately expanding the war in Vietnam by bombing Cambodia, Laos, and North Vietnam, by systematically lying "not only to the [American] public but also to Congress."[24]

For distancing ourselves from any pseudo-history of Islamism, we need to understand that postcolonial Islamist reassertion is a legacy of defeats and humiliation for the *Ummah*. Arab defeat at the hands of Israel in a six-day war of 1967 brought Islamism to where it is today. It is one of the most powerful political ideologies in the Muslim world. We need an understanding of the Muslim psyche vis-à-vis the Muslim experience in Palestine, Kashmir, Iran, Algeria, Libya, Egypt, and among other places, Iraq and Afghanistan. How the Cold War allies—Muslims and the West—turned into adversaries or competitors in uneven elite conflicts and asymmetrical wars in the globalized world for conflicting hegemonies and ideologies demands our attention. A brief discussion of Islam and Muslim in historical perspective takes us closer to the root causes of the age-old Muslim–West conflict.

The first and foremost requirement for understanding the problem is that the Muslim world is actually a loose conglomerate of countries that were once European colonies. With the exception of Turkey (Saudi Arabia and Afghanistan in the very limited sense of the expression), all Muslim-majority countries are postcolonial countries, with all or most characteristics of such countries. These characteristics include: (a) overdeveloped military and bureaucracy, (b) underdeveloped/weak civil societies, (c) divided not cohesive, hierarchical societies stratified by ranks, status, and wealth. While the elites jealously guard their status and privileges, thanks to the exposure to modern education and democratic ideas, masses in the Muslim world are gradually questioning the traditional ruling classes. With two or three exceptions, absolute monarchies and civil/military dictatorships—with nonexistent or feeble human rights and freedom—are the norms in most countries in the Muslim world. Some of these countries are, again, artificial entities. They have inherited artificial boundaries drawn by their colonial masters—British, French, and Dutch—who arbitrarily created new countries, such as Jordan, Lebanon, Israel, Kuwait, Pakistan (and Bangladesh), and lumped ethnically diverse people together (against their will) in countries with arbitrarily designed states.

The process denied the right of self-determination to nations with distinct ethno-national identities: linguistic, racial, tribal, religious, or sectarian. Many of them have simply become stateless or living as members of diasporas across the world. The Kurds, Palestinians, Kashmiris, Pashtuns, Tamils in Sri Lanka, Balochis, Muslims in southern Thailand, and Moro Muslims in Mindanao (Philippines), and crores of Afro-Asian nations (often denigrated as tribes and minorities) may be mentioned in this regard. As Tutsi and Hutu nations live (and kill each other) in artificial postcolonial countries of Burundi and Rwanda, so are the restive Muslim (Berber) Tuareg tribals in Mali, Algeria, Libya, Nigeria, Niger, Burkina Faso, and the Kanuri tribals in Mali, Nigeria, Niger, and Chad. Scholars and laymen frequently ignore the various ethno-national groups struggle for self-determination or equal rights, and opportunities in countries they call home as Islamist militancy and terrorism. We cannot understand the so-called Islamist terrorism without understanding the root causes of the phenomenon. It is time that we use different expressions instead of Islamic/Islamist terrorism to understand underprivileged Muslims' quest for freedom, democracy, self-determination, and equal rights and opportunities. Last but not least, we need to understand that unlike Europe and America, the Muslim world has not gone through an Islamic Reformation/ Renaissance. Most importantly, Muslims have not yet been able to establish nation states by redrawing the boundary lines of Muslim-majority countries. Unless they live in fully decolonized countries in accordance with the desire of each and every ethno-national, linguistic, or sectarian group with full rights and freedom, there will not be any peace in the turbulent parts of South Asia, Northwest and sub-Saharan Africa, Middle East, and parts of Southeast Asia.

Last but not least, we cannot understand violent extremism by looking at it only through the prism of religion. We need to understand how race, ethnicity, identity, and marginalized peoples' yearn for recognition and respect, and their denial or withdrawal humiliate them and may turn them into violent terrorists.[25] We may agree with Karen Armstrong that no religion has so far been able to withstand changes over the last 400 years in science and technology, philosophy and ideas, and sociopolitical and economic systems and structures. Religious revival is not just retrogressive, but an attempt to cope with these changes and challenges of rationalism against myths and superstitions.[26]

Taking cover of religion, race, or nationhood is convenient for the underdogs. Backward, marginalized, latecomers are too weak to compete with more advanced people in the mainstream. They often use religion, Marxism, nationalism, terrorism, and anarchy to reach their goals. When nonviolent methods fail, they resort to violence. Artificial states based on arbitrarily drawn lines across the desert could be breeding grounds for conflicts between neighbors and/or between the colonizers and the original inhabitants. The Palestine problem or the sectarian/communal conflicts in Iraq, Lebanon, Pakistan, and Afghanistan, Russia and India are examples in this regard. The Muslim–West conflict is likely to be intensified after the latter's unsuccessful bid for retaining its weakening hegemony over the unwilling Muslim world. At times, a multiethnic states' unwillingness to recognize the right of self-determination by a section or sections of population leads to conflicts. "Yield to one, lose more" is the Achilles Heel of artificial states. Among others, Pakistan, Afghanistan, India, Russia, China, Iraq, and Turkey are vulnerable to ethno-national separatist threats. Some of these separatist groups use Islam to justify their distinct identities.

Joe Lieberman, a former independent democratic senator from Connecticut, sounds quite reasonable. He affirms this war is not about defeating a broader political ideology, but about destroying al Qaeda and similar terrorist organizations such as the Pakistan-based LeT.[27] We, however, have no clues as to how to reach al Qaeda, which is more of a global movement than an organization. Lieberman is right that since the U.S. is not at war with Islam, it must "encourage and empower the non-violent Muslim majority," who understand "better than anyone else the enormous difference between their faith and the terrorist political ideology that has exploited it."[28] The more radical offshoots of MB—who despise the mother organization (MB) for being too soft and constitutional—such as al Qaeda, Islamic Jihad, Hamas, and their friends in Iran, Syria, Lebanon, and elsewhere will eventually pose a much bigger threat to American and Israeli interests in the region.

However, despite some attempts to understand the Muslim world and Islamist terror threats to America, American politicians and intellectuals deliberately avoid certain embarrassing issues, and do not want to find out the root causes of Islamist threats to their country. One may raise the question if America will ever go against the Israeli Lobby to win over Arab and Muslim heart and mind. While military strategists, war and security analysts know Islamists have no prospects of winning an asymmetrical war against America; those who know the psyche of the proud, ideologically committed and desperate enemy know it quite well that the weaker party can wreak havoc by taking the war to the least expected places by the least expected means and strategies. Nothing is deadlier than an ideologically committed and undeniably wronged and humiliated enemy. America is facing that dreadful enemy in Islamism, which is anything, but declining. Islamists in the coming years are likely to adopt new methods, going beyond terrorism. Some of them have already come to power through elections, and there are others in the pipeline.

Chomsky has aptly called modern wars "trade wars."

> Since trade ignores national boundaries and the manufacturer insists on having the world as a market, the flag of his nation must follow him, and the doors of the nations which are closed against him must be battered down... even if the sovereignty of unwilling nations be outraged in the process.[29]

Trading advantages for colonial and postcolonial powers and the greed of the Military–Industrial Complex have been the main factors behind modern war. Woodrow Wilson's following appraisal of causes of war has got wide currency: "Is there any man, is there any woman, let me say any child here that does not know that the seed of war in the modern world is industrial and commercial rivalry?"

It is important that not only the American but also the Pakistani Military Inc., is a destabilizing factor, both within and beyond the borders of the country. The profit-oriented armed forces of Pakistan, which run industries, banks, and virtually the government (even under civilian administration)[30] have vested interests in keeping the region turbulent to legitimize and further strengthen their position. Thus, Pakistani armed forces are least interested in a durable peace across the Line of Control in Kashmir, or across the Durand Line between Pakistan and Afghanistan.

The Youth Bulge and Demographic Pressure

Both Malthus and Huntington are helpful in understanding the core of the problem of the ongoing Muslim–West conflict. The Western and Muslim worlds represent people having diametrically opposite identities, ideologies, and interests. They represent two different worlds; the West provides better opportunities, freedom, living space, food, clothing, shelter, health care, and dignity to its people than what the Muslim world offers to the bulk of its people. Malthus believed expanding population without corresponding rise in food supply and jobs would lead to catastrophic wars and conflicts. Huntington has also singled out Youth Bulge as an important factor behind conflicts. Youth Bulge occurs when 30 to 40 percent of the male population in a society belong to the fighting age; cohorts from 15 to 29 years of age, and are underemployed/unemployed. Demographic pressure in Western Europe led to the Crusades in the 11th and 13th centuries. Pope Urban II on the eve of the First Crusade (1095) wrote, "For this land…is too narrow for your large population…. Enter upon the road to the Holy Sepulcher; wrest that land from a wicked race, and subject it to yourselves." The Wicked Race Theory is all about undermining other ethnic groups. Friedrich Ratzel (German demographer) in 1897 coined the expression "lebensraum" (adequate living space) for Germany, which later inspired Hitler's expansionism and war against the wicked races.

Major Western powers' several century-long exploitation of global resources, colonization of most Afro-Asian countries, and annexation of North and South America, Australia, and New Zealand are at the roots of the problem. Overpopulated and underdeveloped Muslim and Third worlds for decades have been craving for their *lebensraum* or adequate living space. They want the end of the discriminatory and restrictive immigration laws in resource-rich and sparsely populated North America, Europe, Brazil, Argentina, Australia, and New Zealand. We see the reflection of this feeling of marginalization of the Third World in the late Algerian President Houari Boumediene's U.N. General Assembly speech in 1974:

> One day, millions of men will leave the Southern Hemisphere to go to the Northern Hemisphere. And they will not go there as friends. Because they will go there to conquer it. And they will conquer it with their sons. The wombs of our women will give us victory.[31]

Boumediene's above assertion, on the one hand, reflects Muslim (or the Third World) desperation for equal opportunity and human dignity, presumably denied by the West; on the other, this also conveys the ominous message to the West that the Third World has been aggrieved and willing to fight for their rights and dignity. Contrary to George W. Bush's oversimplification, Muslims do not hate freedom and democracy. The overwhelming majority of Muslim militants and their global supporters do not fight for restoring their so-called golden past, let alone the problematic Shariah codes. Most Islamist terror is about secular issues of good governance, justice, and human dignity. The Taliban and bands of obscurantist Islamist militants represent a miniscule (and fast diminishing) minority of Muslims. The Arab Spring and successful holding of democratic elections in two-third of the Muslim world, since the beginning of the 21st century, belie all trumped up Western allegations about Muslims' contempt for freedom and democracy.

In sum, this work is not going to address all the major issues between the Muslim and Western worlds, the role of Russia, China, India, Pakistan, Iran, Israel, and other major and minor powers in the global conflicts in the coming decades. This study elaborates some of the main factors behind the intra-Muslim and Muslim–West conflicts in global and regional perspectives. It demonstrates why parts of South Asia, Persian Gulf, and North Africa have more inflammable matters than elsewhere in the world. These regions have several eyes of the storm and potential Sarajevos to trigger another world war, while the Hundred-Year War since the First Arab–Israeli War in 1948, has not petered out. Sometimes it only remains latent like a dormant volcano, but erupts quite frequently. While the intra-Muslim conflicts apparently appear to be sectarian, tribal, and ethno-national conflicts, they are actually class wars between the privileged few and the underprivileged millions, from Algeria to Egypt, and Iraq to Indonesia. This study also explains why the Muslim–West conflicts should not become parts of the Huntingtonian cliché of the Clash of Civilizations as they are primarily conflicts of interests and hegemony. For the bulk of Muslims, their not-so-inevitable conflict with the West and its surrogates in the Muslim world is a class war between Western super ordinates and their unwilling subordinates.

It is noteworthy that while the death toll in World War II was between 60 and 85 million; civil wars, genocides, asymmetric warfare, state-sponsored pogroms and last but not least, U.S.-led invasions of dozens of countries since the Korean War, by 2013, led to more than 75 million deaths, mostly civilians. The U.S. invasion of Iraq in March 2003 alone killed more than a million Iraqis by September 2007. Since then hundreds of thousands of Iraqis have died, and as of September 2013, hundreds are dying every week in sectarian violence and at the hands of unknown assailants and Islamist extremists. Although the U.S. has not been solely responsible for all the post-World War II conflicts and civilian deaths in the world, yet the 37 countries it invaded since the Korean War resulted in the violent deaths of 20 to 30 million civilians, 9 to 14 million in Afghanistan alone.[32]

Chapter Breakdown

Chapter 2: Dynamics of Islam and Islamism: Allah's Law versus Mullah's Law

This chapter draws a line between the apparently similar, but diametrically different entities of Islam, the religion, and Islamism, the political ideology. This, in short, is an appraisal of the divergence within Islam. The adherents of the faith are not only divided along ethno-national and class lines, but they are also sharply polarized as members of various sects and schools of thought: Shiites and Sunnis, Sufis and hardcore Islamist radicals, followers and opponents of Shariah, and last but not least, liberal democratic and extremist totalitarian. There is no reason to identify all Islamists as conservative or orthodox as they do not necessarily follow Islamic teachings and traditions. Finally, while all Islamists do not support violent extremism, the average God-fearing Muslim is dead against terrorism and killing of innocent people in the name of religion or any other ideology.

Chapter 3: Global Muslims' Triple Jeopardy: Islamophobia, Israel, and Globalization

This chapter is an appraisal of the Muslim–West conflict in historical as well as contemporary perspectives. It aims at understanding the problem by juxtaposing it against the ongoing, controversial globalization process. Although Islamophobia and Westophobia are not direct derivatives of the globalization process, yet the age-old Muslim–West conflict became more vigorous and noticeable in the wake of globalization. This chapter is a reappraisal of Muslim state of mind in the light of history of Western colonial excesses and postcolonial duplicities vis-à-vis the Muslim world. In sum, it sheds light on the triple jeopardy of the *Ummah* (global Muslims) in relation to Western Islamophobia, American/Western support for Israeli arrogance and excesses against Muslims and Arabs, and the implications of the not-so-benign West-sponsored globalization process, which is good for capital, not for labor.

Chapter 4: Is the American Empire "Exceptional"?

This chapter is a departure from the Western discourse of "what went wrong with Islam." This is about the problematic role America has been playing since long. It is an appraisal of what went wrong with the American Revolution and dreams of America's founding fathers. It is time that we understand the short- and long-term implications of the rise and decline of American hegemony in historical and contemporary perspectives. This chapter raises the following questions in the light of American history: Is America the biggest problem toward world peace? Is not the American legacy of expropriation, mass murder of indigenous people, slavery, and apartheid at the core of the American psyche, while the American dogma of freedom and democracy is quite superficial, not applicable to non-Americans (others)?

Chapter 5: Global Jihad: Philosophies and Flashpoints

We believe that global jihad is a loaded concept. Interestingly, Islamists and Islamophobes seem to have converged on one point that projects global jihad as a threat to civilization in general, the Western civilization in particular. Scholars often portray global jihad as a step toward establishing an alternative Islamic order in the world. Islamophobes promote extreme prejudice against Islam by projecting it as an evil religion and often equate global jihad with real Islam. This chapter is an attempt to understand if global jihad is an ahistorical reconstruction, a mythical concept, and if global jihadists are strong enough to mold public opinion in the Muslim world to challenge Western and other non-Islamic civilizations in the coming years. With a view to understanding the global flashpoints of the so-called global jihad against the West, this chapter has appraised various Islamist organizations/ movements, from Wahhabism to MB, and al Qaeda to Jamaat-i-Islami (JI) and their ilk, in the light of their philosophies, strength, and popularity among the average Muslims within and beyond the Muslim world.

Chapter 6: The Eye of the Storm: "Jihad" and Proxy Wars in South Asia

This chapter is an appraisal of the growing menace of Islamist insurgency, transnational crime, "narco jihad" and state-sponsored terrorism/proxy wars emerging out of Afghanistan, Pakistan, India, and Bangladesh. Transnational conflicts, crimes, and proxy wars always transcend subregional boundaries, and if not contained, they might adversely affect countries beyond particular regions or subregions. This chapter highlights the extra-Islamic dimensions of crime, terror, and proxy wars that are destabilizing South Asia and the adjoining subregions, posing serious threat to global peace. It addresses the issues that have turned Pakistan and Afghanistan into the eyes of the storm, that is, likely to hit the world very badly in the coming years.

Chapter 7: Another Eye of the Storm: The Middle East and Northwest Africa

This chapter appraises the bogey of nuclear threat from Iran and other "rogue states" in the Muslim world that justifies America's post-Cold War diplomacy or hegemonic behavior and military interventions in the Muslim world. As we know, the main challenge to world peace today comes from state-sponsored terrorism; we need to know if only smaller states or superpowers are also responsible in the promotion of state-sponsored terrorism and proxy wars. If the world is heading toward prolonged intra and interstate conflicts in the coming decades than what we have already witnessed since the end of World War II is an important area of discussion in this chapter. This chapter appraises the role of America in intensifying world conflicts—directly or indirectly—through invasions or benign neglect of smaller countries. This, in short, supports the main theme of this study that global jihad is a hackneyed concept, as neither Islam nor Muslims, but Islamist extremism poses the greatest threat to world peace. We need to worry about the implications of the New World Order—to perpetuate America's global hegemony—and the never ending story of Islamist terrorism in the coming decades.

Chapter 8: Conclusion

The concluding chapter is about the importance of understanding the phenomenon of Islamist militancy in its true perspectives without ignoring how Western intolerance and quest for global hegemony have led to various crises, including long-lasting warfare. It appears that American foreign and domestic policies have evolved into permanent war policies. America has spent far more on defense in the post-Cold War years than ever before. While political culture and Islamic traditions determine the political role of Islam in a given territory, elite manipulation, poverty, and bad governance are the most important factors behind the rise of Islamist militancy and terrorism. It explains as to why the post-terrorist world is not going to be the harbinger of global peace and order. It points out that there is nothing benign about Islamist political parties' winning elections in any Muslim-majority country, as Hitler came to power by winning elections. Last but not least, although apparently it appears that the world is polarized between the Muslim and Western worlds, yet the real polarization is taking place between America and new contenders of global hegemony, especially Russia, China, and their allies.

Notes and References

1. Asef Bayat (ed.), Introduction in *Post-Islamism: The Changing Faces of Political Islam* (New York: Oxford University Press, 2013), pp. 7–9.
2. Institute for Economics and Peace, "2012 Global Terrorism Index: Capturing the Impact of Terrorism from 2002–2011," (London, December 4, 2012). Available at: http://reliefweb.int/sites/reliefweb.int/files/resources/2012-Global-Terrorism-Index-Report.pdf (accessed on January 19, 2014).
3. Available at: http://www.visionofhumanity.org/terrorismindex/about-the-gti/ and www.economicsandpeace.org (accessed on February 2, 2013).
4. John Pilger, "The Real Invasion of Africa and Other Not-Made-for-Hollywood Holy Wars," *Truthout* (February 1, 2013). Available at: http://truth-out.org/author/itemlist/user/44655 (accessed on February 3, 2013).
5. Tony Cartalucci, "The Geopolitical Reordering of Africa: US Covert Support to Al Qaeda in Northern Mali, France 'Comes to the Rescue,'" *Global Research* (January 12, 2013). Available at: www.globalresearch.ca (accessed on February 3, 2013).
6. Bernard Lewis, *What Went Wrong?: The Clash Between Islam and Modernity in the Middle East* (New York: Oxford University Press, 2002), passim.
7. Niall Ferguson, "A $492 Billion Bet," *Newsweek* (November 28, 2011).
8. John Kiriakou's interview with RT TV (February 6, 2013). Available at: www.rt.com/usa (accessed on February 7, 2013).
9. Wesley Clark's video interview with *Democracy Now* (March 2, 2007).
10. Paul Craig Roberts, "Is the War on Terror a Hoax?" *Foreign Policy Journal* (September 30, 2011).
11. Samuel P. Huntington, *The Clash of Civilizations and the Remaking of World Order* (New York, Simon & Schuster, 1996).
12. "The Pentagon Papers: Secrets, Lies and Audiotapes," National Security Archive Electronic Briefing Book Number 48, Posted on Tuesday (June 5, 2001). Available at: http://www.gwu.edu/~nsarchiv/NSAEBB/NSAEBB48/ (accessed on February 8, 2013).
13. Fareed Zakaria, "What America Has Lost," *Newsweek*, September 13, 2010.
14. BBC News, "Shoes Thrown at Bush on Iraq Trip," *BBC News* (December 15, 2008). Available at: http://news.bbc.co.uk/2/hi/7782422.stm (accessed on December 6, 2013).
15. David Stout, "Chávez Calls Bush 'the Devil' in U.N. Speech," *New York Times* (September 20, 2006).
16. Evelin Gerda Lindner, "Humiliation as the Source of Terrorism: A New Paradigm," *Peace Studies*, Vol. 33, No. 2.
17. Institute for the Analysis of Global Security (IAGS), "How Much Did the September 11 Terrorist Attack Cost America?" Available at: http://www.iags.org/costof911.html (accessed on February 26, 2013); Eric Wieffering, "Calculating 9/11's Toll on U.S. Economy," *Star Tribune* (September 10,

2011). Available at: http://www.startribune.com/business (accessed on February 26, 2013).

18. Robert Pape, *Dying to Win: The Strategic Logic of Suicide Terrorism* (New York: Random House, 2005), passim; Mia Bloom, *Dying To Kill: The Allure of Suicide Terror* (New York: Columbia University Press, 2005), passim.

19. Available at: http://abcnews.go.com/blogs/politics/2011/09/america-shaken-but-not-broken-by-911-obama-says and http://www.dailymail.co.uk/news/article-2036119/9-11-Anniversary-Obama-rounds-day-remembrance-Kennedy-Center.html (accessed on September 15, 2011).

20. Evelin Gerda Lindner, "Humiliation as the Source of Terrorism: A New Paradigm," *Peace Studies*, Vol. 33, No. 2 (2001).

21. *New York Times*, "Pakistan's Spy Agency Is Tied to Attack on U.S. Embassy," *New York Times* (September 22, 2011).

22. *New York Times* (September 13, 22, 23, 2011).

23. Jerry Z. Muller, "Us and Them: The Enduring Power of Ethnic Nationalism," *Foreign Affairs* (March/April 2008).

24. "The Pentagon Paper: 1971 Year in Review." Available at: http://www.upi.com? Audio/Year_in_Review/Events-of-1971/12295509436546-1/#title (accessed on December 14, 2010); David Frum, *How We Got Here: The '70s* (New York: Basic Books, 2000), p. 43.

25. Evelin Gerda Lindner, "Humiliation as the Source of Terrorism: A New Paradigm," *Peace Studies*, Vol. 33, No. 2 (2001).

26. Karen Armstrong, *Introduction to the Battle for God* (New York: Ballantine Books, 2001).

27. Joseph I. Lieberman, "Who's the Enemy in the War on Terror?" *Wall Street Journal* (June 15, 2010).

28. Ibid.

29. Noam Chomsky, *On Power and Ideology* (Cambridge, Massachusetts: South End Press, 1990), p. 14.

30. Ayesha Siddiqa, *Military Inc.: Inside Pakistan's Military Economy* (London: Pluto Press, 2007), passim.

31. Available at: http://wn.com/HouariBoumediene (accessed on January 30, 2011).

32. More than 1,000,000 Iraqis murdered since 2003 invasion, Opinion Research Business Survey (London, September 16, 2007). Available at: http://www.zcommunications.org/more-than-1-000-000-iraqis-murdered-since-2003-invasion-by-orb.html (accessed on September 19, 2013); James A. Lucas, "Deaths in Other Nations since WW II Due to US Interventions." Available at: http://www.countercurrents.org/lucas240407.htm (accessed on September 19, 2013).

2

Dynamics of Islam and Islamism: Allah's Law versus Mullah's Law

> Surely the Muslims, Jews, Christians and the Sabians, whoever believes in
> God and the Last Day, and whoever does right, shall have his reward with
> his Lord and will neither have fear nor regret.
>
> The Quran, 2:62

> Permission is granted to those (to take up arms) who fight because they
> were oppressed. God is certainly able to give help to those who were driven
> away from their homes for no other reason than they said: "Our Lord is
> God." And if God has not restrained some men through some others,
> monasteries, churches, synagogues and mosques, where the name of God
> is honored most, would have been razed.
>
> The Quran, 22:39–40

Overview

This chapter draws a line between the apparently similar, but diametrically
different entities of Islam, the religion, and Islamism, the political
ideology. This, in short, is an appraisal of the divergence within Islam.
The adherents of the faith are not only divided along ethno-national and
class lines, they are also sharply polarized as members of various sects
and schools of thought: between Shiites and Sunnis, followers of Sufis
and hardcore Islamist radicals, between the followers and opponents of
Shariah or between liberal democratic and extremist totalitarian Muslims.
Although both the liberal and extremists identify themselves as Muslim,

we have differentiated the followers of the Quran, and authentic traditions of Prophet Muhammad as Muslims, from the hardcore illiberal, dogmatic and irrational, and often proponents of violence and terrorism, or Islamists. There is no valid reason to identify an Islamist as conservative or orthodox, as they do not uphold any Islamic tradition or teaching of the Quran and Prophet Muhammad. Unless we understand the difference between the two, there is no way of understanding the intricacies of the problem of violations of human rights and commission of violent crime in the name of Islam. The problem is so baffling that even many Muslims get confused as to how their religion, which literally stands for "peace" and *aslama* or "total surrender to the will of God," can be used for violent crime, anarchist behavior, and terrorism to kill innocent civilians irrespective of faith, race, and ideology. This chapter elucidates the dynamics of spiritual and political Islam by differentiating the two sets of laws, emanating from Allah's and the mullah's, respectively.

The Problem

Islam is the second largest and the fastest growing religion in the world. According to the latest finding by the Pew Research Center,

> The world's Muslim population is expected to increase by about 35% in the next 20 years, rising from 1.6 billion in 2010 to 2.2 billion by 2030. Globally, the Muslim population is forecast to grow at about twice the rate of the non-Muslim population over the next two decades.[1]

There are misperceptions about Islam that most Muslims come from the Arab world, Turkey, and Iran. While around 20 percent of Muslims are Arab, roughly, 40 percent are South Asian, 20 percent Indonesian, and the rest are from other parts of the world. This information is pertinent to our understanding of some of the dynamics of Islam and Islamism with special reference to the growing tension between the Muslim and Western worlds.

There are various Islamist organizations and movements such as Wahhabism, MB, JI, al Qaeda, Harkat ul-Jihad al-Islami (HUJI), LeT, Jemaah Islamiya, and their likes in regional and global perspectives. This is going to highlight the process and consequences of the rise of dogmatism, and the average Muslims' blind reliance on the mullahs (the main promoters and custodians of Shariah) as the sole custodians and interpreters of Islam, who consider man-made Shariah laws to be divine, and justify Islamic State, autocracy, polygamy, subjection, and inferiority of women and non-Muslims, stoning to death for adultery, death for apostasy, and last but not least, Islam to be the only true religion acceptable to God. It also highlights how overpowering is the influence of local traditions and belief systems, or little traditions on scripture-based great traditions of Islam in the light of the case studies of Islamic and Islamist movements in Muslim-majority countries in Africa and Asia.

It is time to draw a line between the apparently similar entities of "Islam," the religion, and "Islamism," the political ideology. It is noteworthy that Muslims are not only divided along ethno-national and class lines, but are also divided as adherents of various sects and schools of thought, between Shiites and Sunnis, moderate Sufis and militant Islamists, ultra-orthodox followers of Shariah law and opponents of the extra-Islamic draconian code practiced in the name of Islam. As the followers of Shariah-based orthodox Muslims are not homogeneous, so are the liberal Muslims. Then again, the overwhelming majority of conservative and orthodox followers of Shariah do not support the creation of Islamic States or a global caliphate. This is an attempt to understand as to how and why most followers of spiritual Islam have remained backward, premodern, fatalist, and next worldly, while sections of them—believing Islam to be a complete code of life—espouse political Islam as the only ideology to run transnational states.

There is no valid reason to identify every Islamist as conservative or orthodox as all of them do not conform to the teachings of Islam. Unless we differentiate the two, we cannot understand the complexities of the problem of human rights violations in the name of Islam. The problem is so puzzling that many Muslims get confused as to how their religion, which stands for "peace and surrender to the will of God," can be abused by anarchists and terrorists who indiscriminately kill innocent people, Muslims, and non-Muslims. We need to know the process and consequences of the rise of dogmatism and the average Muslims' blind reliance on the intolerant mullah, who considers Islam the chosen religion and Muslims the chosen people of Allah.

What Went Wrong?

Despite what Bernard Lewis wrote in his sketchy essay, "What Went Wrong?" with Islam and in his sketchier book having the same title,[2] it is rather time to ask: what went wrong with the West? Lewis's concern with bewildered and pathetically backward Muslims (of the Middle East, as he has excluded the bulk of the global Muslims, who live beyond the Arab world) in the postcolonial era is appalling. Muslims, according to him, have been asking: (a) "Who did this to us?" (b) "What did we do wrong?" and (c) "How do we put it right?" He is right that while some Muslims "attribute all evil to the abandonment of the divine heritage of Islam," advocating return to a real or imagined past, his blaming the Muslims' blame game for holding European colonial rule responsible for their backwardness is appallingly pathetic. He imputes the lack of freedom in Muslim countries to their backwardness, not to European colonial rule. He simply surmises in condescension and contempt that "if Muslims continue on their present path, the suicide bomber may become a metaphor for the whole region."[3]

However, as there were internal factors for the degeneration of the Islamic civilization—tribalism, autocracy, neglect of science and philosophy, and the mass adherence for premodern Shariah code and escapist Sufism—the rise of the Western imperialism was the single-most important cause for the decline of the Islamic civilization. We find Edward Said, Marshall Hodgson, Juan Cole, Aijaz Ahmad, and even Zbigniew Brzezinski more acceptable than the Orientalist discourse of Blame-the-Victim.[4]

Chomsky is equally incisive in the deconstruction of neo-orientalism. He points out the Anglo-American duplicities in Iran. In the 1950s, America worked against democracy by overthrowing the elected government of Dr Mossadegh by bribing ayatollahs to restore the autocratic Shah to control Iranian oil. He cites Western double standard vis-à-vis the suffering of Kurdish minorities. While supporting the Kurdish cause in Iraq under Saddam Hussein, the West remained quiet about the persecution of Kurds in Turkey, a Western ally. His critiquing the historical engineering of the West to the detriment of the Palestinians and the peace process is also enlightening.[5] In short, there are striking parallels between today's Islamism and Europe's radical leftism in the 1960s and 1970s. Both have drawn supporters from alienated angry youth.[6]

Most people do not know that Muslims—Arab, North African, Turk, Iranian, Central Asian, Afghan, and Indian—were once foremost among dominant powers representing the longest surviving civilization in world history. Long after the heydays of Islamic civilization had been over in the 20th century, renowned British historian H.A.R. Gibb saw Islam and its adherents in a positive light:

> No other society has such a record of success in uniting in an equality of status, of opportunity and endeavor so many and so varied races of mankind. The great Muslim communities of Africa, India and Indonesia, perhaps also the small community in Japan, show that Islam has still the power to reconcile apparently irreconcilable elements of race and tradition. If ever the opposition of the great societies of the East and West is to be replaced by cooperation, the mediation of Islam is an indispensable condition.[7]

No other civilization in known history besides the Islamic one sustained for over a millennium, from the mid-7th to early 18th century. Muslims were the dominant power from the Iberian Peninsula (Spain and Portugal) to northwestern and eastern Africa, the Arab world, Turkey, Central Asia, Eastern Europe, Iran, Afghanistan, and India. By the 16th century, the Malay world from southern Thailand to parts of the Philippines converted to Islam. In short, Muslim empires had been the most dominant ones from the shores of the Atlantic to the edge of the Pacific Ocean, the whole of Indian Ocean and the Mediterranean world. Muslims' military and politico-economic dominance also matched their preponderance in the realms of art, architecture, philosophy, and science. Muslims built some of the most magnificent buildings of all times—from the Alhambra to the Taj Mahal—and without their contribution to literature (prose writing and fiction), mathematics, medicine, music, geography, historiography, ship-building, chemistry, astronomy, physics, and philosophy, the Dark Ages of Europe (5th to the 15th centuries) would have lasted much longer. The world owes its debt to Muslim mathematicians for introducing algebra and algorithm and further improvement of the decimal system. They were the first ones to introduce universities in the 9th century, predating Oxford and Cambridge by three centuries.

Arabic, during the 9th and 13th centuries, was the language of any discipline of knowledge. But for the direct contributions of Islamic scholars, and higher seats of learning in Cordova, Granada, Baghdad, Tunis, Cairo,

Isfahan, Samarqand, Bukhara, Delhi, and elsewhere in the heartland of Islam, European Renaissance, Reformation, and geographical discoveries would have been delayed by several centuries. Although some Western scholars believe that had there been the Nobel Prize in the 10th century, Muslims would have taken them all; yet most Westerners are unaware or unwilling to acknowledge their debt to Islam and Muslims for their cultural enrichment and scientific progress. During the Islamic Golden Age in the mid-8th to the mid-13th centuries, Muslims had been the most advanced people in the world. The Arabic roots of many terms in European languages in science, arts, mathematics, music, and other disciplines suggest how pervasive was the Muslim influence in every sphere of knowledge, trade, commerce, industry, and urban lifestyle. From admiral to alcohol, algebra, algorithm, arsenal, cipher, divan, guitar, lute, sofa, magazine, monsoon, tariff, and hundreds of other words in European languages have been derived from Arabic. European scholars during the Dark Age of Europe first read works by Socrates, Plato, and Aristotle through Arabic translations. One may mention the following Muslim luminaries of the medieval period, who have immensely enriched all disciplines of knowledge: Musa al-Khwarismi (d. 846), father of algebra (*al-jabr*) and algorithm (al-Khwarismi); Abu Bakr al-Razi (864–935), his medical work Al-Mansuri or *The Liber Almansoris* was used for centuries in Europe; Ibn Sina/Avicenna (980–1037), his medical encyclopedia was used in Western universities up to the 19th century; Al-Haytham/Alhazen (965–1039) invented camera obscura; Abu Rayhan al-Biruni (973–1050), Indian poet, historian of science, and Sanskrit scholar; Ibn Sina /Avicenna (980–1037), his medical encyclopedia was used in Western universities up to the 19th century; Ibn Rushd/Averroes (1126–1198), commentator on Aristotle, influenced Western philosophy; Ibn an-Nafis (d. 1288) discovered blood circulation; and Ibn Khaldun (1332–1406) wrote world history and is regarded as the father of sociology and modern historiography.

Bernard Lewis, who is otherwise widely known for his orientalist (anti-Arab/anti-Muslim) and Islamophobic viewpoints, seems to be quite objective in the following description of Islam:

> *Islam is one of the world's great religions. Let me be explicit about what I, as a historian of Islam who is not a Muslim, mean by that. Islam has brought comfort and peace of mind to countless millions of men and women. It has given dignity and meaning to drab and impoverished lives. It has taught people of different*

races to live in brotherhood and people of different creeds to live side by side in reasonable tolerance. It inspired a great civilization in which others besides Muslims lived creative and useful lives and which, by its achievement, enriched the whole world. But Islam, like other religions, has also known periods when it inspired in some of its followers a mood of hatred and violence. It is our misfortune that part, though by no means all or even most, of the Muslim world is now going through such a period, and that much, though again not all, of that hatred is directed against us.[8] (emphasis added)

However, very similar to the decline and fall of other empires in history, complacence, lack of creativity, neglect of science and technology, internal feuds due to racial, sectarian, religious, and tribal prejudices, and foreign invasions (the Crusades, Mongol invasions, the inquisition or *reconquista*, and European colonial expansions in Asia and Africa) led to the decline and fall of the Muslim empires and civilization. While mutual fighting on sectarian, racial, and regional lines between Shiites and Sunnis, Hashimites and Umayyads, Arabs and non-Arabs, Turks and Iranians, and Southern and Northern Arabians sapped Muslims' vitality and creativity signaling the rapid decline of Islamic civilization in the East and West; Muslim ruling elites and scholars failed to visualize the rise of European powers in the late 15th and early 16th centuries. Muslims were too arrogant and unwilling to accept that they had anything to learn from the West in science, arts, philosophy, and the art of governance.[9] While the Baghdad-based Islamic Empire (the Abbasids) adopted rational Mutazilite philosophy as the state-creed up to early 9th century, the rule of Caliph Mutawakkil, the Mad Bigot (847–861), desecularized the Empire by promoting ultra-orthodox clerics, legalizing polygamy, and subjugation of women. The Muslim world did not go through its Renaissance and Reformation to adopt secular ideas, science and technology.

Under the overpowering influence of ultra-orthodox scholars, such as Imam Ghazzali (d. 1111), who despised mathematics as intoxicating and philosophy as dangerous, Muslims distanced themselves from modern knowledge and technology. The mighty Ottoman Empire, the hegemon of southeastern Europe, North Africa, and Middle East up to the 19th century, did not introduce printing press till the early modern era. Ottomans had their first university as late as in 1879. While the fall of Granada—the last Muslim kingdom in Spain—in 1492 signaled the beginning of the end of Muslim dominance in the Mediterranean world; the post-Renaissance, post-Industrial Revolution, European colonial onslaught on the Muslim world simply bewildered Muslim rulers, clerics, and laymen. Meanwhile, obscurantist mullahs in Ottoman Turkey had been instrumental in destroying an observatory in Istanbul one year after its erection in 1579. In 1745, mullahs succeeded in stopping the first printing press in Turkey. Ghazzali opposed mathematics and philosophy in *The Incoherence of the Philosophers*, considering them dangerous and intoxicating.[10]

The upshot is almost the total degeneration and stagnation that the global Muslims have been confronting since the 12th century in general, and in the wake of the European Renaissance, Reformation, Enlightenment, Industrial Revolution, the British, French, and American Revolutions in particular. Consequently, the global Muslim community, who represents more than 1.6 billion souls, is among the least developed in the world. A comparison of Muslim achievement in science and technology, and in any branch of knowledge, art, and culture—including health, education, governance, human rights—with the developed world draws an abysmally poor picture of Muslim backwardness. A recent study reveals the following:

> In 2005 Harvard University produced more scientific papers than 17 Arabic-speaking countries combined. The world's 1.6 billion Muslims have produced only two Nobel laureates in chemistry and physics.... By contrast Jews, outnumbered 100 to one by Muslims, have own 79. The 57 countries in the Organization of the Islamic Conference spend a puny 0.81% of GDP on research and development, about a third of the world's average.... Many blame Islam's supposed innate hostility to science. Some universities seem keener on prayer than study. Quaid-i-Azam University in Islamabad, for example, has three mosques on campus, with a fourth planned, but no bookshop.[11]

The glaring contrast between Muslim backwardness and Western and East Asian advancement is simply mindboggling. While the combined annual GDP of 57 Organization of Islamic Cooperation (OIC) countries is less than $2 trillion, the U.S. alone has a GDP of around $14 trillion. Each of China, Japan, and Germany has higher GDP than the combined GDP of the Muslim world. Other glaring differences that dwarf the Muslim world against the developed West and East are in the realm of knowledge. While America alone has more than 5,000 universities, the Muslim world has around 500; none of them is among the top 500 in the world category. While Japan has 5,000 and America has 4,000 scientists per million people, the corresponding figure is less than 250 per million in the Muslim world. In view of the Muslim backwardness, we may impute it to Muslim clerics, backward-looking Muslims, and their governments. One cannot impute Muslim backwardness to foreign occupation and colonialism alone as postcolonial entities, such as South Korea, Taiwan, Hong Kong, Singapore, Argentina, Brazil, Chile, Mexico, Venezuela, and Sri Lanka, among many others, are far more advanced than most Muslim-majority countries in the realms of literacy, development, the rule of law, and freedom.

However, there is not everything so bleak and hopeless in the Muslim world. Since the turn of the century, Gulf countries, especially, Saudi Arabia, Qatar, and Iran, have been spending billions on the development of science and technology. Saudi Arabia's King Abdullah University of Science and Technology (opened in 2009) has a $20 billion endowment that even rich American universities would envy. Of late, Saudi universities have started research collaborations with Oxford, Cambridge, and Imperial College. Qatar spends around $5 billion on research annually. Turkey has also increased research spending by over 10 percent each year. While Turkey's output of scientific papers has gone up from 5,000 to 22,000 between 2000 and 2009, Iran grew from bare 1,300 to 15,000.[12] Things are not that promising in the rest of the Muslim world, especially in Yemen, Sudan, Somalia, Mali, Afghanistan, Pakistan, and Bangladesh, in the realm of research in science and technology. Not only the backward-looking clerics, but some modern-educated Muslim intellectuals in countries such as Pakistan and Malaysia also ridicule scientific research in astrophysics and evolution theories as "chasing wild ideas." We have reasons to believe that due to the overpowering influence of Salafi, Wahhabi, and traditional clerics, the kind of freedom that science demands will remain elusive throughout the Muslim world in general. There is every apprehension that even President Morsi, who holds a PhD in materials science, will not be able to stop the erosion of scientific ideas due to the preponderance of dogmatic Salafists, who espouse a radical and backward version of Islam.[13]

The proud and vainglorious mullah, their ardent followers, and Muslims in general are more or less aware of their glorious past, but they have hardly any clues as to what went wrong with their ancestors, who could not withstand the pressure from the West. They often not only exaggerate Muslim contribution to knowledge but also impute their backwardness and degeneration to Western conspiracy and design. Arabic, Persian, Urdu, and Bengali Muslim poets and writers lamented the Loss of Cordova and the end of the Ottoman and Mughal empires. Muslims need not be told who they lost their golden past to; they know it well that they were European colonial powers and their Jewish and Hindu collaborators. America, since the end of the Cold War, is the new villain in the Muslim world. A Cold War, ally and friend, against the common enemy—communism—has become the new adversary, albeit not without any genuine reasons.

Nevertheless, we have no reason to reject all Western criticism of Islam (as practiced by global Muslims), holding it responsible for Muslim degeneration. We need to take into account how Muslims themselves have been responsible for drawing such a poor picture of them. They are equally responsible for their overall backwardness. Muslim backwardness is mainly due to Muslims' reliance on traditions and Shariah; their unwillingness and opposition to renewal or reformation of faith; blind compliance to half-educated clerics and dated theories and ideologies; their aversion to rational enquiry, objectivity, and, most importantly, lack of tolerance for divergent opinions. We must not lose sight of some Muslims' reservations about democracy, secularism, equal rights, and status for women (and non-Muslim minorities in Muslim majority countries without exceptions) in this regard. The Muslim concept of an Islamic State, and even worse, an equally utopian and ahistorical transnational Khilafat (caliphate) by Sunni Muslims, and the millennial Shiite Global Imamate or the Kingdom of God are retrogressive as well. Likening the ahistorical myth of Islamic State with mirage, Tarek Fatah has aptly demolished the concept in his discourse of Islamic State versus the State of Islam.[14]

Then again, the idea of an Islamic Reformation, Farid Alatas' Protestant Islam is problematic and full of loopholes. As Alatas argues, militancy and terror in the name of Islam is not a classical Islamic, but a modern Islamist problem, if we need to reform anything it should be Islamism, not Islam. He has precisely pointed out that what violent Islamists have been trying to do is not that dissimilar from what Martin Luther did with orthodox Christianity; he got rid of the religious authority of the Pope and clerics to interpret religious texts. Islamist insistence on back to the Quran and new interpretations of Islam through *ijtihad* or reasoning by curbing the authority of the traditional mullah may be considered an attempt toward Islamic Reformation.[15] Paradoxically, Islamist militants—not clerics or Islamic experts, but secular-educated techno-clerics such as Osama bin Laden, Ayman al-Zawahiri, Khaled Sheikh Muhammad, Anwar Aulaqi, and their ilk—have been engaged in global jihad or global anarchy, not Islamic Reformation.

The Muslims in general may be categorized into the following types:

1. Fatalist/escapist/Sufi/mystic (including *Pirs, Tabligh Jamaatis*): Mainly peaceful, puritan, next worldly and ritualistic
2. Islamic modernists/secular and liberal believers in Islam, democracy, and peaceful coexistence with non-Muslims
3. Totalitarian Islamists—not necessarily violent revolutionaries—who aspire for Shariah-based Islamic States through popular support and/or elections under the banner of political parties, such as the MB, JI, and their ilk
4. Militant revivalist and violent revolutionaries with contempt for constitutional politics, who support Islamist outfits, such as al Qaeda, the Taliban, LeT, HUJI, Islamic Jihad, and Jemaah Islamiyah—often offshoots of Wahhabi and Salafi organizations and Islamist parties such as MB and JI—and strive for regional or global caliphates (Sunni) or imamates (Shiite)
5. The anarchic–nihilists—al Qaeda and its ilk— do not necessarily strive for establishing global caliphate or imamate, but want to destroy everything alien to their version of Islam without paying any heed to the teachings of the Quran and having no qualms about killing people indiscriminately, posing the biggest threat to modern civilization
6. Westernized Anglophonic/Francophonic politicians and military dictators in Muslim-majority countries, who nurture Islamism out of political expediency to legitimize their rule by neutralizing more radical and genuine Islamist groups. These pretentious leaders' state-sponsorship of Islam by introducing Islam as the State Religion and/or through alarmist slogans such as Islam-in-Danger inadvertently legitimizes political Islam by culturally Islamizing the polity. Pakistan, Indonesia, Libya, Sudan, Malaysia, and Bangladesh, among others, may be cited in this regard.

The Islamic Faith, Institutions, Laws, and Regulations

Islam is the continuation of the Judeo-Christian faith. Muslims believe that Adam was the first man and prophet of God, followed by several thousand prophets from Noah to Abraham, David, Joseph, Moses, Jesus, and finally Muhammad. The Quran is quite explicit about it: "He established for you the same religion as that, which He established for Noah, that which we have sent to you as inspiration through Abraham, Moses, and Jesus, namely that you should remain steadfast in religion and make no division within it" (42:13). Although similar to Judaism and Christianity, many Westerners have a different perception of Islam—they do not see it in a positive light, especially after 9/11. Islam requires its adherents to believe in strict monotheism. There are six articles of Islamic faith: Allah, Prophets, Revealed Books, Angels, Life after Death, and the Day of Judgment. Some Muslim scholars believe Predestination or the good or evil associated with one's fate to be the seventh article of Islamic faith.

There are five pillars or fundamental principles of Islam. They are:

1. *Imaan* or faith that there is no god but Allah and Muhammad is His messenger
2. *Salat* or prayer— the five mandatory ones per day besides the weekly congregational prayer on Fridays, two Eid prayers annually, and other nonobligatory prayers
3. *Sawm* or obligatory dawn to dusk fasting during the lunar month of Ramadan
4. *Hajj* or obligatory (for those who can afford it) pilgrimage to Mecca and Medina, at least once in one's lifetime
5. *Zakat* or mandatory poor tax, ideally collectible by the state from Muslims to be distributed among the poor and needy

A Muslim must believe in Allah or God as one single omnipresent and omnipotent Supreme Being without having any partners and Muhammad to be the last among the prophets, who revealed the final message of Allah in the form of the Quran carried by angel Gabriel. The message is Islam, which stands for peace and total submission to the will of God. The Quran spells out that neither Muslims are the chosen people of God nor are others destined to go to hell (2:62). The five pillars are not mere rituals, but principles to run a sociopolitical order with justice and equity. Prayer in Islam stands for understanding the message of the Quran by reading sections of the scripture five times a day. The rationale behind congregational prayers in the mosque is to bring people closer to each other irrespective of their race, class, and status. The concept of fasting during the month of Ramadan is aimed at making people understand the pang of hunger. *Zakat* is not that different from income tax and its rate may vary from 2.5 to 50 percent on Muslims' net savings, land/crops, animals (in a pastoral set up like Arabia during the Prophet's time), cash, and gold. While Sunnis believe in giving 2.5 percent of their savings as poor or welfare tax, Shiites believe in giving *khums* or one-fifth of their savings and value of gold, livestocks as *zakat*, exempting land from it. In the heydays of Islamic empires, Muslim rulers also distributed land among landless peasants as *zakat*.[16] While *zakat* or mandatory poor tax ensures social welfare, Hajj aims at bringing global Muslims together for greater understanding, fraternity, and resolving global problems (22:27–28). In short, Islamic rituals are not ends in themselves. The Quran is very explicit about Islam not being a ritualistic faith:

> It is not righteousness that you turn your faces towards East or West…but to spend from your wealth…for your kin, for orphans, for the needy, the wayfarer, for those who ask and for the ransom of slaves; to be steadfast in prayer and *zakat*, to fulfill the contracts which you have made, and to be firm and patient in pain and adversity throughout all periods of panic. (2:177)

Muhammad, the Last Prophet

Muslims believe that Muhammad, the final messenger, prophet, or *rasul* of Allah, was human not a divine being. Muslims neither worship him nor like to be called Mohammedans. Muslims' holy book, the Quran, as Muslims believe, was revealed to Muhammad (570–632) during 610 and 632, in Mecca and Medina. The Quran literally means recitation. There is a consensus among scholars that Muhammad was unlettered, as he could not read or write. He was a posthumous child, first raised by his grandfather and then by his uncle, who never embraced Islam. At 25, Muhammad married a wealthy 40-year-old Arab widow Khadijah.

He did not take another wife until Khadijah died at 65. She was the first convert to the religion of Islam. Most Muslims and non-Muslims do not know that Muhammad did not establish and run a theocracy or Islamic State in Medina. The Medina-based state transcended tribal and religious boundaries. Most of its citizens or members of the *Ummah* (now the expression exclusively denotes the global Muslim community) during the time of the Prophet were Jewish, not Muslims until Jews and Muslims drifted apart due to political differences and the latter's joining hands with the enemies of Islam in Mecca. Contrary to what mullahs, laymen, and most Muslim and non-Muslim scholars of Islam believe, Muhammad did not establish a theocracy or an Islamic State. The Prophet was the first Arab nationalist who created the nation-state of Medina where Jews, Muslims, Christians, pagans, Arabs, and non-Arabs from Persia and sub-Saharan Africa became members of the *Ummah* transcending their tribal and religious boundaries.

The Prophet preached a monotheistic religion eliminating all intermediaries between God and human beings. By demolishing the idols of the Kaaba in Mecca, he destroyed the symbols of power, authority, and the main sources of income of the tribal chiefs, who were also the custodians of their respective idols. He did not rule solely on the authority of his being the Prophet of Allah, but he brought the diverse tribes, races, and communities together with a written constitution or the famous Charter of Medina. The Charter came into being soon after Muhammad's migration to Medina in 622, and was amended several times after the Battle of Badr (624), which Muhammad won with Meccan adversaries. The constitution was based on the principle of one nation of diverse tribes and communities living under the sovereignty of one God.[17] No wonder Carlyle eulogizes Muhammad in glowing terms. "How one man single-handedly, could weld warring tribes and wandering Bedouins into a most powerful and civilized nation in less than two decades" is an enigma to him. He further defends the Prophet as a great man, "Our current hypothesis about Mahomet, that he was a scheming imposter...begins really to be now untenable to anyone. The lies which well-meaning zeal has heaped around this man are disgraceful to ourselves only."[18] From Gandhi to Bernard Shaw, and historian O'Leary, among others, have shattered the myth that Muhammad spread his religion through the sword.[19] Last but not least, Michael Hart has selected Muhammad as the "most influential person" among a hundred people in the world because "he was the only man in history who was supremely successful on both the religious and secular levels."[20]

Although Muhammad is a historical figure, yet thanks to the overreliance on unauthentic Hadis literature and not-so-contemporary accounts of his life through Arab historians such as Ibn Ishaq (702–768), Ibn Hisham (d. 838), and Al Tabari (838–923), the Prophet remains an enigmatic figure, full of contradictions. Ibn Ishaq's *Sirat* or biography of Muhammad written 120 years after the death of the Prophet is full of unsubstantiated accounts of the Prophet's private life; his multiple marriages (including to a seven-year-old Ayesha); warfare; and, last but not least, his alleged permission for cold-blooded killing of several hundred Jews in Medina. The Hadis literature simply contradicts the teachings of the Quran. We cannot accept all *hadises* to be true as they also reflect Sunni, Shiite, and other sectarian and tribal biases, prejudices, popular Arab culture, myths, and traditions which often contradict the teachings of the Quran and the spirit of Islam. In sum, while we learn so little about the life, activities, and sayings of Prophet Muhammad through history, the Hadis literature is full of ahistorical accounts and stories attributed to him. Then again, the bulk of these pseudo traditions have been the cornerstones of the various schools of Muslim jurisprudence, rituals, and codes of conduct reflected in the various schools of Muslim jurisprudence or Shariah law.

Thanks to concocted history and theologians' biased interpretations of the history of early Islam to justify theocracy and the so-called Islamic State, Muslims and non-Muslims across the board believe that as Muhammad ran a theocracy, so did his first four rightful caliphs or successors: Abu Bakr (632–634), Umar (634–644), Usman (644–656), and Ali (656–661). We find Shaban's appraisal of the early caliphate very insightful. Denying the concept of an Islamic State or theocracy as Islamic, he points out that all the first four heads of state, caliphs (*Khalifa*), or successors of Prophet Muhammad (632–661) adopted the title of Amir al-Muminin, or the leader of the believers not Amir al-Muslemin or the leader of the Muslims. According to Shaban, the title being political not religious was a move toward including non-Muslim subjects as members of the newly created polity having Medina as its capital; Amir was not a dictator or commander, but rather a counselor, very much in the tradition of Arab leadership.[21]

The Quran (Koran)

The Quran has a unique style; it is neither prose nor poem, but in rhymes having 114 chapters of unequal length. The Meccan verses, revealed at Mecca up to the Prophet's migration to Medina in 622, are spiritual and ethical; about good and evil, right and wrong, hell and heaven, anecdotal accounts of some historical figures and incidents. The Medinan verses are more about rules and regulations, family law, and code of conduct as citizens of the nascent state of Medina under the Prophet. In short, the Quran is more a book of guidance than a legal code applicable to all Muslims for all times. While there are some specific guidelines and regulations or codes of conduct, applicable universally for all times, there are again many instructions and prohibitions, which were contextual and only relevant to the prevalent situation during the lifetime of the Prophet. The Quran is also a very difficult book to understand as the chapters and verses are not codified chronologically. Those who compiled the book from an authentic copy from the Prophet's family in its present form did not contextualize the verses. Most Muslims do not know that many Quranic verses had exclusive relevance to the time of the Prophet, having very little or no relevance to the modern world.

The Quran is ideally central to Muslims' life, but Hadis, Shariah, and *mazhab*s or sects are equally important for them. The Quran is, however, very difficult to understand, even by native Arabic speakers, who have not learned the skill of understanding figurative poetic expressions from sophisticated scholars or *ulama*. The literal translations and biased interpretations of Quranic verses in support of polygamy, wife bashing, stoning to death for adultery, inferiority of women and non-Muslims, and the average Muslims' inability to contextualize Quranic verses have further aggravated the situation. Consequently, a book of guidance has become a book of law and magical power; many Muslims simply learn the Quran by heart or learn rote learning without understanding a word, let alone any ethical teaching of the Muslim Holy Book.

The Quran does not single out the Muslims as the "chosen people" of God. We rather find in the Quran that God has divided human beings into different races, tribes, and nations. The Quran also considers God-fearing Jews, Christians, and other non-Muslims as believers: "Surely those who believe, and those who are Jews, and the Christians, and the

Sabians whoever believes in Allah and the Last Day and does good, they have their reward with their Lord, and there is no fear for them, nor shall they grieve" (2:62); "And if your Lord had pleased, He would have made people a single nation. And they cease not to differ" (11:118); "O mankind! We have created you male and female, and have made you nations and tribes that you may know one another. The noblest of you, in the sight of Allah, is the best in conduct. Allah is Knower, Aware" (49:13); "There is no compulsion in religion" (2:256); and "To you is your religion, and to me is mine" (109–6).

Hadis (Hadith) and Shariah (Sharia) Law

The Hadis or traditions and sayings of Prophet Muhammad were collected roughly 200 years after his death. Some *hadises* contradict the teachings of the Quran and go against science, common sense, and decency. One may prove almost anything to ones liking through the Hadis literature. As there are Sunni *hadises* so are there Shiite versions of them, often contradicting each other. What is glorified in Sunni tradition could be despised in the Shiite one. Among various renowned Hadis collectors, Imam Bukhari (810–870) is the most renowned besides Muslim, Tirmizi, Ibn Maaja, Abu Dawood, and An Nasai. He collected more than 600,000 *hadises*, and discarded most of them and retained around 7,000 of them considering them *sahih* or authentic. The problem with Hadis collection was that despite the good intentions and objectivity of Hadis collectors, it was humanly impossible to authenticate more than 200 years after the demise of the Prophet whatever were attributed to him. Hadis scholars and Muslim clerics in general argue that since 20 or 50 Rawis or Hadis narrators told the same thing to different Hadis collectors in different times, corroborating a "saying," or tradition of the Prophet, they are authentic. They simply ignore the fact that anything contradicting the Quranic teachings and principles cannot be acceptable to any Muslim. They also ignore the fact that in every community or country there are popular sayings, myths, customs, and beliefs or "little traditions" transmitted through generations, and they are not necessarily authentic and real. Mullahs simply do not know the art of differentiating myths with reality. This is the reason as to why, we find so many ridiculous, vulgar, anti-Quranic, anti-science, and anti-common sense things in the Hadis literature. People said different things attributing them to the Prophet to justify slavery, polygamy, concubines, dozens of wives for rulers, harem, eunuch, or castrated male guards to protect harems, female genital mutilation, *rajm* or stoning to death for adultery by married people (the Quran specifies 100 lashes for both married and unmarried adulterer/adulteress). There are so-called authentic *hadises* in defence of absolute rule, slavery, and patriarchy or subservience of women to men. In this backdrop, we find Fazlur Rahman's appraisal of Hadis literature very balanced and useful to this study. He cites Imam Shafi (the founder of the Shafi sect in Sunni Islam), who believed that no Hadis or Sunnah (sayings and practices of the Prophet, respectively) had ever existed before the 8th century. The Prophet left no Sunnah or Hadis outside the Quran.

Although it is not binding to believe in Hadis and Shariah to remain Muslim, they play important roles in a Muslims' private and social life. Theoretically, the Shariah code has been derived from the Quran, Hadis, *fiqh*, or Muslim jurisprudence based on the individual and collective opinions (*qias* and *ijma*, respectively) of Muslim jurists in the 9th/10th centuries, common sense, and local (pre-Islamic) traditions. Muslim clerics quite authoritatively cite Hadis and specific Shariah code to justify anything from absolute monarchy to slavery, patriarchy, misogyny, and overall subjugation of women to female genital mutilation, stoning to death for adultery to child marriage, concubines, harem, seclusion of women, inferiority of non-Muslims, and even their subjugation by force. In sum, both the Hadis and Shariah codes, at times, contradict the Quran. Consequently, some Muslim feminists decry what the Quran has given to women has been conveniently taken away by the Shariah law.

Since the Quran is a book of guidance not law (one finds only a handful of do's and don'ts in the Quran), and there being no consensus among Muslim scholars on the authenticity of many *sahih* or authentic *hadises*; Shariah is basically a man-made code, subject to revisions and modifications, there is hardly anything divine about it. Shariah is authoritative, not infallible; a Muslim does not have to believe in Hadis, *fiqh*, or Shariah as infallible and sacrosanct as the Quran.[22] The Sunni Shariah code went through major transformation and changes, but only up to the 16th century. Although the Shiite Shariah is still subject to changes and modifications yet only the well-entrenched ayatollahs and *mujtahids* (interpreters of law) can modify it. However, since the Islamic Revolution in Iran, the Shiite clerics do not run the country in the name of Shariah, but by their Divine Providence to establish Khomeini's *Vilayat-e-Faqih* or the guardianship of the Jurist. It appears that Shiites are more respectful of the clerics (and less democratic) than Sunni Muslims. In sum, the moral principles of the Quran outweigh its legal principles. As for example, while slavery, concubines, and polygamy are tolerated in Islam for a specific historical era, the Quran does not promote or encourage these practices. Shariah codes as practiced in various countries are borrowed from the Old Testament and folk traditions, and reflective of Muslim jurists' prejudices and biases against women, religious, sectarian, and ethnic minorities.

The *Sunnah* Muslims practice globally, to a large extent, is pre-Islamic in origin.[23] One Al-Azhar Sheikh elucidates with relevant citations from the Old Testament that the following beliefs and practices among Muslims have been plagiarized from Biblical traditions.

1. Stoning to death for adultery and apostasy
2. Wearing of beards by men and head cover by women
3. Circumcision
4. Displaying holy writings on the wall
5. The belief that Eve was created from Adam's rib and menstruating women are spiritually unclean
6. Prohibiting drawing or sculpting human or animal life forms
7. The ritualized blessing of Amen
8. Animal sacrifice (*aqeeqah*) at the birth of children[24]

A look into the much maligned and abused Shariah law reveals something totally different from what the average mullah, Islamist extremists, and Islamophobics think Shariah is all about—enforcing a totalitarian rule, forced conversion of non-Muslims, or their subjugation to the so-called Islamic State run by brutal force. The six principles of Shariah are not that different from what U.S. Constitution and U.N. Charter of Human Rights have enshrined as inalienable rights of all human beings. As one scholar has pointed out there is no room for killing of infidels, veiling of women, stoning people for adultery, honor killing, and female genital mutilation in Shariah. The six principles of Shariah have been derived from the Quran and all Muslims must adhere to these principles to remain Muslims. They are:

1. The right to the protection of life
2. The right to the protection of family
3. The right to the protection of education
4. The right to the protection of religion
5. The right to the protection of property (access to resources)
6. The right to the protection of human dignity[25]

There are four major Sunni and a couple of Shiite sects. Among the prominent Sunni sects are (a) Hanafi, (b) Shafi, (c) Maliki, and (d) Hanbali. The major Shiite sects are known as *Twelvers* and *Seveners*, or the believers in the 12th and 7th imams, respectively. Both the minority *Seveners* and majority *Twelvers* believe in their respective 7th or 12th imam to be the hidden imams, said to have disappeared in 755 and 874, respectively, and, they believe, will reappear before the Doomsday as the messiah, or Imam Mahdi to establish the Muslim version of the Kingdom of God on earth. There are mutual differences among these sects. What is permissible in one particular sect under its specific Shariah code may not be permissible for other sects.

Besides the adherents of the various sects, there are Muslims, who do not belong to any particular Sunni or Shiite sect. They prefer to call themselves *Ahl-e-Hadis* or people of the Hadis, and do not believe in any Sunni or Shiite imams as sole interpreters of Islamic law or Shariah. Their Shariah is theoretically based on *hadises* and they are not totally free from the influence of local customs and practices of other sects. They proliferate in South Asia and are also known as Indian Wahhabis for their extremist views. Some leading Islamist outfits in South Asia, such as the LeT in Pakistan and the JMB in Bangladesh, belong to the ultra-orthodox *Ahl-e-Hadis* sect.

While the Sunnis recognize all the first four caliphs or early successors of the Prophet as legitimate rulers, the Shiites do not recognize the first three caliphs of Prophet Muhammad as his legitimate successors. They only consider Ali, Muhammad's son-in-law, and the fourth caliph as the only legitimate successor of the Prophet. Shiites, who call themselves followers of Ali, not only consider the first three caliphs as usurpers, deviant, non-Muslims, enemies of Islam, and of the Prophet, Ali and the House of Muhammad, but Shiite priests also ritually curse the first three caliphs—Abu Bakr, Umar, and Usman—invoking Divine retribution on them, in Shiite mosques before the Friday congregation prayers begin. This cursing is quite common in many, if not most, Shiite mosques even today. We also find Shiite *hadises* portraying the first three caliphs and many renowned followers of the Prophet as homosexual, promiscuous, degenerated people. Even Ayesha is not spared from the Shiite vitriol. Both Sunni and Shiite traditions depict her as a wife of the Prophet, who is said to have married her when she was only seven or nine, which again has no historical veracity. One suspects people might have justified pedophile in the name of the Prophet, as so many other vices have Islamic justifications. According to some Shiite traditions, Ayesha was not a believer and alleged to have poisoned the Prophet to death. Shiites are again divided between the followers of the 12th or the 7th imam. Adherents of both the schools believe that the respective last imam (12th or 7th) is not dead, but hidden or has disappeared. Shiite traditions have led them to believe that the hidden imam will appear as the messiah to establish the Kingdom of God before the Doomsday.

Unlike the Sunnis, the Shiite believes in hereditary succession. To the Shiites, Ali and his successors—all known as imams—are considered divine and infallible. Some Shiite extremists believe that Angel Gabriel by mistake carried the message of God to Muhammad instead of Ali to be the last prophet of God. The Shia–Sunni cleavage reached its peak in 680 after the brutal killing of Hussein, a son of Ali and grandson of the Prophet, at Karbala in Iraq at Yezid's order. Yezid was the second king of the Umayyad dynasty, a contender of the caliphate or vice-regency of the Prophet of Islam.

This brief account of the differences between Shiite and Sunni traditions highlights how *hadises* have turned Shiites and Sunnis into sworn enemies, since the killing of Hussein (son of Ali), or the Tragedy of Karbala that took place in 680. An Umayyad contender of the caliphate killed his Hashemite rival Hussein, from the House of Muhammad and Ali. Sunni and Shiite *hadises* often give diametrically opposite interpretations of the Quran, Islamic rituals, belief system, teachings of the Prophet, his lifestyle, character of his companions, and other major and minor events that occurred during the 7th and 8th centuries. As for example, while Sunnis consider *mut'a/segheh* or temporary/contractual marriages (a pre-Islamic custom in Arabia) for a fixed period (for a day, week, month, or a year or two) *haram* or totally forbidden, Shiite Islam allows it. In fact, one may find a partner for *segheh* in Iran through professional matchmakers.

There are yet many other sects, some considered heretics and deviant by Sunni and Shiite Muslims. The Ahmadiyya community in Pakistan, India, Bangladesh, and Indonesia may be cited as an example of such an outcast among Muslims. Pakistan and Indonesia declared them non-Muslim for their belief that Mirza Ghulam Ahmad (1835–1908) was a prophet or spiritually he represented all the prophets sent by God, and was the "Promised One" of all religions. In Pakistan, serious rioting took place in 1953 over the demand by Islamist parties to declare the Ahmadiyyas as non-Muslim. They have inferior rights in Pakistan and Indonesia. Muslim extremists in Bangladesh also demand that Ahmadiyyas be declared non-Muslim.

Besides the ritualistic orthodox schools, there are heterodox mystic orders of Sufism in Islam. Orthodox clerics often despise Sufis considering them heretical and deviant Muslims. Sufis having scores of orders, paths, or *tariqas*, strive for esoteric or hidden meanings of Islam to come closer to God through love and devotion. Contrary to popular belief, all Sufis are not heterodox and peaceful either, some are known as "warrior Sufis." Sufism flourished during the decay of Islamic power from the 12th century onward. Sufis were mostly grassroots-based, people-oriented, believers in egalitarian socioeconomic and relatively democratic or representative political orders. In short, Sufism had the potential to usher in Islamic Protestantism or reformation. However, many, if not most, Sufis also served the interests of Muslim dynasties. Sufism proliferated in North Africa, Central Asia, Turkey, Iran, Afghanistan, and South Asia. Ultra-orthodox Wahhabis despise Sufism. Sufis played the most important role in mass conversion of underdogs into Muslims in Punjab, Sindh, Bengal, Indonesia, and some other parts of Central and South Asia. Some Sufis consider Shariah and ritualistic Islam inappropriate for the more advanced Muslims, who have found the Truth through the Sufi masters—*pirs*, *murshids*, *shaykhs*—while others believe that one reaches *haqiqah* or the Truth or Nirvana only by accepting Shariah, by traveling through *tariqah* or the path under the guidance of a Sufi master.

There is another category of Sunni Muslims, who belong to the *Tablighi Jamaat*, a puritan and nonpolitical Islamic movement to bring Muslims closer to orthodox Islam. This transnational evangelical movement does not aim at converting non-Muslims into Muslims, but primarily transforming non-practicing Muslims into the practicing ones, came into being in North India. It is an offshoot of the ultra-orthodox Deoband Movement (the so-called Indian Wahhabism), established in 1926 in response to Hindu revivalism, to protect the Muslim identity of non-practicing Muslims in India. Now, it has millions of adherents in more than 200 countries. Although it emerged out of the Hanafi School of Sunni Islam, it does not endorse or promote any particular sect and strives for bringing as many Muslims as possible within the fold of Islamic orthodoxy. Many *tablighi*s spend a day per week or a month or 40 days a year to visit Muslim homes across the globe and invite them to mosques. They believe in close bond among global Muslims and do not indulge in (or even talk about) politics.

Millions of Muslims annually gather at *Tabligh Ijtamas* near Dhaka in Bangladesh and near Lahore in Pakistan. These congregations last for a few days and so far as the number of participants is concerned, are second only to the Hajj congregation. Famous British rock-singer Cat Stevens (Yusuf Islam) is amongst the devout followers of the movement. Despite charges of having links with terrorism, the *Tablighi Jamaat* remains a purely evangelical Islamic movement. However, one cannot rule out the possibilities of terrorist use of the *Tabligh* movement as a cover. Nevertheless, the overwhelming majority of the *tablighi*s do not represent the mullah, but modern-educated, semi-literate, or totally illiterate Muslims, who are more next-worldly, apolitical than this worldly and political. However, modern-educated adherents of this ultra-orthodox evangelical Islamic movement have remained intolerant to non-Muslims, and contrary to the teaching of the Quran, believe that only Muslims will go to the paradise and others will burn in hell-fire eternally. Some *tablighi*s could be very offensive to non-Muslims. *Tablighi*s in green turban told a gravely injured Christian patient at a hospital in Karachi to convert to Islam to save himself from eternal hell-fire.[26]

In short, the *tablighi*s represent sections of the ultra-orthodox born-again type Muslims, who are moderate, nonpolitical, and nonviolent. Among the educated *tablighi*s, engineers, medical doctors, and science graduates overwhelmingly outnumber liberal arts and social science graduates. Despite their puritan and orthodox views, some orthodox Muslim scholars consider the *tablighis* heretics. While some scholars portray the *Tablighi Jamaat* as a hidden front of Wahhabism, the *Ahl-e-Hadis* scholars portray it as anti-Deobandi, and the JI finds it a group of deviant Muslims.[27]

The Concept of War and Peace in Islam

The Quran and the great traditions of Islam are much more egalitarian and liberating, than what we find in the Old and New Testaments and in the Hindu or Buddhist scriptures in regard to human and women's rights.[28] Contrary to the popular perception expounded by the mullah as well as by non-Muslim scholars and Islamophobes, the Quran does not propound the theory of Islam's superiority over other religions. It promotes pluralism in creed, color, and culture as the ideal world system, most desirable to God. The concept of Muslims being the chosen people of God, or the only people destined to go to heaven, is anything but Islamic. This is reflective in the following verse: "Surely the Muslims, Jews, Christians, and the Sabians, whoever believes in God and the Last Day, and whoever does right, shall have his reward with his Lord and will neither have fear nor regret" (The Quran, 2:62). However, what is given by the Quran has been taken away by Shariah. There are other misgivings about Islam, especially in regard to the concepts of jihad, terrorism, and suicide attacks. Jihad as holy war is not an Islamic concept;[29] it is purely defensive, permissible to both Muslims and non-Muslims:

> Permission is granted to those (to take up arms) who fight because they were oppressed. God is certainly able to give help to those who were driven away from their homes for no other reason than they said: "Our Lord is God." And if God has not restrained some men through some others, monasteries, churches, synagogues and mosques, where the name of God is honored most, would have been razed. (The Quran, 22:39–40)

In accordance with the Quran noncombatants, especially women and children must not be attacked or killed, the enemy must not be killed by setting them ablaze and cannot be forcibly converted either. The following verses may be cited in this regard: "There can be no compulsion in religion" (The Quran, 2:256); "To you your religion; to me mine" (The Quran, 109:6). Suicide is also forbidden in Islam: "Don't kill yourself; most definitely Allah is most kind to you. And whoever transgresses the limit and kill oneself, most definitely I will punish him/her, which is not difficult for me" (The Quran, 4:29–30).

The Quranic verses, which both militant Islamists and Islamophobes cite to justify violence and demonize Islam, respectively, are problematic. They frequently cite verses from Chapter 9 (*Surah al-Tauba*), totally out of context: "And fight those who fight you wherever you find them, and expel them from the place they had turned you out from" (*Surah al-Baqr*, 2:191). They, for the obvious reasons, do not cite the preceding and following verses: "Fight those in the name of God who fight you, but do not be aggressive; God does not like aggressors" (2: 190); and "If they desist, then cease to be hostile, except against those who oppress" (2:193). Islamist jihadists cite the following verse to justify terrorism in the name of Islam: "Prepare against them [non-believers] whatever arms and cavalry you can muster, that you may strike terror in the hearts of the enemies of God and your own, and others besides them not known to you, but known to God..." (*Surah al-Anfal*, 8:60). Then again, they do not cite the next verse from the same chapter, which promotes peace:

> But if they are inclined to peace, make peace with them, and have trust in God, for He hears all and knows everything. If they try to cheat you, God is surely sufficient for you. It is He who has strengthened you with His help and with believers. (8:61–62)

Islamists and Islamophobes cite another Quranic verse to justify killing of non-Muslims totally out of context: "But when these months, prohibited for fighting are over, slay the idolaters wherever you find them, and take them captive or besiege them and lie in wait for them at every likely place to slay them" (9:5). Here again, the citing is very selective and out of context. This chapter is contextual to the period when Meccan idolaters were busy organizing an attack in collusion with rebels in Medina against the Prophet and his Medina-based government. We find God urging the Muslims to cease fighting if their enemy were treaty-bound and friendly:

> [Fight] except those idolaters with whom you have a treaty, who have not failed you in the least, nor helped anyone against you. Fulfill your obligations to them during the term of the treaty...If an idolater seeks

protection, then give him asylum that he may hear the word of God. Then escort him to a place of safety…as long as they are honest with you be correct with them, for God loves those who are godly. (9:4, 6– 7)

Islamophobes and Islamist militants never cite the following Quranic verses which prohibit killing of innocent people:

> And do not take a life, which God has forbidden, except in a just cause. We have given the right of redress to the heir of the person who is killed, but he/she should not exceed the limits of justice by slaying the killer, for he/she will be judged by the same law. (*Surah Bani Israel*, 17:33)

> That is why We decreed for the children of Israel that whosoever kills a human being, except as punishment for murder or for spreading corruption in the land, it shall be like killing all humanity; and whosoever saves a life, saves the entire human race… (*Surah al-Maidah*, Ch. 5:32–33)

The Quran also prohibits fighting and killing the enemy after they repent and seek peace: "those who repent before they are subdued should know that God is forgiving and kind" (5:34). In sum, the moral principles of the Quran outweigh its legal principles; many Quranic instructions are contextual, meant for a particular time and place, not universal, let alone binding on modern Muslims.

The Mullah Mind-Set

The understanding of the mullah mind-set is very important as its overpowering influence on Muslim masses mold their overall culture and values, including their belief system. The average Muslims' premodern, precapitalist culture, superstitious beliefs and practices, are full of beliefs in supernatural powers of saints and Sufi masters (dead and alive), and in miraculous healing and protective power of amulets given by saints, Sufis, and village mullahs. Thanks to the mullah influence, Muslims have problem in adapting to modernism individually and collectively. The bulk of the mullahs throughout history have been loyal to the rich and powerful as their livelihood depends on them. Hence, the proliferation of extra- and un-Islamic edicts or *fatwas* issued by mullahs justifying extraordinary privileges of the ruling elites and powerful men, including polygamy, slavery, concubines, harem, inferior rights for women, and non-Muslim minorities in the name of Shariah.

The mullah is a generic term, primarily denoting Muslim theologians, but actually connoting all sections of the Muslim clerics, including imams or prayer-leaders and semi-literate madrassa teachers. Mullahs have the sole authority to interpret the Quran and Shariah law, albeit mostly under the dictate of ruling elites. In short, the mullah collectively represents Muslim clerics and Sufis—*ulama*, *maulanas*, and *maulvis* (scholars), *pirs* and *sheikhs* (Sufis), *muftis* (jurists), and *imams* (prayer-leaders). Shiite mullahs, especially in Iran, have been well entrenched for centuries as Shiism, unlike Sunni, Islam upholds the concept of a formal clergy. In Iran, the Shiite mullahs virtually ran their states within state; and since the overthrow of the last Shah in 1979, they have become the state. Conversely, it is altogether a different story in the Sunni world.

With the passage of time, mullahs in the Sunni world have lost their influence, especially in urban areas. Since mullahs played important roles in mobilizing Muslim masses against Western colonial rule, they were least favored—rather despised—by colonial rulers. Colonial rulers introducing secular Western codes and their postcolonial successors' continuing support for such laws have made the mullahs irrelevant in running the governments. In most postcolonial countries in the Muslim world, with a few exceptions—Pakistan, Sudan, and Somalia—the Shariah only regulates certain aspects of Muslims civil and personal laws, mainly in regard to inheritance, marriage, and divorce. Mullahs, for the obvious reasons, have not taken the circumscription of their legal authority as the sole interpreters and dispensers of the Shariah gracefully. They also resent the loss of revenue-free land grants, which they had enjoyed during precolonial Muslim rule in India and elsewhere. The introduction of European codes, languages, and institutions, hard hit the mullahs' social standing as leaders, judges, jurists, and teachers. Hence, the mullahs tremendously hate Western ideologies and their local admirers and agents. Mullahs draw a broad line between the mythical *Dar ul-Islam* (abode of Islam) and *Dar ul-Harb* (abode of war or non-Muslims), which justifies exploitation, subjugation, and even killing of non-Muslims or *kafirs*, the most frequently used expression among *salafi–jihadi* militants everywhere.

It is noteworthy that although there is no formal clergy or intermediary between God and human beings as per Sunni interpretation of Islam, yet mullahs are quite well entrenched among Sunni Muslims. One of the most influential Sunni clerics and philosophers, Imam Ghazzali (d. 1111), and his followers in the Sunni world have been so rustic, misogynic, dogmatic, and irrational that they have opposed everything they have failed to understand or have considered a threat to their vested interests. Ghazzali not only opposed mathematics and philosophy, but also glorified subjection of women in the name of Islam. According to this medieval cleric, the father of Sunni orthodoxy, a wife can never repay her debt to her husband, not even by leaking his infectious wounds. This type of misogynous exposition has crept into popular Islam. Mullahs, especially throughout South Asia, glorify male supremacy, oppose female leadership, justify seclusion, wife bashing, arbitrary divorce by husbands, and inferior rights and status of women in the name of Islam.[30]

While mullahs in the undivided Indian subcontinent considered radio Satanic, they considered the recitation of the Quran over radio un-Islamic, the late Sheikh Gad al-Haq of the Al-Azhar seminary in Egypt justified female genital mutilation as Islamic and another cleric glorified it as antidotal to HIV infection.[31] Somalia-born ex-Muslim, Ayaan Hirsi Ali, gives a vivid account of the cruel custom of female genital mutilation, glorified by Christians, Muslims, Jews, and pagans, in Ethiopia, Kenya, Somalia, and elsewhere in the Arab world (and Southeast Asia). She also tells us from her own experience, growing up as a child in Kenya and Ethiopia, how other girls used to ridicule her and her sister at school until they went through the painful process of circumcision.[32] Another Muslim cleric, late Abdel-Aziz bin Baz, grand mufti of Saudi Arabia, believed that the world was in fact flat and those images provided by satellite to the contrary were nothing but a Western conspiracy against the Islamic world.[33]

The mullah mind-set is again a by-product of mullahs' ignorance and paradoxically their inferiority complex, social envy, and inflated egos due to their political use by opportunistic ruling elites. Mass reverence by both literate and illiterate Muslims also turns mullahs into megalomaniac zealots, reformers, and leaders. What mullahs learn at the premodern madrassas or seminaries—which do not teach any liberal arts, social sciences, and natural sciences to enlighten the students—is also responsible for mullahs' hatred for ideologies, concepts, and practices, which are beyond their comprehension. Mullahs, in general, consider Muslims to be the chosen people of God, only people, who will go to heaven while non-Muslims are hell-bound. Consequently, many Muslims wish eternal hell fire to dead non-Muslims as they have learned from mullahs to hate everything associated with non-Muslim faiths, rituals, and practices.[34] Mullahs across the board live in a romantic ahistorical past, when they believe, due to Muslim piety and fear of God, that Islam is the most advanced and dominant civilization in the world. They justify medieval Muslims' expansionist warfare, conquest, and subjugation of non-Muslim territories, forcible conversion of non-Muslims into Muslims, and accord inferior rights to non-Muslim subjects. Thanks to the mullah's glorification of Muslim conquests and subjugation of non-Muslims in Spain, India, Eastern Europe, and elsewhere in the world in the medieval age, as great achievements by their ancestors. Consequently, there is still vainglorious pride, arrogance, nostalgia, and intolerance toward non-Muslim culture and people among cross sections of Muslims everywhere.

Due to the pervasive influence of Shariah, orthodox, and next worldly mullah, Muslims learn more about death, hell, and heaven and less about enjoying life in this world. The average Muslim learns from the mullah that music, art, drawing animate beings, drama, theater, movies, and other forms of entertainment are simply forbidden in Islam. As per the edicts of the mullah, Muslims glorify plain and frugal living devoid of art, music, and entertainment, seclusion and subjection of women, Islamic schools, and spending more time in praying, fasting, and chanting God's name believing that life is just a transition to the eternal life after death. As a result, the bulk of Muslims, particularly in South Asia and Saudi Arabia (since the establishment of the Saudi dynasty), grow up without developing any liking, let alone any skill, in fine arts, music, dancing, drama, theater, and anything that the mullah considers *haram* or forbidden in Islam. Interestingly, many mullahs in South Asia forbade listening to the radio—not even the recitation of the Quran—as they thought the device was Satanic and Satan spoke through it to mislead people. Many mullahs still have strong reservations against movies, photography, and television. All of them, irrespective of their class, sect, and upbringing are misogynic; opposed to higher education for girls; favor seclusion of women and veiling; child or early marriage; polygamy; unequal inheritance rights for women; and oppose cross-religion marriages, female leadership, and, in short, prefer the Hadis and Shariah to the Quran. In sum, although the mullah justifies his teachings as Islamic, he is an ardent defender of the little traditions of Islam, which are again influenced and molded by local non-Muslim traditions and beliefs (Hindu–Christian–Jewish–animist). However, the mullah is unaware of any un-Islamic influence on what he considers in accordance with the Shariah, including female genital mutilation (as practiced among Muslims in Africa, the Arab World, and Southeast Asia) and stoning to death for adultery. Many mullahs, even today, justify monarchy, military dictatorship, and even slavery as Islamic. Considering power a gift of God, mullahs throughout history justified absolute rule by Muslim caliphs and kings, who after the end of the Early Caliphate (661) were mostly conquerors and military dictators. Mullahs, in the Muslim world, have no qualms about legitimizing the absolute monarchs and military dictators.

However, the mullah is not an undifferentiated monolith. It represents different categories such as urban and rural, rich and poor, educated and uneducated, Sunni or Shiite, Wahhabi or Sufi, close-minded and open/liberal. Most mullahs are apolitical, compliant, and pragmatic enough to understand the implications of going against the ruling elites and rich and powerful as being not so employable, they depend on these classes for sustenance. Consequently, many mullahs advise Muslims not to indulge in politics and anti-state activities under autocratic regimes. They also have certain Hadis to justify obedience to autocratic rulers. The mullahs—irrespective of their background and training—are premodern, superstitious people, who believe in magical healing powers of saints, amulets, and certain mantras or chants at a particular time of the day or night. Their followers—including college-educated Muslims—learn more of devotion and *sawab* or reward from God in the hereafter for one's good deeds. Most Muslims believe that reading the Quran even without understanding a word in Arabic brings *sawab*. The mullah cites a Hadis in support of this belief that each letter of the Quran bears 10 good deeds, pardon from 10 bad deeds and elevation of one's status in the eyes of God by 10 more steps.

Then there is another side of the coin. Despite one's strong reservations about mullahs' regressive and often reactionary role to the detriment of progress and peace, one cannot deny the fact about mullahs' glorious role in anti-imperialist/anti-colonial movements in various parts of the world. As Wahhabism in Arabia in the 18th and 19th centuries was primarily an anti-Ottoman Turk Arab nationalist movement, so were Mahdism in Sudan and various anti-colonial jihads in Somalia, British India, and elsewhere in the 19th century. Dedicated, honest, and brave mullahs in South Asia were the pioneers of anti-British movement. Most mullahs, unlike English-educated secular Muslims, remained steadfast in opposing the creation of Pakistan, the so-called homeland for Indian Muslims. What might be unbelievable today, the bulk of the most orthodox mullahs in British India did not consider Hindus as enemies of Islam. Instead of supporting Jinnah's Two-Nation Theory—which led to the creation of Pakistan in 1947—they championed the cause of a composite Hindu–Muslim nationhood for India.

Thanks to the teaching of the rustic mullah, the average Muslim believes that prayer, fasting, charity, and Hajj clean all their sins. Consequently, there is no dearth of Muslims, who are absolutely corrupt and very strict followers of Islamic rituals at the same time. There seems to be no ethics or philosophy behind such religiosity. Many Muslims simply believe in neutralizing or outweighing sins with rituals, extra prayers, and fasting, chanting, and visiting shrines of dead Sufis and/or performing an *umra* (visiting Mecca and Medina during the season of Hajj). Interestingly, the average Muslims do not have any qualms about the rehabilitation of the most corrupt, cruel, and debauch people as their leaders so long as they publicly display their piety and support for Islam. The acceptance of Zia-ul-Haq in Pakistan, Ershad in Bangladesh, Suharto in Indonesia, and other corrupt and cruel autocrats elsewhere in the Muslim world—in some cases for decades—are examples in this regard. In short, Muslims represent one of the least innovative and most backward communities in the world. They are also facing an enormous demographic pressure and youth bulge, which are among the leading factors behind economic crisis, sociopolitical unrest, including terrorism and insurgency. Arab Muslims are the least creative and innovative among the *Ummah*.[35]

Last but not least, as most Muslims live in postcolonial autocracies, they have little sense of belonging to the state or government, and respect for their laws and regulations. Hence, the violation of government rules is not considered immoral or sinful. Most mullahs do not know that Prophet Muhammad primarily strove for the rule of law or good governance in the name of establishing the supremacy of one omnipotent God. They also do not understand the denial of any intermediary between God and humans in Islam, and its promotion of strict monotheism or the concept of one omnipotent God without any partner amount to Islam's contempt for demigods or absolute rule.

In short, as the mullah symbolizes Muslim backwardness and reliance on a semi-educated priestly class (contrary to the Sunni teachings), so are obscurantist mullahs responsible for the retarded growth and development of the *Ummah* in every sphere of life. It is not coincidental that the bulk of the mullahs during the last millennium have either sided with foreign or indigenous autocrats or espoused unattainable romantic movements, contrary to the wish of the majority Muslims. Egyptian clerics' unflinching support for the autocratic, corrupt, and incompetent Khedives; their Iranian counterparts' support for the Shah and CIA-sponsored coup d'état in 1953, and most Bangladeshi clerics' collaboration with the Pakistani occupation army during the Liberation War of Bangladesh may be cited in this regard. In view of the mullahs' regressive views, non-revolutionary and compliant bend of mind—he is always a defender of the status quo, or even worse, an advocate of restoring premodern, socioeconomic, and political order, including absolute monarchy, slavery, and patriarchy—both militant and progressive Islamist movements are free from the clutch of the mullah. Whenever a mullah favors any change, he aims at going backward to an elusive glorious past of the early Muslim ancestors or the *Salfiyya*. Thus, even the most progressive and anti-Imperialist/anti-Western mullah represents regressive and backward-looking autocracy, or Islamism, in the name of Islam. The mullah lives in his wonderland and his idiosyncratic beliefs, assertions, and practices—at variance with the teachings of Islam—are unbelievable premodern, misogynic, indecent, vulgar, and unscientific. The mullah is at least hundred years behind his time. As many clerics justify female genital mutilation in the Arab world and Southeast Asia in the name of Islam, some of them consider the practice an antidote to HIV infection. The mullah, in general, despises music, fine arts, drama, theater; he teaches his followers to renounce this world and glorify death and prepare them for the hereafter. In sum, the mullah is mainly responsible for the retardation of Muslims. Islamism, in short, is inherent in the wrong interpretations of Islam by the mullah. The relationship between Islam and Islamism is comparable to the relationship between milk and yoghurt. They are different in look and taste, but derived from the same root.

Islamism by Default and Design

Islamism is not the primeval cause of all evils; it is rather a delayed effect of centuries of Western hegemony and duplicities in the Muslim world. Consequently, it is time that instead of asking the pretentious question, *What went wrong?* with Islam, we should be rather asking how to modernize Islam and Muslims; and how to make the West more responsible and accountable to the Muslim world. The expression "Islamism" is not universally acceptable to all Muslims. Non-Muslim critics and admirers of Islam also find it problematic. Muslims, who think Islam is all about politics, and, Islamophobes, who think Islam is all about violent takeover of the world to establish a global caliphate, find the expression loaded and misleading, as both these groups refuse to differentiate Islam from Islamism or political Islam. However, despite the ongoing debate if spiritual Islam is altogether a different ideology from political Islam, we do not find a better expression to denote and understand the dynamics and exigencies of political Islam.

We need to discern the Cold War Islamism from the post-Cold War one. While during the Cold War, Muslims considered the West a suspect-cum-ally, as a friend against their common enemy, communism. In the wake of the Cold War, Muslims no longer consider the West as a friend, but as their main adversary, thanks to Western duplicities and invasions of Muslim-majority countries. Instead of ushering in a new dawn of hope and empowerment for Muslims, the New World Order totally disillusioned them. By 1991, almost all the Muslim-majority countries—barring Turkey, Pakistan, Bangladesh, and Malaysia—had remained autocratic; and by 2003 three of them—Iraq, Sudan, and Afghanistan—had been invaded by Western troops. In short, the cumulative unpleasant post-Cold War Muslim experience has led to the beginning of another Cold War. Islam versus the West has become the new catchword. Meanwhile, premodern, ultra-orthodox, obscurantist forces had gained upper hand in many Muslim-majority countries. Interestingly, enamored by the concept of transnational Muslim solidarity, Muslims in postcolonial societies are grabbing the elusive *Ummah* as their security blanket as weak and marginalized people find security in number.

Then again, radical Islamism is "a modern philosophy, not just a heap of medieval prejudices." Military action cannot destroy any ideology and post-invasion Islamism is much stronger today than before. However,

I do not toe the line of Bernard Lewis, who assumes that Islamism is an offshoot of yester years' European fascism.[36] However, Lewis is right that, "The struggle between these rival systems [Islamic and Christian] has now lasted for some fourteen centuries;" Islam divides the entire world into the House of Islam and House of Unbelief or the House of War; Islam never considers other faiths equal, and Muslims learned anti-Americanism from German writers and philosophers of the 1930s and 1940s. Muslims are angry with the West for loss of domination and authority in their own countries, and for Western-induced empowerment of Muslim women and creation of rebellious children. He imputes the rising tide of Muslim rebellion against the West to its long colonial hegemony, and to America's support for hated regimes in the Muslim world. He, however, is not critical of European colonialism. It seems, he does not understand Western neocolonial misadventures and designs in the Muslim world either.[37] His differentiation of Islam with Islamism, at times, helps us understand the religion. Nevertheless, what Lewis wrote about Islam–West conflict in 1990 is not wholly relevant today. He saw no Cuba, no Vietnam in the Muslim world and no place where American forces are involved as combatants or even as "advisers."[38]

There is no consensus among scholars who study Islam and Muslims in historical, global, and contemporary perspectives if all political movements having an Islamic connection conform to the definition of Islamism. Leading Islamic scholars such as John Esposito, Martin Kramer, Graham Fuller, and Daniel Pipes believe that Islamism, which is synonymous with political Islam, is a modern movement for change and reform of Islam. They differentiate Islamism from the traditional Islamic movements such as Wahhabism in Saudi Arabia. They believe that unlike the Saudi Wahhabis, who strive for the status quo, Islamists strive for total change in every aspect of life within and beyond the Muslim world. Pipes even refuses to consider the Afghan Taliban as Islamists, as very similar to Saudi Wahhabis, are Islamic revivalists spreading, idealizing, and systematizing premodern rural/tribal customs to an entire country. Fuller thinks both pious and Islamist Muslims believe in change, but the latter are by nature activists. Since Islamists in the Arab world oppose Wahhabism and MB for their moderation, some scholars no longer consider Wahhabis and MB.[39] If all Islamists believe in restoring Shariah or some of them want to go beyond it and if Islamism has already entered a post-Islamist phase or has already been fizzled out—are some of the other contentious issues among scholars of Islam.[40]

As mentioned earlier, there are three types of Islamists: (a) non-violent believers in Shariah-based society through popular support or elections; (b) militant revivalists and violent revolutionaries, often offshoots of major Islamist outfits, such as the MB and JI, strive for regional or global caliphates (Sunni) or imamates (Shiite); and (c) the anarchic–nihilists—al Qaeda and its ilk—do not necessarily strive for establishing global caliphate or imamate, but want to destroy first everything they consider anti-Islamic through terror and violence. They have their own interpretations of the Quran, and most of their leaders are technocrats (mostly engineers and medical doctors) not Islamic clerics, who may be classified as techno-clerics. Sayyid Qutb, Osama bin Laden, Ayman al-Zawahiri, Khalid Sheikh Muhammad, Ramzi Yusuf, Hamza al-Masri, and Anwar al-Awlaki (Aulaqi), among others, were/are not Islamic scholars but techno-clerics. Not traditional Islamic scholars, but illiberal techno-clerics pose the biggest threat to modern civilization. Malise Ruthven corroborates our view. He thinks terrorism and extremism in the name of religion are particularly attractive to graduates in the applied sciences (such as engineering, computer programming, and other highly technical trades). Graduates in the arts and humanities who are trained to read texts critically may be less susceptible to the simplistic religious messages put forward by such movements. Technical specializations discourage critical thinking . . . The cultural, emotional, and spiritual knowledge embedded in the religious tradition they inherit has not been integrated with the technical knowledge they acquire by training and by rote.[41]

The Islamists do not represent a homogeneous monolith; they have mutual differences on ideological and strategic lines. Both the Hamas and Taliban, for example, are Sunni extremist groups; the former believes in democracy and female literacy and empowerment; the latter are dead against these concepts. While the neo-Taliban in the Federally Administered Tribal Area (FATA) and Swat bomb girls' schools force female students to wear *burqas*; the Hamas have never done so in Gaza. Again, the Hamas and Taliban have certain things in common: (a) they came into being to liberate their respective homelands; and (b) the U.S. played the most important role in the formation of these groups—the U.S.-backed Israel promoted Hamas to counterpoise secular nationalist

Palestine Liberation Organization (PLO) under Yasser Arafat and the U.S.-supported Prime Minister Benazir Bhutto in the creation of the Taliban to marginalize and eventually eliminate the Iranian-backed Afghan guerrilla leader, Gulbuddin Hekmatyar of the Hizb-e-Islami in 1994; (c) while the Hamas runs its own television channel, Al-Aqsa, the Taliban banned satellite cables and destroyed television sets in areas under their control.[42]

Again, the diversities, differences, and rivalries among the Islamists are well reflected in sectarian, ethno-national, and ideological conflicts. Some Islamist militants' primordial loyalty lies with what they believe to be Islamic, while others primarily fight for protecting their ethno-national or subregional identities. We are still not sure if the Taliban are primarily fighting to promote Pashtun nationalism or are merely supporting bin Laden's global jihad. In sum, Islamism is an ideology emanating out of Islam by default and design. The degeneration of Islam leads to Islamism. Muslims' inability to understand what went wrong with their glorious past and their quest to reverse the process are important factors in the rise of Islamism. As discussed in the next chapter, the globalization process, which has further accentuated inequality, discrimination, and marginalization of the poor and backward, has strengthened Islamism. The demonstration effect of wealth and power of the rich on the poor and powerless—thanks to the IT Revolution—has further reinforced Islamism. State sponsorship of political Islam, including superpower blessings for it during and after the Cold War, has been equally important in the creation of the Islamist Frankenstein's monster.

Meanwhile, due to state sponsorship of Islamism and Muslims expatriate workers' exposure to the Middle Eastern culture, many Muslims, including the diaspora, have been Islamized culturally. *Hijab* has become an important symbol of Muslim identity not only in conservative countries such as Saudi Arabia and post-revolution Iran but also in the diaspora and in Egypt, Palestine, Afghanistan, Pakistan, Southeast Asia, and even in Turkey. The cultural Islamization of a polity could be a prelude to political Islamization. Daniel Pipes, despite his refined Islamophobia, is right that: "It is a mistake to see all of Islam as Islamism. Islamism is a trend within Islam, at the moment a very powerful one...plenty of Muslims hate Islamism. So, it is a mistake to equate Muslims with Islamists..."[43] However, here the agreement ends as Pipes not only compares Islamism with fascism and communism, but also argues in defeating it with every means from bombers to radios, from fighting a hot war to fighting a cultural war. He also does not believe in democracy as an antidote to Islamism as he thinks democratic Turkey is more dangerous to the West than Islamist Iran. He is optimistic about defeating Islamism with the help of educated humanist Muslims to send them back to the Muslim liberal age of 1800–1940.[44]

As we know, terror, anarchy, insurgency, and war in the name of Islam have no relevance to the teachings of the religion, we need to attribute collective Islamist violence in a given society to certain socio, political, and economic factors. Islamist terrorists and insurgents often target autocratic regimes in the Muslim world, which deny freedom of expression and human rights and dignity to Muslims who do not belong to the sects or ethno-linguistic groups preferred by the ruling elites. Since religion is the main identity in all premodern communities, where ethno-linguistic nationalism is not well entrenched, religion becomes the main instrument of political dissent and protest. Since most Muslim communities and Muslim-majority states are still autocratic, quasi-literate, and premodern to a large extent, not surprisingly, political Islam (often in the most violent form) becomes the main vehicle of revolutionary change and transformation. Iran is an example in this regard. Then again, Muslim minority sects and ethno-linguistic communities (including the diasporas in the West) may also cling to political Islam as the last resort to get freedom, dignity, and equal opportunity. We have scores of examples of Islamist terror and insurgency across the world, which in fact reflect marginalized peoples' quest for rights and opportunities. Last but not least, there is no room for denying that since the end of the Cold War, various Islamist movements also draw Muslims as alternative global ideologies of the downtrodden people, while communism is no longer a popular alternative to unbridled capitalism under globalization, or in the "New World Order."

Last but not least, we cannot trace the origin of most Islamist extremist organizations and movements, such as the MB, JI, al Qaeda, LeT, and their ilk, directly to mullahs or traditional Muslim clerics. Except the Taliban and Khomeini's Islamist network in Iran, secular-educated Muslim technocrats or techno-clerics—mostly engineers, scientists, and medical doctors—have been the main architects and founders of Islamist outfits such as the MB and JI and violent Islamist extremist groups such as al Qaeda and, among others, the Moro Islamic Liberation Front (MILF) and the Abu Sayyaf Group (ASG) in the Philippines. As Islamist extremism is not mainly attributable to the mullah but to techno-clerics, I have discussed Islamist extremist groups such as the MB, JI, and al Qaeda in Chapter 5.

It is noteworthy that while the Quran promotes tolerance and peaceful coexistence of other religions besides Islam, and considers Jews, Christians, and other non-Muslims believers or *momeneen* (plural of *momin* or believer), we find the Shariah law and the mullah utterly intolerant toward all non-Muslims, who they believe to be hell-bound, inferior to Muslims, and liable to persecution, expropriation, forcible conversion to Islam, and even death merely because of their lack of faith in Islam. One may cite the following Quranic verses to highlight the differences between Allah's law and the mullahs' law: "Surely the Muslims, Jews, Christians and the Sabians, whoever believes in God and the Last Day, and whoever does right, shall have his reward with his Lord and will neither have fear nor regret" (The Quran, 2:62).

> Permission is granted to those (to take up arms) who fight because they were oppressed. God is certainly able to give help to those who were driven away from their homes for no other reason than they said: "Our Lord is God." And if God has not restrained some men through some others, monasteries, churches, synagogues and mosques, where the name of God is honored most, would have been razed. (The Quran, 22:39–40)

Radical Muslim clerics and "techno-clerics" are mainly responsible for the endemic sectarian violence between Sunni and Shiite Muslims. As some Shiite clerics consider Sunnis heretical, some of their Sunni counterparts consider the Shiites non-Muslims, and even worse than Jews and Christians. Mullahs also promote inferiority of women and misogyny.

Notes and References

1. Pew Research Center's Forum on Religion & Public Life, "The Future of the Global Muslim Population: Projections for 2010–2030" (January 27, 2011). Available at: http://pewresearch.org/pubs/1872/muslim-population (accessed on June 26, 2012).

2. Bernard Lewis, "What Went Wrong?" *The Atlantic Monthly* (January 2002).

3. Bernard Lewis, *What Went Wrong? The Clash between Islam and Modernity in the Middle East* (New York: Perennial, 2003), p. 159.

4. Edward Said, "Orientalism Now" in *Orientalism* (New York: Vintage Books, 1979), See Chapter 3; Marshall G.S. Hodgson, *Rethinking World History: Essays on Europe, Islam and World History* (Cambridge: Cambridge University Press, 1993), Chapters 7 and 10, pp. 97–125, 207–246; Zbigniew Brzezinski, "Terrorized by 'War on Terror': How a Three-Word Mantra Has Undermined America," *The Washington Post* (March 25, 2007).

5. Noam Chomsky, "The Evil Scourge of Terrorism," "Heroes and Devils," and "The 'Peace Process' in the Middle East," in *Necessary Illusions: Thought Control in Democratic Societies* (Toronto: ANANSI, 1989), pp. 269–332.

6. Max Rodenbeck, "The Truth about Jihad," *New York Review of Books*, Vol. 52, No. 13 (2005).

7. H.A.R. Gibb, *Whither Islam?: A Survey of Modern Movements in the Moslem World* (New York: Am Press Inc, 1973), p. 379.

8. Bernard Lewis, "The Roots of Muslim Rage," *The Atlantic* (September 1990).

9. Bernard Lewis, *What Went Wrong? Western Impact and Middle Eastern Response* (New York: Oxford University Press, 2002), passim.

10. Murad Hofmann, *Islam: The Alternative* (Garnet Publishing, 1993), pp. 33–39.

11. *The Economist*, "Islam and Science: The Road to Renewal," *The Economist* (January 26, 2013).

12. Ibid.

13. Ibid.

14. Tarek Fatah, *Chasing a Mirage: The Tragic Illusion of an Islamic State* (Toronto: Wiley, 2008), passim.

15. Syed Farid Alatas, "Contemporary Muslim Revival: The Case of 'Protestant Islam,'" *The Muslim World*, Vol. 97, No. 3 (2007): 508–520.

16. Maulana Muhammad Ali, *The Religion of Islam* (Lahore: The Ahmadiyyah Anjuman Isha'at Islam, 1950), passim.

17. Montgomery Watt, *Muhammad at Medina* (Oxford: Oxford University Press, 1956), pp. 227–228; Uri Rubin (ed.), *The Life of Muhammad: The Formation of the Classical Islamic World* (Brookfield: Ashgate, 1998), Vol. IV, p. 151.

18. Thomas Carlyle, "The Hero as a Prophet—Mahomet: Islam" (May 8, 1840), Lecture II. Available at: http://www.scribd.com/doc/12685866/Hero-as-a-Prophet-by-Thomas-Carlyle- (accessed on February 24, 2011).

19. De Lacy O'Leary, *Islam at the Crossroads* (London: Kegan Paul, 1923), p. 8.

20. Michael H. Hart, *The 100: A Ranking of the Most Influential Persons in History* (New York: Hart Publishing Company Inc., 1978), p. 33.

21. M.A. Shaban, *Islamic History: A New Interpretation* (A.D. 600–750) (Cambridge University Press, 1971), pp. 56–57.

22. Taj Hashmi, "Shariah is neither Islamic nor Canadian" (April 19, 2005). Available at: http://www.mail-archive.com/osint@yahoogroups.com/msg08830-html (accessed on June 6, 2010).

23. Fazlur Rahman, *Islam* (Chicago: Chicago University Press, 1979), pp. 45–47.

24. Sheikh Sultan M. As-Salameh, "Shari'ah Laws Are Plagiarized from the Bible" (December 22, 2008). Available at: http://ourbeacon.com/index. php?p=29433 (accessed on May 21, 2009).

25. Sumbul Ali-Karamali, "Who's Afraid of Shariah?" *Huffington Post* (September 3, 2010). Available at: http://www.huffingtonpost.com/sumbul-alikaramali/ whos-afraid-of-shariah_b_701331.html (accessed on August 15, 2012).

26. Urooj Zia, "No Compulsion in Religion? Convert or Go to Hell: Tablighis Tell Non-Muslim Patients at Govt. Hospitals," NewAgeIslam.com (April 14, 2011).

27. Yoginder Sikand, *Origins and Development of the Tablighi-Jama'at (1920–2000): A Cross-Country Comparative Study* (New Delhi: Sangam Books, 2002), passim; Yoginder Sikand, "The Tablighi Jamaat's Contested Claims of Islamicity" (June 18, 2010). Available at: http://www.newageislam.com/ NewAgeIslamArticleDetail.aspx?ArticleID=3014 (accessed on June 15, 2010).

28. Taj Hashmi, *Women and Islam in Bangladesh; Beyond Subjection and Tyranny* (London: Palgrave-Macmillan, 2000), Chapter 2.

29. Reza Aslan, *No God but God: The Origins, Evolution, and Future of Islam* (New York: Random House, 2006), pp. 80–81.

30. Ibid., Chapter 3.

31. Taj Hashmi, *Women and Islam in Bangladesh* (New York: Palgrave-Macmillan, 2000), pp. 22–23.

32. Ayaan Hirsi Ali, *Infidel* (New York: Free Press, 2007), Chapter 5.

33. Fatemah Farag, "As the World Turns," *Al-Ahram Weekly*, No. 477(April 19, 2000). Available at: http://weekly.ahram.org.eg/2000/477/eg13.htm (accessed on March 12, 2013).

34. Sayyid Qutb, *Milestones* (Karachi: International Islamic Publishers, 1988), passim; Daniel Burns, "Said Qutb on the Arts in America," *Current Trends in Islamist Ideology*, Vol. 9 (November 2009); Taj Hashmi, *Pakistan as a Peasant Utopia* (Boulder: Westview Press, 1992), Chapters 4, 8.

35. UNDP—Arab States, "Arab Performance in Research and Innovation" (2010), Chapter 5. Available at: http://arabstates.undp.org/subpage_ nf.php?spid=13 (accessed on October 6, 2010).

36. Paul Berman, "Why Radical Islam Just Won't Die," *New York Times* (March 23, 2008).

37. Bernard Lewis, "The Roots of Muslim Rage," *The Atlantic* (September 1990).

38. Ibid.

39. "Is Islamism a Threat? A Debate," *Middle East Quarterly* (December 1999). Available at: http://meforum.org/pf.php?id=447 (accessed on February 13, 2008).

40. Ibid.; Oliver Roy, *The Failure of Political Islam* (London: I.B. Tauris, 1994).

41. Malise Ruthven, "'Born-again' Muslims: Cultural Schizophrenia," *openDemocracy* (September 10, 2009). Available at: http://www.opendemocracy.net/faith-islamicworld/article_103.jsp (accessed on April 14, 2011).

42. Hamid Meer, "The West Cannot Differentiate between Hamas and Taliban: Is it the Truth?" *Prothom Alo* (January 31, 2009).

43. Daniel Pipes, "You Can't Fight Islamism with Ideas Coming out of Europe," *Citizen Times* (December 1, 2010). Available at: http://www.citizen-times.eu/you-cant-fight-islamism-with-ideas-coming-out-of-europe/ (accessed on December 6, 2011).

44. Ibid.

3

Global Muslims' Triple Jeopardy: Islamophobia, Israel, and Globalization

After "the war to end war" they seem to have been successful in Paris at making a "Peace to end Peace."

Field Marshal Archibald Wavell on the *Treaty of Versailles*, 1919

So, it turns out that the creation of Israel had not, after all, been a haphazard fight in which the Arabs fled their homes due to the directives of their own leaders. It had been a systematic campaign of ethnic cleansing by the Jewish militia involving massacres, terrorism, and the wholesale looting of an entire nation.

Miko Peled, author of *The General's Son*, 2012

Overview

This chapter appraises the Muslim–West conflict in historical as well as contemporary perspectives. It illustrates the conflict in the backdrop of Muslims' triple jeopardy of hate, humiliation, and marginalization by the West. Since major Western powers—Britain, France, and the Netherlands—had colonies in the Muslim world and Muslims globally feel discriminated against and persecuted by the West in the postcolonial world, it is only natural that there is no love lost between the Muslim and Western worlds. The lack of mutual trust and respect between the two worlds has been further intensified after the emergence of America as the new global hegemon in the wake of World War II. The West being persistently biased against the best interests of the Muslim world—reflected in its invasions of Iraq, Afghanistan and threats against Iran and Pakistan, and support for some of the worst autocrats in the Muslim world—most Muslims despise the West considering it detrimental to Muslim interest. The not-so-subtle justification of Western hegemony in the world by Western leaders, scholars, and media has further alienated Muslim intellectuals, politicians, and masses from the West. This chapter juxtaposes Muslim worlds' triple jeopardy—Islamophobia, Israel, and Globalization—against Western hegemony and neo-imperialism to understand the problem, if the ongoing conflicts between global Muslims and the West will remain the main components of the Hundred-Year War.

The Problem

The discourse of legitimizing Western superiority by its portrayal of Islam and Muslims in the Orient as exotic, deviant, and inferior is known as Orientalism.[1] Western Orientalist scholars during European colonial rule of the Orient—-in the name of studying Oriental history, religion, culture, and language—deliberately denigrated Muslim, Arab, and Afro-Asian people, their culture, and traditions. The end of colonialism did not signal the end of Orientalist prejudice against the East. The postcolonial discourse of hatred of Islam and Muslims is sometimes quite subtle and sometimes very crude and vulgar. The literary and the so-called objective studies with subtle denigration of Islam and Muslims may be classified as neo-orientalism.[2] The provocatively blunt and openly hateful writings, statements, and speeches against Islam and Muslims are simply Islamophobic. Although the postcolonial neo-colonialists in the West are a bit subtle in establishing their hegemony over the Third World, nevertheless they want to perpetuate the same old system of controlling both the market and sources of cheap raw materials and labor in the Third World.

Here, I have appraised the short- and long-term effects of the Islamophobic hatred on the psyche of the Muslim world. As the victims of hate become hateful of those who hate them, hatred also humiliates them, and turns them into unforgiving adversaries. The understanding of the Muslim concept of shame due to the loss of Palestine to the Zionist state of Israel and the Western invasions of Iraq, Afghanistan, and of late

Libya, Syria, and Western threats against Iran and Pakistan is essential to understand why Muslims are so angry with the West. Western promotion and protection of autocratic pro-Western regimes in the Muslim world—Saudi and Gulf monarchies, the Shah of Iran, Suharto, Zia ul-Haq, and Hosni Mubarak, among others—further embittered the Muslim–West relationship. Muslim Westophobia may be explained in these terms. Last but not least, Muslims also resent marginalization of the Muslim world by the West in the name of promoting democracy, human rights, and the deceptive globalization through a New World Order.

The 1970s was a decade of hope and despair for Muslims. The oil boom brought sudden prosperity to oil-producing nations in the Arab world and Iran. Millions of South Asian Muslim workers got the first-hand exposure to the Arab world and Islamism. What started with the Iranian Revolution in 1979—phenomenal resurgence of Islamism in the world—was further intensified after the Soviet invasion of Afghanistan, the same year. Meanwhile, considering the Iranian Revolution purely a Shiite aberration, the West had remained complacent about any such revolution in the Sunni world. Aijaz Ahmad has rightly attributed the rise of Islamism, since the late 1970s, to Carter's and Reagan's Cold War exigencies; while the former organized the jihad against the Soviet Union, the latter considered the mujahedeen as moral equivalents of our [American] Founding Fathers.[3] It is noteworthy that in early 1980, sporting a Pashtun-style turban, Carter's adviser Zbigniew Brzezinski formally declared the jihad against Soviet Union at Peshawar in Northwestern Pakistan. Mamdani may be right that both al Qaeda and the neo-conservatives in the U.S. were Reaganite twins born on the winning side of the Cold War and hell-bent to remake the world through violence. Giving the devil his due, Mamdani even defends Bernard Lewis, who unlike Huntington and other neo-cons does not portray all Muslims as antimodern, tribal, and fascistic. Mamdani thinks George W. Bush invaded Iraq after being influenced by the neo-cons' gurus, Huntington and his ilk, who considered the Green Peril or Islam as the biggest threat to the West.[4]

Despite Western support for the anti-Soviet jihad in Afghanistan, the decade also signaled the alienation of Muslims from the West. The American/NATO invasions of Iraq and Afghanistan further widened the gap between the Muslim and Western worlds. Many sober Muslims started considering the post-9/11 situation of global Muslims as the worst in the 1,400-year-old history of Islam. The 21st century also signaled the new revival of political Islam.[5] We have reasons to agree with the view that: (a) "Islam has established itself as the only transnational force able to resist America's homogenizing power on a global scale;" (b) the West has failed to understand the Islamic idiom inherent in the mobilization of Muslim youths in Egypt, Tunisia, and elsewhere in the Arab world for freedom and justice during the so-called Arab Spring; (c) Western scholars and analysts by solely focusing on Islam as terror/resistance and civil war in Islam have failed to notice the surge of Islamic awakening as the main factor behind Islamist militancy and terror; (d) it is time the West learns the importance of engaging the Muslim world for a durable Muslim–West understanding; and finally, (e) "Islam should not be reduced to Islamic political movements, no matter the numbers they command. *It is far more and far more powerful*" (emphasis added).[6]

Islamophobia and Westophobia—not direct derivatives of the globalization process—became more vigorous in the wake of globalization. As to how and why the globalized New World Order has further widened the gap between the Muslim and Western worlds is an important question. It seems the quest for an alternative benign global order or Social Democratic Globalization for the underdogs is inherent in the globalization process. However, as neither the Muslim world is monolithic, nor is the West homogenous, there is nothing so global about Islam, yet the expressions global jihad and globalized Islam are in circulation for quite some time. Proponents of local jihads often claim to represent the Global Muslim Community or the *Ummah*.[7] This chapter is a reappraisal of the following problematic concepts: Muslims' extraterritorial loyalty, their Westophobia or (alleged) hatred for the West, Islamophobia as something allegedly inherent in Western culture, and Muslims' unwillingness and inability to modernize themselves and indigenize democracy.

We may consider the post-Cold War period as the spring of hope and winter of despair for the Muslim world. This is the period of fulfilling the unfulfilled promises made in the past. The demonstration effect of the positive changes in the wake of the fall of the Berlin Wall has been an important factor behind the rapid growth of Islamism. Whether the *Ummah* is hell-bent to fight the globalization process to liberate itself from Western hegemony, and whether the West is determined to perpetuate its neo-colonial hegemonic designs in the Muslim world are important questions today. I have singled out the three entities: (a) Islamophobia,

(b) Israel, and (c) Globalization at the roots of Muslim–West conflict. We may explain regional and subregional Islamist terror networks of al Qaeda, Taliban, LeT, Jemaah Islamiyah, MILF, HUJI, and other groups, who ominously are coming closer to each other to bleed the West and its allies. In short, the issues of Palestine, Kashmir, Chechnya, Kosovo, and Southern Mindanao, for example, should not be addressed in isolation. They are all parts of the global jihad.

The Muslim world and the West were at loggerheads for centuries. During the 8th and 17th centuries, Muslim caliphates and empires had been the most formidable superpowers from the Indian Ocean to the Mediterranean world. Europeans, in general, either remained awestricken by their Muslim hegemony or hell-bent to turn the table to their own advantage. As Dante's *The Divine Comedy* (written between 1308 and1321) is an epitome of hatred for Islam and its Prophet, so is Voltaire's play *Fanaticism or Mahomet the Prophet* (written in 1736). Hegel, Francis Bacon, Marx, or Max Weber, among other Western scholars, had hardly any kind word for Islam either. Hegel and Marx through their discourse of Oriental Despotism portrayed the Orient, including the Muslim world, as inferior to the glamorous and enlightened West. The orientalists only noticed despotism, splendor, cruelty, and sensuality in the Muslim world to legitimize Western colonial hegemony in the orient.[8] British colonial rulers used expressions such as mad mullah and the noble savage to undermine Muslim rebels and their followers in the Middle East and South Asia.[9] Derrida's call for deconstructing the European intellectual construct of Islam is very pertinent. He rightly ridicules the much-used Western expression Judeo–Christian civilization as ahistorical and prejudicial to Muslims as Islamic culture also enriched Western civilization.[10] Edward Said's *Orientalism* is simply an eye-opener and a pathbreaking deconstruction of the age-old Western Orientalist prejudice against Arabs and Muslims.

Western prejudice against Islam is not altogether unexpected. Many Muslim rulers during the heydays of Islamic empires had been extremely prejudicial, exploitative, and oppressive to their non-Muslim subjects. The subjugation of the Iberian Peninsula (modern Spain and Portugal) and most East European countries by Muslim rulers for four to seven centuries, and the extermination of around a million Armenians by Turks in 1915–1917 may be mentioned in this regard. Muslim clerics' and intellectuals' love for the subjective and faulty interpretations of some Quranic verses to glorify subjugation of non-Muslims have also strengthened Islamophobia in the West. Many Muslim writers still glorify Muslim tyrants and barbaric invaders such as Sultan Mahmud of the 11th and Ahmad Shah Abdali of the 18th centuries, and lament the loss of Islamic empires and the loss of Cordova, Granada, and the Ottoman and Mughal Empires. They love to blame the West for their present state of powerlessness.

Western colonial hegemony over almost the entire Muslim world for a couple of centuries up to the mid-20th century and the postcolonial Western treatment of the Muslims in general and Arabs in particular have further widened the gap between the worlds of Islam and the West. Only Turkey may be singled out as a Muslim-majority country, which ran a parallel and rival colonial empire in Eastern Europe, North Africa, and Middle East for centuries. However, the loss of Turkey's last vestiges of its empire soon after World War I sent two ominous signals to Muslims, especially in the Indian subcontinent, that: (a) while the Muslim world was under European (Christian) domination, Muslim supremacy and conquests of non-Muslim territories had become history; and (b) with the demise of the Ottoman caliphate, Indian Muslims had no one else to help them out of British hegemony. The culture of suspicion and hatred between Muslims and the West is all about fear, based on past experience, present conflicts, and the prospect of their continuation in the future.

European colonial powers arbitrarily drew lines "across the desert," which created artificial states such as Israel, Lebanon, Jordan, Kuwait, Pakistan, Indonesia, and Malaysia, and truncated entities such as Syria and Iraq. They also made Kurdistan, Kashmir, Palestine, Pashtunistan, and Balochistan disappear as independent entities. British Field Marshal Archibald Wavell's observation about the potentially catastrophic effect of the peace or redrawing the map of Europe and the Middle East after World War I had been prophetic: "After 'the war to end war' they seem to have been successful in Paris at making a 'Peace to end Peace.'"[11] The postcolonial Western hegemonic designs in the Muslim world have been equally disastrous for most Muslims. From the establishment of Israel to the overthrow of democratically elected government in Iran (1953), the Anglo–French and Israeli invasions of Egypt in 1956, and the Israeli invasion and occupation of territories in Egypt, Syria, and Jordan in 1967; the overthrow of Saddam Hussein with flimsy excuses, lies, and deceptions; and, last but not least, the America-led vitriolic campaigns against Iran, Syria, and Pakistan may be cited in this regard. The surge in anti-Westernism among Muslims is a byproduct of colonial legacies and their postcolonial experiences of defeats and humiliation at the hands of Western powers.

We find Hamza Alavi's appraisal of postcolonial societies very useful for this study. Alavi has explained that unlike societies that never experienced colonial rule, postcolonial societies have overdeveloped civil and military bureaucracy and underdeveloped civil society. Postcolonial rulers run the top-heavy bureaucratic structure and maintain the old colonial infrastructure to the benefit of the ruling elites.[12] In short, postcolonial states are mostly artificial entities based on arbitrarily drawn borderlines by colonial rulers and have remained fractured on ethnic, tribal, religious, or sectarian lines.

The Problematic New World Order: Islamophobia versus Westophobia

This is an enigmatic question to the West: *What does a Muslim want?* Then again, Islam and Muslims are not monolithic; quite different in Algeria from Afghanistan or Balochistan; and so are Islamisms as Aijaz Ahmad has used the expression as a plural noun.[13] Conversely, most Muslims have little or no understanding of Western culture, norms, and behavior, and above all, have no clues as to what the West wants Muslims to do. This lack of mutual understanding is at the root of the mutual prejudice against each other. Western scholars' demonology to hurt Islam[14] is extremely vile and distressing for Muslims. While Neo-Orientalist Western scholars—Lewis, Huntington, and others—are condescending toward Islam and Muslims, the avowedly anti-Islamic Pope Benedict XVI, Daniel Pipes, Jerry Falwell, Franklin Graham, Geert Wilders, Rush Limbaugh, General (ret.) William Boykin, Glenn Beck, and Pat Robertson, to name only a few, have been promoters of sensational Islamophobia by branding Islam nothing more than an evil and wicked religion. Many of them believe that terrorism derives from the teachings of the Quran and Prophet Muhammad, and that the average Muslim is a potential terrorist supporter, or even worse, a suicide bomber.[15] Interestingly, Lewis has come to a middle ground putting Islam in between a violent and peaceful religion, albeit tacitly supporting the Clash of Civilizations theory.[16] Even one of the most liberal British politicians, William Gladstone (1809–1998), was Islamophobic. He believed that "So long as there is this book [The Quran], there would be no peace in this world."[17]

The wide gap between the American ideals and realities—American means White—may suggest that mainly racism has molded American Islamophobia. Until the phenomenal rise in Muslim immigration since the 1970s, Black American Muslims represented the bulk of the Muslim population in America. As part of the marginalized and grossly discriminated against Afro-Americans, apparently the Black Muslims *did not exist as another category* among the marginalized. The various genres of Islamic movements among the Black Muslims, which mobilized support for anti-White supremacy among their adherents up to the 1980s, never emerged as the Islamic menace to the main stream of Americans. The rise of immigrant Islam, as Jackson explains, "has complicated this enterprise in at least two ways." Firstly, immigrant Muslims did not join the Black Muslims movements as they considered race as Islamically irrelevant. Secondly, their overall acceptance by the mainstream Americans appeased most of them. However, the second generation and new Muslim immigrants have different expectations. They want better job opportunities, living conditions, respect, and dignity. They are going through the same phase which Jewish, Irish, Italians, Chinese, and other immigrants had gone through in the past.[18]

Case studies of alienated and marginalized Muslim diaspora in regards to their support for the global jihad and homegrown terrorism are quite revealing. An American-born Pakistani Muslim medical student in America, for example, did never consider himself American, and was unable to reconcile Islam and refused to be assimilated into some jive, subaltern, "honorary" whiteness. Some second and third generation American Muslims, thanks to racially motivated Islamophobia, belong to a racial non-category. Interestingly, Arab-Turkish-Iranian-Pakistani-Afghan Muslim immigrants do not want to join American Blackness as they consider Black identity a stigma. It seems Muslim immigrants and their children will remain shackled to an explicitly non-American racial identity, anti-immigrant Islamophobia in this country may simply, and sadly, come to know no bounds.[19] The Muslim immigrant experience in Europe is even worse.

Modern Islamophobia in America predates 9/11. The Iranian Revolution of 1979 signaled its ascent. However, the Soviet invasion of Afghanistan and the consequential Muslim–West alliance against the invaders somewhat neutralized the Western hatred of Muslims up to the Soviet withdrawal in 1989. Apparently, during the Afghan jihad, American media, intellectuals, and politicians singled out minority Shiism not Sunni Islam as the main adversary of America. Nevertheless, the growing surge of Islamophobia in America led to the foundation of the American–Arab Anti-Discrimination Committee (ADC) in 1980. By early 1990s, following the ADC, the Council on American Islamic Relations (CAIR) came into being for protecting Muslim civil rights in America.

However, not long after the Russian withdrawal from Afghanistan, Islamophobia got a new lease of life in America. Not only did the leading American media, analysts, and experts on Islam and Middle East impute the Oklahoma City Bombing in 1995 to Arab Islamists, but there had also been a phenomenal rise in American Islamophobia across the board. In 2002, around 38 percent Americans had favorable views of Islam, by 2007 it went down to 15 percent.[20] In July 2012, several Republican politicians under the leadership of Congresswoman Michele Bachmann of Minnesota alleged that the Obama administration had hired several hardcore MB members in the Homeland Security Department. They singled out Huma Abedin (an Arab–American), the Deputy Chief of Staff of Hillary Clinton, as one of the leading Brotherhood supporters, who are said to have penetrated the Homeland Security Department.[21]

Meanwhile Huntington's so-called theory of the Clash of Civilizations and leading Islamophobes' hateful writings and speeches had further widened the gap between White and Neither-White-nor-Black Muslims in America. While Bush Sr. and Clinton had eschewed Huntington's Clash of Civilizations thesis, Bush Jr. and Tony Blair were ardent admirers of the thesis that demonizes Muslims and Asians in general. Many in the West cannot differentiate Muslims and Arabs. The West, in general, believes that Islam is a "uniquely sexist religion, the 'Muslim mind' is incapable of rationality and science, Islam is inherently violent…the West spreads democracy, while Islam spawns terrorism."[22]

While ultra-conservative radio talk-show host Michael Savage wants forcible conversion of Muslims into Christians to turn them into human beings, Daniel Pipes considers Muslim customs more troublesome than most.[23] In 2008, radio talk-show host Rush Limbaugh portrayed Barack Obama as an Arab Muslim not an African American. Republican presidential candidate John McCain's defense of Obama was also problematic. He said Obama was not an Arab but a "decent family man," as if Arabs are not nice family men.[24] Last but not least, George W. Bush once portrayed Islam as the "Green Menace," and later as a "religion of peace." Donald Rumsfeld's equating Islam with "danger," McCain's assertion that America was founded "primarily on Christian principles," and Mike Huckabee's observation that "more Pakistani illegals" than Mexicans were coming across America have been Islaomophobic assertions.[25] Islamophobes talk about the benign neglect of Europe toward radical Islam.[26] Many of them believe that Muslims will eventually wage a jihad against America to establish an Islamic empire.[27]

Not only a serving general, William Boykin (now retired) vilified Islam as an evil religion and the Muslim God as devil, but some politicians are also Islamophobic. Congressman Peter King (R-NY) publicly vilified American Muslims as radicalized and unpatriotic believing that 80 percent mosques in the country were controlled by radical imams. He did not acknowledge the fact that after 9/11, American Muslims helped prevent at least one-third al Qaeda terrorist plots in the country, and that American mosques have been instrumental in de-radicalizing American Muslims.[28] Peter King, who headed the Congressional Hearings on Islamic Radicalism in America in March 2011, once complained that there were too many mosques in America.[29] Days after Peter King's prejudicial remarks about Muslims, a Southwest Airlines employee offloaded a *hijab*-wearing female Muslim passenger at San Diego International Airport on March 13, 2011 for security reasons.[30]

One may mention the offensive cartoons of Prophet Muhammad, which portrayed him as a suicide bomber hiding bombs in his turban; the movement for banning erection of minarets in mosques in Switzerland; the opposition to the building of a mosque two blocks off the Ground Zero in New York; the burning of the Quran by a Christian pastor in Florida; and last but not least, the Dutch Islamophobe Geert Wilders's portrayal of Islam as "Europe's greatest problem—not just today, but already for decades now," and his comparing the Quran with Hitler's *Mein Kampf* may be mentioned to highlight the growing tide of Islamophobia in the West.[31] Pastor Terry Jones of Florida, who publicly burned down copies of the Quran in March 2011, promised a trial of Muhammad.[32] He considers Islam to be a religion of the Devil and all non-Christians, including Jews, Hindus, and Muslims, devils. The burning of the Quran led to widespread violence against Western and Christian interests in Afghanistan and Pakistan. While Afghan mob raided U.N. compound in Kabul and killed seven foreign workers, Pakistanis killed several Christians and burned down churches.[33] As analysts believed the Quran burning had benefited Islamist extremists, General Petraeus considered it posing new dangers for the U.S.-led war efforts in Afghanistan.[34]

While American Fox TV commentator Bill O'Reilly equated the Quran with *Mein Kampf*, Reverend Jerry Vines portrayed Prophet Muhammad as a demon-possessed-pedophile. Reverend Jerry Falwell called the Prophet a terrorist and George W. Bush's pastor Reverend Franklin Graham called Islam "a very wicked religion."[35] The growing popularity of the Born-again-Christian leaders in America, who also hate Islam (their hatred for Obama is due to his race and alleged faith in Islam), is simply widening the gap between the Muslim and Western worlds. The prejudice against everything Islamic and Muslim in America is growing among ordinary peaceful citizens from all walks of life. They mobilize support among people and seek government intervention against building new mosques and Islamic centers by American Muslims. It seems those who oppose the construction of a mosque at the Ground Zero do so to preserve the sanctity of the place, while others oppose building of mosques to save America from the onslaught of Shariah law. Several leading anti-Shariah rather Islamophobic organizations in the U.S. such as ACT for America and The Call have been active in promoting Islamophobia in the name of protecting America from the demonic Shariah law and for establishing the supremacy of Christianity.[36] The Shariah-phobia of Americans has reached such a peak that many of them consider it an existential threat to their country. Unveiling the Report "Shariah: The Threat to America" by the Center for Security Policy, its President Frank Gaffney told his audience in 2010 that Muslim radicals wanted to destroy Western civilization from within by imposing Shariah through force if possible or through a more stealthy technique if necessary. The report claims that: "There is ultimately but one shariah" and "it is totalitarian in character, incompatible with our Constitution and a threat to freedom here and around the world."[37] Raymond Baker believes that sections of American politicians', medias,' and think tanks' projection of Shariah as the main threat to their country indicates that an American empire is in precipitous decline.[38]

The organized protests and agitations against a proposed mosque and Islamic center at Murfreesboro, a small town in Tennessee, may be cited in this regard.[39] The anti-mosque campaign at Murfreesboro since late 2010 has led to a statewide disturbingly hateful campaign against Islam and Muslims in Tennessee. As we see in the media, state Senator Bill Ketron and Rep. Judd Matheny introduced a bill in the Senate and House in Tennessee in February, 2011. Considering Shariah law a danger to homeland security, the bill gives the Attorney General authority to investigate complaints and decide who is practicing it. It exempts peaceful practice of Islam but labels any adherence to Shariah law, including Islamic practices such as feet washing and prayers as treasonous. It claims that Shariah adherents want to replace the Constitution with their religious law. A dozen other states are considering anti-Shariah bills, and there's a federal lawsuit in Oklahoma over one.[40] According to the Tennessee state Senator Ketron, the bill "is an anti-terrorism measure" to stop terrorist acts, including "Sharia Jihad."[41]

The frenzy against Islam and Muslims may be just the tip of the iceberg. One knows how popular some ultra-right Islamophobic talk-show hosts are in America. Rush Limbaugh and Glenn Beck, for example, make around $60 and $33 million per year, respectively.[42] Thanks to Western Islamophobia, al Qaeda and their ilk adhere to extreme tribalism out of their sense of belonging to an exclusive community. Their Hyper-*Asabiyya* or tribalism reflects their post-honor symptom, which leads to their resorting to terrorism against the West.[43]

The alarmist Islamophobic concept of *Eurobia*, which stands for the specter of Arabization of Europe, is a new development in the West. Egyptian-born Jewish writer Bat Ye'or is a leading exponent of this theory. Her thesis is simple. Europe has allowed itself to be taken over by Arab interests as it largely depends on Arabian oil. While Islam in Europe has not been Westernized, Europe has become increasingly compliant to Muslims out of a fear of social unrest and terrorism. She ascribes the growing anti-Semitism and anti-Americanism to the Euro–Arab axis, which she thinks is a threat not just to the existence of Israel, but also to the survival of Europe. Should current trends continue, she warns, the future of Europe could be one of *dhimmitude*, or subservience to their future Muslim masters? [44] In view of the small number of Muslims in Europe—only around 4 percent of the population—the concept of *Eurobia* sounds exceedingly racist and Islamophobic. Although Muslims tend to be more religious and conservative than most Europeans, there are plenty of secular, non-practicing, and non-believing Muslims in Europe.[45] Tariq Ramadan's succinct assessment of the Swiss Minaret Ban is an eye-opener in this regard. "There are only four minarets in Switzerland, so why is it that it is there that this initiative has been launched [sic]?.... The minarets are but a pretext."[46] A German politician publicly asserted that Islam "did not really belong in Germany because it was not rooted in the country's long Christian history and way of life."[47] Recommending the total obliteration of Islam, one Islamophobe suggests:

> This blood-thirsty Muslim mentality has trickled down to the newest convert to Islam be he or she Brown, Black, Yellow or White.... So Islam will have to be the first to be removed from the path of human progress and the reply to Islam to be effective would have to be more blood-thirsty and paranoid than Islam itself.... After Islam is militarily defeated and then destroyed; the need of the day would be to come up with workable creative ideas, for brainwashing the remaining religious fanatics with techniques like anesthesia leading to amnesia and re-education of such brainwashed ex-religious fanatics; or the use of mass lobotomy to achieve the same result.[48]

A pre-9/11 report on the growing Islamophobia in Britain shed light on the main characteristics of the phenomenon. British Islamophobes, according to the report, separate the Muslim "others" from the mainstream population, as "not having any aims or values in common with other cultures;" and as "inferior to the West—barbaric, irrational, primitive, sexist, ... supportive of terrorism, engaged in a clash of civilizations." They justify anti-Muslim hostility as "natural and normal."[49] Some scholars impute Islamophobia in Europe to West Europe's colonial hangover, racism, and xenophobia. They believe that paradoxically growing unemployment as well as White Europeans' self-love and pride at the successful integration of Western Europe through the European Union (EU) have strengthened Islamophobia in Western Europe. They also believe that the post-9/11 War on Terror has been an important factor in this regard.[50]

Of late Western print and electronic media, Christian evangelists, and Hollywood have become quite paranoid about Islam. One may cite dozens of movies, including True Lies, as Islamophobic. Muslims were angry at the promotion of Islam-bashing writings by former Muslims such as Salman Rushdie, Taslima Nasrin, and Ayaan Hirsi Ali. Ehsan Jami, an ex-Muslim member of the Dutch Labour Party (PvdA), is one of the latest to join the Islam-bashers' bandwagon. In late 2008, he produced a 15-minute video, Interview with Muhammad, which most Muslims would consider extremely vulgar and offensive. A Jewish newspaper from New York went further in promoting hatred against Islam: "Moreover, the only way to deal with Islamic terrorists is the same way in which they deal with their victims.... They killed our innocents, and unless we kill theirs, they will go on killing ours."[51] Conservative Republicans and right-wing Christians adore former Muslim Hirsi Ali who publicly asks Muslims to convert into Christians.[52]

Conferring knighthood on Rushdie might have strengthened some Muslims' belief that the West is inherently anti-Islamic, hence a legitimate target. Pope Benedict XVI's inadvertent/careless quoting of a medieval source, which is quite pejorative to Islam, added fuel to the fire. Sherry Jones's controversial novel, *The Jewel of Medina*, an ahistorical depiction of Ayesha, Prophet Muhammad's wife, which is extremely offensive to Muslims is yet another addition to the Islamophobic literature. The ongoing debate on free speech versus blasphemy is a bit problematic as Britain still has blasphemy law, and in the U.S. people sometimes suffer at their workplace just because of their views: (a) Professor Ward Churchill lost his job at the University of Colorado, Boulder, for his very offensive essay on 9/11 in 2007; and (b) in June 2007, the DePaul University denied tenure to Professor Norman G. Finkelstein for his anti-Semitic publications. Paradoxically, while one may go to jail for anti-Semitic writings or statements, one enjoys the impunity for defiling Islam and Muslims in whatever manner one chooses to do so in the West. Interestingly, while Western governments, civil societies, and media have almost forgotten and condoned the famous British-owned bank HSBC's role in money laundering, drug, and terrorist financing to the tune of $881 million in 2012, as one wonders, what would have happened if the HSBC had Islamic/Muslim connections.[53]

Muslim fanatics, on the other hand, are unequivocal about their praise for The Magnificent Nineteen, who took part in the 9/11 attacks. Muslim radicals, Abu Hamza al-Masri, Omar Bakri Muhammad, and Anjem Choudary, among others, may be mentioned in this regard.[54] From Sayyid Qutb's vitriol against everything American—its jazz music to haircut, love for boxing and other violent sports, and free-mixing to animal-like sexual promiscuity—to his modern counterparts' rabid Westophobia, we hardly see any meeting ground for the Western and Muslim minds. Qutb, said to have inspired both bin Laden and Al Zawahiri, was so hateful of the West that he propounded his dogma of jihad not to defend any country by Muslims, but to destroy the Evil West.[55] Consequently, nothing short of considering hate-crime a violation of human rights and dignity is going to resolve the issue. It is time to draw a line between freedom of speech and freedom from humiliation.[56]

However, Islamophobia and Westophobia do not represent the mainstream Western and Islamic populations. As there is a broad difference between what al Qaeda wants and what the vast majority of Muslims aspire for,[57] similarly, the West in general is sensitive to Muslim sentiments although it is equally stubborn about defending peoples' freedom of expression. Despite Samir Amin's portrayal of Islamist organizations as erstwhile collaborators of the West for preferring capitalism to communism during the Cold War,[58] undoubtedly, in the post-Cold War era Islamists visualize an alternative global order to Western hegemony.[59] Nevertheless, Islamists often cooperated and even collaborated with the West, sometimes by playing the Islamic card, and sometimes by championing the causes of Islamic modernism and democracy to fight the common enemy, such as Russians in Afghanistan, Dr Mossadegh's secular nationalism in Iran, and, among others, Saddam Hussein. Nevertheless, the overwhelming Muslims throughout the world have always been against al Qaeda and killing of innocent people under any pretext.

The Iranian example of Islamist–West collaboration in the 1950s is very remarkable. The avowedly anti-Western, Ayatollah Abol-Ghasem Kashani (1882–1962), who had earlier supported the nationalization of Iranian oil, later favored Mossadegh's overthrow and favored the Shah.[60] From the first Iranian president (February 1980–June 1981) Bani-Sadr's own account it appears that "90 percent of the foremost Shiite religious leaders," including Kashani and Khomeini, had earlier opposed the concept of *Vilayet-i-Faqih* or the "sovereignty of the Islamic jurist."[61] Madeline Albright has rightly considered the CIA-sponsored coup against the Mossadegh government in 1953 clearly a setback for Iran.[62] In hindsight, one may assume that but for Western duplicity, including promotion of autocrats in the Muslim world, Islamism would not have been that well entrenched as it is today.

Although Rushdie, among other Islamophobes, blamed Islam for 9/11,[63] many Muslims and non-Muslims held either the U.S. or Israel responsible for the attacks. By late 2010, while 43 percent Egyptians and on the average 7 percent of the world population believed Israel had been behind 9/11; 36 percent Turks, 30 percent Mexicans, and 23 percent Germans blamed the U.S. for the attacks. Globally, around 15 percent people believed the U.S. had orchestrated 9/11.[64]

The Creation of Israel: The Linchpin of the Muslim–West Conflict

The raison d'être for Israel goes beyond the creation of a Jewish homeland. Theodor Herzl's (the Father of Zionism) justified the creation of a Jewish State in Palestine in his famous 1896 pamphlet *Der Judenstaat* (*The Jewish State*) in the following manner: "We should there form a portion of a *rampart* of Europe against Asia, an outpost of civilization as opposed to barbarism." European colonial powers especially Britain was enamored by the idea of Israel, especially during World War I. Besides the Balfour Declaration made by British Foreign Secretary Arthur James Balfour in 1917 favoring the creation of a Jewish State in Palestine, in the wake of the war in 1918, the British did everything possible to settle a large number of armed European Jews in Palestine (which was under British occupation, 1918–1948) paving the way for the creation of Israel in 1948. Despite many leading Americans' opposition to the creation of Israel, President Truman (a Christian Zionist) favored its creation.[65]

Western powers created Israel by using the U.N. (most European colonies in Africa and Asia were not members of the U.N. in 1947–1948) and by condoning the mass expropriation of about a million Palestinians by Jewish settlers from Europe. It seems the main motive behind the creation of Israel was the Western desire to have a rampart of Europe against Asia in the oil-rich Middle East in close proximity to the strategically important Suez Canal. The Anglo–French and Israeli invasion of Egypt in the wake of Nasser's nationalization of the Suez Canal in 1956 may be cited in support of the above assertion. Western and Israeli double standards vis-à-vis the Arabs and the Israeli defense requirements are abysmally striking. On the one hand, Israel is hell-bent to destroy Iran's alleged nuclear program, yet, on the other hand, Israel not only has huge stockpile of nuclear weapons, but in 1975 it also offered nuclear arsenal to South Africa under Apartheid to intimidate its black neighbors.[66] America's *carte blanche* to Israel is at the roots of the latter's dangerously arrogant policy toward the Muslim world.[67] America favored Israeli occupation of Arab lands in 1967 and subsequent invasions of Arab nations and Palestinians in Gaza and the West Bank. Last but not least, America has been supportive of Israel's brazen and unabashed violations of around 90 U.N. Security Council resolutions condemning its violations of human rights, and asking for its unconditional withdrawal from Arab territories it occupied in the 1967 War, which Israel started by invading Egypt, Syria, and Jordan, contrary to the Western and Israeli propaganda. America also condoned the Israeli (aerial and naval) attack on a U.S. Navy Ship during the 1967 Arab–Israeli War in international waters, as a mistake. The attack sank the USS Liberty and killed 34 U.S. soldiers.

One wonders as to why the West does not take cognizance of Arab rebels displaying the Palestinian flag in anti-autocracy rallies during the Arab Spring in the streets of Cairo, Damascus, and Sana'a. While the Palestine issue has been a flashpoint, the West has been consistently supporting Israel since it hurried creation in 1948 following a U.N. Resolution in 1947 in favor of partitioning Palestine between Arabs and Jews. It is noteworthy that the decision to partition Palestine (Resolution 181) was taken at the U.N. General Assembly on November 29, 1947 by 33 votes against 13 with 10 abstentions and one absence, while more than two-thirds of the world (under colonial rule) remained unrepresented in the U.N.[68] The reason of Western/American support for Israel is not far to seek. Days after Resolution 181, on December 11, 1947, British Labor MP Thomas Reid stated in the Parliament the real motive of American support for Israel:

> What is the motive? Let us be frank about it. One of the chief motives is that the Jews have a controlling voice in the election for the President in the States of New York, Illinois, Ohio and elsewhere in America. I suggest that the chief reason for this evil proposal of U.N.O. is that the political parties in America, or their party machines, are partly at the electoral mercy of the Jews. That is public knowledge.[69]

Despite Israel's victory against Arabs and its occupation of Arab territories in the 1967 War, countries such as the USSR, China, India, and the bulk of the Third World and Muslim-majority countries did not condone the Israeli occupation of Arab territories. Until 1991, majority of the U.N. members considered Zionism synonymous with racism. On November 10, 1975, the U.N. General Assembly could muster enough support among members to adopt Resolution 3379 with 72 votes against 35, which determined that Zionism was a form of racism and racial discrimination. Interestingly, Muslim-majority Iran and Turkey, which had diplomatic relations with Israel in 1975, voted for Resolution 3379 and so did China, India (did not formally recognize Israel until 1992), and the USSR. Resolution 3379 also considered Zionism as a threat to world peace and security. Meanwhile, in December 1953, Resolution 3151 of the General Assembly formally condemned the unholy alliance between South African racism and Zionism.[70]

Israel's growing influence in world affairs has been the main catalyst in the fast deterioration of the Muslim–West understanding. By1991, the Israeli Lobby had become so powerful globally that the U.N. General Assembly—for the first time in its history—on December 16 revoked Resolution 3379 by Resolution 46/86 by 111 votes against 25. In 1991, countries that had favored Resolution 3379 in 1975, either abstained/ absented from voting or voted in favor of its revocation. USSR and India, which had voted for Resolution 3379, went against it in 1991.[71] Afterwards all attempts to find out a solution to the Arab–Israeli problem through the good offices of some European and American leaders, including Bill Clinton, failed. They failed as they wanted to find a solution without compelling Israel to leave all occupied territories, including Jerusalem, in accordance with U.N. Resolution 242 of 1967.

After Bill Clinton—who had a better image than most American presidents had in the Muslim world—Obama sounded quite reassuring to the Muslim world through his pathbreaking Cairo Speech on June 4, 2009, and his insistence in May 2011 that the Palestinian State would be based on the pre-1967 War borders. In Cairo, he asked Israel to recognize the Palestinians' right to have a state of their own, and reiterated boldly: "The United States does not accept the legitimacy of continued Israeli settlements [in the occupied West Bank]." In Washington, on May 19, 2011, on the eve of Israeli hawkish Prime Minister Netanyahu's arrival, he called for Israel's return to the pre-1967 borders.[72] He asked Israel to accept the pre-June 1967 boundaries as the basis for negotiations for a lasting peace with the Palestinians. He wanted full and phased withdrawal of Israeli military forces from the West Bank in coordination with Palestinian security forces for a viable Palestine, a secure Israel. "The dream of a Jewish and democratic state cannot be fulfilled with permanent occupation," he stressed. Instead of asking Israel to demolish the illegal Jewish settlements in the West Bank, he advised Israelis and Arabs to do "land swaps to accommodate Israel's large settlement blocs."[73]

Meanwhile, Israeli Prime Minister Yehud Olmert claimed that he had offered quite a pragmatic solution to the Arab–Israeli problem to the Palestinian President Mahmoud Abbas, on September 16, 2008, in Jerusalem. According to Olmert, the plan "granted the Palestinians a state with a land area equal to 99.5 percent of the West Bank and Gaza." He is said to have promised that Israel would only annex 6.3 percent of Palestinian territory, and would compensate the Palestinian State "with Israeli lands equivalent to 5.8 percent, as well as a corridor that would connect the two regions" of Gaza and West Bank. The plan is said to have also earmarked Jerusalem as a "shared capital" of the Jewish and Palestinian states.[74] However, the apparently generous promise of conceding 99.5 percent of the West Bank and Gaza to the Palestinian State with a corridor to connect the West Bank and Gaza through Israel was nothing, but a dead letter. Later, quite conveniently, Olmert said he had not heard anything from Abbas again, while the former has been waiting ever since. Elliott Abrams, George W. Bush's deputy national security adviser, who tried to negotiate an Israeli–Palestinian settlement, writes that "rather than ignoring the proposal, the Palestinians asked for clarifications about it and then claimed it was they who never heard back" from Israel. Abrams also believes that Olmert's so-called "offer" was never made public or shown to anyone to attest to its accuracy.[75]

Since it is least likely that Israel would pay heed to Obama's advice, and that Arabs would accept Jewish settlements in the West Bank and part with Jerusalem, the Arab–Israeli conflict is likely to remain unresolved for decades. The day after his speech, Obama met with the Israeli Prime Minister Netanyahu at the White House. Netanyahu publicly rejected the idea of Israel's going back to the 1967 border as impractical and, hence, unacceptable to Israel. Obama's speech was full of sound and fury and not so palatable to Palestinians for suggesting Palestinians to swap Jewish settlements in prime real estate in the West Bank with patches of desert. It, however, stirred up pro-Israeli Americans. Conservative American analysts and politicians—from Glenn Beck to Sarah Palin—ridiculed the idea of Israel's withdrawing from the territories it occupied in 1967, and likened it with the absurd idea of America's returning Texas and other territories it occupied in wars with Mexico. Israel and its American supporters have also rejected the idea of any peace talk between Israel and the Palestinian authorities having links with Hamas, which does not recognize Israel's right to exist as an entity, and publicly condemned the killing of bin Laden.[76]

Days before evoking some controversy by his Cairo Speech, Obama mended fence with the Israel Lobby and Israel through his American Israel Public Affairs Committee (AIPAC). Speaking to the AIPAC, America's largest pro-Israel lobby, Obama said that America's support for Israel remained ironclad and that his emphasis on 1967 borders was misrepresented and his words were neither controversial nor new. He said he wanted Israel and the Palestinians to negotiate a border that would be "different from the one that existed on June 4, 1967."[77] He also asserted that Israel was not under any obligation to sign peace with Hamas unless it recognized Israel as an entity, and that he wanted the Palestinians and Israelis to swap lands (allowing Israel to retain the Jewish Settlements in the West Bank). What the pro-Israeli Obama administration did to the Palestinian cause contradicted his Cairo Speech of June 2009, where he promised to turn America into a benign soft-power: "Indeed, we can recall the words of Thomas Jefferson, who said: 'I hope that our wisdom will grow with our power, and teach us that the less we use our power the greater it will be.'"[78] As King Abdullah II of Jordan has explained, while the State Department and the Pentagon have been soft on the Palestinians, Obama under the influence of his pro-Israeli Middle-East adviser Dennis Ross has been soft on Israel.[79]

Consequently, despite all the brouhahas about Obama's Cairo Speech, the Muslim world has not much to expect of the U.S. administration, which cannot go against American public opinion to force Israel to accept the 1967 lines as its borderlines with Palestine. Days after Obama's advice to Israel to accept the 1967 border as the basis of Arab–Israeli border, on May 24, 2011, Israeli Prime Minister Netanyahu addressed a joint session of the U.S. Congress. He told the audience that his country was not going to accept a divided Jerusalem and that the issue of a Palestinian State was least important, while the security for a Jewish state was of prime concern to Israel and America. He "reportedly got 59 rounds of applause—including 29 standing ovations"—for (in effect) telling Obama to shove off his suggestion to start the peace process on the basis of 1967 borders.[80]

What is noteworthy is Obama's volte-face at the end of the day. On September 21, 2011 his so-called soft corner for Palestine simply evaporated on the floors of the U.N. General Assembly. The Israeli Lobby in America—possibly more powerful than the Military–Industrial Complex—forcefully retaliated against Obama's harsh policy against Israel. Consequently, the U.S. president, supposed to be the most powerful head of state in the world, was forced to eat his words. In his U.N. General Assembly speech in September, 2011, Obama unabashedly pooh-poohed Palestinian National Authority's President Mahmoud Abbas's proposal of granting formal U.N. membership to Palestine. Obama, as one analyst tells us, in an empty and arrogant sermon to the U.N., which evoked no applause for a single line in his speech, suggested that a Palestinian State would emerge only after "negotiations between the parties," the Israelis and the Palestinians.[81] He simply ignored the fact that decades of negotiations between the two parties had been fruitless and futile. In the same speech, Obama concocted history and simply refrained from telling the truth to the world body. He told that (a) Israel's neighbors had waged repeated wars against it; and (b) in Bahrain, steps have been taken toward reform and accountability.[82] Not long after Obama's U.N. speech, America condemned the United Nations Educational, Scientific and Cultural Organization (UNESCO) for formally admitting the Palestinian State as a member and cut U.S. funding for the world body—worth $60 million per year.[83] In this backdrop, it seems the Palestinian State will remain ever elusive unless "'something' that will 'somehow happen,'" to paraphrase Mark Danner, who is critical of both the U.N. and U.S. administration for their pro-Israeli bias.[84]

It is evident again that the overwhelming majority of Americans do not know anything about the plight of the Palestinian people at the hands of Israel, let alone the history of Zionism and Israel. As America does not seem to realize the gravity of the Arab–Israeli problem, the mother of all conflicts in the Arab world, so is the Muslim world unwilling to accept Israel's legitimacy. It is noteworthy that despite many secular Israelis' public assertion that their country can deal with their enemies and that they do not need American support, the hawkish side of Washington is more than willing to give Israel a bear hug. It is, again, no longer a secret that George W. Bush sabotaged the Israeli–Palestinian peace talks by favoring the rightist Likud Party of Israel and the Right-of-Likud policy of Jewish settlements in the West Bank.[85] Americans simply do not understand that if the conflict persists, democratic and Islamist Arab governments will take a strong stand against Israel. What is most striking is conservatives' and other pro-Israeli Americans' total inability to understand the Arab and Muslim discourse on Israel—which redraws the pre-1948 map of Palestine—meaning the total obliteration of the Zionist state. Last but not least, the Israel Lobby is so well entrenched in the U.S. administration that even Obama has to concede undue advantages to the Zionist nation. Obama's inability to reverse the pro-Israeli U.S. policy—and his helplessness in this regard—is well reflected in a private conversation with President Sarkozy (which journalists overheard as the microphone was on) at the G20 Summit in Cannes on November 3, 2011. On Sarkozy's terse comment on Benjamin Netanyahu, "I cannot stand him, he is a liar," Obama replied, "You're fed up with him, but I have to deal with him every day."[86]

In view of the emerging changes in the Arab world since the Spring of 2011, which have emboldened Islamist Hamas and other groups, they are least likely to cooperate with the West that is committed to protect the Zionist state to the detriment of more than 10 million expropriated, humiliated, and stateless Palestinians in the world. Meanwhile, Islamist parties are emerging powerful in Egypt and Tunisia. The fate of the rest of the Arab world will not be that different in the coming years; anti-Israel public opinion will remain a feature of Middle-Eastern politics until a final and equitable peace treaty is struck.[87] Even secular Turkey—a NATO member having diplomatic ties with Israel—is not immune to the growing anti-Israeli sentiment that one notices in the Arab world, Iran, and elsewhere in the Muslim world. Turkish Prime Minister Recep Tayyip Erdogan reflected his country's strong reservations about Israel without any ambiguity. In an interview with the *Time* magazine he favored Palestine's full membership to the U.N.; condemned Israel's violations of U.N. Security Council's "more than 89 resolutions on prospective sanctions related to Israel;" and killing of nine Turkish activists by Israel on the *Mavi Marmara*, one of the Turkish ships that the Israeli military stopped from reaching the Gaza Strip with humanitarian aid in 2010. He categorically denied that Iran was becoming nuclear or posing any threat to anybody. He posed the question: "Is it Israel or the countries in the vicinity of Israel that are under threat?" And he added, "Israel has nuclear weapons."[88]

However, despite the growing influence of the Israel Lobby on the Congress, many American security analysts and even a general consider Israel a threat to the U.S. national security. In January 2010, General David Petraeus in his brief to Admiral Michael Mullen, the Chairman of the U.S. Joint Chiefs of Staff, depicted Israel as a security threat to America.[89] Despite many Americans' strong reservations about Israel and the perils that Israel poses to America's national security, the Congress remains unperturbed about having Israel as America's main ally in the Middle East. America's failure to understand why they (Muslims) hate Americans is unbelievable. As Ehsan Ahrari has pointed out, "It took the American policy makers more than fifty years to realize that the Arab–Israeli conflict has been a core Muslim issue." And one cannot agree more with him that although Saddam Hussein was no one's hero in the Muslim world, yet the U.S. invasion of Iraq in 2003 made the average Muslim very angry at America.[90] What the West has persistently failed to understand that despite its avid promotion of democracy, Western tolerance of unpopular autocrats in the Muslim world, along with its pro-Israeli and, by implication, anti-Arab/anti-Muslim policy, secular democracy has become synonymous with Western hedonism, materialism, and Godlessness, as we find in the writings of Sayyid Qutb and his ilk.

There is no room for taking Iraqi journalist Muntadar al-Zaidi's shoe throwing at President Bush in isolation or condescendingly, as Condoleezza Rice attributed it to the confirmation of the democratization of Iraq. Zaidi's emergence as a hero not only in the liberated and democratic Iraq but also in the entire Arab and Muslim world for his public display of courage and hatred for the West tells us a thousand tales and reveals the hidden transcripts of the Muslim world. Muslims across the board, the vast majority being peace-loving ordinary people, love to glorify anyone, who hits the West, symbolically or literally.[91] This incident and its positive repercussion in the Muslim world should be an eye-opener to Western policymakers. The mass protests in the Muslim world against Israeli air raids in Gaza in 2008–2009, and Israeli commandos' killing nine Turkish civilians in the Gaza-bound aid flotilla in May 2010, and the Muslim mass support for Hezbollah's war against Israel in 2006 simply reflect Muslims' contempt for Israel and the West. Mahathir

Mohamad, among many leading Muslims, condemned the Israeli attack on the unarmed Turkish flotilla as "most cowardly and deserving only of brutes, not civilized people." He also portrayed Israel as a rogue state.[92] As the West condones Israeli retaliatory air raids as acts in self-defense, Muslims in general have no qualms about justifying Hezbollah or Hamas rocket attacks against Israel to kill indiscriminately. It is noteworthy that while the Western media in general, and the ones run by the neo-cons in particular—Fox News, for example—portrayed the Israeli bomb victims in Gaza as Palestinian militants,[93] most other sources confirmed the bulk of the victims as non-combatant civilians, women, children, and the elderly.

The Israel Lobby is so influential that America, which propounds the freedom of expression as a sacred constitutional right, and its mainstream media shy away from publishing anti-Israeli news and views. It did not give any coverage to what Carter's former Security Advisor Zbigniew Brzezinski said in a speech to the National Iranian American Council in November 2012 about Israel's belligerent policy towards Iran, and reprimanded the U.S. for following Israel "like a stupid mule whatever the Israelis do."[94] As Alison Weir, the executive director of "If Americans Knew," believes that due to the influence of the Zionist Lobby, Americans can lose their jobs by simply criticizing Israeli atrocities, especially killing of Palestinian civilians and children by the Israeli Defense Forces,[95] few Americans dare go against the Zionist Lobby. Many conservative Congressmen and analysts stigmatized Obama's Defense Secretary Senator Chuck Hagel as anti-Semite for his criticism of Israel's highhandedness.[96]

The Arabs and Muslims, in general, despise Israel so much that even pro-Western Saudi Arabia and Jordan publicly supported all Arab–Israeli wars between 1948 and 1973, the latter took part in all of them. Pledging a billion dollars to rebuild Gaza at the Arab summit in Kuwait in January 2009, King Abdullah of Saudi Arabia said, "each drop of Palestinian blood [is] more precious than anything in the world." Other Arab leaders at the Summit also condemned Israel in unambiguous terms.[97] It is noteworthy that senior members of the Saudi Royal Family no longer shy out from publicly condemning Israel, U.N., and even the U.S. for the sufferings of the Palestinians. "America is not innocent in this calamity," asserts Saudi Prince Turki al-Faisal. He also mentions the growing Shia–Sunni rapprochement, including President Ahmadinejad's public recognition of Saudi Arabia as the leader of the Muslim world.[98]

The pro-Western Arab rulers' public support for Palestine against Israeli encroachment reflects their insecurity and desire to buy legitimacy at home. Conversely, Arab disunity and Arab states' past experience of catastrophic defeats at the hands of nuclear-armed and U.S.-sponsored Israel are important factors behind Israeli conceit and complacence. However, the prospect of revolutionary regime changes in pro-Western Arab countries is a potential threat to Israel in the long run. Most importantly, anti-Israeli secular and Islamist militant groups have already been enjoying wide grassroots support among the *Ummah*, well beyond the Arab world. We may consider the Palestine conflict as the mother of all conflicts in the Muslim world. The diametrically opposite Muslim and Western discourses on Palestine and Israel make our investigation difficult. Nevertheless, we need to understand that this lack of convergence is the key to our understanding of the problems of Islamophobia and Westophobia.[99]

Unless Israeli leaders abandon the belief that the harder you beat the Palestinians, the softer they will become,[100] there is no hope for any durable peace between Islam and the West. With the rising popularity of Hamas among Muslim masses, the standing of Arab leaders suffered due to their silence and duplicity.[101] Shiite Hezbollah and Mahdi Army and Sunni Hamas are forging ties under the aegis of Iran while the vast majority of liberal Muslims are turning anti-Western.[102] What is likely to be a perpetual headache for Israel in coming decades is the Hamas–Fatah Memorandum of Understanding (MoU), signed in Cairo on May 3, 2011. Although Secretary of State Hillary Clinton refused to rule out further negotiations with a Palestinian side that includes Hamas, Israeli Prime Minister Netanyahu refused to negotiate with any Palestinian side that did not renounce violence and recognize Israel.[103] Israel's refusal to come to an agreement with the Palestinians will not only eventually kill the peace process, a united Hamas-Fatah front with the blessings of post-Mubarak Egypt and other Arab neighbors will also further delegitimize the Jewish State. One Western analyst believes that "the pen that launched the reconciliation between Fatah and Hamas is likely to have more of an impact on U.S. policy toward the Israeli–Palestinian conflict than the bullet that ended Osama bin Laden's life."[104] As it was bad news in 2009 that negotiations over a two-state solution to resolve the Israeli–Palestinian conflict had reached a dead end,[105] Israel's refusal to stop Jewish Settlement in the West Bank under different pretexts has further aggravated the situation. Meanwhile, by early 2011 Mahmoud Abbas, the embittered president of the amorphous Palestinian State, had lost faith in Obama's neutrality and any hope of getting American support for a Palestinian State.[106]

In view of Israeli stubbornness and American vacillation and bias against the Palestinian State, the average Muslim from Morocco to Indonesia and beyond has become avowedly anti-American. To most Muslims, Israel has been an illegitimate entity and will remain so for an indefinite period. It was evident in the anti-Ben Ali movement in Tunisia. Tunisians denounced the dictator for hosting Israeli Prime Minister Ariel Sharon in Tunisia. Their contempt for Egypt's Hosni Mubarak and his predecessor, Anwar Sadat, was also due to their forging diplomatic ties with Israel. Israeli illegitimacy and arrogance are at the core of Arab hatred for pro-Western autocrats in the Arab world. For the pro-democracy Arabs, Israel's secret hotline to Arab autocrats has been a stumbling block to their aspirations for freedom.[107] The overthrow of the Mubarak regime has brought changes in Egypt's policy toward Israel. The military regime in Cairo declared to open its only crossing with the Gaza Strip in May 2011, significantly easing a four-year blockade on the Hamas-ruled territory but setting up a potential conflict with Israel.[108] One Israeli analyst has described the plight of the underemployed/unemployed Palestinians who live in crammed Gaza strip, and are regular victims of Israeli bombing, and questions her own government in the wake of 2012 Israeli bombing of Gaza:

> What does it mean that a girl from Gaza—whose school was bombed and her best friend was killed before her eyes that they, too, are human beings? And how has a nation that has occupied other people's territory for forty-five years continued to tell itself, with such deep conviction, that we are the single and ultimate victim in this story? And the evil of the occupation has become so banal that no one sees the evil anymore.[109]

While 73 percent of Arabs in 2002 in six Arab countries considered the Palestinian issue as one of the most important issues, the corresponding figure in mid-2008 rose to 86 percent.[110] Interestingly, the substantial rise in Arab support for the Palestinian cause took place in the wake of the U.S.-led invasion of Iraq. What is most disheartening from the Western/U.S. viewpoint is that two surveys in 2006 and 2008 in some Arab countries revealed that three-quarters of Muslims based their judgment of America: (a) on its policies, not on its values; (b) the vast majority of them considered the U.S. and Israel as the most threatening states; (c) the vast majority of Sunni Muslims in these countries considered Hassan Nasr Allah of Hezbollah and other anti-Israel/anti-American Shiite leaders as their most favorite; and (d) the vast majority of them did not trust the U.S. as an honest broker.[111]

Former President Ahmadinejad of Iran emerged as the most ardent champion of the jihad for Palestine. While on the one hand, the inherent extraterritoriality of Islam is the driving force behind this global solidarity for the liberation of Palestine, on the other hand, Muslim populist leaders use the Palestine issue as their red herring and fig leaf to hide their incompetence. A recent Brookings research based on 24-nation study reveals that the Palestine–Israeli conflict still matters a lot for the average Muslim in the Middle East.[112] Consequently, it appears that the Muslim–West understanding requires Israel's abandoning the policy of security for Israel, but no Palestinian State.[113] Some analysts rightly believe: Israeli complacence and Western tacit support for Israeli occupation of Arab lands and Arab resentment against peace with Israel will eventually be catastrophic to world peace in the coming decades.[114]

Israeli nervousness at the political upheavals in the Arab world and the MB's demand for a plebiscite in post-Mubarak Egypt to decide the controversial peace with Israel are some of the indications in this regard. British politician William Hague believes that if Israel abandoned the Peace Process to reach the "two-state-formula" in Palestine, Arabs would be forced to abandon the Process; and this would eventually lead to a bloody war for a "one-state-solution" in the coming years.[115] Thomas Friedman reflects similar views:

> Today, I believe President Obama should put his own peace plan on the table, bridging the Israeli and Palestinian positions, and demand that the two sides negotiate on it without any preconditions. It is vital for Israel's future—at a time when there is already a global campaign to delegitimize the Jewish state—that it disentangles itself from the Arabs' story as much as possible. There is a huge storm coming, Israel. Get out of the way.[116]

One believes it is time the West realizes "Israel cannot for long endure as a colonial project. It must choose between wars—and destruction—or transition to a state for all its peoples."[117] Thanks to Israeli complacency and the overpowering influence of the Israel Lobby in America, the Arab–Israeli problem remains in backburner. Meanwhile, following the overthrow of the Mubarak regime in Egypt, Arabs throughout the Middle East are calling for a *Third Intifada* (anti-Israeli mass demonstrations), which is likely to involve Arabs within and beyond Israel and Palestine.[118] The denial of basic human rights to Palestinians in Gaza and the West Bank—human dignity and security, health care, education, employment opportunities, and clean drinking water—will never keep the status quo in perpetuity in favor of Israel. It seems no durable peace is possible without recognizing the right of self-determination and the right of return to millions of Palestinian refugees and diaspora in the West.

The growing American–Israeli–Indian nexus, which China and Pakistan do not consider a friendly triumvirate, is another factor behind the growing Muslim resentment against America and its allies. As Pankaj Mishra has elucidated, Obama does not mention why his country is callous about the relentless tyranny of governments that deny their citizens dignity, particularly America's closest allies and Israel, the only democracy in the Middle East, and India, the largest democracy in the world. We hear the same story about Kashmir again and again, narrated by hundreds of analysts, journalists, and others about India's brutal occupation of Kashmir with more than 700,000 troops. One account reveals 70,000 civilians died and 8,000 disappeared in occupied Kashmir in 10 years up to 2010, where systematic torture by Indian armed forces (according to the Red Cross) is normative. Last summer, soldiers fired at demonstrators, killing 112 civilians, mostly teenagers (Kashmir has many of its own Hamza al-Khatibs), reveals the same source.[119] India and Israel have developed a strong military relationship. Hindu nationalists admire Israel's uncompromising attitude to Muslim minorities. In 1993, the then Israeli foreign minister, Shimon Peres, reportedly advised the Hindu nationalist leader L.K. Advani to alter the demographic composition of the mutinous Kashmir valley by settling Hindus there.[120]

In view of the turbulent situation in Palestine and Kashmir—two sore points in the Muslim psyche—Obama's ambivalence and unequivocal support for Israel and India have convinced the *Ummah* that neither there is any peaceful solution to their problems nor they have any genuine friend to help them out in the East or West. One analyst argues:

[P]resident Obama spoke at a time when U.S. influence in the region is at an all-time low in modern history. A new PEW survey...finds that the rise of pro-democracy movements has not led to an improvement in America's image in the region...in other predominantly Muslim countries, views of the U.S. remain negative.[121]

Last but not least, Professor Jerome Slater has convincingly argued, irrespective of what people think of Zionism—as racism or not—there is no denying that "to an alarming degree, an increasing number of Israelis are [racist]," that Israel is not a Jewish refuge (as most Jews do not want to live in Israel), and that the concept of a Jewish State is inconsistent with democracy. He considers Prime Minister Netanyahu's demand for a "formal Palestinian recognition of Israel as a Jewish state as a precondition for negotiations" as full of cynicism. He thinks Netanyahu and Israeli Zionists have "*neither the intention nor the capability of reaching a two-state settlement under any conditions*" (emphasis added). Slater believes that Palestinians are more flexible on the issue of the two-state solution than Israelis; provided Israel accepts the principle of the "right to return" to the Palestinian diaspora across the world.[122] In this backdrop, it appears that no Arab–Israeli peace is on the cards in the foreseeable future.

Global Jihad under Globalization

Notwithstanding the controversy about the globalization process, there is sort of a consensus among scholars about the broad definition of the concept, which theoretically stands for the growing integration of economies and societies around the world to eliminate state-enforced restrictions on exchanges across borders. Global jihad or globalized Islam, on the other hand, are loaded concepts. Interestingly, Islamists and Islamophobes seem to have agreed that global jihad stands for the destruction of the West. Now, to find out if Islam is "irreconcilable" with free trade, market economy, democracy, human rights, and gender equality, we may consider the facts that throughout the precolonial medieval world during the 8th and 17th centuries, Muslims represented the most powerful and resourceful global powers.

One Western/Israeli scholar observes,[123]

In the year 1000, the Middle East was the crucible of world civilization. One could not lay acclaim to true learning if one did not know Arabic, the language of science and philosophy. This [Islamic] supremely urbane civilization cultivated genius. Had there been Nobel Prizes in 1000, they would have gone exclusively to Moslems.

While Ernest Gellner considers Islam to be the only global, credible political system, Akbar Ahmed finds similarities between Islam and Protestantism: radical, ascetic, anti-magical and disciplined, not incompatible with capitalism.[124] To Gellner,

[T]he secularization thesis does not apply to Islam. In the course of the last one hundred years, the hold of Islam over the minds and hearts of believers has not diminished and, by some criteria, has probably increased.... Christianity has its Bible belt: Islam is a Qur'an belt.[125]

Juergensmeyer is equally incisive and thinks that much of the world "neither understands nor finds 'secular state' attractive;" and that religious nationalism is a fact of life and will be with us for a long time to come, and we should not demonize religious nationalism, and it is time to reconstruct, not deconstruct.[126] The overwhelming majority of the Muslims want to be integrated with the global system, aspiring for Islamic Modernism, if not Westernization. They do not want to remain marginalized in the periphery. Then again, as per Islamic ethics, there is not much room for profligacy in Muslim culture. Majid Rahnema has spelled it out as a vice of modernism, "A modern person is one with unlimited needs," and this is not acceptable to the average Muslim.[127]

We cannot understand Muslim reservations about globalization unless we understand as to why well-informed people in the Third World, in general, and Western scholars and leaders, having broader worldview and sympathy for the Third World, are also opposed to the process if not to globalization per se. Globalization is a process as well as a revolution, and revolutions affect religions. Very similar to how the geographical discoveries, Renaissance, industrial and French revolutions, nationalism, socialism, Fascism, Nazism, the world wars, and the postcolonial world orders affected religions globally, the post-Cold War globalization process has been doing the same to premodern cultures and nations, including Muslims. James Kurth shows how premodern religions perceive ideas and systems emerging out of globalization as threats to their existence.

By invoking theology, custodians and followers of such religions join the anti-globalization bandwagon. He argues that the anti-globalization movement by premodern people represents the conflict between the insecurity of the premodern order and the postmodern globalization, a conflict between theology and new ideology. He also believes that Muslim and Hindu revivals are not necessarily anti-globalization, but they reflect their failures to cope with globalized modernism and secularism. Nevertheless, he has aptly argued that the failure of Arab and Iranian nationalisms led to Islamic revival, and that Islamic revivalists not by design but by default are opposed to globalization, which represents the neo-imperialist interests of the West, backed by the IMF and WTO. He also ascribes this opposition to too much of democracy, secularism, and unbridled capitalism associated with globalization.[128]

While premodern Muslims' reservations about secularism and democracy might have heightened their opposition to globalization, nevertheless the not-so-benign designs of those who promote globalization have deflated the balloon of globalization. Some analysts believe that globalization neither signals the end of history nor the advent of free trade and a flat world. By restricting the free flow of labor and by only allowing the free flow of capital, globalization has widened the north-south gap. It has also globalized terrorism. Relative modernization of certain Muslim-majority countries due to the positive effects of globalization is least acceptable to sections of ultra-conservative and backward Muslims.[129]

Globalizations' predatory role is a big factor behind its rejection by people in the Third World. Some analysts believe that: "Each year, for every $1 of aid money over the table from rich to poor countries, the West gets back $10 of ill-gotten gains under the table and, for good measure, lectures the rest on corruption."[130] Growing number of academics, intellectuals, and some politicians are getting disillusioned by globalization.[131] Despite the rhetoric, globalization has hardly any positive correlation with (free) market economy. American farm subsidy to millions of rich farmers adversely affects poor cultivators from Haiti to Hondurus, Brazil to Bangladesh, Egypt, Equador, and Pakistan to the Philippines. Annually, American farmers get more than $200 billion subsidy to keep the price of their produce—corn, cotton, wheat, rice, soybean, and other crops— artificially low. In the process, what happens is anything but capitalism or market economy. Analysts attribute hunger in Haiti and terrorism and

Islamist resurgence in Egypt and Pakistan to U.S. farm subsidy. In March 2010, President Bill Clinton, as U.N. Special Envoy to Haiti, publicly apologized to Haitian farmers for destroying their rice farming through farm subsidy to U.S. farmers under his administration.[132] Surprisingly, the Global Connectedness Index reveals that the world in 2012 was less integrated than it was in 2007.[133]

Notwithstanding the controversy about the globalization process, it has enlightened and emboldened people across the globe by providing new information, especially postmodern ideas to question and challenge hegemonic ideas, institutions, and entities.[134] One should not expect "postmodernization of cultures," which amounts to a decline in high culture and "pluralization of lifestyles," in the Muslim world. The Muslim world is yet to have gone through its Renaissance and Reformation.[135] As Akbar Ahmed explains, while modernism is elitist, postmodernism is mass-oriented,[136] and we know, the bulk of the *Ummah* is still under the spell of clerics and despots, who despise change and hate democracy. Ironically, declassed elites with ultra-radical (often anarchist-nihilist) Islamist ideologies have been striving for Muslim masses' due share in the global arena by force. Islamist radicalism not only reflects Muslim aspirations for complete access to the market and free flow of labor along with capital, but it is also reflective of Muslim identity crisis and quest for autonomy, dignity, and freedom. Muslims believe that in precolonial days they had their own heydays of globalization where they had been dominant economically, politically, and culturally. Islamism is mainly all about restoring that lost glory stolen by the West.

Muslims' bad experience with pro-Western governments in their countries turned them into anti-Western, first under leftist influence during the Cold War and later under the influence of the mullah. Mullahs and village elders oppose mass education, secularism, and the concept of equal rights to women both out of ideological and pragmatic considerations. Firstly, they consider democracy, secularism, and women's liberation un-Islamic, and, secondly, they oppose mass adoption of modern health-care system, secular education, and empowerment of women apprehending losing their clients to Western-donor sponsored development practitioners. As the village mullah, who runs mosque-bound religious schools (*maktabs* or madrassas), is not willing to lose students to secular schools, the village quack is dead against modern clinics and health-care centers in the countryside. Village moneylenders and other vested-interest groups also oppose NGOs and microcredit for the obvious reason. Thus, apparently Western donor-driven NGOs and Islam at the grassroots have negative correlations. Some Pakistani mullahs' successful campaigns against polio vaccine as un-Islamic in remote northwestern Pakistani tribal areas and their Bangladeshi counterpart's issuing *fatwas* against secular law, schools, and NGOs may be mentioned in this regard. Again, there is no denying of NGO corruption and NGOs, including Grameen Bank, charging exorbitantly high interest from poor borrowers. One may cite examples of NGO extortion from Bangladesh in this regard. The over-glorified Grameen Bank of Dr Muhammad Yunus, Bangladesh Rural Advancement Committee (BRAC), PROSHIKA, ASA, and other Western donor-driven NGOs charge exorbitantly high rates of interest, around 20–30 percent and even more, from poor borrowers (mostly rural women).[137] Ironically, despite the neo-moneylenders impunity, lack of accountability and transparency, Western leaders, donors, analysts, academics, pundits, and experts—from the Clintons to Queen Sofia of Spain—glorify these successful entrepreneurs (who again, are exempt from income tax for running charities). Western leaders, bankers, and donors put them on par with Mother Teresa. Dr Yunus has already become a Nobel Laureate and, in 2009, the British Queen knighted Mr Abed of the BRAC, an NGO-runner in Bangladesh. One wonders if it is Western arrogance, ignorance, or insensitivity about Muslim resentment that it glorifies Islamophobes such as Salman Rushdie (also knighted by the Queen) and controversial NGO-business runners in the Muslim world. This is in no way only a conflict of cultures, but mainly an elite conflict for hegemony between the rich and powerful Western and the marginalized Islamic/leftist elites in the Third World.

It is noteworthy that not only orthodox Muslims and mullahs are critical of the NGO-culture and other IMF-World Bank or Western donor-driven projects in the Muslim world, but presently marginalized, former leftist intellectuals, and activists are also vocal against the globalization process. There seems to be a growing Mullah–Marxist nexus within and beyond the Muslim world. British–Pakistani Marxist Tariq Ali even praised Hezbollah and Hamas for their anti-Western stands and glorified the Taliban as freedom fighters championing Pashtun Nationalism.[138] The flip side of the opposition to Globalization-cum-Westernization is also due to peoples' genuine fear and bad experience with extortionist NGOs. Former Chief Economist and Senior Vice President of the World Bank Nobel Laureate Joseph Stiglitz is quite emphatic about how Western donors, and even the IMF's "intrusiveness smacked of a new form of colonialism."[139] His further demonizing the globalization process for its inherent corrupt systems and methods is enlightening. He has pinpointed flaws in Western banking system, the mortgage scam, and other corrupt practices—which he describes as "The Great American Robbery"—which do not bode well for the West-sponsored globalization process.[140]

Since globalization has become synonymous with Westernization—which is again an anathema to most Muslims for espousing unbridled materialism, secularism, and hedonism—Muslims are apprehensive of what is known as the Davos Culture. Muslims are paradoxically optimistic and pessimistic about their future at the same time. While radical Islamists talk about "taking over the White House one day," the vast majority of Muslims having some understanding of the global system strives for equal opportunity in global perspective and is more than willing to integrate with Wallerstein's World System. Interestingly, not-so-radical but socially conservative Islamists are not opposed to participating in the global system either, as most of them during the Cold War had no qualms about actively collaborating with the West favoring the capitalist world order.[141] A survey of Muslim public opinion vis-à-vis globalization in seven countries—Egypt, Turkey, Azerbaijan, Iran, Indonesia, the Palestinian Territories, and Nigeria—revealed that around 63 percent of Muslims viewed globalization not as a threat and around 80 percent favored maintaining minimum standards for working conditions for the laborers.[142] However, as globalization stands for total triumph of capitalism, downtrodden people in the South are least enamored by this "part-promise, part-reality, and part-imagination."[143]

Is There an Alternative Discourse toward Muslim–West Understanding?

Although the West still controls less than 15 percent of the world population, a sharp decline from 40 percent in 1900, the Muslim share went up from 4 percent in 1900 to 13 in 1990, likely to be 19 by 2025. Optimistic Muslims are striving to do things for their own benefit in their own way, not the Western way any longer.[144] Then again, Muslims are not the only critics of globalization. As Mahathir Mohamad blamed globalization for creating confusion and despair for Muslims, so did Kofi Annan portray it "not as an agent of progress but as a disruptive force" for "destroying lives, jobs, and traditions."[145] Being disillusioned with the outcome of globalization, Joseph Stiglitz asserts that "globalization has not succeeded in reducing poverty," nor has it been able to ensure global stability. He also agrees with its critics that globalization has further empowered hypocritical Western countries, which have pushed poor countries to eliminate trade barriers, but kept up their own barriers to the detriment of the developing countries. He favors "saving Globalization from its advocates."[146] Pepe Escobar, deeply influenced by Hobsbawm, Wallerstein, and Samir Amin, is another bitter critic of globalization. Singling out the immoral neo-cons for global crises—including global jihad—echoing Wallerstein, he asserts that capitalist global order cannot guarantee any autonomy to the poorer states and that America's reticence to "multipolar anarchy" will eventually lead to a "nonstop Liquid War." He also subscribes to Amin's views on American imperialism, which instead of aiming at integrating the various economies in the world "aims only at looting their resources."[147]

Other Western critics of globalization, former French President Sarkozy and Walden Bello, for example, believe globalization is responsible for "the death of laissez-faire capitalism." They advocate Global Social Democracy (GSD), which includes massive aid program or another Marshall Plan from north to the south to eliminate poverty, and for a Second Green Revolution especially in Africa. De-emphasizing military action, the GSD wants the West to emerge as a soft power to benefit the global poor.[148] Portraying globalization as Disaster Capitalism and spelling out Shell and BP, Haliburton and Blackwater, Naomi Klein blames politicians and industrialists for "playing the bait-and-switch game to rip off the world" during the periods of wars and global economic crises.[149]

The World Social Forum (WSF), since its inception in 2001, with its passionate agenda against the Davos-based World Economic Forum is another anti-globalization move led by neoliberals and left-oriented people such as Noam Chomsky. The WSF is trying to get the global Muslim support to work together against the U.S. and so far has organized a successful WSF conference in Karachi in March 2006, attended by 20,000 people from 58 countries. The rallying points of the conference, also attended by Iranian and Palestinian delegates, included fighting for the rights of the Palestinians, protecting Iran's sovereignty, and opposing "anti-Muslim imperialism."[150]

The inadequate market accessibility is not exclusively a Muslim problem but an important issue dogging the North–South relationship or what Gunder Frank spelled out as *the core-periphery conflict*. Some apparently modern and rich countries with the latest amenities and technology are only partially integrated with globalization. Culturally they are the least integrated with modern and postmodern ideas and institutions. The Muslim world is the least integrated with the globalization process. The Muslim world also shares the stigma of not being able to institutionalize democratic governance except a handful of Muslim-majority countries. Let us see if Islamic culture has something to do with the retarded growth of democracy in the Muslim world.

In view of the repeated violations of the principles of democracy and freedom by the West since the end of World War I, nothing could be more politically incorrect than raising the question: Is Islam compatible to democracy? The Western discourse of democracy, especially what it highlights as the so-called differences between Christianity (West) and Islam (Orient) in regard to the compatibility of democracy in Islam, is Islamophobic. The West has never singled out catholic incompatibility for the lack of democracy in Latin America. The West hardly acknowledges the secular identities of Muslims as Bengalis, Nigerians, Indonesians, communists, agnostics, or atheists. Far from conforming to rigid Islamism, let alone Islamist ideologies, most Muslims share the common cultural traits of their non-Muslim neighbors.[151]

While assuming Islam's incompatibility with democracy analysts lose sight of the history of the evolution of democracy in the West, which became democratic and home of first nation states in history after going through the Renaissance, Reformations, Enlightenment, Capitalism, Industrial Revolutions, and through the revolutionary changes in Britain, America, and France. The level and maturity of representative governments also depend on economic stability everywhere, including the Muslim world.[152]

Again, all Muslim parties and groups are not inimical to democracy. Then again, the West denied their legitimacy and the right to form government in Algeria, Egypt, and the truncated leftover of Palestine in Gaza and the West Bank. The denial of democratic outlets to Islamists often leads to the radicalization process of Islamist organizations.[153] Western irritation at the 28-year-old Ahmed Maher, who started a web-based revolution for democracy in Egypt in April 2008, was quite puzzling. Maher captured the imagination of millions of young and not-so-young Egyptians who aspired for liberal democracy and the removal of Hosni Mubarak from power.[154] Of late, the overthrow of Tunisian dictator Ben Ali and Hosni Mubarak of Egypt by freedom- and democracy-loving people belie the prejudicial assumption about Muslims' so-called dislike for democracy.

Contrary to the wrong perception that Muslims despise freedom and democratic institutions, some of their heroes fought and died for democracy, such as the celebrated Sufi master Mansur Hallaj, executed for propounding the theory that every individual is the depository of *haqq*, truth or God, and hence necessarily sovereign. He was tortured and burned alive in Baghdad in the early 11th century.[155] The pious caliphs or *khalifas* in early Islam were not hereditary monarchs. After the demise of Prophet Muhammad, they presided over the Medina-based nascent Islamic domain up to 661 as the representatives of the Prophet and were accountable to the *Shura* or council of elders. The introduction of hereditary monarchy by Muawiyah, the founder of the Umayyad dynasty in 661, was a departure from the Islamic tradition. Historians consider Muawiyah to be the first Muslim king. The Shiite concept of the infallible imam with absolute temporal and religious authority is a heresy, a sacrilege to Sunni Islam.

Since the Muslim world has not yet gone through its Renaissance or Reformation, very similar to medieval Europeans, traditional Muslims, especially in the Arab world, consider freedom (*al-hurriyya*) synonymous with disorder, and freedom of religion (*al-hurriyya al-diniyya*) is permissible with one sole condition: do not leave Islam. Interestingly, there is no Arabic word for democracy. Arabs use the Greek word *dimuqratiyya* to denote democracy. *Jumhuriyya* (*gumhuriyya* or *jamhuriyyat*) again, does not connote democracy but the bulk of the people, also the "most noble of them."[156] Both in Arabic and Urdu, secularism stands for *ladiniyyah* or the pejorative absence of religion. Sir Muhammad Iqbal (1877–1938), renowned Urdu poet, philosopher, and politician—also known as the Dreamer of

Pakistan—considered politics devoid of religion equivalent to Chengis Khan's autocracy: "Juda ho deen siyasat se, To reh jati hai Changezi."

While most Muslim oligarchs and monarchs oppose democracy and some legitimize their rule through referendums—à la Nasser, Ayub Khan, Zia ul-Haq, Ziaur Rahman, and Saddam Hussein—ordinary Muslims ask for democracy, if not secularism. It is very significant that while Muslims under secular despots opt for Islamism, Muslims who are living or have lived under Islamist tyrannies aspire for democracy.[157] Paradoxically, the West throughout the Cold War was friendly with pro-Western secular and Islamist despots in the Muslim world. In sum, secularism and Muslim democracy coexist in Turkey, Pakistan, Bangladesh, Maldives, Indonesia, and Malaysia.[158] Of late, Iraq, Afghanistan, Tunisia, Libya, Egypt, and Yemen have become democratic. Since the transition to democracy and secularism depends on the growth of liberalism, the not-so-liberal Muslim world will have to wait for a few more years—if not decades—before it is ready for democracy. As Fareed Zakaria argues, liberalism, the rule of law and respect for individual freedoms, must precede democratic transition, not the other way round. Otherwise, what we get is illiberal democracy or unaccountable oligarchy or dictatorship to cast a shadow on democratic governance. As Western Europe's evolutionary transition to democracy took centuries, while in 1830 Britain allowed only 2 percent of its population to vote for the House of Parliament, raising it to 7 percent in 1867 and around 40 percent in the 1880s,[159] we should not pay heed to the demand for overnight democratization of the Muslim world.

We need to understand the concept of historicism or cultural relativity, that social and cultural phenomena are determined by history (or historical accidents). Otherwise, as Islamists' election victories in Algeria (1991), Gaza (2006), and Egypt (2012) have remained problematic, the outcome of the West-sponsored democracy in Iraq and Afghanistan will not be that different either. The Shiite and Sunni Arabs and Sunni Kurds in Iraq and the various ethno-linguistic and sectarian groups in Afghanistan are hardly prepared for national democratic governments by transcending their ethno-national and sectarian identities. Most postcolonial Muslim-majority countries are artificial entities not nation states, they suffer from tremendous identity crisis and are vulnerable to centrifugal or ethno-national separatist forces. Consequently, anti-Western Islamism, a legacy of colonial days, prevails there as an alternative to secular democracy.

Most importantly, the biggest hindrance to the democratization of the Muslim world is not the Muslim, but the Western ambivalence about the transition. As Shadi Hamid elaborates,

> [F]or decades, U.S. policy toward the Middle East has been paralyzed by "the Islamist dilemma"—how can the United States promote democracy in the region without risking bringing Islamists to power? Now, it seems, the United States no longer has a choice. Popular revolutions have swept U.S.-backed authoritarian regimes from power in Tunisia and Egypt.... If truly democratic governments form in their wake; they are likely to include significant representation of mainstream Islamist groups.[160]

The inherent unpredictability of Islamist-led democracies in the Arab world could hurt U.S. security interests in the region. Nevertheless, America's "entering into a strategic dialogue with the region's Islamist groups and parties" could bring rich dividends for all of them. Hamid rightly points out that: "It will be better to develop such ties with opposition groups now, while the United States still has leverage, rather than later, after they are already in power."[161] We, however, cannot agree with him that since the 1990s Islamists in the Arab world favor democracy, popular sovereignty, and have given up calls for Islamic States. Nevertheless, since America is mainly responsible for the retardation of democracy and the rise of Islamist parties such as the MB, Ennahda, and JI in the Muslim world, it should have the stomach to digest the bitter pill of Islamism, which has emerged as the only viable political ideology for many Muslims across the world.

To wrap up this chapter, we may cite Asef Bayat, who thinks:

> [P]ost-Islamism is not anti-Islamic or secular; a post Islamist movement dearly upholds religion but also highlights citizens' rights. It aspires to a pious society within a democratic state. Early examples of such movements include the reform movement in Iran in the late 1990s and the country's Green Movement today, Indonesia's Prosperous Justice Party, Egypt's Hizb al-Wasat, Morocco's Justice and Development Party (PJD), and Turkey's ruling Justice and Development Party (AKP). Each was originally fundamentalist but over time came to critique Islamist excess, its violation of democratic rights, and its use of religion as a tool to sanctify political power.[162]

Post-Islamism is not only a condition but also a project, "a conscious attempt to conceptualize and strategize the rationale and modalities of

transcending Islamism in social, political, and intellectual domains."
While Islamism is all about Islam and Muslim responsibility toward
establishing an Islamic political order, post-Islamism, on the other hand,
is about the coexistence of Islam with people's rights and liberty. The
post-Islamist quest for pluralism, democracy, and justice has signaled
a departure from Khomeini's Vilayet–e-Faqih (or guardianship of the
Islamist jurist) in Iran, Kemalist authoritarian state in Turkey, and Shiite
supremacy in Lebanon.[163]

However, the democratic transitions in the Muslim world—in Iraq,
Afghanistan, Pakistan, Bangladesh, Indonesia, and Malaysia, among
others—and the Arab Spring, despite its limitations, have narrowed the
gap between Hope and Change in the Arab world. We may agree with
one analyst that:

> Far from celebrating a historic revolution, we should now be asking whether
> anything has changed at all—and if it has, has it been changed for the better?
> Yes, there is significant change. My heart tells me that it is likely to be for
> the good in the long term; but my head tells me that it is far too soon to tell.
> There is reason for both great optimism and tremendous fear. And there
> is also room for confusion—the upheavals in the Arab world are taking
> shape in starkly different ways in the various countries of the region.[164]

Our experience tells us that neither the West is prepared to engage the
Muslim world, particularly the not-so-friendly Islamist parties and groups,
nor are Muslims in general and Islamists in particular willing to modernize
their religion and traditional ways of thinking as they are apprehensive of
losing their identity, culture, and freedom to the dominant West. In spite
of globalization, the prevalent identity crisis, lack of freedom and rights
of self-determination for Muslims, especially in the Arab world, both
the modern/secular and traditional/Islamic streams of Muslim thought
are going through a period of crisis and transition. We may share Tariq
Ramadan's optimism that despite the rise in Saudi and Qatari sponsored
Salafi influence in the post-Arab Spring North Africa, "...the Islamists
are put into a situation where they can lose everything," and that their
"winning might be the beginning of losing," as they "are acting against the
interests of every single country—in Tunisia, Egypt, now all of a sudden
in north Mali."[165]

However, unless the West becomes proactive and an honest broker
to protect the *Ummah*'s rights, interests, and honor, peace will remain

ever elusive, and global jihads and crusades will continue to destabilize the world for decades. The way America and its conservative Arab allies toppled the democratically elected Morsi in Egypt and have been promoting anti-Assad rebels (many committed to al Qaeda's extremist ideology), do not bode well for democracy in the Arab world in the short-run. Nevertheless, since the world has already entered the post-terrorist phase of history, freedom and fundamental rights-oriented post-Islamism will eventually call the shots across the Muslim world. However, this is not going to happen overnight, and not in a peaceful way.

In sum, the preponderance of Israel as the most powerful nation in the Middle East (and its endless violation of international law and human rights with impunity) does not negate the fact that the Muslim world is coming closer to each other. We have reasons to believe that: "The Middle East today is a complex region that is changing fast. Grand generalizations about it are likely to be undone by events. *But it is a more vibrant, energetic and democratic place than it was a generation ago*" (emphasis added).[166]

Notes and References

1. Edward Said, *Orientalism* (New York: Vintage Books, 1979).
2. M. Shahid Alam, *Challenging the New Orientalism: Dissenting Essyas on the "War Against Islam"* (North Haledon, New Jersey: IPI, 2007).
3. Aijaz Ahmad, "Islam, Islamisms and the West," *Socialist Register* (February 2, 2006): 2–5.
4. Mahmood Mamdani, *Good Muslim, Bad Muslim: America, the Cold War, and the Roots of Terror* (New York: Doubleday, 2005), pp. 10–23; "Al Qaeda and the Neocons Are Both Determined to Remake the World through Political Violence," *Boston Review*, Vol. 30, No. 1 (2005). Available at: http://connection.ebscohost.com/c/articles/15967980/national-interest-al-qaeda-neocons-are-both-determined-remake-world-through-political-violence (accessed on February 22, 2014); Mamdani's Interview with a Muslim Blogger "Naseeb Vibes," (December 2, 2004). Available at: http://www.nasseb.com/naseebvibes/printArticle.php (accessed on July 26, 2009).
5. Raymond W. Baker, "The Paradox of Islam's Future," *Political Science Quarterly*, Vol. 127, No. 4 (2012): 519.
6. Ibid., pp. 519–525.
7. Patrick Sookhdeo, *Global Jihad: The Future in the Face of Militant Islam* (Three Rivers, Michigan: Isaac Publishing, 2007); Sarah E. Zabel, "The Military Strategy of Global Jihad" (October 2007). Available at: www.

StaretegicStudiesInstitute.army.mil; "WWIII, Islam's Imperialist Dream, Suicide Bombing Islamic, to Conquer Europe and America." Available at: http://www.science.co.il/arab-israeli-conflict/articles/Global-Jihad.asp; Efraim Karsh, *Islamic Imperialism: A History* (Yale University Press, 2007); Bruce Riedel, "Terrorism in India and the Global Jihad," *Foreign Policy* (November 30, 2008); Fawaz A. Gerges, "Iraq War Fuels Global Jihad: US Intervention Infuriates even Mainstream Muslims, Giving Al Qaeda and other Jihadists a Boost," *YaleGlobal* (December 21, 2006); Oliver Roy, *Globalized Islam: The Search for a New Ummah* (Columbia University Press, 2004).

8. Edward Said, *Orientalism* (New York: Vintage Books, 1979), passim.

9. Akbar S. Ahmad, *Discovering Islam: Making Sense of Muslim History and Society* (New Delhi: Vistaar Publications, 1990), pp. 117–140.

10. Ibrahim Kalin, "Islamophobia and the Limits of Multiculturalism," in John Esposito and Ibrahim Kalin (eds) *Islamophobia: The Challenege of Pluralism in the 21st Century* (New York: Oxford University Press, 2011), p. 3.

11. Anthony Padgen, *Worlds at War: The 2500-Year Struggle between East and West* (New York: Oxford University Press, 2008), p. 407.

12 Hamza Alavi, "The State in Post-Colonial Societies: Pakistan and Bangladesh," *New Left Review*, Vol. 74, (July–August 1972).

13. Ahmad, "Islam, Islamisms and the West."

14. M. Shahid Alam, *Challenging the New Orientalism: Dissenting Essays on the "War Against Islam"* (North Haledon, New Jersey: IPI, 2006), pp. 3–39.

15. Ibid.; Akbar S. Ahmad, *Postmodernism and Islam: Predicament and Promise*, (New Delhi: Penguin Books, 1993), pp. 1–50; "Anti-Muslim Comments by Evangelist Denounced by Progressive Religious Leaders: Interfaith Network Calls for Graham to Apologize to Muslim Community." Available at: http://jmm.aaa.net.au/articles/1159.htm (accessed on October 15, 2009).

16. Gordon Adams, "Seven Questions: Bernard Lewis on the Two Biggest Myths about Islam," *Foreign Policy* (August 2008). Available at: http://www.foreignpolicy.com/articles/2008/08/19/seven_questions_bernard_lewis_on_the_two_biggest_myths_about_islam (accessed on January 19, 2014).

17. "Gladstone's Thinking towards Islam," Christopher Parish (Gladstone's great grandson) and Professor Richard Aldous discuss the 200th birthday of William Gladstone, BBC Radio (January 23, 2009).

18. Sherman A. Jackson, "Muslims, Islam(s), Race, and American Islamophobia," in John Esposito and Ibrahim Kalin (eds) *Islamophobia: The Challenge of Pluralism in the 21st Century* (New York: Oxford University Press, 2011), pp. 93–101.

19. Ibid., pp. 100–105.

20. Pew Research Center surveys between 2002 and 2007.

21. CNN News (July 17, 2012) (CNN News on TV).

22. Deepa Kumar, "Framing Islam: The Resurgence of Orientalism during the Bush II Era," *Journal of Communication Inquiry*, Vol. 34, No. 3 (April 2010).

23. John Esposito and Ibrahim Kalin (eds), Introduction to *Islamophobia: The Challenge of Pluralism in the 21st Century*, by John Esposito (New York: Oxford University Press, 2011), pp. XXI–XXII.

24. Jackson, "Muslims, Islam(s), Race, and American Islamophobia," pp. 102–104.

25. Juan Cole, "Islamophobia and American Foreign Policy Rhetoric: The Bush Years and After," in John Esposito and Ibrahim Kalin (eds), *Islamophobia: The Challenge of Pluralism in the 21st Century* (New York: Oxford University Press, 2011), pp. 127–137.

26. Bruce Bawer, *While Europe Slept: How Radical Islam Is Destroying the West from Within* (London: Doubleday, 2006); Melanie Phillips, *Londonistan* (New York: Encounter Books, 2007).

27. Steven Emerson, *America Jihad: The Terrorists Living among Us* (Washington, D.C.: Free Press, 2003), passim.

28. Sally Steenland, "Congressional Hearings May Inflame Islamophobia" (February 3, 2011). Available at: http://www.americanprogress.org/issues/2011/2.

29. "Mr King's Sound and Fury," *New York Times* (March 11, 2011). Available at: http://www.politico.com/blogs/politicolive/ (accessed on March 16, 2011).

30. "Muslim Woman Sues Southwest Airlines after Being Taken off Flight," *Los Angeles Times* (October 5, 2011). Available at: http://latimesblogs.latimes.com/lanow/2011/10/a-muslim-woman-from-san-diego-is-suing-southwest-airlines-after-being-taken-off-a-flight-in-march-after-crew-members-deemed-h.html (accessed on January 19, 2014).

31. *Spiegel* Interview with Geert Wilders, "Merkel Is Afraid" (November 9, 2010).

32. CBS News (September 8, 2010) (TV News Bulletin); Terry Jones, *Islam Is of the Devil* (Lake Mary, Florida: Creation House, 2010).

33. *New York Times* (April 1, 2011). Available at: http://www.JihadWatch.org/2011/03/Pakistan-two-more-christians-killed-churches-burned-as-muslims-respond-to-florida-quran-burning.html (accessed on April 2, 2011).

34. *The Wall Street Journal* (2011).

35. Akbar S. Ahmed, *Islam under Siege* (Cambridge: Polity Press, 2003), p. 36.

36. *The Tennessean* (November 12, 2011).

37. Raymond W. Baker, "The Paradox of Islam's Future," *Political Science Quarterly*, Vol. 127, No. 4 (2012): 545.

38. Ibid., p. 547.

39. "Unwelcome: Muslims as Neighbors," CNN (March 27, 2011) (a documentary).

40. "Tennesse Bill Would Jail Shariah Followers," *USA Today* (February 23, 2011). Available at: http://usatoday30.usatoday.com/news/nation/2011-02-23-tennessee-law-shariah_N.htm (accessed on January 19, 2014).

41. *The Tennessean* (February 23, 2011).
42. "Newsweek's Power 50," *Newsweek* (November 8, 2010). Available at: http://www.newsweek.com/newsweeks-power-50-list-69843 (accessed on January 19, 2014).
43. Akbar S. Ahmed, *Islam under Siege* (Cambridge: Polity Press, 2003), p. 16.
44. Bat Ye'or, *Eurabia: The Euro-Arab Axis* (Rutherford, New Jersey: Fairleigh Dickinson University Press, 2005), passim.
45. Khaled Diab, "The Mythical European Umma," *The Guardian* (August 21, 2009).
46. Tariq Ramadan, "Islam Is a European Religion" (December 18, 2009). Available at: http://en.qantara.de/webcom/show_article.php/C-476/nr-1266/i.html (accessed January 5, 2010).
47. Editorial, "How Can He Do the Job?" *New York Times* (March 8, 2011).
48. Available at: http://www.historyofjihad.org/globaljihad.html (accessed on October 16, 2010).
49. Runnymede Trust Report, "Islamophobia: A Challenge for All," Summary of the Report (London 1997).
50. Alex Rhys-Taylor, "Xenophobia: Europe's Death Knell," *openDemocracy* (May 10, 2011). Available at: http://www.opendemocracy.net (accessed on May 12, 2011).
51. Lawrence Kulak, "The Appropriate Response to Islamic Terror," *Five Towns Jewish Times* (December 12, 2008), pp. 59–61. Available at: http://www.unwatch.org/site/c.bdKKISNqEmG/b.1289203/apps/s/content.asp?ct=6829271 (accessed on March 12, 2009).
52. Pankaj Mishra, "When Will Those Brave Critics of Islam Decry This Mob Hate?" *The Guardian* (September 1, 2010).
53. Omid Safi, "What if HSBC Had Been Muslim? A Two-Tiered Justice System Bought and Sold." Available at: http://omidsafi.religionnews.com/2012/12/13/what-if-hsbc-had-been-muslim-a-two-tiered-justice-system-bought-and-sold/ (accessed on January 14, 2013).
54. Fareed Zakaria GPS, CNN (September 5, 2010).
55. Sayyid Qutb, *Milestones* (Karachi: International Islamic Publishers, 1988), pp. 67–70, 114–42; Richard Wike and Brian J. Grim, "Widespread Negativity: Muslim Distrust Westerners More than Vice Versa," Pew Forum on Religion & Public Life. Available at: http://pewforum.org/docs/?DocID=257 (accessed on October 30, 2007).
56. Karin Maria Svana, "Freedom of Speech vs. Freedom from Humiliation," *openDemocracy* (February 27, 2009).
57. *What Does Al-Qaeda Want? Unedited Communiques* (Berkeley: North Atlantic Books, 2004). Available at: http://www.muebooks.com/what-does-al-qaeda-want-unedited-communiques-terra-nova-series-PDF-839151/ (accessed on January 19, 2014); John Esposito and Dalia Mogahed, *Who Speaks for Islam? What a Billion Muslims Really Think* (New York: Gallup Press, 2007), passim.

58. Samir Amin, "Political Islam in the Service of Imperialism," *Monthly Review* (December 2007).

59. Nikki Keddie, *An Islamic Response to Imperialism: Political and Religious Writings of Sayyid Jamal ad-Din al-Afghani* (Berkeley: University of California Press, 1968), pp. 84–97.

60. Ira Lapidus, *A History of Islamic Societies* (New York: Cambridge University Press, 1993), p. 587.

61. Abol Hassan Bani-Sadr, *My Turn to Speak: Iran, the Revolution & Secret Deals with the U.S.* (New York: Brassey's (US), Inc., 1991), p. 10.

62. Stephen Kinzer, *All the Shah's Men: An American Coup and the Roots of Middle East Terror* (New York: John Wiley & Sons, 2003), p. 212.

63. Salman Rushdie, "This is About Islam," *New York Times* (November 2, 2001).

64. "International Poll: No Consensus on Who Was Behind 9/11." Available at: http://www.worldpublicopinion.org/incl/printable_version.php?pnt=535 (accessed on November 11, 2010).

65. Available at: http://www.archives.gov/education/lessons/us-israel/ and http://www.mideastweb.org/us_supportforstate.htm (accessed on November 1, 2011).

66. Sasha Polakow-Suransky, *The Unspoken Alliance: Israel's Secret Relationship with Apartheid South Africa* (New York: Pantheon Books, 2010).

67. M. Shahid Alam, *Israeli Exceptionalism: The Destabilizing Logic of Zionism* (New York: Palgrave-Macmillan, 2009).

68. UN General Assembly Resolution 181 (November 29, 1947).

69. *Hansard*, Vol. 445 (British Parliamentary Proceedings) (December 11, 1947). Available at: http://hansard.millbanksystems.com/sittings/1947/dec/11#commons (accessed on January 19, 2014).

70. UN General Assembly Resolutions, 3151, 1953 and 3379, 1975.

71. UN General Assembly Resolution, 46/86, 1991.

72. *New York Times* (May 20, 2011).

73. *Washington Post* (May 19 and 20, 2011).

74. Nathan Thrall, "What Future for Israel?" *The New York Review of Books* (August 15, 2013).

75. Ibid.

76. CNN News (May 20–22, 2011).

77. Obama AIPAC Speech 2011: "President Seeks to Smooth out U.S.-Israel Tensions," *Huffington Post* (May 22, 2011). Available at: http://www.huffingtonpost.com/2011/05/22/obama-aipac-speech-2011-p_n_865198.html (accessed on December 6, 2013).

78. *New York Times* (June 4, 2009).

79. *Christian Science Monitor* (May 22, 2011) and *Huffington Post* (May 22, 2011), web editions; *New York Times* (May 21, 2011).

80. CNN News and NPR Radio (May 24, 2010); *Washington Post* (May 26, 2011).

81. Bill Van Auken, "Obama at the UN: The Arrogant Voice of Imperialism." Available at: www.wsws.org/articles/2011/Sep2011/boun-s22.shtml (accessed on September 26, 2011).

82. White House Press Release (CNN News, September 21, 2011).

83. "US Cuts UNESCO Funds over Vote for Palestinian State," BBC News, Middle East (October 31, 2011). Available at: http://www.bbc.co.uk/news/world-middle-east-15527534 (accessed on January 19, 2014).

84. Mark Danner, "The Politics of Fear," *The New York Review* (November 22, 2012).

85. Fania Oz-Salzberger, "With Friends Like These...," *Newsweek* (September 18, 2011); MJ Rosenberg, "How the Lobby Chills Middle East Debate" (May 27, 2011). Available at: http://politicalcorrection.org/fpmatters/201105270008 (accessed on October 31, 2011).

86. Mark Landler, "Journalists Overhear Private Exchange between Obama and Sarkozy," *New York Times* (November 7, 2011).

87. Shadi Hamid, "The Rise of the Islamists: How Islamists Will Change Politics, and Vice Versa," *Foreign Affairs* (May/June 2011).

88. Recep Tayyip Erdogan, "10 Questions for Recep Tayyip Erdogan: Turkish Prime Minister Recep Tayyip Erdogan on Palestinian Statehood, Israel and Unfriending Syria's Dictator," *Time* (October 10, 2011).

89. "The Petraeus Briefing Biden's Embarrassment Is Not the Whole Story." Available at: http://mideast.foreignpolicy.com/posts/2010/03/14/the_petraeus_briefing_biden_s_embarrasment_is_not_the_whole_story (accessed on February 8, 2011).

90. Ehsan Ahrari, "The Post-9/11 American Conundrum: How to Win the War of Ideas in the World of Islam," *Mediterranean Quarterly*, Vol. 19, No. 2 (2008).

91. BBC News, "Iraq Rally for Bush Shoe Attacker" (December 15, 2008); "Demand for Shoes Made Famous by Bush," *Dawn* (Pakistan daily) (December 23, 2008); "Arab World Hails Shoe Attack as Bush Farewell Gift," AFP, Baghdad (December 16, 2008).

92. Mahathir Mohamad, "Israel the Rogue State." Available at: http://globalresearch.ca/index.php?context=va&aid=19472 (accessed on June 1, 2010).

93. Fox News (December 28, 2008) (from Fox TV News).

94. Kevin Barrett, "Brzezinski: US Must Stop Following Israel 'Like a Stupid Mule.'" Available at: http://www.infowars.com/brzezinski-us-must-stop-following-israel-like-a-stupid-mule/ (accessed on February 21, 2014).

95. Available at: http://kouroshziabari.com/2013/01/criticize-israel-and-lose-your-career-interview-with-alison-weir/alison-weir/ (accessed on February 3, 2013).

96. Philip Weiss, "Casual Slander of Hagel as Anti-Semite puts Elliott Abrams on Hot Seat," Mondoweiss (January 12, 2013). Available at: http://mondoweiss.

net/2013/01/casual-slander-elliott.html (accessed on February 17, 2013); Paul Craig Roberts, "Hagel Is a Victim of the Israel Lobby," Interview with the Russian TV (February 16, 2013). Available at: http://www. informationclearinghouse.info/article33966.htm#.USBfZwfm_yo.reddit (accessed on February 17, 2013)

97. "Arab Summit Debates Gaza Response." Available at: http://www.aljazeera. com/news/middleeast/2009/01/200911951538123422.html (accessed on February 21, 2014).

98. Turki al-Faisal, "Saudi Arabia's Patience Is Running Out," *Financial Times* (January 23, 2009).

99. See Jimmy Carter, *Palestine: Peace Not Apartheid* (New York: Simon & Schuster, 2007); John J. Mearsheimer and Stephen M. Walt, *The Israel Lobby and US Foreign Policy* (New York: Farrar, 2007), passim.

100. Johann Hari, "The True Story behind This War Is Not the One Israel Is Telling," *The Independent* (December 29, 2008).

101. Kamran Bokhari and Reva Bhalla, "Hamas and the Arab States," Stratfor Geopolitical Intelligence Report (January 7, 2009). Available at: http:// www.stratfor.com/weekly/20090107_hamas_and_arab_states (accessed in February 2014); Michael Slackman, "Ordinary Arabs Fume over Israeli Invasion," *IHT* (January 10, 2009).

102. Tim Mcgirk, "Can Israel Survive?" *Time* (January 19, 2009).

103. *New York Times* (May 5, 2011).

104. Ron Kampeas, "For Israeli-Palestinian Conflict, Hamas' Pen Is Mightier than bin Laden Bullet," JTA, The Global News Service of the Jewish People (May 3, 2011). Available at: www.jta.org/news/article/2011/05/03 (accessed on May 5, 2011).

105. Nathan Brown, "Palestine and Israel: Time for Plan B," Carnegie Endowment for International Peace, Policy Brief No. 78 (February 2009).

106. Dan Ephron, "The Wrath of Abbas," *Newsweek* (May 2, 2011).

107. Sam Bahour, "Palestine Is the Key to Arab Democracy," *The Guardian* (February 8, 2011); Tim Ross et al., "Israel's Secret Hotline to the Man Tipped to Replace Mubarak," *The Telegraph* (February 8, 2011).

108. *Washington Post* (May 25, 2011).

109. Nomika Zion, "It's Not Just about Fear, Bibi, It's about Hopelessness," *The New York Review of Books* (January 10, 2013).

110. Shibley Telhami's Analysis Paper, "Does the Palestinian-Israeli Conflict Still Matter?" Presented at the Saban Center for Middle East at Brookings, Washington, D.C. (July 1, 2008). Available at: http://www.brookings.edu/ research/papers/2008/06/middle-east-telhami (accessed on February 21, 2014).

111. Ibid.

112. Ibid.

113. Robert Fisk, "Obama Was Unconvinced by Bibi's Desire for Peace," *The Independent* (February 21, 2009).

114. Hussein Agha and Robert Malley, "Who's Afraid of the Palestinians?" *The New York Review of Books* (February 10, 2011).
115. BBC World News (February 8, 2011).
116. Thomas Friedman, "BE—Before Egypt, AE—After Egypt," *New York Times* (February 2, 2011).
117. M. Shahid Alam, "Running out of Solutions—Israel: A Failing Colonial Project?" *Counterpunch* (July 9–11, 2010).
118. *New Age* (Bangladeshi daily) (May 13, 2011).
119. Pankaj Mishra, "In India and Israel, the Burden of Protest Falls on the Victims of Injustice," *The Guardian* (June 6, 2011).
120. Ibid.
121. Abdus Sattar Ghazali, "Obama's Reset Rhetoric Is Unlikely to Translate into Meaningful Policy Change in the Middle East," Countercurrents.org (May 22, 2011).
122. Jerome Slater, "Zionism, the Jewish State, and an Israeli–Palestinian Settlement: An Opinion Piece," *Political Science Quarterly*, Vol. 127, No. 4 (2012): 609–617.
123. Martin Kramer, "Islam's Sober Millennium," *The Jerusalem Post* (December 31, 1999).
124. Akbar Ahmed and Hastings Donnan (eds), *Islam, Globalization and Postmodernity* (London: Routledge, 1994), pp. 1–13.
125. Ernest Gellner, Foreword to *Islam, Globalization and Postmodernity* (London: Routledge, 1994).
126. Mark Juergensmeyer, *The New Cold War? Religious Nationalism Confronts the Secular State* (University of California Press, 1994), pp. 1–8, 18–39; *Global Rebellion: Religious Challenges to the Secular State from Christian Militias to al Qaeda* (California University Press, 2008).
127. IDRC (Canada), "Economy and the Riches of the Poor" (October 20, 1998). Available at: www.idrc.ca/en/ev (accessed on March 2, 2009).
128. James Kurth, "Religion and Globalization," *Foreign Policy Research Institute*, Vol. 7, No. 7 (May 1999).
129. Nevzat Soguk, *Globalization and Islamism: Beyond Fundamentalism* (Lanham, Maryland: Rowman and Littlefield Publishers, 2010); Rohan Gunaratna, "The al-Qaeda Threat and the International Response," in David Martin Jones (ed.), *Globalization and the New Terror: The Asia Pacific Dimension* (Northampton, Maryland: Edward Elgar, 2004), pp. 51–69; Faisal Devji, *Landscape of the Jihad: Militancy, Morality and Modernity* (Ithaca: Cornell University Press, 2004).
130. Jorge Heine and Ramesh Thakur, "Exposing Globalization's Dark Side," *Japan Times* (January 20, 2011).
131. Stefan Theil, "Europe's Philosophy of Failure," *Foreign Policy* (December 13, 2007). Available at: http://www.foreignpolicy.com/articles/2007/12/13/europes_philosophy_of_failure (accessed on December 11, 2013).

132. CNN News (November 1, 2011); "'We Made a Devil's Bargain': Former President Clinton Apologizes for Trade Policies that Destroyed Haitian Rice Farming." Available at: http://www.democracynow.org/2010/4/1/clinton_rice (accessed on November 1, 2011).

133. "DHL Global Connectedness Index 2012." Available at: http://www.dhl.com/en/about_us/logistics_insights/studies_research/global_connectedness_index_2012.html (accessed on February 3, 2013).

134. Akbar S. Ahmed and Hastings Donnan, "Islam in the Age of Postmodernity," in Akbar S. Ahmed and Hastings Donnan (eds), *Islam, Globalization and Postmodernity* (London: Routledge, 1994), pp. 1–13; Akbar S. Ahmed, *Postmodernism and Islam: Predicament and Promise* (New Delhi: Penguin Books, 1993), Chapter 1.

135. Bryan S. Turner, Preface to *Orientalism, Postmodernism & Globalism* (London: Routledge, 1994).

136. Akbar S. Ahmed, *Postmodernism and Islam: Predicament and Promise* (New Delhi: Penguin Books, 1993), pp. 6–9.

137. Taj Hashmi. "NGOs and Empowerment of Women" and "Militant Feminism, Islam and Patriarchy," in *Women and Islam in Bangladesh*, (New York: Palgrave-Macmillan, 2000).

138. Imtiaz Baloch, "Tariq Ali Praises Taliban and Hezbollah, Mocks Baloch and Sindhi National Movements" (November 21, 2008). Available at: http://groups.yahoo.com/group/socialist_pakistan_news/message/13764 (accessed on December 30, 2008).

139. Joseph Stiglitz, "Broken Promises," in *Globalization and its Discontents* (New York: W.W. Norton & Company, 2002).

140. Joseph Stiglitz, *Freefall: America, Free Markets, and the Sinking of the World Economy* (New York: W.W. Norton & Company, 2010), Chapters 2, 4, and 5.

141. Samir Amin, "Political Islam in the Service of Imperialism," *Monthly Review* (December 2007).

142. "Muslims Positive about Globalization, Trade." Available at: www.worldpublicopinion.org (accessed on August 29, 2008).

143. Akbar S. Ahmed, *Islam under Siege: Living Dangerously in a Post- Honor World* (Cambridge, UK: Polity, 2003), p. 48.

144. Fouad Ajami, "The Clash," *New York Times Sunday Book Review* (January 6, 2008).

145. Akbar S. Ahmed, *Islam under Siege* (Cambridge, UK: Polity, 2003), p. 49.

146. Joseph E. Stiglitz, "The Promise of Global Institutions," "Broken Promises," "The IMF's Other Agenda," and "The Way Ahead," in *Globalization and its Discontents* (New York: W.W. Norton & Company, 2002); *Making Globalization Work* (New York: W.W. Norton, 2007), passim.

147. Pepe Escobar, *Globalistan: How the Globalized World is Dissolving into Liquid War* (Ann Arbor, Michigan: Nimble Books, 2007), pp. 12–36; *Obama Does Globalistan* (Ann Arbor, Michigan: Nimble Books, 2009), passim.

148. Kartin Benhold, "Sarkozy Sees French Way to Globalize: Collectively," *International Herald Tribune* (August 30, 2007); Walden Bello, "The Coming Capitalist Consensus," *Foreign Policy in Focus* (December 24, 2008) and "Global Social Democracy Is Possible Now" (February 13, 2009). Available at: www.socialdems.com/page.asp?PID=1528 (accessed on March 26, 2009).
149. Naomi Klein, *The Shock Doctrine: The Rise of Disaster Capital* (New York: Metropolitan Books, 2007).
150. South Asia News, "Delegates at World Social Forum Urge Muslim Unity against US." Available at: www.monstersandcritics.com/news/southasia (accessed on February 19, 2009).
151. Aijaz Ahmad, "Islam, Islamisms and the West," *Socialist Register* (February 2, 2006): 2–5.
152. Saliba Sarsar and David Strohmetz, "The Economics of Democracy in Muslim Countries," *Middle East Quarterly*, (2008): 3–11. Available at: http://www.meforum.org/article/1921 (accessed on February 20, 2014).
153. Tamara Cofman Wittes, Husain Haqqani, Hillel Fradkin, Tarek Masoud, Bassam Tibi et al., "Islamist Parties and Democracy," *Journal of Democracy*, Vol. 19, No. 3 (2008): 7–54.
154. Samantha M. Shapiro, "Revolution, Facebook-Style," *New York Times* (January 25, 2009).
155. Fatima Mernissi, *Islam and Democracy: Fear of the Modern World* (New York: Addison-Wesley Publishing Company, 1992), pp. 19–20.
156. Ibid., pp. 45–53, 71–72.
157. Oliver Roy, *Globalized Islam: The Search for a New Ummah* (New York: Columbia University Press, 2004), pp. 2–3.
158. M. Hakan Yavuz, *Secularism and Muslim Democracy in Turkey* (Cambridge: Cambridge University Press, 2009); Bernard Lewis, "Why Turkey Is the Only Muslim Democracy," *Middle East Quarterly* (March 1994): 41–49.
159. Fareed Zakaria, "The Rise of Illiberal Democracy," *Foreign Affairs* (November 1997).
160. Shadi Hamid, "The Rise of the Islamists: How Islamists Will Change Politics, and Vice Versa," *Foreign Affairs* (May/June 2011).
161. Ibid.
162. Asef Bayat, "The Post-Islamist Revolutions: What the Revolts in the Arab World Mean," *Foreign Affairs* (Snapshot) (April 26, 2011).
163. Asef Bayat (ed.), *Post-Islamism: The Changing Faces of Political Islam* (New York: Oxford University Press, 2013), pp. 3–30, Chapter 1.
164. Nathan J. Brown, "Hope and Change," *Foreign Policy* (May 18, 2011).
165. "Tariq Ramadan Interviewed post-Arab Spring," *open Democracy* (December 5, 2012).
166. Fareed Zakaria, "Where the Past Is Not Prologue: Turmoil Is a Constant in the Middle East, but the Region Is Strengthening," *Time* (December 10, 2012).

4

Is the American Empire "Exceptional"?

Truth is treason in the empire of lies.... There is an alternative to national bankruptcy, a bigger police state, trillion-dollar wars, and a government that draws ever more parasitically on the productive energies of the American people.

Ron Paul, U.S. Presidential Candidate, 2008 and 2012

Washington's empire extracts resources from the American people for the benefit of the few powerful interest groups that rule America. The military-security complex, Wall Street, agri-business and the Israel Lobby use the government to extract resources from Americans to serve their profits and power.... That is how the American Empire functions.

Paul Craig Roberts, Assistant Secretary of Treasury, 1981–1982

Overview

We know in the post-terrorist phase of history today, the main challenge to world peace comes from state-sponsored terrorism, death squads, and proxy wars. If the world is heading toward prolonged intra and interstate conflicts in the coming decades, then what we have already witnessed since the end of World War II is an important question. This chapter appraises the role of America as an empire in intensifying world conflict through invasions, interventions (such as regime change), or benign neglect of smaller countries. We need answers to the following questions with regard to the Muslim world: (a) Is the Muslim–West conflict a derivative of American imperialism? (b) Are there better options for America? (c) Can America be a dependable friend to the Muslim world? This chapter supports the main theme of this study that global jihad is a hackneyed cliché, and that neither Islam nor Muslims pose the greatest threat to world peace, rather whatever is wrong with the West-sponsored New World Order has been the biggest challenge to human civilization since the end of World War II. Last but not least, America, to a large extent, has been responsible for the promotion of Islamist terror and anarchy in the world by directly and indirectly promoting them since the early days of the Cold War.

Is America an Empire and on the Path to "Permanent War"?

It is noteworthy that even the British Empire at its zenith in the 19th century did not consider itself an empire. America is no exception in this regard. Since the costs of direct imperialism (such as colonial annexation, temporary military occupation, or overt military intervention) are high, I don't think states prefer to use imperialism. So you have to be fairly desperate to resort to it. When states are already economically dominant, they're not as desperate. And since they already exert sufficient control on the world, they don't need imperialism. An analogy is a big corporation. Big corporations prefer free markets, they already have the capital and resources to beat out smaller competitors on a so-called fair-playing field (which of course is not really fair, which is why big corporations prefer them). When they don't already have the advantage, they're more likely to cheat in order to secure profit and market share. I think of states and imperialism similarly. If a state already dominates the world, it prefers the status quo, and it doesn't want to shake things up by being overtly imperialistic. Alternatively, when that state is declining, imperialism makes more sense as a way to retain dominance.

Britain went through this in the 19th century and the U.S. has done the same in the 20th century. The evidence for this is that the U.S. has engaged in more overt military actions (invasions and occupations) during its period of economic decline (roughly the 1970s through the 1990s until the present) than when it was economically hegemonic (after World War II through the early 1970s).

Soon after the end of World War II, America chose the path to permanent war[1] as its destiny. It put the Cold War exigencies as the justifications for maintaining the most powerful military machine in the world. Paradoxically, "when the United States became more secure, it became more forceful", and since the end of the Cold War, "it has spent far more than any other country or coalition to build armed forces; it has sent forces into combat more frequently than it did in the era of much bigger threats to national security."[2] Interestingly, according to the 2012 Global Terrorism Index, America is not the most terror-infested country in the world; it ranked 41 out of 158 nations.[3] In fact, in comparison to the Cold-War years, America has faced far fewer attacks at home and abroad after 9/11. In view of the growing belligerence of America toward countries and entities, such as Iran, Syria, al Qaeda, and their alleged promoters, it is no longer sensational to assume that the ongoing Muslim–West conflict will possibly end up in another Hundred-Year War. As discussed earlier, the Hundred-Year War had already begun in the 1948 Arab–Israeli war following the creation of Israel.

As we will find out later, empires are all about their founders' quest for wealth, power, and glory, which they achieve by overpowering the ubiquitous others through deception, arrogance, and violence. Then again, imperialists also live in a state of fear of losing out what they acquire by force to other contenders or even to the vanquished people. Thus, an understanding of American imperialism requires an understanding of its brief history. Most importantly, we must understand as to how elites manipulate truth and culturally hegemonize mass consciousness to legitimize their hegemony with "false consciousness." In sum, we have no reason to believe that American policy has aimed at stabilizing the world "in order to prevent dangers from arising."[4]

Inconvenient Truths and Unresolved Questions

This chapter is a departure from the Western discourse of "*What Went Wrong* with Islam." This is about the problematic role America and its allies have been playing since long; an appraisal of what is wrong with their hegemonic designs and warfare that led to Islamist terrorism and insurgencies in global perspective. America initiates a major war after every 10-year or so since the end of the Cold War. Thus, it is time that we understand the short- and long-term implications of the rise and eventual decline of American hegemony in the coming decades. We may raise the following questions for understanding the problem:

1. Is America the biggest problem toward world peace? Is not the American legacy of expropriation and mass murder of indigenous people and slavery and apartheid at the core of the American psyche, while the American dogma of liberty and equality is quite superficial, not applicable to non-Americans?
2. Will America remain a hostage to its own Military–Industrial–Congressional (and Israel) lobbies, which have been at the roots of all wars that America has initiated since the end of World War II, and in the coming decades as well?
3. Will the growing American belligerence toward Muslim-majority countries—such as Iran, Syria, and Pakistan—in the wake of its invasions of Iraq and Afghanistan, unite Sunni and Shiite, liberal and extremist Muslims against America in the near future? Or, will the Sunnis and Shiites under the Saudi and Iranian regimes, respectively, start another cold war within the fold of Islam?
4. Will American high handedness in the Middle East, Africa, Central and South Asia initiate another cold war between America, Western Europe, India, Israel, Australia, Saudi Arabia, and other Gulf Cooperation Council (GCC) countries on one side, and Russia, China, Pakistan, Iran, Iraq, Syria, Afghanistan, Turkey, Egypt, and their allies, within and beyond the Muslim world, on the other?

We need answers to all the above questions for a comprehensive understanding of what really went wrong with America and as to how and why the richest and most powerful country, which came into being in the name of liberty and democracy, turned into another rapacious empire. What is very puzzling is that unlike European colonial powers in the past—Britain, France, Spain, Portugal, the Netherlands, or Belgium—America has no reason to be an Empire as it has fertile land, natural resources, and a huge indigenous market. Despite all these, greed and the delusion of grandeur of the ruling classes, military, and mercantile elites have made America an empire. Despite America's generosity, open arms policy toward immigration, and contributions to knowledge, science, and technology, it is definitely the most hated country in the world. Many sensible Americans are aware of it. They know, America's brutal invasions that resulted in more than a million deaths in Indo-China alone were not that different from what Hitler did to Jews and fellow Europeans, and Japan did to China, Korea, and others during World War II. As America's brutal and unnecessary killing of more than a hundred thousand Japanese men, women, and children at Hiroshima and Nagasaki by incinerating them into pulp and ash was sort of war crime, so have been the series of unprovoked American invasions of countries from Cuba to Nicaragua, Vietnam, Laos, Cambodia to Grenada, Panama, Afghanistan, Iraq, and Libya.

America's quest for an empire of liberty goes back to Thomas Jefferson but the limits of power restrained it from promoting an empire beyond North America. While Theodore Roosevelt and Woodrow Wilson did not pursue the idea of turning America into an empire out of sheer pragmatism, with the emergence of America as the most powerful nation on earth after the end of World War II, America emerged as an empire both by design and default. The polarization of the world between pro- and anti-America blocs during the Cold War further paved the way for the Empire. However, with the demise of the Soviet Union and its communist allies in Europe and Central Asia—that signaled the end of the Cold War—the Empire lost its legitimacy and support among its erstwhile allies. The promise of a New World Order and a globalized world with better rights, freedom, and opportunity for all in the early 1990s resulted in an extraordinary rise in people's hope level across the world. However, neither globalization nor the so-called New World Order delivered the much sought freedom and opportunities to the masses, especially in the South and the Muslim World. The disenchantment of the Muslim and Third Worlds delegitimized the American Empire.

While the world wants the Americans to shun self-righteous arrogance and vainglorious attitude for turning their country into a soft and smart power, the average American is the least informed and grossly immodest person in the Western world. Tocqueville has the following unflattering words for Americans as he found them to be as early as in the 1830s:

The Americans, in their intercourse with strangers, appear impatient of the smallest censures, and insatiable of praise. The most slender eulogism is acceptable to them, the most exalted seldom contends them: they unnecessarily harass you to extort praise, and if you resist their entreaties, they fall to praising themselves.... If I say to an American that the country he lives in is a fine one, "Ay," he replies, "there is not its equal in the world."[5]

In the backdrop of Tocqueville's observations about American super-narcissist, self-righteousness, it is difficult to be a critic of America's foreign policy. The average American is not prepared to believe that her/his country is imperialistic and has been destabilizing the world since long. Interestingly, Tocqueville criticized American narcissism but praised America's so-called aversion to wars:

The Americans have no neighbors, and consequently they have no great wars, or financial crises, or inroads, or conquest, to dread; they require neither great taxes, nor large armies, nor great generals; and they have nothing to fear from a scourge which is more formidable to republics than all these evils combined, namely military glory.[6] (emphasis added)

The average American also does not question the utility of spending billions on their armed forces at home and abroad, in Europe, Pacific, Middle East, Africa, Latin America, and North America. As renowned security analyst Richard Betts explains:

For some time after the collapse of the Soviet Union and Marxist ideology, unipolarity obscured the crucial difference between war and law enforcement.... U.S. military force was an instrument that could be used to impose law, democratic norms, and world order—in effect, the United States could be "globocop."[7]

Betts further criticizes America's futile attempts to exert its influence as a global cop and empire through conventional and unconventional wars at home and abroad (such as counterterrorism), and humanitarian interventions and deterrence or provocation in distant lands. He believes that America's failure to make a cost-benefit analysis of overstretching its military and economic powers has led to Washington's loss of control of policy decisions at home and abroad, leading to the unsustainable policy of control without control. He advises Washington to follow Calusewitz's advice that it "should not try to jump across most ditches," but when it does, it "should not jump halfway."[8]

Nevertheless, the fact remains that since the 1950s, America has been directly or indirectly invading countries, toppling regimes, and has been the biggest promoter of not-so-democratic to dictatorial regimes, who violate human rights, terrorize their own people, invade neighbors, and promote proxy wars. The list of autocracies that America promoted (and still promotes) is quite long. They include regimes run by Franco, Pinochet, Shah of Iran, Yahya Khan, Zia-ul-Haq, Suharto, Marcos, Papa and Baby Doc, Saddam Hussein, and the Arab monarchies, especially the Saudi Dynasty. America and its allies have killed more than two million civilians across the world since Hiroshima in the name of freedom and democracy. In sum, what Frederick Douglas (an ex-slave) told a White audience at Rochester, New York, in 1852 is still relevant today: "There is not a nation on the earth guilty of practices more shocking and bloody than are the people of the United States, at this very hour."[9] Martin Luther King Jr. also portrayed the American government as "the greatest purveyor of violence in the world today."[10] Being the last country to abolish slavery, the second last to abolish apartheid in the Western world and for its hegemonic imperialistic behavior across the world, America has not yet emerged as the real champion of liberty, equality, and fraternity. The sooner Americans pay heed to Tocqueville's advice to America and other democracies in the 1830s on the evils of war, the better.

> No protracted war can fail to endanger the freedom of a democratic country.... War does not always give over democratic communities to military government, but it must invariably and immeasurably increase the powers of civil government; it must almost compulsorily concentrate the direction of all men and the management of all things in the hands of administration. If it leads not to despotism by sudden violence, it prepares men for it more gently by their habits. *All those who seek to destroy the liberties of a democratic nation ought to know that war is the surest and the shortest means to accomplish it.*[11] (emphasis added)

As slave-owning founding fathers of America were not champions of freedom and human dignity, selective and indiscriminate killing of people, plundering wealth and territories by American soldiers and civilians did not start in Vietnam. Killing of President Diem, the lies behind the Gulf of Tonkin incident and the Mai Lai massacre in Vietnam, the Abu Ghraib episode, Guantanamo Bay, U.S. Marines' urinating on a dead Taliban or the killing of Afghan villagers, including women and children by American soldiers, have been just the tips of the iceberg. Paradoxically, the only country that has ever used nuclear weapons is against nuclear proliferation by other countries such as Iran and North Korea. Surprisingly, no American President since the assassination of John F. Kennedy has ever raised a finger against Israel for acquiring nuclear weapons. There is nothing surprising about America's covert support for Israel because American foreign policy has always been duplicitous, and after Kennedy, it is virtually running by the powerful Military–Industrial Complex and the Israel Lobby.[12]

The ongoing tension and the lack of mutual trust and respect between the worlds of Islam and the West are likely to escalate further. Ultra-orthodox obscurantist forces have gained upper hand in several Muslim-majority countries. Interestingly, the newly liberated polities in Tunisia, Egypt, and Libya are not free from the growing influence of political Islam. Islamist parties in Tunisia, Egypt, and Libya have already demanded the introduction of misogynistic illiberal law, including polygamy and child marriage.[13] Although soft and liberal democratic through transformation or because of pragmatic reasons, Islamist parties have two things in common: their contempt for Western hegemony and aversion to accepting Israel as a legitimate entity. Even the most liberal Islamist parties in Turkey are no exceptions in this regard. The American-led liberation of Iraq and Afghanistan has paradoxically empowered Islamist forces, especially in Iraq where pro-Iranian Shiite majority is calling the shots. It is noteworthy that post-Saddam Iraq and post-Taliban Afghanistan are closer to America's archrival Iran than ever before. American protégés, Prime Minister Nouri al Maliki of Iraq and President Hamid Karzai of Afghanistan, have excellent relations with President Ahmadinejad of Iran, and successors of Maliki and Karzai are most likely to maintain cordial relations with Iran in the coming years.

Thanks to American promotion of military dictators and obscurantist forces, Pakistan has emerged as the most powerful citadel of Islamist extremism in South Asia. While liberal democratic and secular values are fast disappearing in Pakistan, sectarianism and extreme intolerance of non-Muslims and liberal Sufi Islam have been institutionalized through judicial and legislative measures. America's growing friendship with Pakistan's sworn enemy, India, and killing of Pakistani civilians and soldiers through drone attacks and aerial bombing by the U.S. military have also been counterproductive. Let us find out what has been dogging the American polity. I have avoided citing Muslim and left-oriented scholars with strong anti-American bias and agendas in my portrayal of America. I have mostly relied on Western/American scholars, politicians, journalists, retired generals, and analysts who have singled out America as an awkward, cumbersome, hypocritical, malevolent, and unmanageable empire.

George W. Bush told the U.S. Congress in the aftermath of the 9/11 attacks: "Americans are asking: [W]hy do they hate us? They hate our freedoms—our freedom of religion, our freedom of speech, our freedom to vote and assemble and disagree with each other." This is not true. The 9/11 attacks had nothing to do with American freedom but everything to do with the U.S. policies and actions in the Muslim world.[14] Then again, "If there is a single power the West underestimates, it is the power of collective hatred."[15] However, Americans are so narcissistically self-righteous that even Senator Fulbright, who critiqued American arrogance of power in the 1960s, believed that with her deep-rooted democratic traditions, America was not likely to dominate the world in the manner of a Hitler or Napoleon. He also believed that "America will escape these fatal temptations of power."[16] What the Senator wrote in 1966 has not eventually passed the acid test as soon afterwards America emerged as the most reckless, belligerent nation in the world. Its war machine in less than 10 years killed more than two million people in Vietnam alone.

Ultra-Right guru of American neo-cons, Bernard Lewis—who justified the U.S. invasion of Iraq—gives an evasive answer as to why Muslims hate America.

> That's the wrong question.... You have this millennial rivalry between two world religions, and now, from their point of view, the wrong one seems to be winning.... More generally...you can't be rich, strong, successful and loved, particularly by those who are not rich, not strong and not successful. So the hatred is something almost axiomatic. *The question which we should be asking is why do they neither fear nor respect us?* (emphasis added)

The so-called Lewis Doctrine—"Get tough or get out"—is all about justifying Western hegemony in Muslim lands.[17] What neo-cons fail to realize is that the ongoing Muslim–West conflict "has the potential to last beyond our children's lifetime and to be fought mostly on U.S. soil."[18] However, due to America's long-drawn involvement in the $3 trillion wars in Afghanistan and Iraq, the wealth and influence of the so-called "1 percent" of the population are growing, while the middle class is shrinking and more people are joining the marginalized classes across America. Paul Krugman believes that the concentration of wealth in the hands of few threatens American democracy, in the long run.[19]

John Tirman singles out what Mel Gibson, Paris Hilton, and their ilk represent collectively as signs of American degeneration. He thinks, "Mel Gibson most exudes one thing that is quintessentially Hollywood-American: violence", and Paris Hilton "may be the apotheosis of a menace—the trash celebrity."[20] Thanks to the manipulation of the media, education system, and deification of movie stars, sportsmen and women, and celebrities, many Americans are least informed and interested in national and global politics. The powerful Military–Industrial Complex's glorification of wars America has fought and is still fighting since the Korean War—on phony issues against imaginary enemies—in distant corners of the world has turned depoliticized Americans into warmongers as well. The upshot is the simultaneous denigration and demonization of the others—Muslims, Arabs, Iranians, Afghans, and Pakistanis—and whoever ill-informed Americans think as the enemies of freedom. The level of American cultural backwardness has been well reflected in their support for warmongers, such as Reagan and Bush (both Sr and Jr.), Sarah Palin, and the Tea-Party conservatives, especially, in the most reactionary parts of the country—central Georgia, rural Kentucky, etc., as Chomsky uses the expression. American ruling elites never expose their imperialist designs to the average Americans who, consequently, are always available to fight and die for "freedom and liberty."

To be fair, one can only pity not blame the backward Americans for their belief system and willingness to preserve the vested interests of the rich and powerful. Chalmers Johnson has explained the situation quite succinctly: "Once upon a time, you could trace the spread of imperialism by counting up colonies. America's version of the colony is the military base."[21] And America has more than 750 of them worldwide.

Scholars are, however, not sure if America is an imperialist, neo-imperialist, or neo-colonialist entity. The U.S. is not only an artificial entity (not a nation-state such as France or Germany) but also a hegemonic power. Most definitions of colonial and imperialist relationships between countries fit in well with America's relationship with countries in the Third/developing world. We find the New Oxford American Dictionary very helpful in understanding imperialism, a policy of extending a country's power and influence through diplomacy or military force. Nevertheless, American imperialism is not all about plundering foreign lands and creating overseas market for American goods and services. We find President Reagan's Assistant Secretary of Treasury (1981–1982) Paul Craig Roberts's analysis very useful in understanding the real nature of American imperialism:

> America's wars are very expensive. Bush and Obama have doubled the national debt, and the American people have no benefits from it. No riches, no bread and circuses flow to Americans from Washington's wars. So what is it all about? The answer is that Washington's empire extracts resources from the American people for the benefit of the few powerful interest groups that rule America. The military-security complex, Wall Street, agri-business and the Israel Lobby use the government to extract resources from Americans to serve their profits and power. The US Constitution has been extracted in the interests of the Security State, and Americans' incomes have been redirected to the pockets of the 1 percent. That is how the American Empire functions.[22] (emphasis added)

Then again, America is not all about wars and invasions, slavery, apartheid, and the Klu Klux Klan. It is also a land of inventions, discoveries and innovations, grace, compassion, and love for fellow human beings and even animals. It is in short, a land of freedom and fairness. From Thomas Edison to the Wright Brothers, Abraham Lincoln to Martin Luther King Jr., Helen Keller to Albert Einstein, Ernest Hemingway to Harper Lee, Noam Chomsky to Muhammad Ali, Bill Gates, and Steve Jobs; thousands of great men and women who have immense contributions to human civilization are Americans. Very few nations in the world can match American philanthropy. Annually, the Americans raise about $250 billion for charity, averaging about $1,000 per head nationwide.[23] Oil-rich Arab autocracies do not come near America with regard to the latter's philanthropy and open-door immigration policy. Whatever racial profiling and Islamophobic behavior one encounters in America are not unexpected in the wake of 9/11 and scores of attacks on American lives and properties by deviant Muslims, including American citizens such as Anwar Aulaki and Major Nidal Hassan. Despite some American Muslims' promotion of conspiracy theories and hate crime against America (which they love to hate for various reasons), the American government and people in general have remained tolerant and respectful of American Muslims. While several hundred mosques came up in America in the wake of 9/11, the Saudi government does not allow the erection of a single church, synagogue, and temple in Saudi Arabia. The Saudi government even does not allow non-Muslim visitors in the holy cities of Mecca and Medina. One may juxtapose the level of religious freedom that Muslims enjoy in America against the absence of similar rights for the non-Muslims in Saudi Arabia, Egypt, Pakistan, Indonesia, and some other countries in the Muslim world. Then again, the problem of America's imperialist adventures, which have killed millions of innocent people across the world, remains unresolved. The following accounts help us understand how the legacy of White supremacy influences modern imperialists in America to subjugate and kill others. They not only plunder their own people in the name of freedom and fighting their "war on terror" but also invade foreign lands for wealth, influence, and grandeur.

The Empire of Fear, Arrogance, and War

The inherent fear of losing out the empire is the main reason why imperialists justify their over lordship by invoking God, democracy, freedom, peace, and justice or whatever they deem necessary. Columbus justified slavery and dehumanization of slaves in Haiti in the name of Christianity. He justified keeping slaves naked because they showed no more embarrassment than animals. He also wrote: "Let us in the name of the Holy Trinity go on sending all the slaves that can be sold."[24] Howard Zinn gives plenty of evidences in support of European and American White slave traders' barbaric methods of shipping slaves in small cage-like containers from Africa to the shores of America.

> [B]lacks were chained together [in cages on board the ships] and the slaves [were] in different stages of suffocation, many dead, some having killed others in desperate attempts to breathe. Slaves often jumped overboard to drown rather than continue their suffering. To one observer a slave-deck was "so covered with blood and mucus that it resembled a slaughter house."

The accounts of annexation of territories by White settlers of America are also very disturbing. The new settlers occupied New Mexico, Utah, Nevada, Arizona, California, Colorado, and Texas from Mexico by brutal force. Zinn cites Colonel Hitchcock who in his diary gives an account of how in 1845 General Taylor's soldiers annexed Mexican territories: "I have said from the first that the United States are the aggressors.... We have not one particle of right to be here.... My heart is not in this business... but, as a military man, I am bound to execute orders." What is even more surprising is that Abraham Lincoln, who later was instrumental in the abolition of slavery, in 1848 glorified General Taylor as "the hero of the Mexican war."[25]

Although modern American leaders do not publicly say what Theodore Roosevelt spelled out in the late 19th century about the superiority of White civilization, yet they glorify war to promote American hegemony. There is no secret about the real motive behind American invasions of Iraq in 1991 and 2003. One American general is said to have observed that had Kuwait grown carrots, not oil, America would not have bothered to send troops to liberate the country. And by now the whole world knows how the Bush administration lied about the so-called weapons of mass destruction as a pretext to invade Iraq in 2003. So, at the end of the day, it is all about strategic importance, trading, and speculating in natural resources that motivate America to wage wars in distant lands. However, the sustainability of the empire depends on how well the ruling elites maintain the balance between military and the statecraft. American leaders from the very beginning realized the importance of maintaining this (precarious) balance.

President George Washington in his Farewell Address to the nation on September 17, 1796 felt that: "Overgrown military establishments are under any form of government inauspicious to liberty, and are to be regarded as particularly hostile to Republican liberty."[26] One hundred and sixty-five years later, President Eisenhower echoed Washington's reservations about having overgrown military establishments in his Farewell Address to the nation on January 17, 1961:

> This conjunction of an immense military establishment and a large arms industry is new in the American experience. The total influence—economic, political, even spiritual—is felt in every city, every statehouse, every office of the federal government. We recognize the imperative need for this

development. Yet we must not fail to comprehend its grave implications. Our toil, resources and livelihood are all involved; so is the very structure of our society. In the councils of government, we must guard against the acquisition of unwarranted influence, whether sought or unsought, by the Military–Industrial Complex. The potential for the disastrous rise of misplaced power exists and will persist. We must never let the weight of this combination endanger our liberties or democratic processes. We should take nothing for granted.[27]

One eminent scholar asserts, "Until we rein in what Eisenhower originally called the 'military-industrial-congressional complex,' we will never have a peace-based economy."[28] The original draft of the speech had Congressional Complex as a part of the now famous Military–Industrial Complex. Susan Eisenhower, granddaughter of the President, corroborated this in the "Real Time with Bill Maher" show on July 25, 2009 that: "The 'congressional' part was taken out because the President felt that he'd had excellent relations with a Democratic Congress and didn't want to get into name-calling on his way out." One analyst believes that: "By the 1950s, members of Congress had insinuated themselves into positions of power in the complex, so that one is well justified in calling it the military–industrial–congressional complex (MICC) during the past 40 years."[29]

While the Cold-War era was the best of times for American warmongers, they have not done so badly in the wake of the Cold War. What Berkeley Professor Robert B. Reich—Former Economic Adviser to President Obama and Labor Secretary in Clinton administration for four years—has demonstrated is how wasteful, counterproductive, and warmongering the MICC has been for decades. He has listed 10 mega military hardware manufacturers in America, including the Lockheed Martin, Northrop Grumman, Boeing, and Raytheon, who in 2010 alone made more than $73 billion by selling their products to the U.S. government.[30] P.W. Singer is very pertinent in understanding why the privatized military industry, military contractors, and mercenaries cost billions to the American economy. We learn from his work that more than 20,000 private American soldiers or mercenaries fought in Iraq in 2003, and that thousands of "soldiers for hire" work for American "Military Corporations" to fight for American allies from the Balkans to Central Asia, West Africa, and beyond. He raises the ethical questions about the profit motive of private armies, who have also been violating the principles of democracy and human rights. And in the name of national security, they cost billions to the American taxpayers.[31] This writer heard from his former Iraqi students (brigadiers)—who insisted on remaining anonymous—at a Department of Defense (DoD) college in Honolulu (APCSS) about the alleged atrocities committed by members of the Blackwater—a private American military company formed in 1997, renamed Xe Services LLC in 2009—in Iraq. Members of this privately run mercenary militia are alleged to have killed large numbers of Iraqi civilians and top military officers since the NATO occupation of the country in 2003. These highly paid private troops also enjoy capitulatory rights or immunity from being arrested by Iraqi or Afghan police and trialed by the Iraqi and Afghan courts. These appraisals are relevant in understanding the problem of the American Empire.

Renowned historian Chalmers Johnson believes that mercenaries are "at work" behind the government machinery in America. He finds no rationale behind America having more than 750 military bases outside America in and around 130 countries. They cost America more than $100 billion a year, heighten tension between America and countries that feel threatened by the presence of U.S. troops in their neighborhood, and perpetuate patron–client relationships between America and its client states. Despite all these, America feigns that it is not secure from rogue states such as Iraq under Saddam Hussein and Iran under the ayatollahs. Former Defense Secretary Rumsfeld wrote months after the American invasion of Iraq in 2003: "Today, we lack metrics to know if we are winning or losing the global war on terror."[32] In view of this, Americans and freedom-loving people across the world need to raise the question as to why (as of 2010) America deploys approximately 300,000 troops besides 90,000 sailors at 761 sites in foreign countries by keeping America in a perpetual state of war. It is time that Americans ask America to stop "reinventing wars" for the sake of global peace.[33] Jimmy Carter and Colin Powell describe what American invasion of Lebanon before the 1983 suicide attack on U.S. Marine barracks in Beirut entails:[34]

> We sent Marines into Lebanon and you only have to go to Lebanon, to Syria or to Jordan to witness first-hand the intense hatred among many people for the United States because we bombed and shelled and unmercifully killed totally innocent villagers—women and children and farmers and housewives—in those villages around Beirut.... As a result of that...we became kind of a Satan in the minds of those who are deeply resentful. (Carter)

The USS New Jersey started hurling 16-inch shells into the mountains above Beirut, in World War II style, as if we were softening up the beaches on some Pacific atoll prior to an invasion. What we tend to overlook in such situations is that other people will react much as we would. (Powell)

The Military–Industrial Complex has kept alive the Russian bogey in America even after the demise of the Soviet Union and the consequential disorientation, political and economic crises that befell Russia. American warmongers invented the Islamic bogey and Saddam Hussein as immediate security threats to America, along with China as the main adversary in the long run. Reagan's Secretary of Defense Casper Weinberger reminded Americans:

As time goes on, the threat posed by NBC [Nuclear, Biological, and Chemical] weapons will only get worse—so get used to it.... We must also remember that right now—not three to five years or a decade away—a Russia with twenty-five thousand nuclear warheads could destroy the United States in an afternoon.[35]

Weinberger and his coauthor lamented the drastic cut in America's defense expenditure, which they felt had turned America into a sitting duck in relation to the most likely invasions by North Korea, China, Iran, Russia, and even by Mexico and Japan. They were critical of Bill Clinton and even Bush Sr. for allegedly slashing the defense budget. They predicted a North Korean invasion in 1998, the Iranian one in 1999, and the Russian and Japanese invasions of America in 2006 and 2007, respectively. Interestingly enough, Margaret Thatcher wrote an equally alarmist foreword for the book.[36]

As George Friedman argues, "America was born out of war and has continued to fight to this day at an ever increasing pace. Norway's grand strategy might be more about economics than warfare, but U.S. strategic goals, and U.S. grand strategy, originate in fear,"[37] American conservatives glorify wars. Since the beginning of the 21st century, America is at war 100 percent of the time and is likely to do so in the coming decades.[38] One is not sure if by 2020, it will not be an Islamist but very different challenges that the U.S. military will be facing, including from Russia and others.[39] There is no logic in Friedman's projection of Russia, Turkey, Japan, Mexico, and Poland as emerging security threats to the U.S. However, as the founder of a private intelligence firm Stratford, which "is closely aligned with Pentagon planners…as a private wing of the Pentagon," his views reflect what military contractors and think tanks do all the time.[40] They legitimize the Military–Industrial Complex's inventions of threats to the Homeland.[41]

John Tirman has listed a hundred ways of America screwing up the world. He has cited examples of American leaders' stupid ideas. While George W. Bush opposed the Kyoto Protocol believing that it "would have wrecked" the U.S. economy, Reagan was naïve enough to assert that "trees cause more pollution than automobiles do." Reagan also considered Philippines's Marcos as one of the most democratic rulers in Asia and Angola's warlord Savimbi, Zaire's mass murderer Mobutu and Pakistan's Islamist military dictator General Zia-ul-Haq as America's best friends in the world. As discussed earlier, America befriended many dictators, and CIA removed elected governments in various countries. It is noteworthy that in the early 1960s, Saddam Hussein was a CIA agent engaged in toppling the pro-Soviet Iraqi regime of General Karim Qassim.[42]

Chalmers Johnson, who worked for the CIA for six years (1967–1973), blamed the overgrown Military–Industrial Complex for dragging America into unwinnable and unnecessary wars. He considered Bush Jr. a sophomoric ignoramus. He is, however, shocked at President Clinton's cruise missile attack on a pharmaceutical plant in Khartoum, Sudan, and the 1999 bombing of the Chinese Embassy in Belgrade.[43] He was disappointed with the successor to the worst president in American history, as Obama failed in abandoning warmongering Americans' infatuation with imperialism. Obama neither closed down the extrajudicial detention camp at Guantanamo Bay nor did he replace Bush's top military generals and advisers, including General David Petraeus and Defense Secretary Robert Gates, he pointed out.[44]

Despite being the biggest proponent of free market economy and globalization, America has been violating the fundamentals of the free market through agricultural subsidies to American farmers, which cost the developing world $350 billion per year, while America donates around $50 billion annually as foreign aid to the Third World. There is no reason to condone America allowing the export of genetically modified (GM) seeds to Third World countries to the detriment of their agriculture—damaging their crop diversification programs—and turning them perpetually dependent on GM seeds.[45] The oversold "Food for Peace" program

(PL 480), often glorified as the Marshall Plan for the Third World, is another way of giving billions of dollars as farm subsidy to rich American farmers and to sell fertilizers and chemicals to the Third World for the benefit of American corporations, doubling the gap between the rich and poor nations from 1960 through 1989.[46]

Media Lies and Government Deceptions

As Americans live in a state of ignorance about their politics, economics, domestic and foreign policies, they are indifferent about the exploitation by the rich and powerful "1 percent" of the poor and disempowered "99 percent" Americans. Although the *New York Times* might be the best daily newspaper in the world and the *Washington Post* is not far behind, they are not so when the terrain is U.S. foreign policy or the issue is about protecting the interests of the jobless and poor Americans, observes Chomsky. He has rightly portrayed the mainstream American media as anti-poor and pro-war and pro-globalization. It considers the anti-globalization forces as anti-progress and the wretched of the earth. Two years after the American invasion of Iraq, the *New York Times* in 2005 estimated around "500 civilian deaths attributable to coalition forces" in the country, while the actual number had exceeded 100,000.[47] Yet in another story, the *New York Times* in August 2004 (three months before the Presidential Election, which re-elected George Bush) published a fabricated story about al Qaeda's alleged plots to bomb several buildings in the financial district of New York, and the World Bank and the IMF buildings in Washington, D.C.

> The headlines were grand, with photos of Special Forces guarding the buildings.... It was strongly implied that there were domestic jihadist operatives...and that it only reinforced the unwarranted fears that conveniently earned George W. Bush a second term three months later, was never part of the story in the *Times* or the *Post*.[48]

No American scholar has possibly done a better job than Chomsky in exposing American duplicities, political corruption, imperialistic designs, and war crimes committed globally in the name of democracy and freedom. He has convincingly elaborated and analyzed the American art and science of controlling the public mind to "tame the bewildered herd" by engineering opinion and manufacturing consent through the government's public relations agencies and privately owned media. He has illustrated the facts in the light of history and contemporary records. He gives account of President Wilson's propaganda commission, called the Creel commission, which within six months in 1916 cleverly manipulated the overwhelmingly pacifist Americans by turning them into a "hysterical, warmongering population" to hate and destroy everything German in the name of patriotism.[49] George Creel, who headed the Commission, reveals that the Wilson administration spent about five million dollars and engaged 75,000 speakers, operating in 5,200 communities, made 755,190 speeches in favor of American participation in World War I.[50]

Chomsky also mentions renowned thinker and journalist Walter Lippmann, who believed that democracies should manufacture consent of the public as the common interests always "elude the general public."[51] As Chomsky argues, "The public sees no reason to get involved in foreign adventures, killing, and torture. So, you have to whip them up. *And to whip them up you have to frighten them*" (emphasis added).[52] In view of the successful arousal of mass hysteria in America by the Bush administration against Saddam Hussein since the 9/11 attacks, we have reasons to believe that fear mongering by manipulating facts and sheer lies and deceptions by rulers is essential to justify unjust wars. American leaders successfully used media and its propaganda machine to frighten the average Americans to justify its destructive wars in distant lands. London-based Iraqi banker Ahmad Chalabi, who came to the limelight as the future leader of Iraq after the defeat of Saddam Hussein, observed in 1991 that the U.S. was "waiting for Saddam to butcher the insurgents in the hope that he can be overthrown later by a suitable officer" (through a pro-U.S. military coup).[53]

Reagan and the cohorts of his supporters of gunboat diplomacy, also glorified war and believed in instilling in people respect for martial value. They simply wanted to kill the sickly inhibitions against the use of military force in the collective psyche of America after the disaster in Vietnam. Reagan and his associates aptly named it the Vietnam Syndrome or the mass inhibitions against mobilizing American troops in foreign lands. Thanks to the successful use of media and government manipulations, the average Americans since the presidency of Reagan are more vigorous than before in supporting American war efforts anywhere in the world. Many American students at a prestigious university in Massachusetts responded to a survey in 1991 estimating that around 100,000 Vietnamese had died during the decade-long American invasion of that country, while the official figure is about two million and the actual figure is probably three to four million.[54]

In the backdrop of growing American belligerency toward new enemies—mostly reconstructed or invented by its ruling elites and media—every 10 years or so, we need to understand: (a) as to how the necessary illusions or thought control work in democracies; and (b) why the continuation of this process would lead to more wars and invasions of new targets by America and its allies in the foreseeable future. The imperialist follows the motto of same war, different targets,[55] albeit with mass support through media manipulation. Amartya Sen might be right that democracies do not go to war with one another, but democracies invade countries in the name of democracy and freedom.

Soldier-turned-academic Bacevich believes that Americans "have fallen prey to militarism, manifesting itself in a romanticized view of soldiers… with utopian ends had established itself as the distinguishing element of contemporary U.S. policy." He thinks that the New American Militarism has evolved over decades, not just in the wake of 9/11, and that the marriage of military metaphysics with eschatological ambition would lead to endless wars. He has agreed with Robert Kagan that "America did not change on September 11, it only became more itself," that is, America started glorifying its legacy of militarism developed not in the past six decades but "for the better part of the past four centuries." Bacevich also cites Michael Ignetieff and Madeleine Albright. While Ignetieff believes that "Empire has become a precondition for democracy," Albright is said to have asked Colin Powell: "What's the point of having this superb military that you're always talking about, if we can't use it?"[56]

Consequently, American military budget grew by more than 12 percent annually between 2001 and 2009, when the country was run in accordance with the Weinberger Doctrine. Reagan's Defense Secretary Casper Weinberger did not want America to commit the Vietnam mistakes. In accordance with this doctrine, America used overwhelming force for a swift and decisive victory for America in Iraq in 1991 and 2003. America's 1992 Defense Planning Guidance (DPG) reflected Weinberger strategy. In the name of benevolent global hegemony, America started spending more on defense to prevent the reemergence of a new rival. By 2007, America started spending $622 billion on defense per year, which amounts to spending $2,065 per capita against $1,000 in Britain, $845 in France, $430 in Germany, and about $340 in Japan. America's overseas use of military (in invading countries) rose phenomenally in the first 15 years after the fall of the Berlin Wall, more than what it had done during the 45 years of the Cold War.[57] In 2011, America spent $739.3 billion on defense, equivalent to 45.7 percent of what the rest of the world spent on defense in that particular year.[58]

Tirman is right that:

> [A]s a result, the U.S. relations with many countries are shaped by their ability to buy this expensive military hardware, which they don't need any more than we do.... What does America care about? The profitability of Lockheed Martin and Halliburton and all the rest.

Last but not least, defense contractors' "tight grip on members of Congress...and the presidency itself" does not allow any "change of course that could correct or limit the damage of these practices." The onset of the War on Terror further strengthened the Military–Industrial Complex, which will remain the new normal in the coming years.[59] The Military–Industrial and Congressional lobbies, on a regular basis, overrule and outmaneuver the President. Obama's abysmal failure to close down the Guantanamo Bay prison camps (despite his promises since the first Presidential Campaign in 2008) is an example of the preponderance of the Congress, which opposed the closing down proposal in June 2013.[60] The trial of U.S. Army private Bradley Manning at a military court since his arrest in 2010 for leaking 700,000 documents of torture and casualties of Iraqi civilians at the hands of U.S. troops to the Wikileaks may be cited as another example of the overpowering influence of the U.S. military on the civilian government. The U.S. media hardly circulates this news.[61] Ron Paul, a Republican Presidential Candidate in 2008 and 2012, believes that whistleblower Bradley Manning should be released, as he believes, Manning "has done us [Americans] a great service by letting the people know the truth...his goal was to inform the American people of the truth about what was happening in the Iraq/Afghanistan Wars."[62] Ron Paul also considers Manning and Edward Snowden (another whistleblower wanted by Washington, who published thousands of documents implicating America in spying against its own citizens) as victims of the American

Empire, which wants to hide things from its own people. Paul likens them with Daniel Ellsberg who in 1971 released the top secret Pentagon Papers that revealed American lies and deceptions about the Vietnam War.[63]

As Tirman is provocative and incisive so is Chomsky passionate about peace. One may disagree with them for their extreme views nevertheless they deserve our respect and attention for their extreme love for peace and justice. Chomsky tells us how American warmongers invent a New Hitler on a regular basis. "They've got to keep coming up one after another. You frighten the population, terrorize them, intimidate them so that they're too afraid to travel and cower in fear. Then you have a magnificent victory over Grenada, Panama, or some other defenseless third world army," observes Chomsky.[64] Michael Leedin of the American Enterprise Institute has aptly observed that every 10 years or so, America needs to "pick up some crappy little country and throw it against the wall, just to show the world that we mean business." In accordance with this logic, shortly after the First Gulf War ended, North Korea emerged as "the next renegade state."[65] A White House spokesman in July 2003 mentioned Syria, along with Libya and Cuba, among the "junior varsity axis of evil."[66]

Wars and conflicts fetch windfalls for the Military–Industrial Complex. The economics of militarism has its own unique way of flouting the market rules and regulations most arbitrarily, in accordance with bureaucratic decisions uninfluenced by market forces but often quite responsive to insider influence and crony capitalism. Military contractors and manufacturers of military hardware, including Kellogg Brown & Root, are subsidiaries of the Halliburton Company and the Bechtel Group. Not coincidentally, Brown & Root is former Vice President Dick Cheney's old company and Bechtel has old connections with the CIA and high-ranking Republican politicians. The Congress simply doles out public money to these companies. It gave $7.4 billion to a company for missile defense in 2004. Lockheed Martin and Boeing are among the prime contractors, who make billions in the name of defending America.[67] While Tomahawk cruise missiles, for example, cost $1/$1.5 million apiece, the U.S.-led forces on the first day of the invasion of Libya in March, 2011 launched 112 of them against Qaddafi loyalists. That is, America spent $112 to $168 million on cruise missile alone on the first day of the attack on Libya.[68] Some other military hardware are even costlier: a single F-22 Raptor costs $135 million, one single AC-130U Gunship costs $190 million, the cost of a single F-117A Nighthawk is $122 million, and that of a single B-2 Stealth Bomber is a whipping $2.2 billion. The Pentagon's latest, staggering estimate of the lifetime cost (over the next 50 years) of the F-35 will be $1.51 trillion.[69]

So, going to war as well as making military hardware are all about making money. "The hidden agenda is to create a new legitimacy, opening the door for a 'revitalization of the nation's defense' while also providing a justification for direct military actions by the US in different parts of the World," argues Chossudovsky. He believes,

> [T]his new direction of the U.S. economy will generate hundreds of billions of dollars of surplus profits, which will line the pockets of a handful of large corporations. While contributing very marginally to the rehabilitation of the employment of specialised scientific, technical and professional workers laid-off by the civilian economy, this profit bonanza will also be used by the U.S. corporate establishment to finance—in the form of so-called "foreign investment"—the expansion of the American Empire in different parts of the World.[70]

Since war is business, America had no qualms about selling weapons to Iran through Israel to release American hostages captured by the Army of the Guardians of the Islamic Revolution (known as the Iran-Contra-Gate affair) in 1985. America also sold chemical weapons to Saddam Hussein, which he used against Iran and Kurdish rebels in the 1980s.[71]

American media bias against Arabs, Palestinians, and Muslims in general is well known. William Safire's double standard may be cited in this regard. While he wrote favorably of Kurdish freedom fighters' rightful aspirations to autonomy and respect for their culture, he had no qualms about portraying PLO leader Yasser Arafat as one who embraced the Ayatollah in Iran because Arafat wanted not only the sovereignty of the Israeli-occupied territories but also claimed the whole of Israel as the Palestinian State.[72] In view of such distortion of facts, we cannot agree more that the world needs a New World Information Order to diversify media access for alternative global media system free from Western domination.[73]

We, however, know how the West demonizes any dissenting voice and even a relatively pro-Arab media network Aljazeera (which is not an autonomous media conglomerate) for its projection of the other side of the coin, especially with regard to Israeli invasions of Gaza and Lebanon, and American/NATO invasion of Iraq. It may be mentioned that the Nixon administration wanted to bar the publication of the *Pentagon Papers* in 1971 and considered free press "a cantankerous press, an obstinate press, a ubiquitous press" for exposing some of the lies American governments had fed their people from time to time, especially with regard to the Vietnam War. As Truman ruled with the help of a small number of Wall Street lawyers and bankers, so has democracy in America been dysfunctional since Reagan's presidency. Since major or elite media in America are corporations catering to the needs and interests of the privileged audiences, true democracy has remained retarded.[74]

There are many American scholars who do not believe in what their government tells them about wars and interventions their country undertakes in foreign lands. They are not communists, anti-Semitic bigots, and secret admirers of al Qaeda or conspiracy theoreticians. Noam Chomsky, Chalmers Johnson, Howard Zinn, Andrew Bacevich, and William Blum do not fit in any of the above categories. Thus, one just cannot trash Blum's skepticism about the U.S. government version of 9/11 attacks as rubbish. He tells the world:

> I'm very aware of the serious contradictions and apparent lies in the Official Government Version (OGV) of what happened on that fateful day. (Before the Truthers can be dismissed as "conspiracy theorists," it should be noted that the OGV is literally a "conspiracy theory" about the fantastic things that a certain 19 men conspired to do.) It does appear that the buildings in New York collapsed essentially because of a controlled demolition, which employed explosives as well as certain incendiary substances found in the rubble.[75]

He does not stop at calling the attacks an inside job, he rather raises the question: "What if the government, with its omnipresent eyes and ears, discovered the plotting of Mideast terrorists some time before and decided to let it happen—and even enhance the destruction—to make use of it as a justification for its 'War on Terror?'"[76] We do not have to agree with what Blum thinks of 9/11 attacks. However, his skepticism reflects one thing: many American intellectuals simply do not believe the government version of any story relating to wars, conflicts, and terrorism where the U.S. government is the perpetrator or victim.

The Israel Lobby and the Israeli Exceptionalism

One can figure out the importance of Israel in America's foreign policy from the influence of the Israel Lobby in the country. Although it is almost a taboo in America to point fingers at Israel as a problem to world peace and America's long-term security, a few people have dared to expose Israel as the biggest threat to world peace and America's security. The Israel Lobby is so powerful that American politicians seem to be competing against each other in demonstrating their love and concern for the Zionist state, the beacon of light, only democracy in the Middle East, and a victim of anti-Semitism. While John Edwards in 2004 assured Israel that "your future is our future," former House Speaker Newt Gingrich felt that "Israel is facing the greatest danger for [sic] its survival since the 1967 victory." In 2007, Hillary Clinton in her address to the powerful American-Israel Public Affairs Committee (AIPAC) meeting in New York expressed that Israel was going through "great difficulty" and "great peril," and that it was a "beacon of what's right in a neighborhood overshadowed by the wrongs of radicalism, extremism, despotism and terrorism."[77]

It is noteworthy that Barack Obama, who sometimes talks about the plight of the Palestinians, was unequivocal in his praise for Israel in 2007, promising that if elected to the presidency, he would "do nothing to change the U.S.–Israeli relationship."[78] In view of this, we should not take any American politician seriously whenever we hear them talking about a Palestinian State (what seems unattainable) or asking Israel to vacate those territories it occupied from Arabs during the 1967 War. Obama said these sorts of things soon after becoming the President in Cairo in June 2009. He promised a "new beginning between the United States and Muslims around the world" and urged Islamic nations to embrace democracy, women's rights, religious tolerance, and the right of Israel to coexist with an independent Palestinian State. This initially pleased many Muslims around the world.[79] As a senior Aljazeera political analyst said, "[The speech] was about willingness to engage in soft power while keeping the military option alive." Another Arab analyst felt that:

> [H]is [Obama's] call for stopping settlement and for the establishment of
> a Palestinian state, and his reference to the suffering of Palestinians…is a

clear message to Israel that a just peace is built on the foundations of a Palestinian state with Jerusalem as its capital.[80]

However, as discussed in Chapter 3, Israeli Prime Minister Benjamin Netanyahu rejected President Obama's suggestion made in a speech at the State Department in May, 2011 that a future Palestinian state must be based on the 1967 borders. Netanyahu said those borders, which existed before the 1967 Middle-East war, were indefensible. An estimated 500,000 Israelis live in settlements built in the West Bank, which lies outside those borders.[81] Soon afterwards, addressing an AIPAC meeting in Washington, Obama made it clear that the Jewish state would likely be able to negotiate keeping some settlements in any final deal with the Palestinians. Obama, as expected, simply succumbed to the pressure of the Israel Lobby.[82] The U.S. rejection of the proposed Palestinian statehood by President Mahmoud Abbas (of the Palestinian National Authority, not State) in 2011 further strengthens the notion that the tail (Israel) actually wags the dog (U.S.). What Susan Rice, the American ambassador to the U.N., said is noteworthy. She felt that there was no greater threat to "U.S. support and funding of the U.N. than the prospect of Palestinian statehood being endorsed by member states," and that the U.S. "could withdraw funding from U.N. if Palestine state is recognized." Obama conveyed the same message to Abbas.[83]

As Tirman explains, "The AIPAC is the apotheosis of the lobbying group as a representative of a foreign country. Few lobbies have been more powerful. Few have more single-mindedly pursued a narrow agenda in U.S. foreign policy, and few have done more damage." He has also pointed out that the AIPAC represents the right wing of Israeli political spectrum, not the mainstream American Jews, and an ultra-right American think tank, the Washington Institute for Near East Policy, runs the organization.[84] Paul Findley, a former Congressman from Illinois, is also very candid in this regard. He reveals that the AIPAC spies on Congressmen and finds out if they say anything against Israel even in private conversation. He thinks,

> It is no overstatement to say that AIPAC has effectively gained control of virtually all of Capitol Hill's action on Middle East policy. *Almost without exception, House and Senate members do its bidding, because most of them consider AIPAC to be the direct Capitol Hill representative of a political force that can make or break their chances at election time.*[85] (emphasis added)

Findley reveals that American State and Defense employees since Eisenhower administration are being suborned and bribed on a wide scale by the Mossad to work for Israel. He cites an Ohio Congressman who was distressed at American policymakers' inability to distinguish between our national interest and Israel's national interest because of the AIPAC influence.[86] In sum, AIPAC has an almost unchallenged hold on Congress. And no wonder Ehud Olmert (a former Israeli Prime Minister) was so grateful to the outfit: "Thank God we have AIPAC, the greatest supporter and friend we have in the whole world."[87]

Thus, it appears that the Israel Lobby in America is as "American as an apple pie." However, the Lobby's interests hardly converge with those of America's. The Israel Lobby can reward or punish politicians through campaign contributions, which has been its main weapon. Thus, the Lobby is responsible for dragging America into wasteful and unpopular wars and conflicts in the Middle East, including the Iraq wars and conflicts with Iran and Syria. The Lobby is said to have been mainly responsible for Iran's nuclear ambitions.[88] Some other findings about the Israel Lobby's extraordinary influence on the U.S. administration corroborate Shahid Alam's arguments about Israeli Exceptionalism which defies all laws, logics, commonsense, and norms of international law and relations.[89]

The following examples are simply mindboggling: (a) Israel has the sole privilege of borrowing from American commercial banks at lower rates than other borrowers, (b) Israel is the only recipient of American foreign aid that does not have to account for how it is spent, (c) America gives $3 billion to Israel each year, one-sixth of America's total foreign aid, which amounts to giving $500 to each Israeli citizen against $20 for each Egyptian, and $5 for each Pakistani and Haitian citizen, (d) Israel also receives a donation of $2 billion from American citizens each year, which is the only tax deductible donation by U.S. citizens to a foreign country due to a special clause in the U.S.–Israel income tax treaty.[90] Last but not least, one takes the risk of getting branded as anti-Semitic by merely pointing out Israel as a big threat to world peace, its excesses, double standards, and the extraordinary influence of the Israel Lobby on the U.S. administration. Mearsheimer and Walt have pointed out how difficult it was to get a publisher for their book in America and even journals and magazines simply refused to publish their article critiquing the Israel Lobby in America on flimsy grounds.[91] Nobel Laureate German poet Gunter Grass has become a persona non grata in Israel for his poem (in German), "What Must Be Said," which came out in the *Suddeutsche Zeitung* on April 4, 2012. Grass questions Western hypocrisy about nuclear proliferation and Israel, and as to why he took so long to write about Israel, which is a threat to world peace.

> Why only now, grown old,
> and with what ink remains, do I say:
> Israel's atomic power endangers
> an already fragile world peace?
> Because what must be said
> may be too late tomorrow....
> And granted: I've broken my silence
> because I'm sick of the West's hypocrisy.[92]

In view of America's unconditional support for Israel, one wonders if the Zionist state has been an asset or liability to America. Israel during the Cold War might have provided some helpful intelligence to America against Soviet Union, but they did not decisively affect the course of the Cold War. Conversely, the Arab oil embargo due to Western support for Israel adversely affected American economy. However, Israel has the capability to counter some rogue states in the Middle East to preserve Western interests in the region. Then again, Israel has become a strategic burden and indirectly a security threat to America. The Palestine issue is at the root of all conflicts in the Middle East, and America's unqualified support for Israel is the main factor behind Muslim/Arab hatred for America.[93] America's duplicitous policies, especially its vetoes against Palestinian and Arab interests and shying out from playing the role of an honest broker to resolve the Palestinian problem, may be mentioned in this regard. More than 80 percent Arabs consider Arab–Israeli conflict very important in determining their relations with America. They believe America to be a "partner in Israeli expansionism." Most Arabs consider Israel as the root cause behind Muslim support for al Qaeda.[94]

As Steven Kull elaborates, Muslims overwhelmingly believe that 9/11 attacks are contrary to the teachings of Islam, but they also believe that America is reviving the spirit of the Crusades among Western Christians against Islam, as after 9/11 instead of backing away from the Muslim world it invaded Afghanistan and then Iraq and expanded its forces in the Gulf. It appears that al Qaeda's intended goal of the 9/11 attacks was to make Muslims retaliate against the American backlash to precipitate their global jihad. And America unwittingly is doing what al Qaeda wants it to do.[95] Again, the American administration simply does not pay much heed to the argument that Islamist terrorists have been mainly targeting American/Western interests by exploiting the plight of the Palestinians. The Palestine issue has remained as an open sore and Israel an unassimilated lump in the Arab world.

America, a Hostage to Its Own Arrogance

As World War I had not put an end to all wars, so did World War II not signal the end of hostilities between nations. Due to the unrelenting belligerence between major powers and smaller states since the Korean War it seems the world had already entered the phase of another Hundred-Year War. Chossudovsky and Cunningham are convincing that America's design to perpetuate its global hegemony in the name of humanitarian undertaking is the biggest threat to peace as the superpower is determined to go for a long war against rogue states and while embarked on a military adventure is not hesitant to use nuclear weapons. Harold P. Smith, U.S. Assistant Secretary of Defense under Clinton administration, observed in 1997 that the B61-11 would be the nuclear weapon of choice against rogue states such as Libya.[96]

Although the Carter administration in 1978 specified that if a nonnuclear weapon state—not "already in bed with a nuclear weapon power"—invaded America, the latter would not retaliate against it with nuclear weapons. However, by 1995, the Pentagon reversed the Carter-Clinton policy of not using nuclear weapons against a nonnuclear state having no links with a nuclear power. By 1997, Iran and Libya, among other Third World countries, had become prime potential targets of nuclear attacks by America. Kristensen in 1997 raised some important questions as to who was in charge of America's nuclear arsenal: "Does the State Department know that the Pentagon is incorporating nonnuclear Non-Proliferation Treaty (NPT) countries into U.S. nuclear targeting?"

He also asked the question if President Clinton was aware of what the STRATCOM's policy was in this regard. The answers to the questions were: "probably not."[97] In view of this, there is nothing sensational about the assumption that America is likely to trigger a nuclear attack on nonnuclear countries such as Iran or Syria to prolong the long war. The long war, or what we may consider the continuance of the war that began in Korea, is likely to continue beyond the middle of this century, and the use of nuclear weapons by countries such as the U.S., Israel, and possibly China, India, and Pakistan in some of the major conflicts in the coming decades cannot be simply ruled out as least likely.

If we define the long war as the amalgamation of the major global conflicts in the post-Cold War era, then Saddam Hussein's Kuwait invasion in August 1990 heralded its beginning. He was quite prophetic in classifying the U.S.-led invasion of Iraq in 1991 as the "Mother of All Battles." During the Cold War, America and the Soviet Union did not cross swords although they were engaged in their four-decade-long proxy wars in Korea, Vietnam, Afghanistan, and elsewhere. However, things have changed since the end of Cold War. America since 1991 has been directly confronting its main challengers, rogue states and non-state actors. As American- and NATO-occupied countries in the Muslim world are fast becoming laboratories for global jihad, the nature of the conflict between America and the self-styled global jihadists has made it difficult for America to develop an effective winning strategy.[98] CIA veteran Michael Scheuer thinks that American leaders refuse to accept the obvious: that is, America is fighting a "worldwide Islamic insurgency—*not criminality or terrorism*—and our policy and procedures have failed to make more than a modest dent in enemy forces" (emphasis added).[99] He believes that since America has lost all other means to fight the Islamic insurgency, the military is now America's only tool. He argues that American policies and actions were bin Laden's only indispensable allies, and that Arab oil has turned America into a blind supporter of Islamist regimes such as Saudi Arabia, "whose goals—unlike bin Laden's—can be met only by annihilating all non-Muslims."[100]

In view of the depressive backdrop it is time to answer the questions Senator Fulbright raised in the 1960s: if "America can close the gap between her capacity and performance," and if America can "be confident but also tolerant, to be rich but also generous, to be willing to teach but also willing to learn, to be powerful but also wise."[101] Then again, he also sounded very pessimistic about the lack of commonsense and goodwill toward others among American leaders, "There is a kind of voodoo about American foreign policy. Certain drums have to be beaten regularly to ward off evil spirits.... Certain pledges must be repeated everyday lest the whole free world go to rack and ruin."[102] Surprisingly, very little has changed in the voodoo foreign policy. One may cite what the State Department did vis-à-vis the Maldives coup in February 2012 in this regard. After recognizing the military-backed government of Waheed Hussain, who had toppled the democratically elected President Mohamed Nasheed, within 72 hours, America backtracked from its swift recognition of the new regime.[103] It seems, being hostage to its own arrogance and ignorance, America will continue behaving erratically in foreign affairs. Thus, "Unveiling of the American Empire," as Chalmers Johnson has used the expression, is necessary for durable peace.[104]

It is time that Americans realize their country dominates the world through its military, not through any ideology or inherent virtue of the republic. Americans have no reason to be complacent about their so-called victory in the Cold War. We know 9/11 has changed the world. However, to be precise, the attacks produced a dangerous change in the thinking of American leaders, who began to see the republic as a genuine empire, a new Rome, the greatest colossus in history, no longer bound by international law. Even worse, this transformation from republic to empire may well prove irreversible, and slowly but surely the Department of Defense is obscuring and displacing the Department of State as the primary agency for making and administering foreign policy.[105] It is time to shatter the myth that since America spends around 4 percent of its GDP on defense against 6.3 percent by Eritrea, 9 percent by Oman, or 6.7 percent by the U.A.E., America is not overspending on defense. The 4 percent smokescreen (and other gimmicks) by the U.S. administration cannot justify America's spending more than $700 billion defense budget. We agree with Preble that America's ubiquitous enemy does not come from outside, but it is America's "waste, fraud, and abuse." America's power is a "problem because it costs too much," and America has far more power than it needs to defend itself.[106]

Obama administration has not deviated much from George W. Bush's War on Terror policy. In 2002, Bush asked Americans to be prepared to wage wars against as many as 60 countries. And not only the military lobby and hawks in the U.S. administration welcomed the scenario of waging wars against 60 countries, but analysts, journalists, think-tank operators, and even academics were also excited about their country becoming the gyroscope of world order and taking on "the role of successor to the British Empire," to paraphrase Christopher Preble. The list of the empire lovers includes conservative analysts such as Charles Krauthammer, Robert D. Kaplan, and Walter Russell Mead of the Council on Foreign Relations. Some other ideologues (direct descendants of Woodrow Wilson) want America to emerge as a humanitarian imperialist power for making the world safe for democracy. These soft imperialists even suggest using expressions such as postmodern imperialism, neo-imperialism, or liberal imperialism to justify America's right of humanitarian intervention anywhere outside the perimeters of America. What is evident that irrespective of which party controls the Congress or the White House, the military with a huge budget does actually call the shots. When General Anthony Zinni commanded the CENTCOM, he had 20 ambassadors serving under him, various U.S. command chiefs—avoiding the service chiefs— directly reported to the President. There is at least one example of a general who even publicly contradicted the President on an important international issue. While President Clinton condemned General Pervez Musharraf's military takeover in Pakistan, General Zinni ignored the Congressional sanctions against Pakistan and became a strong supporter of Musharraf [107] We also have the example of General Stanley McChrystal saying unflattering things about Vice President Joe Biden in June 2010 in an interview with the *Rolling Stone* magazine, which is reflective of the U.S. military mind-set, not always respectful of the civilian authority.[108] Another serving general William Boykin—born-again-Christian—got away with very offensive comments on Islam and Muslims in 2003. He even called Allah, God in Arabic, "an idol," not the real God. While President Bush condoned his comments, Secretary of Defense Rumsfeld defended his comments as his "freedom of expression."[109]

Now, instead of asking the question: Why do they hate us [Americans]? Americans should simply pay heed to Senator Fulbright's advice:

Maybe we are not really cut out for the job of spreading the gospel of democracy.... Maybe it would profit us to concentrate on our own democracy instead of trying to inflict our own particular version of it [on others].... In our excessive involvement in the affairs of other countries we are not only living off our assets...we are also denying the world the example of a free society enjoying freedom to the fullest.[110]

The above discussion leads us to think beyond the hackneyed and clichéd scenario, "What if America goes down the hill." It is simply a myth that American military muscle saved the free world from the curse of communism. As American carpet-bombing of Vietnam, Laos, and Cambodia could not stop these countries from adopting communism, so did American military play no role in the end of communism in Russia and Eastern Europe. As American military supremacy did not prevent 9/11, did not intimidate Saddam Hussein and bin Laden, could not stop North Korea's nuclear program, it does not coerce Iran or Syria into submission either. America's military machine, on the contrary, has corrupted American government. American policymakers must realize that their military is "dominant, but not omnipotent."[111] It is least likely that America will achieve anything through gunboat diplomacy, especially under the changed exigencies of the post-Cold War era.[112] One wonders if American policymakers could reflect on what Lord Kennet told the House of Lords in 1966: "America speaks all of peace, but bombs China's neighbor.... China speaks all of war, but there is not a single Chinese soldier outside China."[113] As we know, America takes longer than others to shed premodern institutions and mind-set. It was last among Western nations to abolish slavery and second last to abolish apartheid. However, we may agree with Churchill that, "You can always count on Americans to do the right thing, after they've tried everything else."[114]

Nevertheless, Obama's bellicose statements toward China in late 2011, portraying the latter as a "military threat to the hemisphere that the United States was ready to confront," further convinces us that America's spawning militarism might lead to World War III.[115] And even worse, as a former Head of the CIA's Bin Laden Unit (up to 2004) predicts: "This war has the potential to last beyond our children's lifetimes and to be fought mostly on U.S. soil." He also believes that America will be eventually defeated at the hands of Islamist militants due to its arrogance, neglect, and denial of the reality. Thanks to their intoxicating pride, American leaders are very good at declaring victory after every messy invasion of countries such as Iraq and Afghanistan. America has not won any war between the Korean stalemate (1953) and the Afghan jihad (due to the Soviet withdrawal in 1989).[116] Again, in view of the growing mistrust between America and the Muslim world, and America's prolonged economic recession, we can visualize America launching mega wars to salvage its economy. As it is least likely that the Congress will undertake any economic planning to the annoyance of the rich 1 percent, waging mega wars remains as the only option for America in the coming years. We do not think there is any exaggeration in Scheuer's prediction about the life span of the Muslim–West conflict—beyond our children's lifetimes. One may, however, disagree with him that in the long run Islamists will defeat America and that the wars will be fought mostly on the U.S. soil. Then again, he is not the first or only American analyst to point out how American policymakers love to invent enemies to justify invasions of countries to the benefit of the Military–Industrial Complex. William Blum (former State Department employee) may be cited in this regard:

> The engine of American foreign policy has been fueled not by a devotion to any kind of morality, but rather by the necessity to serve other imperatives, which can be summarized as follows: making the world safe for American corporations; enhancing the financial statements of defense contractors at home who have contributed generously to members of congress; preventing the rise of any society that might serve as a successful example of an alternative to the capitalist model; extending political and economic hegemony over as wide an area as possible, as befits a "great power."[117]

There are some other doomsday projections about the state of American economy and the state of global peace in the coming years. Princeton's Nobel Laureate Economist Paul Krugman has pointed out that although World War II boosted government spending to 42 percent of total U.S. output, the Iraq and Afghanistan wars, which peaked at around 1.2 percent of GDP, have not stimulated the U.S. economy much. Although Krugman is not a warmonger, he believes that "the United States needs to spend on a scale similar to World War II [in peaceful development projects] in order to escape an extended economic slump."[118] One wonders, while China and other Asian countries have been the major consumer goods producers for America and around 10 percent of Americans are out of job, if America has any other alternative to waging more wars—mega wars on much bigger scales than the Iraq and Afghanistan wars—to keep its faltering economy running. In this backdrop, do we have reasons to believe that America will be on warpath before or after it withdraws its last soldier from Afghanistan by 2014? According to the Russian Academy of Science estimate, although America will substantially recover from its severe economic instability by 2017–2019, the superpower will confront a severe crisis in global perspective:

> [T]he economic revival will, in 2016–2020, likely entail serious shifts in the global power balance and serious military-political conflicts involving both the global heavyweights and the developing countries. The epicenters of the conflicts will supposedly be located in the Middle East and the post-Soviet Central Asia.[119]

As the prevalent institutionalized corruption benefits corporate business—including the Military–Industrial Complex and farmers—through regressive taxation, monopolies, and subsidies, America does not have many options to keep its economy running. Although in absolute terms China's $6.9 trillion GDP is dwarfed by America's $15 trillion (in 2011), in Purchasing Power Parity (PPP) China's $11.3 trillion GDP is not far behind America's $15 trillion. In the coming years, China's GDP in PPP terms is likely to surpass that of America, which is likely to narrow the gap between the two in terms of military capability. China's accelerated defense expenditure, which is growing at 12 percent per year, is going to match America's defense budget in the coming years. In view of the higher costs of living and living standards in America, that reflect in pays and perks of American troops and defense contractors; the high cost of American-made military hardware; the cost of running 700-odd military bases across the world; and last but not least, America's spending billions of dollar on overseas invasions and warfare since the First Gulf War (1991), one has no reason to be awestricken by America's defense budget. China, Russia, and India, among others, can raise and maintain a well-equipped military at a much lower overhead cost.

America not only perpetuates it global empire through its military and regional vassals and subcontractors—autocratic rulers and military dictators—but it also controls the world through unfair trade deals and promotion of genetically modified seeds (GMO) and phony ideas and institutions, such as microfinance, Grameen Bank (in Bangladesh), and unaccountable NGOs. It may be mentioned that Monsanto, the largest manufacturer and promoter of GMO in the world, has been an active proponent of microfinance and the Grameen Bank, along with America's mega corporations and financial institutions such as Morgan Stanley and Citibank. Meanwhile, by early this century, Monsanto launched the GMO Revolution with its cozy relations with Washington. And Washington is bent on pursuing the policy of creating The U.S. Lebensraum (literally living space) by applying the motto "Food is Power" in the Third World. One may cite the example of U.S. military's total destruction of the Iraqi seed treasure in this regard.[120]

We have no reasons to question the assumption that America has been behaving like an empire. And we know empires survive through occupying new territories or by subduing old and new adversaries. An empire needs wars for its sustenance and glory. Americans, possibly the only patriotic people in the developed world, love to glorify their country as the most powerful nation on earth. However, as Krugman's statistics suggest, America's simultaneous invasions of a couple of Third-World countries are not likely to boost government spending by more than 1 or 2 percent of its output per year, while the tottering economy needs a rise in government spending by 40-odd percent, which is possible only through another world war. Since America is a democracy, despite the overwhelming influence of the Military–Industrial Complex, the growing antiwar sentiment among the people is likely to prevail. The President and the Congress cannot just go for a mega war or a nuclear showdown with another superpower to signal the beginning of World War III. This, however, does not mean that American warmongers will fail to invent new enemies to justify their invasions, as it has been doing since the 1940s. The list of countries that America had been at war with and bombed since 1945 is self-explanatory: China, 1945–1946, 1950–1953; Korea, 1950–1953; Guatemala, 1954, 1967–1969; Indonesia, 1958; Cuba, 1959–1960; The Belgian Congo, 1964; Peru, 1965; Laos, 1964–1973; Vietnam, 1961–1975; Cambodia, 1969–1970; Grenada, 1983; Libya, 1986, 2011; El Salvador, 1980s; Nicaragua, 1980s; Panama, 1989; Iraq, 1991–1999, 2003–2010; Bosnia, 1995; Sudan, 1998; Yugoslavia, 1999; and Afghanistan, 2001–2014(?). America invaded all these countries in the name of defending its interests or with the pretext that the country concerned had attacked America or its overseas interests. Although a mega war would boost America's economy in the short run, it would morally, socially, and economically bankrupt the nation.

In sum, those who argue that American Empire has been different from the British, French or Dutch empires should understand that despite America's promotion of democratic institutions in the Philippines and Puerto Rico (and of late in Iraq and Afghanistan), America since the end of World War II has mostly promoted autocratic and unaccountable regimes in the Third World. The end of the Cold War did not stop America from supporting autocratic regimes of Saudi Arabia, Pakistan under General Musharraf, Bahrain, and other unaccountable monarchies in the Arab world. I have already discussed America's unconditional support to Israel, which as an occupying entity has been violating human rights of Arabs since its inception in 1948. We should also remember that all hegemons try to legitimize themselves by promoting certain universal values in their colonies for the sake of open, if not, free trade, as they benefit most from such trade due to their comparative advantage. We have no reasons to believe that America under Obama—and afterwards in the coming decades—is least likely to shred its colonial hangover, close down its overseas bases, stop invading countries, and stop promoting autocratic regimes in the Middle East and elsewhere in the Third World. As many analysts believe, America will further intensify its drone attacks under hawkish John O Brennan, the new CIA chief under Obama. The way Brennan defended drone attacks and targeted killing and refused to provide information about the death toll in drone strikes at the Senate hearing on his confirmation as the CIA chief may be mentioned in this regard.[121]

As both the British and American empires denied they were empires and became "*more imperialistic when they were weak rather than when they were strong*" (emphasis added), with the visible decline in America's economic dominance in the world since the 1970s, it has been turning more imperialistic every day. Renewed U.S. aggression since then has become more visible.[122] In this backdrop, we have reasons to expect further escalation in U.S. aggression in different names and excuses in different parts of the world, especially in the Latin American and Afro-Asian continents. However, the Empire is not that well entrenched among its own people. Only around 10 percent of Americans trust the Congress, while a sitting president's popularity hovers in the 30s and 40s. Then again, what is alarming is that around 70 percent of Americans trust their media. And we know media along with the mega corporations, financial organizations, including the IMF and World Bank, help run the American Empire. World

Bank whistleblower Karen Hudes (fired and arrested for trespassing the World Bank headquarters in April 2013 and released after one month) has revealed World Bank corruption in the Third World. She believes that $900 million went to corrupt people in the Philippines through World Bank officials—corrupt from top to down—and that American mega corporations are ripping off the poor in the Third World. She thinks American people are not aware of the political clout of mega corporations and corporate corruption in their country, and organizations such as the Bank of America and Goldman Sachs control the U.S. government, and, most importantly, are above the law.[123]

As cited above, Paul Craig Roberts has argued, "Washington's empire extracts resources from the American people for the benefit of the few powerful interest groups that rule America," the Obama administration has not flinched from declaring whistleblowers such as William Assange, Edward Snowden, and Bradley Manning as enemies and spies. They have leaked classified State, CIA/NSA, and Defense documents exposing the U.S. government's unethical and illegal practices at home and abroad, including mass surveillance of American citizens, killing and torture of civilians in Iraq and Afghanistan. The U.S. government's reaction to the whistleblowers smack of its imperialist behavior, as Assange, Snowden, and Manning have exposed the dark side of the U.S. administration, which has been assiduously justifying unjust foreign invasions, Guantanamo Bay, and its phony War on Terror. In sum, the American Empire is not that different from what were once British, French, or Dutch Empires, democratic at home, autocratic and tyrannical abroad. America's physical occupation of Afghanistan and Iraq blurs whatever differences it had with the traditional empires of the past. Last but not least, as Russian President Putin has told Americans bluntly, they should stop portraying themselves as exceptional, as doing so is "extremely dangerous."[124] The sooner America realizes that the days of the empire are over, the better.

Notes and References

1. Andrew J. Bacevich, *Washington Rules: America's Path to Permanent War* (New York: Metropolitan Books, 2010).
2. Richard K. Betts, "From Cold War to Hot Peace: The Habit of American Force," *Political Science Quarterly*, Vol. 127, No. 3 (2012): 353.

3. "The Global Terrorism Index Systematically Ranks 158 Countries According to the Impact of Terrorism." Available at: http://www.visionofhumanity.org/terrorismindex/about-the-gti/ (accessed on December 7, 2013) and "Global Peace Index." Available at: http://economicsandpeace.org/ (accessed on December 7, 2013).

4. Richard K. Betts, "From Cold War to Hot Peace: The Habit of American Force," *Political Science Quarterly*, Vol. 127, No. 3 (2012): 353–354.

5. Alexis de Tocqueville, *Democracy in America*, in Richard D. Heffner (ed.) (New York: Penguin Books, [1835] 1984), p. 252.

6. Ibid., pp. 128–129.

7. Richard K. Betts, "From Cold War to Hot Peace: The Habit of American Force," *Political Science Quarterly*, Vol. 127, No. 3 (2012): 360.

8. Ibid., pp. 363–368.

9. Howard Zinn's Foreword in John Tirman's *100 Ways America is Screwing Up the World* (New York: HarperCollins, 2006), pp. xvi–xvii.

10. Ibid., p. xviii.

11. Alexis de Tocqueville, *Democracy in America*, in Richard D. Heffner (ed.) (New York: Penguin Books, 1984), p. 278.

12. John J. Mearsheimer and Stephen M. Walt, *The Israel Lobby and U.S. Foreign Policy* (New York: Farrar, Straus and Giroux, 2007).

13. Mona Eltahawy, "Why Do They Hate Us? The Real War on Women in the Middle East," *Foreign Policy* (May–June 2012).

14. Michael Scheuer, Preface in *Imperial Hubris: Why the West Is Losing the War on Terror* (Dulles, Virginia: Potomac Books, 2005), p. x.

15. Ibid., p. 1.

16. Senator J. William Fulbright, *The Arrogance of Power* (New York: Random House, 1966), p. 4.

17. Peter Waldman, "A Historian's Take on Islam Steers U.S. in Terrorism Fight: Bernard Lewis's Blueprint—Sowing Arab Democracy—Is Facing a Test in Iraq," *The Wall Street Journal* (February 3, 2004).

18. Michael Scheuer, *Imperial Hubris: Why the West is Losing the War on Terror* (Dulles, Virginia: Potomac Books, 2005), p. xi.

19. Paul Krugman, "Oligarchy, American Style," *New York Times* (November 3, 2011).

20. John Tirman, *100 Ways America is Screwing Up the World* (New York: HarperCollins, 2006), pp. 166–168, 232, 248–257.

21. Chalmers Johnson, *Dismantling the Empire: America's Last Best Hope* (New York: Metropolitan Books, 2010), p. 114.

22. Paul Craig Roberts, "How the New American Empire Really Works," *Counterpunch* (March 27, 2012). Available at: http://www.counterpunch.org/2012/03/27/how-the-new-american-empire-really-works/ (accessed on December 7, 2013).

23. Tirman, *100 Ways America Is Screwing Up the World*, pp. 249, 254.

24. Howard Zinn, *A People's History of the United States: 1492—Present* (New York: HarperCollins, 2005), p. 4.

25. Ibid., pp. 29, 151–153.

26. Chalmers Johnson, *The Sorrows of Empire: Militarism, Secrecy and the End of the Republic* (New York: Holt Paperbacks, 2005), p. 39.

27. Ibid.

28. Phil Tajitsu Nash, "Ending the Military-Industrial-Congressional Complex," *Asian Week* (September 10, 2007). Available at: https://www.google.com/#q=Phil+Tajitsu+Nash%2C+%E2%80%9CEnding+the+Military-Industrial-Congressional+Complex%E2%80%9D%2C+ (accessed on December 7, 2013).

29. Robert Higgs, "World War II and the Military-Industrial-Congressional Complex," *Freedom Daily* (May 1995). Available at: http://www.independent.org/publications/article.asp?id=141 (accessed on December 7, 2013).

30. Robert B. Reich, "Help End the Military-Industrial-Congressional Complex," YouTube Video (June 2, 2011).

31. P.W. Singer, *Corporate Warriors: The Rise of the Privatized Military Industry* (Ithaca: Cornell University Press, 2003), passim.

32. Chalmers Johnson, *Dismantling the Empire: America's Last Best Hope* (New York: Metropolitan Books, 2010), pp. 93–106, 109–132.

33. Andrew J. Bacevich, *Washington Rules: America's Path to Permanent War* (New York: Metropolitan Books, 2010), pp. 19–25, 152–155.

34. William Blum, *Freeing the World to Death: Essays on the American Empire* (Monroe, Maine: Common Courage Press, 2005), p. i.

35. Casper Weinberger and Peter Schweizer, *The Next War* (Washington, D.C.: Regenery Publishing, 1996), p. XV.

36. Ibid., passim.

37. George Friedman, *The Next 100 Years: A forecast for the 21st Century* (New York: Doubleday, 2009), p. 40.

38. Ibid., pp. 40–49.

39. Ibid., pp. 5–13, 38, 79–87, 155–192.

40. Finian Cunningham, "Syria—The Western Deception Over Regime Change Unravels," *Global Research* (March 8, 2012). Available at: www.globalresearch.ca/index.php?context=va&aid=29660 (accessed on December 7, 2013).

41. Howard Zinn's Foreword in *100 Ways America is Screwing Up the World*, (New York: HarperCollins, 2006), pp. xii–xiv.

42. Tirman, *100 Ways America is Screwing Up the World*, pp. 4–5, 29, 44–45, 70–79.

43. Chalmers Johnson, *Dismantling the Empire: America's Last Best Hope* (New York: Metropolitan Books, 2010), pp. 4–5.

44. Ibid., pp. 5–8.

45. Ibid., pp. 26–27.

46. Noam Chomsky, *World Orders, Old and New* (London: Pluto Press, 1994), pp. 124–129.

47. Ibid., pp. 168–170.

48. Ibid., p. 171.

49. Noam Chomsky, *Media Control: The Spectacular Achievements of Propaganda* (New York: Seven Stories Press, 2002), pp. 11–30.

50. George Creel, *How We Advertised America* (1920) (Kindle Edition 2010).

51. Chomsky, *Media Control: The Spectacular Achievements of Propaganda*, pp. 14–15.

52. Ibid., p. 30.

53. Chomsky, *World Orders, Old and New*, p. 9.

54. Chomsky, *Media Control: The Spectacular Achievements of Propaganda*, pp. 33–45.

55. Ibid., pp. 74–75.

56. Andrew J. Bacevich, *The New American Militarism: How Americans Are Seduced by War* (New York: Oxford University Press, 2005), pp. 2–7, 13–25.

57. Christopher A. Preble, *The Power Problem* (Ithaca: Cornell University Press, 2009), pp. 8, 24–39, 90.

58. *The Economist* (April 7, 2012).

59. Tirman, *100 Ways America Is Screwing Up the World*, p. 107.

60. Thomas Joscelyn, "Obama, Not Congress, Is the Reason Guantánamo Is Still Open," *Daily Beast* (May 3, 2013). Available at: http://www.thedailybeast.com/articles/2013/05/03/obama-not-congress-is-the-reason-guantanamo-is-still-open.html (accessed on June 7, 2013); Russian TV (June 5, 2013).

61. "Bradley Manning Trial Begins with Clash of Interpretations over Soldier's Actions," *The Guardian* (June 3, 2013); "The Bradley Manning Trial: A Short(ish) Guide to Understanding the Case," NPR News (June 5, 2013). Available at: http://www.npr.org/blogs/thetwo-way/2013/06/05/188938313/the-bradley-manning-trial-a-short-ish-guide-to-understanding-t (accessed on June 7, 2013).

62. Breanna Edwards, Ron Paul: Manning "Should Be Released," *Politico* (August 22, 2013). Available at: http://www.politico.com/story/2013/08/ron-paul-chelsea-manning-95819.html#ixzz2clveuEgE (accessed on August 22, 2013).

63. Ron Paul's Interview by Larry King, RT News (August 22, 2013).

64. Chomsky, *Media Control: The Spectacular Achievements of Propaganda*, pp. 44–45 and 74–75.

65. Bruce Cumings, Ervand Abrahamian, and Moshe Ma'oz, *Inventing the Axis of Evil: The Truth about North Korea, Iran and Syria* (New York: The New Press, 2004), pp. 3, 93.

66. Ibid., p. 157.

67. Chalmers Johnson, *The Sorrows of Empire: Militarism, Secrecy, and the End of the Republic* (New York: Holt Publishers, 2005), pp. 308–309.

68. "$112 Million Worth of Tomahawk Missiles Already Launched in Libya Operation." Available at: http://washingtonexaminer.com/politics/beltway-

confidential/2011/03/112-million-worth-tomahawk-missiles-already-launched-libya (accessed on March 30, 2012).

69. *Chicago Tribune* (April 2, 2012).
70. Michel Chossudovsky, "War is Good for Business," *Global Research* (September 16, 2001). Available at: http://globalresearch.ca/articles/CHO109D.html (accessed on April 8, 2012).
71. Ari Ben-Menashe, *Profits of War: The Sensational Story of the World-Wide Arms Conspiracy* (Australia: Allen & Unwin, 1992), pp. xvi, 91.
72. Noam Chomsky, *Necessary Illusions: Thought Control in Democratic Societies* (Toronto: Anansi Press Inc., 2003), p. 286.
73. Ibid., p. 1.
74. Ibid., pp. 2–8.
75. William Blum, "The 9/11 Truth Movement: The Anti-Empire Report," *Foreign Policy Journal* (October 2, 2010).
76. Ibid.
77. John J. Mearsheimer and Stephen M. Walt, *The Israel Lobby and U.S. Foreign Policy* (New York: Farrar, Straus and Giroux, 2007), p. 4.
78. Ibid.
79. "Barack Obama Pledges New Beginning between US and Muslims: US President Tells Israel 'It Is Time for Settlements to Stop,'" *Guardian* (June 4, 2009).
80. Available at: http://www.outsidethebeltway.com/obamas_cairo_speech/ (accessed on April 18, 2012).
81. "Israeli PM Netanyahu Rejects Obama '1967 Borders' View," BBC News (May 20, 2011). Available at: http://www.bbc.co.uk/news/world-middle-east-13465133 (accessed on April 12, 2012); "Israeli Rebuke of Obama Exposes Divide on Mideast," Reuters (May 20, 2011). Available at: http://www.reuters.com/article/2011/05/20/us-obama-mideast-netanyahu-idUSTRE74I7L720110520 (accessed on April 19, 2012).
82. "Obama Eases Israeli Anger on Mideast Peace Vision," Reuters (May 22, 2011). Available at: http://www.reuters.com/article/2011/05/23/us-usa-israel-idUSTRE74L0D020110523 (accessed on April 19, 2012).
83. *The Telegraph* (June 24, 2011 and September 22, 2011).
84. Tirman, *100 Ways America is Screwing Up the World*, p. 155.
85. Paul Findley, *They Dare to Speak Out: People and Institutions Confront Israel's Lobby* (Chicago: Lawrence Hill Books, 1989), p. 25.
86. Ibid., pp. 49 and 147.
87. John J. Mearsheimer and Stephen M. Walt, *The Israel Lobby and U.S. Foreign Policy* (New York: Farrar, Straus and Giroux, 2007), p. 162.
88. Ibid., pp. 13–18.
89. M. Shahid Alam, *Israeli Exceptionalism: The Destabilizing Logic of Zionism* (New York: Palgrave Macmillan, 2009), passim.
90. John J. Mearsheimer and Stephen M. Walt, *The Israel Lobby and U.S. Foreign Policy* (New York: Farrar, Straus and Giroux, 2007), pp. 26–29.

91. Ibid., p. vii.

92. *Guardian* (April 5 and 8, 2012); Tunku Varadarajan, "Provocative Poetry, Prohibitive Cheese," *Newsweek* (April 16, 2012).

93. Eric S. Margolis, *American Raj: Liberation or Domination?* (Toronto: Key Porter Books, 2008), pp. 4, 19.

94. Steven Kull, *Feeling Betrayed: The Roots of Muslim Anger at America* (Washington, D.C.: Brookings Institution Press, 2011), pp. 89–101.

95. Steven Kull, "Why Muslims Are Still Mad at America" (September 6, 2011). Available at: http://www.worldpublicopinion.org/incl/printable_version.php?pnt=691 (accessed on September 12, 2011).

96. Michel Chossudovsky, "Towards a World War III Scenario: The Dangers of Nuclear War," E-Book Series No. 1.0 (Montreal: Global Research Publishers, 2011); Michel Chossudovsky and Finian Cunningham (eds), "The Globalization of War: The 'Military Roadmap' to World War III," *Global Research* (February 10, 2012).

97. Hans Kristensen, "Targets of Opportunity: How Nuclear Planners Found New Targets for Old Weapons," *The Bulletin of the Atomic Scientists*, Vol. 53, No. 5 (1997): 22–28.

98. Ehsan Ahrari, "Why the Long War Can and Cannot be Compared to the Cold War," *Comparative Strategy*, Vol. 26, No. 4 (July 2007): 275.

99. Michael Scheuer, *Imperial Hubris: Why the West Is Losing the War on Terror* (Dulles, Virginia: Potomac Books, 2005), pp. ix–xi.

100. Ibid., pp. x–xi.

101. Senator J. William Fulbright, *The Arrogance of Power* (New York: Random House, 1966), p. 27.

102. Ibid., p. 32.

103. Associated Press (February 10, 2012).

104. Chalmers Johnson, *The Sorrows of Empire: Militarism, Secrecy and the End of the Republic* (New York: Holt Paperbacks, 2004), pp. 1–15.

105. Ibid., pp. 3–5.

106. Christopher Preble, *The Power Problem: How America's Military Dominance Makes US Less Safe, Less Prosperous, and Less Free* (Ithaca: Cornell University Press, 2009), pp. 64–87.

107. Ibid., pp. 5–6, 67–7, 124–125.

108. *Washington Post* (June 20, 2010).

109. *Los Angeles Times* (October 16, 2003) and CNN.com (October 17, 2003).

110. Andrew J. Bacevich, *Washington Rules* (New York: Metropolitan Books, 2010), p. 113.

111. Christopher Preble, Introduction to *The Power Problem: How America's Military Dominance Makes US Less Safe, Less Prosperous, and Less Free* (Ithaca: Cornell University Press, 2009).

112. Stanley E. Spangler, *Force and Accommodation in World Politics* (Maxwell Air Force Base, Alabama: Air University Press, 1991), p. 293.

113. Senator J. William Fulbright, *The Arrogance of Power* (New York: Random House, 1966), pp. 144, 153.

114. Mackubin Thomas Owens, *US Civil-Military Relations after 9/11: Renegotiating the Civil-Military Bargain* (New York: Continuum, 2011), p. 192.

115. Ibid.

116. Michael Scheuer, *Imperial Hubris: Why the West Is Losing the War on Terror* (Dulles, Virginia: Potomac Books, 2005), pp. ix–xi, xv, 181.

117. William Blum, "A Brief History of U.S. Interventions: 1945 to the Present," *Z Magazine*, Vol. 13, No. 6 (June 1999).

118. Paul Krugman, "U.S. Economy Needs 'The Financial Equivalent of War,'" *Huffington Post* (September 28, 2011).

119. Viktor Burbaki, "Why the US Needs a Major War," *Strategic Cultural Foundation* (online journal) (January 4, 2012). Available at: http://www.strategic-culture.org/news/2012/01/04why-the-us-needs-a-major-war.htm (accessed on December 7, 2013).

120. F. William Engdahl, *Seeds of Destruction: The Hidden Agenda of Genetic Manipulation* [2007], *Global Research* (Centre for Research on Globalization, Montreal), pp. 3–15, 105–107, 152–172, 202–204.

121. David Cole, "13 Questions for John O Brennan," *The New York Review* (2013); "Brennan Defends Drone Strike Policies," *Washington Post* (February 7, 2013).

122. Julian Go and Alex Doherty, "The United States—An Exceptional Empire?" New Left Project. Available at: http://www.newleftproject.org/index.php/site/article_comments/the_united_states_an_unexceptional_empire (accessed on February 8, 2013).

123. "World Bank Whistleblower Karen Hudes Arranged to Federal Court on 13 June," NSNBC International (June 12, 2013). Available at: http://nsnbc.me/2013/06/12/world-bank-whistleblower-karen-hudes-arrainged-to-federal-court-on-13-june/ (accessed on June 23, 2013); RT News (June 22, 2013).

124. Vladimir V. Putin, "A Plea for Caution From Russia: What Putin Has to Say to Americans About Syria," *New York Times* (September 11, 2013).

5

Global Jihad: Philosophies and Flashpoints

Jews and Christians...should be forced to pay Jizya [poll tax] in osrder to put an end to their independence and supremacy so that they should not remain rulers and sovereigns in the land. These powers should be wrested from them by the followers of the true Faith [Islam], who should assume the sovereignty and lead others towards the Right Way. That is why the Islamic state offers them [non-Muslims] protection, if they agree to live as Zimmis by paying Jizya...it is the duty of the true Muslims to exert their utmost to bring an end to their wicked rule and bring them under a righteous order.

Abul A'la Maududi (1971), Founder of the Jamaat-i-Islami

The Muslim Brotherhood has not changed; only Western opinion of it has. As it was since its founding in 1928, the group is committed to empowering and spreading Sharia law—a law that preaches hate for non-Muslim "infidels," especially Islam's historic nemesis, Christianity, and allows anything, from lying to cheating, to make Islam supreme.

Raymond Ibrahim, Middle East Forum, June 25, 2012

Overview

Global jihad is a loaded concept. Interestingly, Islamists and Islamophobes seem to have convergence on one point that projects global jihad as a threat to civilization in general, Western civilization in particular, and that it is a means toward establishing an alternative Islamic global order. Islamophobes promote extreme prejudice against Islam by projecting it as an evil religion and often equate global jihad with real Islam. This chapter is an attempt to understand if global jihad is an ahistorical reconstruction, a mythical concept, and if global jihadists are strong enough to mold public opinion in the Muslim world to challenge Western and other non-Islamic civilizations in the coming years. This chapter raises the important question and tries to answer it: Does the average Muslim hate America and the West and want their destruction? This is an appraisal of the state of global jihad and its potentials in the light of case studies of Islamist movements in Egypt, Saudi Arabia, Iran, Afghanistan, and Pakistan, in historical, contemporary, and future perspectives.

Muslim Quest for Alternative Orders

American presidents from Eisenhower to Obama have been responsible for the phenomenal rise of Islamist forces throughout the Muslim world. Hillary Clinton and some top American diplomats and politicians have publicly admitted that the Cold War exigencies had led their country to support Islamist forces, including the Afghan Mujahedeen and those who later founded al Qaeda. We also know that in 1953, while Eisenhower flirted with the ayatollahs on the eve of the CIA-led military coup that toppled a democratically elected government in Iran, both Carter and Reagan legitimized General Zia ul-Haq's pro-JI Islamist military dictatorship in Pakistan (1977–1988). American leadership during Eisenhower and Nixon years preferred the MB to Nasser, for the latter's avowedly anti-Western and anti-Israeli stand, and his close ties with the Soviet Union. America continued to support the soft-on-Islam President Anwar Sadat and the MB till the killing of Sadat by Islamist radicals in 1981. Some critics of the American foreign policy also portray the MB as an offshoot of the CIA. MB founder Hassan al-Banna's son-in-law Said Ramadan (father of Tariq Ramadan) is said to have been a CIA agent in the 1950s.[1] Many analysts believe that the Cold War understanding between America and Islamists—the MB, JI, and Afghan Mujahedeen—did not end with the end of the Cold War. They believe that MB leaders in Egypt and Syria, including Dr Morsi, are pro-American.[2] As a Western analyst puts in plain words, America and its allies are "funding, arming, while simultaneously fighting al Qaeda from Mali to Syria" to serve their long-term geopolitical interests in the Muslim world.[3] In view of the controversial role America, NATO, and its allies have been playing in the various conflict zones of jihad and counter-jihad in northwest and East Africa, Middle East, and Afghanistan, one has reasons to believe that the West has been playing a dubious role. For example, on the one hand, we find top U.S. leaders, NATO, and ISAF commanders telling the world that they are fighting terrorists/insurgents in Afghanistan, and, on the other, we find them acquiescing in to the public cultivation of poppy and narcotic trade in and beyond Afghanistan, which benefit drug lords, Taliban and al Qaeda.

Irrespective of whether Mohamed Morsi and top MB leaders have had ties with America or not, the ground reality is that the average Egyptian Muslims do not favor either America or Israel. And thanks to decades of civil and military dictatorship (1952–2011), the Egyptians never had the exposure to liberal democracy and human rights. Thus, for the bulk of Egyptian Muslims, Islamism or political Islam has emerged as the main alternative to military dictatorship and as the most powerful ideology to ensure civil liberty and human rights. However, as we know from people's experience of living under Shiite and Sunni theocracies in countries such as Saudi Arabia, Iran, Afghanistan, and to some extent, in Pakistan, Islamism never ensures civil liberty, human rights, and democracy. In view of this, I am briefly introducing the MB, JI, al Qaeda, Khomeinism/Iranian Islamism, Taliban, Wahhabism, and some minor Islamist outfits in the Muslim world to facilitate the understanding of the impending threat of militant Islam and Muslim democracies in the Muslim world. Ominously, Muslim-majority countries—from West Africa to North Africa, and the Middle East to South and Southeast Asia—have been going through turbulent phase in their history and are on the threshold of big transitions toward modernism and good governance (if not democracy) in the post-Cold War era of globalization and the promised New World Order.

The level of support for Islamism varies from country to country. Islamist organizations and movements such as the MB and Wahhabism flourish better in countries lacking in political freedom and democratic institutions than in free and democratic countries. Islamist organizations-cum-movements, such as the MB and Wahhabism, fill in the political and cultural space in countries without political parties and secular sociocultural associations and institutions. Thus Islamist organizations are well entrenched throughout North Africa and Middle East. Although relative political and cultural freedom in Pakistan (even under military dictators) has allowed the proliferation of non-Islamic (if not totally secular) political parties and cultural organizations, yet Islam being the raison d être for the creation of the state has special political importance in the country. Islamism has lesser space in the political arena of Bangladesh as the country emerged out of Pakistan in the name of secular Bengali nationalism, which was a departure from Islam-based state ideology of Pakistan.

Far from being united under a common banner, the Muslim militants are least capable of challenging Western hegemony. Again, they have more intra-Muslim conflicts to sort out before they can pose any substantial threat to Western civilization. As there are flashpoints so are there dormant volcanoes in the Muslim world. Most importantly, Islamists proliferate under autocratic regimes, which by default or design promote Islamism. Examples abound. While Saudi Arabia promotes Wahhabi Islam as the state ideology to legitimize Saudi autocracy, military dictators in Pakistan and Bangladesh legitimized Islamism (although not the militant version of it) in league with Islam-loving politicians and clerics to legitimize military rule. Islamism flourished by default in countries, such as Egypt and Iran, where disgruntled Muslims and the relatively free (and influential) clerics clung to Islamism for an alternative order. This explains the rise of the MB and Khomeini.

Muslim Brotherhood, Jamaat-i-Islami, and Global Jihad

Muslim Brotherhood (MB)

The understanding of Islamist flashpoints of global jihad requires an understanding of major Islamist movements, their brief history, ideologies, and strategies. We may begin with the MB or Ikhwanul Muslemeen, the most prominent Islamist party in the world, which may be considered as "the mother of al Qaeda." It had a humble beginning. Hassan al-Banna (1906–1949), son of an imam and mosque teacher in Cairo, used to repair watches and having interest in Islamic traditions wrote books on Islam.

In March 1928, the 22-year-old al-Banna founded the Society for Muslim Brothers and within 10 years it drew 500,000 Egyptians as active members. By 1945 the figure rose to two million. Thanks to 9/11 al Qaeda seems to have stolen the thunder, while the MB remains the most organized and largest transnational Islamist organization in the world.

It is noteworthy that 19th century Islamic thinker Jamal al-Din Afghani's Egyptian "great-grand-disciple" al-Banna was the founder of the MB, and al-Banna's disciple Sayyid Qutb directly inspired Ayman al-Zawahiri, "who in 1967 established the first jihadist cell in the Arab world."[4] Despite al-Banna's nonviolent "Fifty-Point Manifesto," which mainly emphasized "transnational Islamic reforms," the MB under Sayyid Qutb in the 1940s and 1950s emerged as an out and out transnational "jihadist" organization. Afterwards, for decades, it promoted violence and hatred against the West, non-Muslims, and "deviant" Muslims. However, as later the MB discarded political violence and terrorism, some analysts believe that instead of changing the existing political system, it ended up being changed by the system. Some even believe that since the MB renounced violence as a means to capture political power in the 1980s, despite its name it is largely secular.[5] Some analysts believe that the post-Mubarak Egypt and other Arab nations are most likely to be post-Islamist democracies in the coming decades.[6] Despite the growing surge of Islamism in Egypt, there is no likelihood of an MB–al Qaeda understanding. As the MB leaders do not approve of terrorism, al Qaeda despises them as nothing but "cowards, aliens, deviants, Crusaders and Jews."[7]

Nevertheless, the average Egyptian Muslims since the debacle of the 1967 War against Israel, and especially since the death of Nasser in 1970, have turned Islamic. While in the 1970s, one would hardly come across an Egyptian woman in *hijab*, today almost 95 percent of them wear it considering it an Islamic requirement. Interestingly, one week after the overthrow of Mubarak, hardcore MB leader Imam Qaradawi told thousands of cheering Egyptians at the Tahrir Square in Cairo that their revolution had remained unfinished; Islamists must take over the country's administration.[8] Although the Brotherhood has discarded violent means to capture power, it is still a formidable political force as Mubarak stifled the growth of liberal democratic parties during his rule. The Brotherhood has similarities with the JL in South Asia. Indian (Pakistani after 1947) Islamist Maulana Maududi (1903–1979), who founded the JL (Party of

Islam) in 1941, was influenced by the Brotherhood. His writings later influenced MB leaders and activists. However, the Jamaat and Brotherhood have differences as well. While Maududi admired Fascism, al-Banna had admiration for socialism and wanted social justice for the poor. Interestingly, although the Egyptian Brotherhood holds a supranational ideology, most Islamist outfits, such as the FIS in Algeria, have been primarily Islamo-nationalist movements.[9]

Far from being an offshoot of Wahhabism, which predates it by almost 200 years, the MB was derived out of a liberal Islamic modernist movement called Pan-Islamism. An avid admirer of European civilization and French culture, Jamal al-Din Afghani (1838–1897) was the founder of Pan-Islamism. He championed the cause of Muslim unity and freedom of the Muslim world from European colonial rule. Sheikh Muhammad Abduh (1849–1905) was a disciple of Afghani. He, like Afghani, championed liberal Islam and close ties between Islam, Christianity, and Judaism. It is noteworthy that Pan-Islamist Afghani's Egyptian "great-grand-disciple" Sayyid Qutb directly inspired Ayman al-Zawahiri, "who in 1967 established the first jihadist cell in the Arab world."[10] In view of this, it appears that al Qaeda is an offshoot of the MB, not of Arabian Wahhabism. Radical MB followers seem to have embraced Afghani's anti-imperialist Pan-Islamism but with certain modifications. They have totally discarded the nonviolent aspect of Pan-Islamism and have gone even several steps ahead of radical MB leaders—who vacillate between constitutional (peaceful) and unconstitutional (violent) methods—by declaring an all-out war against the West and its followers, especially among Muslims.

No sooner had the MB come into being than it started promoting terrorism: (a) its leaders disseminated the message of Hitler's *Mein Kampf* among their followers, (b) in 1948 one MB activist killed Egypt's Prime Minster Nukrashi Pasha, (c) in 1952 party workers burnt down around 750 nightclubs, theaters, and hotels in Cairo alone, (d) the same year, it supported the military takeover of Egypt, and (e) last but not least, it advocated establishing a caliphate, stretching from Spain to Indonesia. In short, the MB did not start as a political party but as an Islamist movement for establishing a global caliphate through violence.[11] The radical MB leader Sayyid Qutb (1906–1966) was the main proponent of jihad against the West. In fact, al Qaeda is a radical offshoot of the MB, not Wahhabism. There are striking similarities between Sayyid Qutb's and al Qaeda's anti-Western positions. As a schoolteacher in Egypt, he went to a college in Colorado to get a diploma in education in 1948. He wrote books and articles on jihad and on what he thought of American society, politics, and culture. He does not have any kind word for America. He despises the American girl; Americans' love for sports, including boxing; their materialism; hypocrisy; haircut; music; and in sum, he declares it mandatory to fight the West and its followers in Egypt and everywhere in the Muslim world. He divides the world between the domains of Islam or wisdom and of un-Islam or ignorance (*jahiliyyah*) and prescribes offensive jihad, virtually against the whole world.[12]

Despite some similarities between Wahhabism and Qutb's support for violent jihad, Wahhabism did not influence him ideologically. Initially, he was an admirer of America, but his two-year-long exposure to the country was enough to turn him into its bitter critic. He supported the Nasser-led military revolution against the pro-Western Egyptian monarchy. However, Nasser and Qutb had different visions for Egypt; the former championed secular Arab nationalism and the latter favored Islamic rule. Qutb also favored transformation of the entire world through global jihad. He believed that jihad was not defensive, but an offensive total war against non-Muslims and whatever represented *jahiliyya* or ignorance. In short, Qutb considered truce or peace undesirable and continuous jihad the most desirable thing for a good Muslim.[13]

In view of the apparent transformation of the MB into a pro-democracy party, Tariq Ali believes it to be "not too different from Christian Democratic Parties in Western Europe."[14] Former CIA agent and author Bruce Ridedel, among others, believes that since the MB has long renounced violence there is nothing to fear this Islamist outfit.[15] President Carter expressed similar views. However, Anthony Martin seems to be right that since Egypt, like other Muslim nations in the region, has thoroughly embraced fundamental Islam, Carter's optimism about the MB smacks of his lack of understanding of Islamism in the Arab world.[16] The MB has not given up its transnational jihad. We should not forget the legacy of the MB, which is anything but democratic. It aims at establishing a global caliphate through violence. I think "the true intentions of the Brotherhood are far more sinister than the lovely speeches" its leaders give, and that they "dream of a worldwide, all powerful Islamic Caliphate," and that "they look forward to the day they can tear up the peace treaty with Israel."[17] Then again, the MB leaves no stone unturned to project itself as a liberal democratic organization. Its webpage conveniently projects bin Laden's criticism of the organization for discarding Sayyid Qutb's hard-line policy to support MB's "liberal credentials."[18]

The MB's radical offshoots have been more dangerous than the parent organization. These include the *Al Gama'a al-Islamiyya* in Egypt, *al Takfir wal Hijra* in the Arab world, Hamas in Gaza, and last but not least, al Qaeda. Many analysts believe that the MB has ceased to be an Islamist threat and Salafist al-Nour is a bigger threat to peace than the pro-MB Freedom and Justice Party of Egypt, which captured 47 percent of votes in the parliamentary elections of 2011/12. President Mohamed Morsi asserted in April 2012 that he was for a "United States of Arabia" with Jerusalem as its capital. He, however, gave mixed and contradictory signals about his party's actual aims and objectives.[19] In short, at least in rhetoric, the MB is not a political party but a movement for global caliphate through jihad. Some scholars ridicule people who consider the MB as moderate Islamist and democratic. They find Obama administration's perception of the MB as "largely secular" and "pluralistic" problematic. One analyst asserts that the party has neither denounced jihad against takfir (who have denounced Islam) nor has it renounced the concept of establishing an Islamic State by force. Morsi is said to have asserted that he would conquer Egypt "for the second time, and make all Christians convert to Islam, or else pay the jizya."[20]

Although there are uncertainties about the future of Shariah and the MB in Egypt and their implications on democracy, human rights, women, non-Muslims, and Western interests in the country,[21] there is hardly any Arab country—from Morocco to Iraq—without MB followers and active members. Interestingly, although primarily a Sunni Muslim organization committed to establishing a Sunni global caliphate, the MB has Shiite followers and sympathizers in Iran and elsewhere. Even Chechen rebels in Russia consider the MB their role model. Thousands among the Muslim diasporas in North America and Europe are MB sympathizers. Although Hafiz al-Assad crushed the MB during the 1982 Hama uprising by killing around 25,000 Syrian sympathizers of the outfit, yet thanks to American and Arab League support, the MB regained some lost ground in Syria during the anti-Bashar Assad rebellion in 2012.[22] Then again, the MB in

Syria is not an independent entity. It heavily relies on guidance from MB leaders in Cairo.[23]

The MB is ambivalent about its methods of capturing power: (a) it believes in Islam to be a complete system to regulate every aspect of a Muslim's private and public affairs; (b) it is not a nationalist but a supranationalist organization, aiming at establishing a global caliphate where Shariah will remain the sole basis of government; (c) as Sayyid Qutb explains, the MB considers the world beyond the realm of Islam as *jahiliyya* or ignorance, which could only be transformed into the Kingdom of God through physical power and jihad by outmaneuvering the wicked powers of Jews and Christians; (d) there are, however, MB leaders who disagree with Qutb's radicalism. Some Al Azhar sheikhs even declared him a deviant. Nevertheless, Sayyid Qutb's writings have profoundly influenced radical Brothers and al Qaeda supporters.

Although it is difficult to foresee if Egypt will become another Iran or Algeria in the near future, yet there is every likelihood that Islam if not Islamism will mold Egypt's domestic and foreign policies in the coming years. And this development will not be palatable to either America or Israel. Although the creation of Israel did not hurt Egypt economically, yet Egyptians fought four wars against Israel. The vast majority of Egyptian Muslims—irrespective of their ideology and level of commitment to their faith—are unwilling to recognize Israel. This pathological hatred for Israel might lead to another war against the Zionist state in the future. A country without any liberal democratic traditions, with more than a quarter of unemployed youth, poverty, and unequal distribution of wealth, and, last but not least, under the growing influence of Islamist supremacists, Egypt is destined to rise as a flashpoint of global jihad. The apparently transformed MB with a new name, Freedom and Justice Party since April 2011, has not renounced the old MB credo: "God is our objective; the Quran is our constitution, the Prophet is our leader; Jihad is our way; and death for the sake of God is the highest of our aspirations."[24] Despite its setbacks in the wake of the July 2013 military coup that toppled the Morsi regime, one cannot rule out the reemergence of the MB with new vigor and possibly with a new name.

In view of the phenomenal rise of the MB in Egypt, as we have no reasons to be optimistic about the country's peaceful transition to democracy, so do we have no reason to be that alarmist about an immediate Islamization of the polity. The country is sharply polarized between Islamists and secular Arab nationalists who believe in Christian–Muslim understanding. However, in view of the growing violence against Christians and liberal Muslims since the overthrow of Mubarak, it was evident soon after Morsi's election as the President that he would not be able to appease liberal Muslims, Christians, Islamist extremists, and the powerful Egyptian military at the same time. Morsi's decision to welcome President Ahmadinejad of Iran, who was "deeply unpopular with Egyptian citizens and political players," on February 5, 2013 was his strange gamble, as one analyst has rightly pointed out.[25] Morsi's hobnobbing with the Iranian regime, which is a bête noire to America and Saudi Arabia, was a big factor behind the overthrow of his regime through a mass upheaval-cum-military takeover. There is no reason to believe that the July coup was purely a military takeover by Mubarak loyalists and anti-Islamist forces in the country. Secretary John Kerry indirectly confirmed his country's tacit support for the military rulers of Egypt, whom he praised for restoring democracy in the country.[26]

The ongoing bloody conflict between MB followers, on the one hand, and the military, Salafists, and liberal Egyptians, on the other, has all the potentials to drag Egypt into a long-drawn civil war. Egypt does not have any leader with Nasser's charisma, foresight, and honesty to nip Islamists in the bud. He not only dissolved the MB after the first signs of its support for terrorism and radical Islamization of Egypt, but he also arrested some 15,000 MB members and executed many, including Sayyid Qutb. We may agree with the view that: "It would have been so much easier to stop Hitler, say *before* he crossed the Rhine—but how many voices were there then insisting he was just a tin-pot dictator who would never be a serious threat to anyone?"[27]

The MB is very different from other political parties. One just cannot become a member without going through a five/eight-year stringent indoctrination process to prove one's loyalty and commitment to its ideology. Very similar to the JI, the MB believes in gradual infiltration of its ideology among the masses and portrays itself as a believer in democracy. During the anti-Mubarak movement in Egypt, far from emulating Ayatollah Ruhollah Khomeini, they [MB leaders] channeled Thomas Paine, calling for civil liberties, religious equality, and an end to Mubarak's dictatorship.[28] As one senior JI leader of Bangladesh told me in 1991, the Jamaat would come to power through other means not elections, it seems Mohamed Morsi conveyed the same message to his interviewer in 2010: "Our program is a long-term one, not a short-term one. If we are rushing things, then I don't think that this leads to a real stable position."[29] Irrespective of what we believe about the MB, (a) its alleged long-term plan for establishing Islamic theocracies across the Middle East; (b) its suspected American connections (America is said to have undertaken the project to promote MB, JI in South Asia and Saudi Wahhabism to contain Iran and Islamist extremists such as al Qaeda), we cannot ignore what the grassroots in the Muslim world really want. They sometimes go ahead of their leaders and do things beyond their expectations and control. The grassroots across the Muslim world want democracy, freedom, human rights, and dignity, not theocracy and American hegemony.

Jamaat-i-Islami (JI) in Pakistan and Bangladesh

Maulana Abul Ala Maududi (1903–1979), an India-born madrassa-educated journalist, author, and political thinker, was the founder of the JI or Party of Islam. It came into being in 1941 in British India. Maududi started the organization with a view to promote Islamic values and practices in the light of his way of interpreting the Quran and Hadis. He was a maverick, his ideas being quite radical and different from the mainstream Sunni *ulama* or clerics in the Indian subcontinent. Interestingly, like most leading Muslim clerics in British India, he was opposed to the concept of Pakistan, as he did not believe that Mohamed Ali Jinnah, a secular Shiite Muslim, along with his Anglo-Mohamedan associates, would establish an Islamic State. He knew it well that Jinnah and his associates strove for a Muslim not Islamic Pakistan in Muslim-majority territories to be carved out of British India. Although he decided to stay back in India after the Partition of 1947, with no signs of abatement in the Great Punjab Killing (which started immediately before the Partition), as a Muslim he no longer felt safe in the Indian Punjab and migrated to Pakistan. Afterwards, till his death in 1979, he worked for establishing an Islamic State in Pakistan. In early 1950s, Pakistan went through mass agitations and anti-Ahmadiyya rioting in the Punjab, especially in Lahore. Maududi incited Pakistani

Muslims to demand that the Ahmadiyya Muslim Community (also known as Qadianis) be declared a non-Muslim minority because of their alleged disbelief in Prophet Muhammad as the last prophet of God. The 1953 rioting in Lahore was followed by mass arrests of agent provocateurs; leading among them was the JI chief, Maududi. The court found him guilty and condemned him to death for inciting anti-Ahmadiyya rioting, but soon he got clemency.

We find ideological similarities between the MB and JI. Like Qutb, Maududi also strove for God's sovereignty. Maududi, however, came up with a new theory of democracy. It was theodemocracy or a theocracy run in a democratic manner. He also wanted to establish a caliphate to run the Islamic system of governance. In his theodemocratic caliphate, minority non-Muslims would remain as *zimmis* or protected people with inferior rights. Interestingly, he was willing to accept inferior rights or *zimmi* status for minority Muslims in Hindu-majority India. He also believed that Islam was not just another religion about faith and rituals, but a movement, a comprehensive code of ethics, a government manual and guidance about running our life from cradle to grave. He was quite ambivalent about the concept of jihad. On the one hand, he did not consider jihad to be a holy war, and, on the other, he considered the 1965 Indo-Pakistan war a jihad par excellence. Like the MB, JI also believes that Muslims and Islam transcend national boundaries. Considering jihad to be the best of all prayers, Maududi believed that his theodemocratic transnational caliphate was only attainable through global jihad. His theodemocratic caliphate would be capitalistic with welfare and social justice.[30] Interestingly, according to Maududi's son Sayyid Farooq Haider Maududi, his father established a transnational fascist party in the name of Islam.[31] However, despite being influenced by the MB, the FIS in Algeria is not transnational; it has been primarily an Algerian nationalist movement for Islamo-nationalism.[32]

Despite their democratic rhetoric and apparent transformation into democratic organizations, the MB and JI believe in millennial Islamic movement to establish their cherished global caliphate or God's Kingdom, where women and minorities would not enjoy equal rights and opportunities. Their lip service to democracy and apparent acquiescence to secular law reflect their pragmatism, not their transformation into liberal democratic organizations. One finds JL's fascist blueprint in some of its founder Maududi's writings. His totalitarian Islamic State would eventually devour the sovereignty of all neighboring states run by non-Muslims or not in accordance with Shariah:

> Muslim groups will not be content with the establishment of an Islamic state in one area alone. Depending on their resources, they should try to expand in all direction.... If their Islamic state has power and resources it will fight and destroy non-Islamic governments and establish Islamic states in their place.[33]

He also believed that:

> Jews and Christians...should be forced to pay Jizya [poll tax] in order to put an end to their independence and supremacy.... These powers should be wrested from them by the followers of the true Faith...the Islamic state offers them protection, if they agree to live as Zimmis by paying Jizya, but it cannot allow that they should remain supreme rulers in any place and establish wrong ways and establish them on others...it is the duty of the true Muslims...to bring an end to their wicked rule and bring them under a righteous order.[34]

As with Fascism, Islamist extremist parties mostly flourish in countries under autocracy and corruption with mass unemployment and poverty. These parties strive for the Islamist secularization of society by raising socioeconomic rather than Islamic issues as the biggest problems confronting the Muslim world. Interestingly, unlike the MB, Wahhabis, and their ilk, Islamist parties in Turkey seem to be more secular than Islamic. Under secular-educated leadership, they are quite comfortable with traditional Turkish culture, music, food, and festivals.[35] Again, Islamist parties do not necessarily flourish under poverty. Some of them grow in affluent societies drawing well-to-do people within their folds. Al Qaeda is a glaring example in this regard. However, it is difficult to draw a line between Islamist parties that are designed and those who have emerged by default due to bad governance and poverty. While al Qaeda and its ilk are in the designed category, ideologically motivated to oppose democracy, human rights, and equal rights for women and minorities; pragmatic Islamists such as the MB and JI fall in the latter category with ideological orientation as well. They apparently call for democracy and some rights for women and minorities, but oppose the freedom of expression and secular law and institutions. It is noteworthy that America has been trying to make friends with the MB and Jamaat, because they take part in elections and condemn terrorism.[36]

America also has the friendliest tie with Saudi Arabia, where Wahhabism prevails as the state ideology. Despite their anti-Western rhetoric, the MB and JI are inherently pro-Western but premodern and antimodern at the same time. Many of them are no longer the Islamist parties in the strict sense of the expression. The Bangladesh JL, no longer the JL of Bangladesh, is a good example in this regard. Although it favors establishing Allah's Law, it no longer supports establishing Allah's Sovereignty but Islamic social justice and public welfare only through constitutional means, not violence. The party wants to enforce God-fearing, honest, and efficient leadership through democratic methods, instead of the inefficient and dishonest ones.[37] It is, however, noteworthy that the JI in Bangladesh runs 12 different Islamist parties, including the Islami Oikko Jote, Khilafat Majlis, and Khilafat Andolon.[38] Thus, proscribing the JI would not end its political influence in Bangladesh. As it has happened in Egypt, the MB since the overthrow of Mubarak in 2011, by adopting a new name, Freedom and Justice Party, is promise-bound to implement the same old Islamist ideology of the MB; the JI in Bangladesh would be doing the same thing in the event of its proscription.

Apprehending silent Western dominance of Arab countries that went through the Arab Spring, Samir Amin believes that the right-wing Islamist parties such as Ennahda in Tunisia and the MB in Egypt will be close allies of the West. He is right that America and dictators such as Sadat and Mubarak nurtured Islamist groups in Egypt as last resorts to preserve the status quo. "This is why I argued that political Islam did not belong to the opposition block, as claimed by the MB, but was an organic part of the power structure," asserts Amin.[39] Portraying the MB not as an Islamic but primarily as a reactionary party, he believes that it "will represent the best security for the imperialist system," and that the post-revolutionary Arab countries under political Islam will stagnate for another 50 years or so, just as what has happened to Islamic Iran. Since Salafism, the fulcrum of the MB, rejects the idea of liberty and glorifies fatalist Islam, or the slave-master relationship between human beings and God, democracy will remain elusive under Islamist rule. Islamist regimes' promotion of science, computer, and business management does not amount to their promotion of modern education either. Last but not least:

"The Muslim Brotherhood and imperialism operate in conjunction, and with a division of tasks. The Muslim Brotherhood needed a 'certificate' of democracy, which Obama gave them, and to that end they had to distance themselves from the 'extremists,' the Salafis."[40] Thus, not Islamist MB or JI but Salafist extremists are the biggest threats to liberal democracy and Western interests in the Muslim world.

Al Qaeda: Is it on the Run or Coming Back?

Al Qaeda has been the most known, feared, hated, and enigmatic terror outfit in the world. Some scholars and laymen soon after 9/11 questioned if al Qaeda and its enigmatic leader Osama bin Laden had been behind the attacks or if they had the capabilities to execute the carnage (some still raise these questions). There are, however, convincing proofs about al Qaeda masterminding and executing the attacks. Now, whether al Qaeda is an organization or a movement or franchise is another question among scholars. Security analyst Ehsan Ahrari considers it a franchise. Peter Bergen believes that after 2001 the terror outfit has been reorganized into "al Qaeda 2.0," which is a decentralized movement rather than a centralized organization, with abysmally poor support from global Muslims. A former CIA analyst Mark Sageman believes that al Qaeda is no longer the main threat to the West; more immediate threat comes from marginalized Muslim immigrants and citizens in the West. Retired U.S. Marine officer Bruce Hoffman believes that al Qaeda's networks are intact and still poses a big threat to America. Many analysts, on the other hand, believe that al Qaeda's inability to attack America since 9/11 proves its inability to undertake any major attacks on Western interests in the near future.[41]

While many consider bin Laden to be the founder and Saudi Wahhabism as its inspiration, al Qaeda is actually an offshoot of the MB and Abdullah Azzam, a Palestinian Islamic scholar and mentor of bin Laden, was its founder. He was disillusioned with the Palestinian leadership who emphasized on politics and nationalism rather than on Islam. Qutb's writings on total war had influenced Azzam. After teaching at a Saudi university for a few years, in early 1980s, he joined the Afghan jihad against the Soviet Union. He worked together with bin Laden and established al Qaeda with direct Pakistani military intelligence (ISI) support. In 1988, Saudi money, American arms, and Pakistani training and logistics helped the formation of this stateless army of Sunni militants who wanted to establish global caliphate transcending Afghanistan and Pakistan. The ISI had another motive behind arming and training al Qaeda fighters; it was to fight India, mainly in Indian-occupied Kashmir.[42] Soon after the formation of al Qaeda, Azzam had strong differences with the ISI, which had been backing several other mujahedeen groups in Afghanistan in the late 1980s. Azzam asked some top al Qaeda leaders, including bin Laden and al Zawahiri, to support him to open a united front against Pakistan, which they declined. Soon in late 1989 Azzam got killed in a bomb blast, which some believe was planted by bin Laden and his associates.[43]

From the inner struggles and cleavages within al Qaeda's top leadership from the very beginning, it appears that it has been primarily a political not Islamic organization in content and nature. After Azzam's death, we have not seen any cleric at the helm of al Qaeda affairs. Senior and middle-ranking leaders of this Islamist terror outfit have been mostly techno-clerics, not Islamic clerics or mullahs, sheikhs, or imams. The organization has mostly been overrated since August 1998 for simultaneous bombing of the U.S. embassies in Daressalam and Nairobi in Africa. 9/11 attacks heightened al Qaeda's stature as the most powerful terror outfit in the world. By 2004, experts believed that the organization had as many as 18,000 fighters worldwide. However, the way al Qaeda almost fizzled out in and around Afghanistan not long after the U.S.-led invasion of Afghanistan in 2001, and as it appeared from bin Laden's private documents, captured by U.S. troops who killed him in May 2011, the organization was practically finished by 2007 and had been in serious financial crisis and shortage of fighters. After 2001, al Qaeda leaders were in hiding, waging a virtual war through video and Internet. Having its own media network, *al Sahab* (The Cloud), presumably based in Pakistan, bin Laden and al Zawahiri used to circulate their messages, full of sound and fury, through videotapes and Internet for America and its allies. Interestingly, days before the 2004 Presidential Election—which gave George W. Bush his second term—bin Laden issued an ominous warning to America through a videotaped speech, shown on the U.S. media. After the killing of bin Laden, it appears (apparently though) that al Qaeda had practically died out a few years earlier than bin Laden's death in 2011. Due to the cataclysmic 9/11, which the average Muslims abhorred as Satanic acts in the name of Islam, al Qaeda had very little to almost nonexistent support and sympathy among global Muslims.

As we look back, we see al Qaeda and the Mujahedeen not as self-sustaining organizations. America, Saudi Arabia, and Pakistan had been their main promoters. As CIA and the State Department had no qualms about promoting anti-communist autocrats—Franco, Pinochet, Reza Shah, Salazar, Marcos, Suharto, Zia ul-Haq, and others—they were also enthusiastic about promoting ultra-rightist terror outfits such as the Contra, al Qaeda, and the Mujahedeen. The Taliban came out of several Pashtun Mujahedeen groups. It is noteworthy that America considered the Saudi version of Islam an asset during the Cold War, and Washington still has a soft corner for Saudi Wahhabism, which since World War I has been a traditional ally of the West. The Soviet invasion of Afghanistan was the main catalyst in furthering Washington's interest in radical Islam and the Mujahedeen. Reagan once compared the Mujahedeen with America's founding fathers for their service to the cause of freedom.

However, soon after the Soviet withdrawal in 1989, the U.S. rejoiced and left war-torn Afghanistan to itself, infested with more than 30 Mujahedeen factions divided on ethnic, sectarian, and ideological lines; among them, al Qaeda being the most deadly, organized, and politically motivated transnational terror outfit emerged as the number one. Meanwhile, bin Laden's reputation grew tremendously after the Russian and American withdrawal from Afghanistan.[44] In view of the rise of al Qaeda, the Taliban, and the various Mujahedeen groups in Afghanistan, northwestern Pakistan, and Central Asia, we think America played both an active and passive role in their creation. But for its generous financial and military support, there would not have been any significant resistance against the Soviet Union, let alone any al Qaeda or Taliban. Similarly, without America's abrupt leaving the armed gangs of unemployed Mujahedeen to themselves, there would not have been any chaos or civil war in Afghanistan, which paved the way for the Taliban takeover in 1996. After the Soviet and American withdrawal in 1989, al Qaeda singled out Israel, America, and the secular regimes in the Muslim world as the main enemies of Islam. Pakistan's ISI, which runs a parallel government in the country, added India as another very important enemy of Islam, for its occupation of Muslim-majority Kashmir. Meanwhile, American oil companies had forged ties with several Islamist outfits in Afghanistan and adjoining subregion in hopes of building an oil pipeline from Central Asia to the Indian Ocean through Afghanistan. American benign neglect to the reconstruction of the war-ravaged Afghanistan to a large extent led to the rise of al Qaeda, bin Laden, and the Taliban.[45]

Ayman al Zawahiri, a radical Egyptian medical doctor, who was once arrested for his role in the assassination of President Sadat, is a cofounder of al Qaeda. He is said to be the main organizer of the organization, which was led by the charismatic bin Laden. As per al Zawahiri's advice, bin Laden organized al Qaeda as an umbrella organization to accommodate different ethnic groups within its fold. Thus Arab, Bangladeshi, Chechen, Chinese Uigher, Pashtun, Baloch, Punjabi, Indian, Burmese, Indonesian, Filipino, Somali, Kenyan, and even American and European Muslim militants joined al Qaeda. Most of the recruits came from the former bands of the Mujahedeen. Zawahiri wanted Afghanistan and then Pakistan to become the core of the caliphate or al Qaeda's Global Islamic Empire. Bin Laden also wanted to forge ties with Hezbollah, a Shiite militia in Lebanon. Al Qaeda wanted to fight not only the West and Israel, but also Saudi Arabia, especially because of its allowing U.S. troops in the kingdom.[46]

Zawahiri's Egyptian connection was an asset for al Qaeda as he had connections with Egypt's once powerful Islamist group Gamaah al Islamiyya or the Islamic Group (IG). The IG, which was responsible for the assassination of Sadat, disintegrated in 1997. In 1991, Zawahiri broke with IG as he did not approve of killing Christians and tourists in Egypt and in 1996 formed the Egyptian Islamic Jihad (EIJ). After the Taliban takeover, he went to Afghanistan. Bin Laden after his expulsion from Sudan in the wake of the U.S. Embassy bombings, in 1998, went to Afghanistan. They began a new chapter in the name of a global jihad under the aegis of al Qaeda in Afghanistan under the Taliban administration of semiliterate Mullah Umar, another veteran of the Afghan jihad. Zawahiri was instrumental in the 1998 merger of the EIJ with al Qaeda. Soon, in September 2001, al Qaeda performed the least predictable and possibly the most catastrophic terrorist act in history.[47]

Following the 9/11 attacks, in November 2001, the U.S. retaliated against Afghanistan and toppled the Taliban regime for harboring top al

Qaeda leaders. However, instead of finishing the job in Afghanistan by eliminating al Qaeda completely, America turned its attention to Iraq to topple Saddam Hussein. The American-led invasion of Iraq gave some respite to al Qaeda elements to reorganize themselves in Afghanistan, Pakistan, and elsewhere. Meanwhile al Qaeda infiltrated anti-government forces in Yemen, the anti-Assad forces in Syria, and tribal and Islamist rebels in Mali and elsewhere in Northwest Africa. By January, al Qaeda and its ilk became so powerful and visible in a vast region from Somalia to Sudan, Nigeria, Chad, Mali, Algeria, and Libya in Africa that some analysts coined a new expression "Afrighanistan" to denote a second Afghanistan in terms of the growth in Islamist militancy and terror by al Qaeda and similar Islamist groups.[48]

Terrorists and transnational crime syndicates collaborate with each other. Various Islamist, ethno-nationalist, Marxist, anarchist, and narco-terrorist groups having common enemies in America have already come closer to each other. Menacingly to America's long-term security, various Latin American terrorists, narco-terrorist and well-armed insurgent groups, including the FARC, have forged ties with al Qaeda. The al Qaeda–FARC drug alliance has been an ominous development, within and beyond the Americas.[49] Narco-terrorism and narco-jihad along with state-sponsored proxy wars through non-state actors are fast replacing the traditional suicide bomber.

Somalia used to be the most volatile, al Qaeda-infested country in the world up to early 2011. Yemen has been another safe haven for al Qaeda. The America-born radical engineer-turned-cleric Anwar Awlaki, also known as the bin Laden of the Internet, used to be the main organizer of al Qaeda till his death in a U.S. drone attack in September 2011 in Yemen. However, Awalaki's death weakened the al Qaeda's support base in the country; nevertheless, it is still quite active in the region. There were several suicide attacks in Yemen in early 2012. Al Qaeda claimed the killing of a Yemeni general in one such attack in June 2012.[50] Besides the never ending threat of Islamist terror, secessionists in the south pose the existential threat to united Yemen. They want South Yemen to become a separate country again, as it existed before the merger with the north in 1990. The Southern Separatist Movement or al-Herak is again divided into socialist and pro-Iranian factions. Al Qaeda and its ilk are fighting al-Herak in the south and the central government in the north. The overthrow of the dictatorial President Abdullah Saleh in 2012 and his replacement by a Southerner, Mansour Hadi, has not resolved either the Islamist or the separatist problem in Yemen. In view of this, one is not sure which is worse for the north: southern secession or al Qaeda?[51]

Unlike the MB or JI, al Qaeda is more of a franchise than a well-organized Islamist party based in particular countries or regions. Thus, we find its prototypes operating in different parts of the world, sometimes independently on their own. Northern Algeria's Boko Haram has been the leading anarchist Islamist terror outfit in Africa. In 2002, Muhammed Yusuf (1970–2009), a Western-educated northern Nigerian ideologue, established the Boko Haram, also known as the *Jama'atu Ahlis Sunna Lidda'awati wal-Jihad*, which in Arabic means "people committed to the propagation of the Prophet's teachings and jihad." In 2009, Nigerian law enforcers killed him in custody. He belonged to the Kanuri tribe, whose members live across Nigeria, Niger, Chad, and Cameroon. Boko Haram or the Nigerian Taliban is more anti-Western and antimodern than the Taliban. It prohibits or considers it *haram* (forbidden) to take part in any political or social activity, including voting in elections, wearing shirts and trousers, and receiving Western/secular education. Boko Haram is striving for the revival of the Sokoto Caliphate that existed in parts of northern Nigeria, Niger, and eastern Cameroon until abolished by the British in 1903. Boko Haram's obscurantist program and violent attacks on Christians, deviant Muslims, U.N. offices, and government forces reflect poor and marginalized tribesmen's political aspirations. So far, the militants have confined their activities within Nigeria.[52] One, however, cannot rule out the possibilities of its turning transnational engulfing the entire Northwestern Africa, initially among the aspirational poverty-stricken Kanuri tribesmen across Northern Nigeria, Niger, Chad, and eastern Cameroon. Hundreds of Boko Haram militants had been in Timbaktu fighting government troops of Mali up to the defeat of Islamist militants in northern Mali by French troops in late January 2013. Boko Haram militants have links with al Qaeda and Islamist terror groups in Afghanistan and Algeria.[53]

By late 2011, al Qaeda had started operating in West Africa, in Mali, Mauritania, Niger, Nigeria, and Algeria. By mid-2012, al Qaeda's main sanctuary in West Africa was in northern Mali where it helped the secessionist Tuareg tribesmen in establishing their independent Islamic State of Azawad. More than 250,000 square miles of West African territory,

> including the legendary city of Timbaktu—risks turning into an outland much like the remote areas of Afghanistan, Pakistan, Somalia, and Yemen where terrorists linked to al Qaeda seek safety from U.S. and other efforts to hunt them down, according to European diplomats, academic experts, and reports from the region.[54]

It appears that al Qaeda is well entrenched in the Islamic State of northern Mali, which is bigger than France in landmass. It has been under strict Shariah law since its unilateral declaration of independence from Mali. Tuareg fighters, who served Qaddafi till his last days as mercenaries, along with some other Salafist and secular groups having the common enemy in the government of Mali, have been the mainstay of al Qaeda in Islamic West Africa or Maghreb (AQIM). As some analysts believe, while Mali is emerging as the New Libya, another fractured state and failed state; al Qaeda's gaining ground in West Africa is turning the entire subregion into another Afghanistan, a conflict zone between the AQIM and America, and a battlefield for the proxy war of hegemony between China and the U.S. in the coming years.[55]

According to a senior European diplomat, the Islamic State in northern Mali provided for the first time a territorial base for al Qaeda in the AQIM. He discussed the situation on the condition of anonymity with *Washington Post*. "Every week that goes by is important because it gives AQIM more time to implant itself," he said.[56] Al Qaeda's resilience, ability to fish in troubled water by exploiting ethno-national conflicts, its adaptability, and above all, its transnational network easily outwit and bypass government intelligence and security systems. As Niger's President Mahamadou Issoufou reported in June 2012, jihadi fighters from Pakistan and Afghanistan were training members of Islamist groups in northern Mali.[57] One is not sure if the African Union and the Economic Community of West African States (ECOWAS) will be able to overpower the Islamic State of Azawad in the long run. They are quite well-armed with the leftover of Qaddafi's arsenal. Again, a secular group of separatists/freedom fighters under the banner of the National Movement for the Liberation of Azawad (MNLA) have forged ties with Ansar Eddine, a local franchise of al Qaeda, which has money and international connections. The MNLA has agreed to an Islamic State against the will of many of its followers. However, there is no reason to panic as this landlocked huge territory of northern Mali with 1.3 million people cannot sustain long after Mali stabilizes following the March 2012 military rebellion in the south. An al Qaeda-run government in northern Mali or independent Azawad is not going to get any Western support.[58]

In view of the contradictory and exaggerated accounts of the rise of Islamist militancy in Nigeria, Mali, Somalia, and Yemen one is not sure if an Islamist takeover of these countries is on the cards. Without undermining the growing Islamist threat in parts of Africa and Arab world, we need to understand the secular aspects of violent crime and insurgencies or revolts from the margins on class, ethnic, and sectarian lines.[59] Meanwhile by late January 2013, French-led troops defeated and expelled the Islamist rebels in northern Mali. The poverty-stricken and marginalized nomadic Tuareg people in northeastern Mali, along with other marginalized and fractured communities/tribes (who are dispersed in several countries) such as the Kanuri tribesmen in Nigeria, Niger, Chad, and Cameroon; Somali refugees in Kenya and Ethiopia (along with marginalized Ethiopian Muslims); Arab/Muslim nomads in Sudan and South Sudan; and last but not least, Islamist rebels in and from Algeria and Libya, are not going to sign peace with the autocratic regimes in the vast regions of northwest and East Africa, and with the French and British invaders in the foreseeable future. Consequently, we have reasons to agree with analysts who believe that terrorism in Algeria and Mali demonstrates the increasing reach of Islamist extremism in Africa. Islamist groups such as al Qaeda in the Islamic Maghrib (West Africa) or the AQIM and the Movement for Unity and Jihad in West Africa (MUJAO), the hydra-headed Boko Haram in Nigeria, and the dormant but not totally annihilated Islamists in Libya and Somalia are going to destabilize and terrorize Africa for decades. We may agree with the view that: "Both action by jihadists and action against jihadists could exacerbate the dangers."[60] Last but not least, the overthrow of the Qaddafi regime in October 2011 led to the exodus of thousands of pro- and anti-Qaddafi Islamist (Libyan and foreigners, mostly from several African countries) from Libya into neighboring countries. On the 11th anniversary of 9/11 on September 11, 2012, al Qaeda–linked Ansar al-Sharia attacked the U.S. consulate at Benghazi and killed four

Americans, including Ambassador Christopher Stevens. Several other anti-Qaddafi Islamist groups are active throughout northwestern Africa.[61] Despite initial French victory against Tuareg Islamist rebels in Mali in January 2013, jihadists are gaining grounds in neighboring countries. Niger is also a fertile breeding ground for sustained Islamist/tribal militancy and terror. Many Tuareg militants fled to Niger. "Given Niger's weak government structures, they also pose a serious security threat to the country as a whole," observes one analyst.[62] After signing a power-sharing agreement in March 2012 with three jihadist militants—al Qaeda in the Islamic Maghreb, Ansar Dine, and the Movement for Oneness and Jihad in West Africa—they found Niger an appealingly easy target. Its secular political elite lack legitimacy among illiterate and deeply religious tribesmen. Niger's rampant corruption and bad governance have further aggravated the situation. The perpetual conflicts with neighboring Nigeria and the presence of marginalized Tuareg tribesmen in Niger, which has a weak and unpopular military and unguarded checkpoints along the border with Nigeria, have allowed for an influx of radical Islamic preachers into the country. Boko Haram and Niger's homegrown Islamist terror outfits have forged ties. The outbreak of a jihad in Niger could drag the West into a long-drawn military engagement in the region.[63] It would adversely affect French interests as it gets roughly three-quarters of its energy from uranium mined in northern Niger. We may agree with the view that:

[U]nsurprisingly, France has already deployed soldiers to protect those resources, and China is said to have done the same at its uranium mine near Azalik. Niger is also an oil exporter, and production is expected to grow significantly in coming months. Rebel movements and Islamic militants are within reach of Niger's mines and oil fields, which they could use to fund their rebellion. Further attacks on Nigerian and Algerian territory remain a distinct possibility.[64]

Then again, like war-torn and/or fractured Afghanistan, Chechnya, and Dagestan, Somalia, Yemen, and Pakistan al Qaeda can destabilize the entire Maghreb and adjoining areas from Azawad. Al Qaeda has widespread networks from the north and northwest to the southwest, central, and eastern regions of Africa and the Middle East, which bin Laden and al Zawahiri systematized in the 1990s. Al Qaeda paid more attention to Africa than Afghanistan, especially to the Islamic West Africa, to turn the continent into its safe haven, even before the overthrow of the Taliban regime in Afghanistan in 2001. As planned by Zawahiri, al Qaeda infiltrated into various West European countries from Africa. Al Qaeda took full advantage of the crackdown on Islamist parties by the military-backed Algerian government in the 1990s. It forged ties with Algerian radical Salafist Group for Preaching and Combat (GSPC).[65] Despite GSPC's limited appeal among Algerian Muslims, there is no authentic figure about its strength in the subregion.[66] America's Africa Command (Africom, formed in 2008) has intensified its military operations against al Qaeda and its affiliates from northwest Africa to central and eastern Africa. The U.S. drone attacks in Somalia and Yemen have not been able to eliminate al Qaeda bases; rather by killing innocent civilians along with a handful of al Qaeda leaders have alienated people from America.[67] American and Western post-Cold War interventions in Africa and the Muslim world in general have failed to win the hearts and minds of the average Muslims. The French invasion of Mali in January 2013, in the name of crushing Islamist terrorists, has not brought peace to the region. French justification for the invasion in the name of protecting France from Mali-based terrorists does not hold water as France in December 2012 was the 63rd terror-infested country in the world.[68]

Al Qaeda or any other terrorist group does not need thousands of fighters to destabilize a superpower such as the U.S. Terrorism is all about asymmetric warfare, which mostly favors terrorists to the detriment of counterterrorist/counterinsurgent measures by governments everywhere. We may cite the example of Chechnya. Al Qaeda-backed Chechen separatists in this tiny patch of land with 1.3 million people not only killed several thousand civilians in schools, theaters, sidewalks, and marketplaces in Chechnya and Russia since 2000, but by 2010 they also killed 15,000 Russian troops. Russia lost more troops in Chechnya in 10 years than what they had lost in Afghanistan during the decade-long Afghan jihad.[69] The general perception is that (a) the Anglo-French intervention in Mali is U.S.-sponsored; (b) Uranium, gold, and other minerals are the main factors behind their intervention; (c) America and Qatar covertly supported al Qaeda in northern Mali to justify a European invasion of Mali; (d) Algeria and other countries in the region will be the next targets of Western invasions in the name of containing terrorism.[70]

We are not sure if al Qaeda is alive only across the African continent or it has more than a dormant presence in Asia, Europe, and America. As American analysts and experts tend to overestimate or underestimate actual or perceived threats to their country, we can hardly rely on their appraisal if al Qaeda is a spent force or it has the potential to stage more mega attacks on America. Following the overthrow of Saddam Hussein in 2003, President Bush declared America's victory in the War on Terror, and we know how gross that overestimation was. Thus, we have every reason to be skeptical about what Obama proclaimed after the death of Osama bin Laden: "We have put al Qaeda on a path to defeat." We believe that al Qaeda is not on the "brink of defeat." Its "fingerprints are increasingly evident" in Syria, Iraq, Yemen, the Maghreb, Somalia, Nigeria, and Egypt. After bin Laden's death, al Qaeda conducted more than 200 attacks in Iraq alone and killed more than a thousand Iraqis.[71] Ahmed Rashid thinks that far from being dead, the post-Laden al Qaeda is "now a far looser and more amorphous terror network." It has branches in every European country and has penetrated Muslim communities in the U.S. as well.[72]

Seth Jones is right that (a) far from being a sign of its weakness, al Qaeda's forging ties with various terror groups in North Africa, Middle East, or South Asia is a sign of its strength and indispensability to other terrorist outfits; (b) although most Muslims despise al Qaeda, it enjoys enough support among Muslim populations in almost every continent to target umpteen number of countries, including America; (c) far from being an anti-Shiite organization, al Qaeda is quite close to various Shiite militant groups, including Hezbollah; and (d) last but not least, for al Qaeda, Iran is a refuge. Any American or Israeli invasion of Iran is likely to bring al Qaeda closer to Iran against their common enemies, particularly America and Israel.[73] Finally, we should never forget al Qaeda is not a well-structured organization but a movement inspired by an evil terrorist ideology. There will always be some takers of the ideology. The Arab Spring has opened some opportunities for al Qaeda to infiltrate various Islamist organizations, including the MB. Finally, al Qaeda and its followers have the potential to destabilize the entire Muslim world by exploiting the cause of global jihad in the name of an inchoate caliphate.[74]

In sum, as discussed above, far from being a spent force, the post-9/11 al Qaeda morphed into a movement or franchise. Since then its presence is felt beyond the so-called heartland of the outfit, beyond Afghanistan,

Pakistan, Iraq, and Somalia. Following the killing of Osama bin Laden in May 2011, al Qaeda entered the post-bin Laden phase of its history. Belying the initial euphoria of the U.S. administration following the death of bin Laden, al Qaeda, the so-called defeated network of terror, emerged as an important component of the anti-Assad forces in Syria. After attacking the U.S. Embassy at Benghazi in Libya on the 11th anniversary of 9/11 in 2012—killing several Americans including Ambassador Christopher Stevens—al Qaeda did not look back. By mid-2013, America and its allies realized "how diffuse the [al Qaeda-led] terrorist phase has become, and how difficult it is to guard against." They realized that the new al Qaeda, a decentralized loose movement, was even more unpredictable if not deadlier than what it had been in September 2001.[75] After intercepting electronic communications of al Qaeda agents who discussed attacks on American and Western overseas interests by American spy agencies in August 2013, the U.S., Canada, Britain, France, Germany, and Norway decided to close several diplomatic missions in North Africa, Middle East, and elsewhere for few days.[76] While the Obama administration successfully intercepted the al Qaeda communications and prevented attacks on Western overseas interests by taking precautionary measures to err on the side of caution,[77] yet the closing down of Western embassies after the threat was reasonable, but not a long-term solution. Again, the surge in al Qaeda activities across the continents despite the more than a decade-long Global War on Terror indicates the failure of the U.S.-led counterterrorism operations against al Qaeda. Meanwhile, the Interpol attributed the series of jailbreaks in July 2013 in Libya, Iraq, and Pakistan to al Qaeda. Some news agencies, including the CNN, revealed that al Qaeda was also involved in several jailbreaks in Colombia and some other countries in Europe and South America in 2013 that led to the release of around 1,500 dangerous terrorists.[78]

We may cite what Frederick Kagan of the American Enterprise Institute has said in this regard:

> The war against al Qaeda is not going well.... The killing of Osama bin Laden has not been followed-up in Pakistan with disruption to the leadership group there on the scale of operations that preceded the Abbottabad raid. Al Qaeda affiliates in Iraq, Syria, Yemen, and West Africa have dramatically expanded their operating areas and capabilities since 2009 and appear poised to continue that expansion. Progress against al Shabaab, the al Qaeda

affiliate in Somalia, is extremely fragile and shows signs of beginning to unravel. New groups with al Qaeda leanings, although not affiliations, are emerging in Egypt, and old groups that had not previously been affiliated with al Qaeda, such as Boko Haram in Nigeria, appear to be moving closer to it. Current trends point to continued expansion of al Qaeda affiliates and their capabilities, and it is difficult to see how current or proposed American and international policies are likely to contain that expansion, let alone reduce it to 2009 levels or below. Americans must seriously consider the possibility that we are, in fact, starting to lose the war against al Qaeda.[79]

The "Shiite Bomb" and the Shia–Sunni Conflict

Iran is allegedly developing nuclear weapons. This is making headlines quite frequently across the world. Although these are debatable propositions if Iran is justified in having nuclear arsenal, or if it is already in the process of making nuclear weapons, it is, however, not a contentious issue that the energy-rich, strategically located Iran run by a millennial Shiite ideology is very important for the Middle East and the world at large both for the right and wrong reasons. The Iranian hand in the growing Shiite assertion and the Shia–Sunni conflicts in Syria, Iraq, the Gulf and Pakistan, and Afghanistan is as important as Iran becoming a nuclear power. However, as President Carter has spelled out, even if the Iranian leadership becomes insane and invades Israel, Iran would be almost totally destroyed by nuclear-armed Israel and America.[80] As per the conventional wisdom, Saudi Arabia, Egypt, and Turkey, not Israel, have reasons to worry about a nuclear Iran. However, according to a report by the Center for New American Security (CNAS), a prestigious American security think tank, published on February 19, 2013: "The conventional wisdom is probably wrong." The report's authors include Colin Kahl, a former deputy assistant U.S. Secretary of Defense for the Middle East, and Melissa Dalton, a foreign affairs specialist with the secretary. The report reveals that although there is some risk that Saudi Arabia would seek an atomic bomb, it would more likely rely on its ally, the U.S. to protect it or buy a bomb from another ally, Pakistan. The report also argues that Egypt does not see Iran's nuclear ambitions as an existential threat and that Turkey already has a nuclear deterrent in the form of its NATO security guarantees.[81]

We need an understanding of the inherent causes of Shia–Sunni conflict and the implications of the Shiite revival since the Iranian Revolution to understand the implications of a nuclear-armed Iran for the Gulf subregion.[82] Unlike Sunni Islamists, Khomeini and his followers did not aim at replacing the secular autocracy of the Shah with a Shariah-based government. Ayatollah Khomeini (1902–1989) established not the rule of Shariah but a *Vilayet-i-Faqeeh* or Kingdom of the Jurist, a theocracy based on absolute rule by the cleric. Ayatollah Khomeini till his death remained the supreme ruler and lawmaker in Iran. As the main spiritual leader of Shiite Muslims of Iran, he was the *marja al-taqlid* (source of imitation) for the people, whose authority could not be questioned or challenged by anybody. He graduated from a seminary in Qom; was a teacher and writer; studied Islamic philosophy, law, and ethics; held liberal views about Greek philosophy; and even considered Aristotle the founder of logic. Plato also influenced him a lot. He wrote mystic, political, and social poems as well. After becoming an ayatollah (an expert in Islamic jurisprudence, ethics, and philosophy) in 1961, Khomeini started mobilizing clerics against the Shah's White Revolution (which was detrimental to clerics' tax-free estates) and to boycott the referendum on White Revolution in 1963. The Shah arrested him in 1963 and released him after bloody rioting in 1964. He spent 14 years in exile in Iraq, Turkey, and France. He inspired Iranians from exile through his taped speeches on audio cassettes. Finally, Iranians overthrew the Shah and in February 1979 Khomeini returned to Iran and established his *Vilayet-e-Faqih*. He inspired both Shiite and Sunni Muslims throughout the world for his simultaneous opposition of America and of Saddam Hussein. His advocacy of global Islamic Revolution and portrayal of America as the "Great Satan" may be mentioned in this regard.[83] However, as Foucault has argued:

> ...for Iran, one must talk about Shi'ism before talking about Islam, that Shi'ism and not ethnicity is the foundation of the national identity and consequently of the legitimacy of all power...the modernity of the Shah as a form of archaism to the extent it was imposed by brute force are very relevant: the Shah didn't understand a thing about social control (but perhaps that's why a revolution was possible, which leaves many fine days ahead for modern and subtle governments).[84]

Was the Iranian Revolution a "political revolution or revolution against politics?" is the question. The Iranian Revolution reflects how society successfully went against the autocratic state, without any framework for an alternative order. The masses had only one program, which was well reflected in their demand, "the Shah must go."[85]

Since the Revolution, clerics are running the theodemocracy in the country under Ayatollah Khamenei's dictates. President Mahmoud Ahmadinejad is answerable to the Ayatollah. Nevertheless, Iran is far more democratic than the Arab countries. However, although Iran does not sponsor terrorism and has not invaded any country in the past decades, Israeli and American/Western belligerence toward the Islamist regime has destabilized the entire region. Being worried about the growing Iranian influence on their Shiite minority populations (majority in Bahrain), Saudi Arabia and other Arab kingdoms in the Gulf, on the one hand, are engaged in an arms race with Iran, and, on the other, are promoting rebels to topple the pro-Iranian Assad regime in Syria. The Iranian regime has profound influence on Iraqi government and on the Hezbollah militia in Lebanon, and has good relations with the Afghan government as well. In view of Iraq's and Afghanistan's friendly relations with Iran, which America considers a big threat to its best interests in the region, it appears that America has little control over countries (Iraq and Afghanistan) it liberated in the recent past. Further, destabilization of Syria is likely to destabilize Lebanon, signaling civil wars in Syria, Lebanon, Iraq, and elsewhere in the Arab world.[86] The Shia–Sunni conflict in post-Saddam Iraq is a new phenomenon. Juan Cole attributes it to American machination: "The kind of sectarian fighting we're seeing now in Iraq is new in its scale and ferocity, and it was the Americans who unleashed it."[87]

The decades-long marginalization of Shiites in Sunni-majority countries in the Arab world has further intensified the Shiite–Sunni conflict. Not only the Saddam Hussein regime discriminated against the majority Iraqis who are Shiites, but Sunni regimes in Saudi Arabia, Bahrain, Kuwait, and the U.A.E. have also been discriminatory against Shiite citizens. Bahraini Shiites, despite being the majority of the population in the sheikhdom, have been restive against the Sunni monarch. Following the overthrow of Saddam Hussein, in 2003 the Jordanian-born Sunni extremist Abu Musab al-Zarqawi came to Iraq and merged his outfit Tawheed wal-Jihad with al Qaeda, which was afterwards known as al Qaeda in Iraq (AQI). The AQI unleashed a reign of terror in Iraq, especially by indiscriminate killing of Shiites, till his death in 2006. The Sunni monarch of the Shiite-majority Bahrain brutally subdued a Shiite revolt with tacit support of America and Saudi Arabia's moral and military support in early 2012.

However, things changed drastically in Iraq after the formation of a democratic government in 2006. From the Prime Minister Nouri al-Maliki to most key members of the administration all are Shiites. The ascendancy of the hitherto marginalized, poor, and unemployed Shiites along with the growing Iranian influence has alarmed many Sunni Iraqis. The continuation of the Sunni backlash against the Shiite majority in the country is imputed to Prime Minister Maliki's alleged discriminatory policies against the Sunni minority. Sporadic bomb attacks on Shiite mosques, shrines and killing of Shiites at home, work, or in the marketplace have been quite common. Sections of the marginalized Sunni Muslims have swelled the ranks of anti-Shiite death squads. One analyst blames the Prime Minister's prosecution of Sunni Vice President Tareq al-Hashemi and other Sunni officials for further alienating Sunni Iranians from his government.[88]

Meanwhile, the onset of the so-called regime-change operation against the pro-Iranian Assad government in Syria in early 2012 under the aegis of America, Israel, and the Arab League—Saudi Arabia, Kuwait, and Qatar in particular— which some radical Islamist groups such as the MB and al Qaeda also joined, has further aggravated the Shia–Sunni conflict in the Gulf region. America's main interest in waging a war against Assad is to weaken Iran and protect Israeli interests.[89] Due to the Iranian regime's belligerence toward its Sunni neighbors in the Gulf who happen to be in league with America (and indirectly with Israel) and the formidable anti-Iranian coalition backed by America, Israel, and Saudi Arabia, it is least likely that the region will enjoy any stability or durable peace. Neither the onslaught against Syria nor the ongoing sanctions against Iran (and the threats of an Israeli attack on the country) is going to dissipate very soon.

One must not ignore the undercurrent of establishing a Shiite-majority oil-rich state in the Arabian Peninsula. While the overthrow of Saddam Hussein has already established a Shiite homeland in Iraq under Iranian tutelage, some Shiite clerics and itinerary preachers/propagandists are campaigning for a Shiite homeland in the Gulf. They point out that oil-rich Sunni Arab kingdoms do not have oil in Sunni-majority provinces or subregions in Saudi Arabia, Kuwait, Qatar, Bahrain, or elsewhere in the Gulf. They urge Shiites to strive for the Greater Bahrain (*Bahrain al-Kubra*), which includes Kuwait, Qatar, Oman, U.A.E., and parts of Saudi Arabia, which would become a Shiite majority and oil-rich state in the Arabian Peninsula.[90] The ongoing Shia–Sunni conflict in Pakistan, which frequently leads to mass killing of rival sect members (mostly Shiites) in mosques and public places, is a Wahhabi–Salafi legacy initiated by Saudi Arabia and some Gulf countries following the Islamic Revolution in Iran. General Zia ul-Haq's Islamization program, which totally excluded the Shiite jurisprudence from the program, and America's hostility to the Shiite regime in Iran are important factors in the marginalization and persecution of Shiite minorities in Pakistan. The anti-Shiite role of the Taliban, al Qaeda, Deobandi/Wahhabi clerics, and rabidly anti-Shiite outfits such as the Lashkar-e-Jhangvi (LeJ), Ahl-e-Sunnah Wal Jamaat (ASWJ), Tahrik-e-Taliban Pakistan (TTP), and Sipah-e-Muhammadi Pakistan (SMP) may be mentioned in this regard. Consequently, there is a growing demand by Sunni extremists in Pakistan for declaring all Shiites as non-Muslim minorities in the country.[91] In 1974, the government declared the Ahmadiyya Muslims a non-Muslim minority in Pakistan.

However, despite the ongoing Shia–Sunni conflict—a proxy war between Iran and Saudi Arabia—Sunni Taliban and Shiite Iran are coming closer to each other against their common enemies, the West and pro-Western regimes in the Muslim world. In June 2013, a Taliban delegation from Qatar went to Tehran to hold talks with Iranian security officials. Several Taliban leaders including a minister and governor of Maidan Wardak province of Afghanistan under Taliban rule had earlier met with high Iranian officials. President Hamid Karzai of Afghanistan, who had been eager to talk with the Taliban for a peaceful settlement of the Afghan conflict, told in March 2013 that the Taliban wanted to talk with the Afghan government.[92]

Wahhabism and the Saudi Flashpoint

Contrary to popular belief, Wahhabism is not the mother of al Qaeda or the Taliban. Nevertheless, it violates human rights, denies freedom and democracy. The Wahhabi-run Saudi Arabia is much more regressive and repressive than the Iranian theocracy under ayatollahs. It was primarily an anti-Turkish Arab nationalist movement. Muhammad ibn Abd al Wahhab (1703–1792), an Islamic scholar, was the founder of the new and purified version of Sunni Islam. He emphasized strict monotheism, prohibiting showing excessive reverence to the Prophet and saints. In 1740, al-Wahhab met Muhammad bin Saud, a tribal chief in Nejd (Central Arabia), and they made a pledge to implement al-Wahhab's teachings in Arabia, and agreed that while Ibn Saud and his family would remain the temporal leaders, al-Wahhab would retain the spiritual leadership of the movement. They challenged the Ottoman hegemony in Arabia, but were almost decisively defeated by the Turks in early 19th century.[93]

However, after about a century's hibernation, from 1902 onward the Wahhabis started gaining ground and after capturing most areas in the Arabian Peninsula in 1932, they established the Kingdom of Saudi Arabia. With the discovery of oil in the 1930s, gradually the poverty-stricken backward kingdom emerged as a welfare state. It has the largest oil and sixth largest gas reserve in the world. However, due to mass illiteracy and lack of any technological skill up to early 1970s, Saudi Arabia heavily depended on Western—mainly American—technocrats for mining, refining, and marketing its oil and gas, and in the overall infrastructure development of the country.[94] Minority Shiite communities enjoy inferior rights and non-Muslims (foreigners) cannot build churches, temples, or synagogues and cannot legally enter the Holy Cities of Mecca and Medina. The Saudi autocracy, run by a few thousand members of an extended family and friendly tribesmen, projects itself as the Custodian of the Two Holy Mosques in Mecca and Medina for legitimacy from its subjects. However, there are dissidents in the country who want to overthrow the Saudi regime.[95]

The presence of strong anti-Saudi dissident groups is self evident in the rise of a Saudi national, Osama bin Laden, as the chief of al Qaeda. It is noteworthy that many Saudi nationals have been funding Islamist militant groups in various countries, including the Taliban. Again, 15 (of a total of 19) of the 9/11 terrorists were Saudi nationals. And we know al Qaeda is not under Saudi control; it aims at going beyond implementing the strict Shariah code a la Saudi Arabia or Afghanistan under Taliban rule. While Saudi rulers—possibly with the exception of King Faisal (1964–1975)—have been pro-American, al Qaeda is avowedly anti-American and anti-Saudi as well. Many Saudi nationals have strong dislike for America. The U.S. invasion of Iraq led to some Wahhabi clerics' declaration of jihad against America.[96] Despite the generosity of the Royal Family, which runs a tax-free welfare state, the 40 percent youth unemployment rate does not bode well for the future of the kingdom and its ties with America.[97]

Meanwhile, Saudi Arabia is going through lots of changes since the Iranian Revolution and pro-Khomeini militants' taking over the grand mosque of Mecca in 1979. The Saudi rulers thought that their generous support for the Afghan jihad against Soviet Union would boost their power and legitimacy but it backfired soon after the Soviet withdrawal from Afghanistan. The Afghan jihad absorbed more than 20,000 Saudi young men. They had been with Osama bin Laden, who later formed al Qaeda. Most of them after the jihad returned to Saudi Arabia. In August 1990, Iraq invaded Kuwait and the Saudi government allowed American and allied troops into Saudi Arabia to fight the Iraqi occupation army in Kuwait. Although a section of Wahhabi clerics approved of Western troops into Saudi Arabia, many of them were dead against any Western troop mobilization in the kingdom.[98]

However, more than two decades after the liberation of Kuwait, there are still thousands of American troops in Saudi Arabia. Apparently, the presence of American troops in Saudi Arabia was bin Laden's casus belli against America, Saudi Arabia, and their allies. As the Saudi dynasty badly needs American troops to defend itself from Sunni and Shiite dissidents, so does America need a friendly regime in a country having the largest known oil reserve in the world. America's safest bet in the Gulf is to go for preserving the status quo to avert any revolutionary regime change in the region. America's pro-regime change policies in Iran and Syria and its opposition to similar changes in friendly Saudi Arabia and Bahrain will further destabilize the region. Nevertheless, in the wake of the Arab Spring, no Arab country seems immune to revolutionary changes. Iran, having well-entrenched position in Iraq and Syria, is not necessarily going to be the main beneficiary of these changes as more avowedly anti-Shiite Islamists might come to power in countries around Iran. As Hugh Eakin observes, while Saudi Arabia has been using its influence in the Gulf Cooperation Council, an alliance of Gulf monarchies, "to pull together support for the beleaguered royal houses of Morocco and Jordan," the White House has remained silent. He blames the U.S. for only caring about oil security, stability, and counterterrorism, not human rights violations by Saudi Arabia.[99] One may agree with Eakin that, "With continued oil and U.S. backing, it [Saudi Arabia] may continue to do so for years to come. But as soon as Saudis start to believe that the promise is no longer being kept…then the future for the Al Saud may be precarious."[100]

Jihad in the West, in the "Lands of the Infidel"

Islamist extremists and jihadists are not only actively engaged in preaching their intolerant ideas in the Muslim world and in countries such as India, Thailand, Philippines, Kenya, Ethiopia, and other Afro-Asian countries with substantial Muslim population, but they are also espousing the cause of jihad in the West, especially in West European countries such as Britain, France, Germany, the Netherlands, Sweden, Norway, and Denmark. There is a huge Muslim diaspora in West Europe countries, which have very liberal immigration and asylum laws. Of late, West Europe has witnessed several Islamist terrorist attacks in London, Madrid, and elsewhere. Throughout West Europe, attacks on individuals for their alleged blasphemies against Islam and its Prophet are not that uncommon. The nearly coordinated and simultaneous attacks on trains in Madrid (2004) and London (2005), the killing of a Dutch filmmaker in 2004, the Cartoon Riots in Denmark, riots in French suburbs in 2005, and rallies of Islamist radicals and jihadists on the street in major European cities may be mentioned as examples.

As indicated in Chapter 3, children of Muslim immigrants, who were born in Europe, have been the main participants in jihadist terrorism in Europe. Several studies reveal that about 80 percent of new recruits of jihadists in West Europe are children of immigrants. There has been an increasing trend of extremism among the youth in Muslim diasporas in Europe. The U.S. and Canada are not immune to this trend where children of the first generation immigrants join jihadist networks. A U.S.-born Major Nidal Hassan—son of a Palestinian immigrant—who killed several American soldiers at Fort Hood, Texas, in 2009 exemplifies that America is not immune to homegrown Islamist terror or jihad as terrorists love to glorify their crime. Problems of Palestine, Iraq, Afghanistan or Pakistan, and U.S. and West European domestic and foreign policies have been the main concerns of the alienated Muslim youths in the West. These nowhere-men pose potential threats to most Western nations, especially the U.S., Canada, Britain, France, and Germany.[101] Another American-born jihadist Anwar Awlaki waged his jihad against America and got killed in the U.S. drone attack in Yemen in September 2011.

We just cannot ignore the following facts, which might pose security threats to the West, as mere Islamophobic propaganda: (a) the Muslim diaspora in Europe is the largest diaspora community in the EU; (b) Muslim immigrants and their children—20 million strong—are the least integrated people in Europe; (c) they have the highest population growth rate in France, Germany, and the U.K.—more than three times the national average; (d) by 2050, Muslims will constitute 20 percent of EU population.[102] We may look into a recent investigative report in a British daily which highlights the growing jihadist threat in Britain. Some alienated jihadists, such as Anjem Choudary from Pakistan, are publicly propagating the cause of jihad against the West, and by taking full advantage of the freedom of expression in the West, they are asking their followers to defy Western law, strive for Shariah, and even kill leaders such as President Obama, Prime Minister Cameron, and leaders in Egypt and Pakistan.[103]

Conclusions

To understand the future of global jihad we must look beyond the precarious stability that prevails in Saudi Arabia and the Gulf monarchies. These countries do not provide good examples of durable peace in the Muslim world or anywhere. American and NATO security umbrellas are not big enough to protect every autocratic regime in the Muslim world in the long run from the growing wrath and disenchantment of its own underdogs, millions of underemployed and unemployed youths inspired by Islamist and other radical, anarchist, and nihilist ideas. This is the crux of the issue. Islamism is not an existential threat to modern civilization. As Fuller has argued, the Islamists cannot overpower the West in the foreseeable future, unlike what they did to the Soviet Union by forcing it to pull out of Afghanistan. Islamism is neither monolithic nor is it all about violence. "Islamism includes Osama bin Laden and the Taliban but also moderates and liberals;" however, pushing secularism by the West will not work in the Muslim world. Rather the West should first empower the silent Muslim majority that rejects radicalism and violence. We may share Fuller's optimism: "The result could be political systems both truly Islamist and truly democratic." Given the dire situation in the Muslim world, given the opportunity, Muslims would have embraced some other ideology to improve their lot. There is nothing inherently wrong with Islam or Islamism.[104]

Notes and References

1. Eric Draitser, "Syria, Egypt and Beyond: Unmasking the Muslim Brotherhood," *Counterpunch* (December 13, 2012).
2. Ibid.
3. Tony Cartalucci, "The Geopolitical Reordering of Africa: US Covert Support to Al Qaeda in Northern Mali, France 'Comes to the Rescue,'" *Global Research* (January 15, 2013).
4. Fawaz A. Gerges, *Journey of the Jihadist: Inside Muslim Militancy* (New York: Harcourt, Inc., 2006), p. 37.
5. Abigail Hauslohner and Andrew Lee Butters, "The Brotherhood," *Time* (February 21, 2011); Jamie Dean, "What's in a Name?" *World Magazine* (February 12, 2011).
6. Asef Bayat, "Egypt, and the Post-Islamist Middle East," *openDemocracy* (February 8, 2011). Available at: http://www.opendemocracy.net/print/57934?utm_source=feedblitz&utm_medium=FeedBlit... (accessed on February 9, 2011).
7. Christopher Dickey and Babak Dehghanpisheh, "Inside the Brotherhood," *Newsweek* (February 14, 2011); "Clarifying the Muslim Brotherhood" (February 2, 2011). Available at: http://www.ikhwanweb.com/print.php?id=27979 (accessed on February 10, 2011).
8. National Commission on Terrorist Attacks, *The 9/11 Commission Report: Final Report of the National Commission on Terrorist Attacks Upon the United States* (Authorized Edition) (New York: W. W. Norton & Company, 2004), *Christian Science Monitor* (February 18, 2011), pp. 53–54.
9. Ibid., pp. 129–130.
10. Fawaz A. Gerges, *Journey of the Jihadist: Inside Muslim Militancy* (New York: Harcourt, Inc., 2006), p. 37.

11. Richard P. Mitchell, *The Society of the Muslim Brothers* (New York: Oxford University Press, 1993), passim; Brynjar Lia, *The Society of the Muslim Brothers in Egypt: The Rise of an Islamic Mass Movement, 1928–1942* (Ithaca, New York: Ithaca Press, 2006), p. 53; Jeffrey Herf, *Nazi Propaganda for the Arab World* (New Haven: Yale University Press, 2009); Lawrence Davidson, *Islamic Fundamentalism* (West Port: Greenwood Press, 1998), pp. 77–78.

12. Sayyid Qutb, *Milestones* (Chicago: Kazi Publications, 1964), pp. 11–21, 45–46,60–62, 70–72, 82–91; Paul Berman, "The Philosopher of Islamic Terror," *New York Times* (March 23, 2003); Robert Irwin, "Is This the Man who Inspired Bin Laden?" *Guardian* (October 31, 2001); Daniel Burns, "Said Qutb on the Arts in America," *Current Trends in Islamist Ideology* (November 18, 2009), Vol. 9.

13. Natana J. Delong-Bas, *Wahhabi Islam: From Revival and Reform to Global Jihad* (New York: Oxford University Press, 2004), pp. 218–265.

14. "British Marxist Writer Tariq Ali's Interview," *Outlook Magazine* (April 23, 2012). Available at: http://www.outlookindia.com/printarticle.aspx?280564 (accessed on May 21, 2012).

15. Bruce Riedel, "Don't Fear Egypt's Muslim Brotherhood," *Daily Beast* (January 27, 2011). Available at: http://www.thedailybeast.com/articles/2011/01/27/muslim-brotherhood-could-win-in-egypt-protests-and-why-obama-shouldnt-worry.html?cid=bs:archive1 (accessed on May 22, 2012).

16. Anthony Martin, "Does Carter's Statement on the Muslim Brotherhood Miss the Point?" *The Examiner* (February 27, 2011). Available at: http://www.examiner.com/article/does-carter-s-statement-on-the-muslim-brotherhood-miss-the-point (accessed on May 22, 2012).

17. "Truth or Consequences—The Two Faces of the Muslim Brotherhood. Part Two," *The Inquisitr* (April 14, 2012). Available at: http://www.inquisitr.com/219967/truth-or-consequences-the-two-faces-of-the-muslim-brotherhood-part-two/ (accessed on May 22, 2012).

18. Marwan Bishara, "Islam Cannot Always Be Blamed: It Appears Islam Is Not an Appropriate Scapegoat after All" (January 19, 2010). Available at: http://www.ikhwanweb.com/article.php?id=22699 (accessed on May 15, 2012).

19. Al-Nas TV, Egypt (May 1, 2012, 04:18). Available at: http://www.memritv.org/clip/en/3431.htm (accessed on December 7, 2013); BBC News "Muslim Brotherhood Sets up New Party Mohammed al-Mursi Insisted the New Party Would Not be Theocratic" (April 30, 2011). Available at: http://www.bbc.co.uk/news/world-middle-east-13249434 (accessed on December 7, 2013).

20. Raymond Ibrahim, "The Evils of the Muslim Brotherhood: Evidence Keeps Mounting," *Middle East Forum* (June 25, 2012). Available at: http://www.meforum.org/3272/muslim-brotherhood-evils (accessed on June 26, 2012).

21. Nathan J. Brown, "Egypt and Islamic Sharia: A Guide for the Perplexed," *Carnegie Endowment* (May 15, 2012). Available at: http://carnegieendowment.org/2012/05/15/egypt-and-islamic-sharia-guide-for-perplexed/argb (accessed on May 17, 2012).

22. "Syria's Muslim Brotherhood Is Gaining Influence over Anti-Assad Revolt," *Washington Post* (May 12, 2012).
23. Eric Draitser, "Syria, Egypt and Beyond: Unmasking the Muslim Brotherhood," *Counterpunch* (December 13, 2012).
24. Available at: http://www.fas.org/irp/world/para/mb.htm (accessed on February 24, 2013).
25. Max Fisher, "Mohamed Morsi's Strange Gamble on Iran and Ahmadinejad," *Washington Post* (February 5, 2013).
26. "Kerry Says Egypt's Military Was 'Restoring Democracy' in Ousting Morsi," *New York Times* (August 2, 2013).
27. Raymond Ibrahim, "Muslim Brotherhood: 'Impose Islam…Step by Step,'" *Middle East Forum* (June 26, 2012). Available at: http://www.meforum.org/2995/muslim-brotherhood-impose-islam (accessed on June 26, 2012).
28. Eric Trager, "The Unbreakable Muslim Brotherhood: Grim Prospects for a Liberal Egypt," *Foreign Affairs* (September/October 2011).
29. Eric Trager, "The Muslim Brotherhood's Long Game: Egypt's Ruling Party Plots its Path to Power," *Foreign Affairs* (July 5, 2012).
30. Seyyed Vali Reza Nasr, *The Vanguard of the Islamic Revolution: The Jamaat-I Islami of Pakistan* (Berkeley: University of California Press, 1994), pp. 3–27, 47–80, 103–147.
31. Available at: http://www.youtube.com/watch?v+763DfYwyyKQ&sns+em (accessed on December 7, 2013).
32. Oliver Roy, *The Failure of Political Islam* (London: I.B. Tauris Publishers, 1994), pp. 129–130.
33. Abul A'la Maududi, *Haqiqat-i-Jihad [The Reality of Jihad]* (Lahore: Taj Company Ltd, 1964), p. 64.
34. Abul A'la Maududi, *The Meaning of the Qur'an* (Lahore: Islamic Publications Ltd, 1993), Vol. 2, pp. 183, 186.
35. Graham E. Fuller, *The Future of Political Islam* (New York: Palgrave-Macmillan, 2004), pp. 33–36.
36. John Mintz and Douglas Farah, "In Search of Friends among the Foes: US Hopes to Work with Diverse Group," *Washington Post* (September 11, 2004).
37. Available at: http://www.jamaat-e-islami.org/en/aboutus.php (accessed on February 24, 2013).
38. *Kaler Kantho* (Bengali daily) (February 24, 2013).
39. Samir Amin, "Political Islam in the Service of Imperialism," *Monthly Review*, Vol. 59, No. 7 (December 2007).
40. Ibid.
41. Peter Bergen, *Holy War, Inc: Inside the Secret World of Osama Bin Laden* (New York: Free Press, 2001), pp. 195–235; Mark Sageman, *Understanding Terror Networks* (Philadelphia: University of Pennsylvania Press, 2004), passim and *Leaderless Jihad: Terror Networks in the Twenty-First Century* (Philadelphia: University of Pennsylvania Press, 2008), passim; Bruce Hoffman, *Inside Terrorism* (New York: Columbia University Press, 2006), passim.

42. *9/11 Commission Report*, pp. 55–58; Peter Bergen, *The Osama bin Laden I know: An Oral History of al Qaeda's Leader* (New York: Free Press, 2006), p. 75.

43. Jonathon White, *Terrorism & Homeland Security* (Belmont, California: Wadsworth, 2012), p. 381.

44. *9/11 Commission Report*, pp. 53–54.

45. Jonathon White, *Terrorism & Homeland Security* (Belmont, California: Wadsworth, 2012) pp. 382–389.

46. Ibid.

47. Ibid.

48. "Afrighanistan? The Real Danger Is That the World Turns Its Back on Another Poor Place Threatened by Jihadists," *The Economist* (January 26, 2013). Available at: http://www.economist.com/news/leaders/21570704-real-danger-world-turns-its-back-another-poor-place-threatened/comments (accessed on January 19, 2014).

49. Anissa Haddadi, "Al Qaeda and the FARC in Drug Alliance," *International Business Times* (November 16, 2011).

50. CCTV and CNN News (June 18, 2012).

51. "Unrest in Yemen: Southern Grumps," *The Economist* (April 13, 2013). Available at: http://www.economist.com/news/middle-east-and-africa/21576113-which-worse-north-southern-secession-or-al-qaeda-southern-grumps (accessed on January 19, 2014).

52. Anti-Defamation League, "Boko Haram: The Emerging Jihadist Threat in West Africa" (December 12, 2011). Available at: http://www.adl.org/combating-hate/international-extremism-terrorism/c/boko-haram-jihadist-threat-africa.html (accessed on February 10, 2013); BBC News, "Who Are Nigeria's Boko Haram Islamists?" (January 11, 2012). Available at: http://www.bbc.co.uk/news/world-africa-13809501 (accessed on February 10, 2013); Andrew Walker, "What Is Boko Haram?" (May 2012), Special Report of the US Institute of Peace. Available at: http://www.usip.org/publications/what-boko-haram (accessed on February 10, 2013).

53. "Al Qaeda Ties Seen for Nigeria Group," *Wall Street Journal* (August 13, 2011). Available at: http://online.wsj.com/article/SB10001424053111904332804576540501936480880.html (accessed on February 10, 2013); Habeeb I. Pindiga, With Agency Report, "Nigeria: Boko Haram Training Camps Found in Mali," *Daily Trust* (February 6, 2013). Available at: http://allafrica.com/stories/201302060749.html (accessed on February 10, 2013); "Afrighanistan," *The Economist* (January 26, 2013).

54. Edward Cody, "In Mali, an Islamist Extremist Haven Takes Shape," *Washington Post* (June 7, 2012).

55. Eric Draitser, "Mali, Al Qaeda, and the US Neo-Colonial Agenda," *Global Research* (July 16, 2012). Available at: http://www.globalresearch.ca/ (accessed on December 7, 2013).

56. Ibid.

57. VoA News (June 7, 2012). Available at: http://blogs.voanews.com/breaking-news/2012/06/07/ (accessed on December 7, 2013).

58. "Secession in Mali: An Unholy Alliance," *The Economist* (June 2, 2012).

59. Paul Rogers, "The Thinning World: Mali, Nigeria, India," *openDemocracy* (July 12, 2012). Available at: http://www.opendemocracy.net/paul-rogers/thinning-world-mali-nigeria-india (accessed on July 12, 2012).

60. "Jihad in Africa: The Danger in the Desert," *The Economist* (January 26, 2013).

61. *New York Times* (September 12, 2012).

62. Sebastian Elischer, "After Mali Comes Niger," *Foreign Affairs* (February 12, 2013).

63. Matthew Bey and Sim Tack, "The Rise of a New Nigerian Militant Group," Stratfor: Global Intelligence (February 21, 2013). Available at: http://www.stratfor.com/weekly/risenewnigerianmilitantgroup?utm_source=freelistf&utm_medium=email&utm_campaign=20130221&utm_term=sweekly&utm_content=title&elq=42ecd02aa31e4a8d887b7f9820d62ae1 (accessed on December 7, 2013).

64. Ibid.

65. BBC News, "Algerian Group Backs al Qaeda" (October 23, 2003); Islamism, Violence and Reform in Algeria, International Crisis Group Report (July 30, 2004).

66. Craig Whitlock, "Al-Qaeda's Far-Reaching New Partner: Salafist Group Finds Limited Appeal in Its Native Algeria," *Washington Post* (October 5, 2006).

67. Craig Whitlock, "U.S. Expands Secret Intelligence Operations in Africa," *Washington Post* (June 13, 2012).

68. Matthew Bey and Sim Tack, "The Rise of a New Nigerian Militant Group."

69. Jonathan R. White, *Terrorism and Homeland Security* (Belmont, California: Wadsworth, 2012), pp. 231–237.

70. *Washington Post* (March 23, 2012); "Pentagon Prepares Military Operation in Mali," *Global Research* (December 25, 2012); Ernst Wolff and Alex Lantier, "France Launches War in Northern Mali" (January 14, 2013). Available at: http://www.wsws.org/en/articles/2013/01/14/mali-j14.html (accessed on February 10, 2013); Tony Catalucci, "The Geopolitical Reordering of Africa: US Covert Support to Al Qaeda in Northern Mali, France 'Comes to the Rescue,'" *Global Research* (January 15, 2013). Available at: http://www.globalresearch.ca/geopolitical-reordering-and-dirty-tricks-us-covert-support-to-al-qaeda-in-northern-mali-france-comes-to-the-rescue/5318614 (accessed on February 10, 2013); Nicola Nasser, "Qatar, Sponsor of Islamist Political Movement, Major Ally of America," *Global Research* (January 23, 2013). Available at: http://www.globalresearch.ca/qatar-sponsor-of-islamist-political-movements-major-ally-of-america/5320105 (accessed on February 10, 2013).

71. Seth G. Jones, "Think Again: Al Qaeda—A Year after Osama bin Laden's Death, the Obituaries for His Terrorist Group Are Still Too Premature," *Foreign Policy* (May/June 2012), pp. 47–48.

72. Ahmed Rashid, *Pakistan on the Brink: The Future of America, Pakistan, and Afghanistan* (New York: Viking Penguin, 2012), p. 4.

73. Seth G. Jones, "Think Again: Al Qaeda—A Year after Osama bin Laden's Death, the Obituaries for His Terrorist Group Are Still Too Premature."

74. Ehsan Ahrari commented on "Al-Qaida versus the Arab Awakening: The Muslim World's Past and Future," Strategic Paradigms, comment posted May 7, 2011. Available at: http://www.ehsanahrari.com/2011/05/07/al-qaida-versus-the-arab-awakening-muslim-world's-past-and-future/ (accessed on July 4, 2012).

75. Mark Mazzetti, "19 U.S. Diplomatic Missions to Stay Closed This Week over Threat," *New York Times* (August 5, 2013).

76. Ibid.; Agence France-Presse, *US Extends Closure of Mideast Missions over Qaeda Fear* (August 5, 2013). Available at: http://www.globalpost.com/dispatch/news/afp/130805/us-extends-closure-mideast-missions-over-qaeda-fear (accessed on August 5, 2013).

77. "With Embassy Closures, the U.S. Errs on the Side of Caution," Stratfor: Global Intelligence. Available at: http://www.stratfor.com/analysis/embassy-closures-us-errs-side-caution (accessed on August 5, 2013).

78. AFP, "Interpol Suspects Al-Qaeda in Recent Jailbreaks" (August 3, 2013). Available at: http://www.foxnews.com/world/2013/08/03/interpol-suspects-al-qaeda-in-recent-jailbreaks/ (accessed on August 5, 2013); CNN News (August 5, 2013).

79. Frederick W. Kagan, Statement before the House Committee on Foreign Affairs Subcommittee on Terrorism, Nonproliferation, and Trade on "Global al-Qaeda: Affiliates, Objectives, and Future Challenges: The Continued Expansion of Al Qaeda Affiliates and their Capabilities" (July 18, 2013). Available at: http://foreignaffairs.house.gov/hearing/subcommittee-hearing-global-al-qaeda-affiliates-objectives-and-future-challenges (accessed on December 7, 2013).

80. President Jimmy Carter's Interview with Piers Morgan, CNN (February 21, 2013).

81. Angus McDowall, "Iran Nuke Unlikely to Start Mideast Arms Race: Report," Reuters (February 20, 2013). Available at: http://mobile.reuters.com/article/idUSBRE91J0G820130220?irpc=932 (accessed on February 21, 2013).

82. Vali Nasr, *The Shia Revival: How Conflicts within Islam Will Shape the Future* (New York: W.W. Norton & Company, 2006), Chapters 1 and 2.

83. Ibid., pp. 119–146.

84. Oliver Roy, "Enigma of the Uprising: Foucault and Iran," *Vacarme*, Vol. 29 (2004). Available at: http://www.vacarme.org/article1366.html (accessed on 2 June, 2013).

85. Ibid.

86. Ibid., pp. 185–226.
87. HNN Staff, "What Is the Difference between Sunni and Shiite Muslims—and Why Does It Matter?" History News Network (September 9, 2002). Available at: http://hnn.us/articles/934.html (accessed on February 15, 2011).
88. *Foreign Policy*, Morning Brief (June 13, 2012). Available at: http://www.google.com/#q=Foreign+Policy%2C+Morning+Brief%2C+June+13%2C+2012 (accessed on January 19, 2014).
89. Michel Chossudovsky, "Confronting Iran, 'Protecting Israel': The Real Reason for America's War on Syria," *Global Research* (June 8, 2012). Available at: http://www.globalresearch.ca/confronting-iran-protecting-israel-the-real-reason-for-america-s-war-on-syria (accessed on December 7, 2013).
90. "Sheikh Al-Habib Calls for a Shia Uprising in the Greater Gulf Region" (February 2, 2012). Available at: https://www.youtube.com/watch?v=zHtb1Y5OmFg&feature=related (accessed on June 12, 2012).
91. Huma Yusuf, Sectarian Violence: Pakistan's Greatest Security Threat? (July 2012), Report of the Norwegian Peace-Building Resource Centre (NOREF); Hassan Abbas, "Shiism and Sectarian Conflict in Pakistan: Identity Politics, Iranian Influence, and Tit-for-Tat Violence" (September 2010), Occasional Paper, Combating Terrorism Center, Washington, D.C.
92. "Afghan Taliban Reportedly Sends Delegation to Iran for Talks," CBS News (June 3, 2013). Available at: http://www.cbsnews.com/news/afghan-taliban-reportedly-sends-delegation-to-iran-for-talks/ (accessed on December 7, 2013).
93. Alfred Felix et al., "History of Arabia," *Encyclopaedia Britannica* (online). Available at: http://www.britannica.com/EBchecked/topic/31568/history-of-Arabia (accessed on February 11, 2013).
94. William Ochsenwald, *The Middle East: A History* (New York: McGraw Hill, 2004), p. 700.
95. Robert Fisk, "Saudis Mobilise Thousands of Troops to Quell Growing Revolt," *The Independent* (March 5, 2011); BBC News, "Saudi Arabia Accused of Repression after Arab Spring" (December 1, 2011). Available at: http://www.bbc.co.uk/news/world-middle-east-15977980 (accessed on February 11, 2013).
96. *Frontline*, "House of Saud," PBS TV (February 8, 2005). Available at: http://www.pbs.org/wgbh/pages/frontline/shows/saud/.
97. Ellen Knickmeyer, "Idle Kingdom," *Foreign Policy* (July 19, 2012); Hugh Eakin, "Will Saudi Arabia Ever Change?" *The New York Review* (January 10, 2013).
98. Thomas Hegghammer, *Jihad in Saudi Arabia: Violence and Pan-Islamism since 1979* (Cambridge: Cambridge University Press, 2010), Chapters. 4–8.
99. Hugh Eakin, "Will Saudi Arabia Ever Change?" *The New York Review* (January 2013). Available at: http://www.nybooks.com/articles/archives/2013/jan/10/will-saudi-arabia-ever-change/?pagination=false (accessed on February 24, 2014).

100. Ibid.
101. Sedat Laciner, "Identity and Terror in Western European Muslim Diasporas," *The Journal of Turkish Weekly* (June 2009). Available at: http://www.turkishweekly.net/news/80105/identity-and-terror-in-western-european-muslim-diasporas.html (accessed on February 24, 2014); Jerrold M. Post and Gabriel Shaffer, "The Risk of Radicalization and Terrorism in US Muslim Communities," *The Brown Journal of World Affairs*, Vol. XIII, No. 2 (2007); Robert S. Leiken, "Europe's Mujahedeen: Where Muslim Mass Immigration Meets Global Terrorism," Backgrounder, Center for Immigration Studies, Harvard University (April 2005).
102. Robert S. Leiken, "Europe's Mujahedeen: Where Muslim Mass Immigration Meets Global Terrorism."
103. "Claim Jobseeker's Allowance and Plan Holy War: Hate Preacher Pocketing £25,000 a Year in Benefits Calls on Fanatics to Live off the State," *Daily Mail* (February 17, 2013). Available at: http://www.dailymail.co.uk/news/article-2279972/Anjem-Choudary-Hate-preacher-pocketing-25-000-year-benefits-calls-fanatics-live-state.html (accessed on February 17, 2013).
104. Michel Chossudovsky, "Hidden US-Israeli Military Agenda: 'Break Syria into Pieces,'" *Global Research* (June 16, 2012). Available at: http://www.globalresearch.ca/index.php?context=va&aid=31454 (accessed on December 7, 2013); Scott Taylor, "Syria Strategy Looks like Bloody Repeat," *Global Research* (June 18, 2012). Available at: http://www.globalresearch.ca/index.php?context=va&aid=31476 (accessed on June 22, 2012).

6

The Eye of the Storm: "Jihad" and Proxy Wars in South Asia

The jihad in Kashmir will soon spread to entire India. Our Mujahideen will create three Pakistans in India. We feel that Kashmir should be liberated at the earliest. Therefore, Indian Muslims should be aroused to rise in revolt against the Indian Union so that India gets disintegrated.

Hafiz Muhammad Saeed, Founder of the LeT

Thanks to Barack Obama and the killing of Osama bin Laden, it is now clear that Pakistan is in the very eye of the storm.... You couldn't truly fight terror while working with Pakistan, the greatest shelter for terrorists.

Bernard-Henri Levy, Author of *American Vertigo*, 2007

Overview

This chapter appraises transnational jihad, narco-jihad, proxy wars, and crime–terror nexus across Afghanistan and Pakistan, and Pakistan and India. Of late, narco-Islamist terror nexus has emerged as the new threat to transnational security within and beyond South Asia. The transnational drug–terror–Islamist nexuses in northwestern South Asia are parts of the new Great Game between America and two superpowers, Russia and China, and the perennial India–Pakistan conflict. The drug–terror–Islamist nexuses have links with al Qaeda, Taliban, LeT, and other Islamist outfits committed to the establishment of a transnational caliphate in South and Central Asia. This is an appraisal of the rise of political Islam in Pakistan and Afghanistan—by design and default, respectively—in historical, contemporary, and futuristic perspectives, with special reference to American role in the rise of Islamist extremism, Islamist–West conflict, and its long-term impact on America's relations with South Asia in general, Pakistan and Afghanistan in particular. Last but not least, this is also an appraisal of the long-term impact of the ongoing proxy wars between India and Pakistan in Afghanistan, and India and Pakistan's mutual promotion of terrorists and insurgents to bleed each other. While there are evidences of Pakistani sponsorship of Islamist and separatist groups, who have been attacking and killing innocent civilians in India on a regular basis, there are similar evidences of Indian sponsorship of terrorist groups against Pakistan. The important questions to be raised are: (a) will superpowers such as the U.S., Russia, and China refrain from sponsoring their client states/groups to use them against each other or against the least favored countries/regimes in South Asia? and (b) will India, Pakistan, and Afghanistan resolve their mutual differences and help contain religious and secular extremist groups by ensuring good governance, equal opportunities, human rights, and human dignity to minority and marginalized communities?

South Asia in the Shadows of Anarchy

Rogue states and rogue elements in government machinery along with non-state actors can destabilize neighboring countries and countries beyond a particular region. In South Asia, Islamist terror networks, drugs, and arms syndicates pose the main transnational threat to countries within and beyond the region. Various global, regional, and local factors contribute to the rise of Islamist extremism and drug mafias in South Asia. Bad governance and leaders' opportunistic use of mafias and terrorist groups against neighboring countries in proxy wars have been the main destabilizing factors in South Asia. The last decade of the Cold War (1980–1990) witnessed the large-scale reliance on drug mafias and Islamist terror networks—glorified as Mujahedeen—in and around Afghanistan by countries within and beyond South Asia, especially by Pakistan and America. The so-called War on Terror has further intensified transnational crime and insurgencies across the Afghan borders. The

Western promotion of Tajik and Uzbek warlords and criminals against the Taliban and al Qaeda elements, mainly manned by Pashtun tribesmen, has not only kept the decades-old ethno-national conflicts alive but has also forced the Taliban to forge ties with transnational drug-lords and Mafias. NATO and ISAF troops' controversial support and even promotion of opium cultivation and drug trafficking along Afghan borders have also promoted transnational drug trafficking, and paradoxically strengthened the narco-jihadist networks in the entire region.[1]

Ever since the beginning of the drug-Islamist nexus in South Asia, analysts have coined the expressions narco-Islamism and narco-jihad to denote a new type of transnational crime and insurgency. Ehsan Ahrari believes that a narco-jihad is being funded by the opium-related system of trade in Afghanistan and Pakistan and that in Pakistan the strength of the narco-jihad is still growing. He imputes the sustained growth in narco-jihad activities to the iron triangle of warlords, corrupt government officials, and the Taliban–al Qaeda nexus in Afghanistan.[2] Unilateral U.S. drone attacks and military action in the subregion will not prevent the region from becoming a safe house for transnational terrorists. The only way to defeat the terrorists is to starve them of the opium cash. American troops' withdrawal from Afghanistan will be as disastrous as American unilateral military action in the subregion. However, America has already decided on ending its longest war and is keen on engaging the Taliban. Meanwhile, Pakistan has emerged as the most important country for the wrong reasons: extensive terror attacks on Pakistani military, law-enforcers and civilians, ISI's promotion of Kashmiri and Pashtun insurgents, sectarian killings, and insurgency in the northwest.

The Soviet invasion of Afghanistan in 1979 turned into a frontline state for a decade. After 9/11, it again became the most important country for America and its allies, first to fight the Taliban and then to restore order in Afghanistan. While during the resistance against Soviet Union, jihad and mujahedeen were terms of endearment in Washington; not long after the end of the jihad, both jihad and mujahedeen became the most repugnant expressions in the West. While the Taliban takeover and the consequential violations of human rights in Afghanistan were shocking to the West, the Taliban's harboring of al Qaeda leaders was the proverbial last straw for Afghanistan. However, soon after the overthrow of the Taliban regime in Afghanistan, thanks to Pakistan-based Taliban, LeT, Taliban of Pakistan or

Pakistani Taliban or Tehrik-e-Taliban Pakistan (TTP), and other Islamist terror groups' activities, mainly across the border in Afghanistan and India and even Europe and America, Pakistan reemerged as the most important country for America. The bogey of Islamist takeover of Pakistan and/or the possible acquisition of Pakistan's nuclear arsenal by extremist elements have further alarmed America and its allies. The ISI's running an invisible government, which is more powerful than the one run by civilians, and its alleged promotion of Islamist terror groups to bleed India, Afghanistan, and even American and NATO troops within and outside Pakistan are important issues in this regard.

While some Muslim clerics wanted liberal Islam as the state ideology of Pakistan, some Deoband clerics and the JI, among others, wanted total Islamization of Pakistan. Some extremist Wahhabi clerics promoted the extremist *Ahl-e-Hadis* (people of the Hadis) sect. Some radical Islamist terror groups, such as the LeT in Pakistan and the HUJI-B or the Movement for Jihad-Bangladesh and the JMB or the Party of Mujahedeen Bangladesh, are offshoots of the *Ahl-e-Hadis* branch of Indian Wahhabism. Pakistan government proscribed the LeT in 2002, and in Bangladesh, due to stern government measures, Islamist extremists groups, the HUJI-B, and JMB in particular are not posing any immediate threat to the country since 2007.[3] However, due to rampant corruption, bad governance, and sharp polarization between secular and Islam-loving political parties, Bangladesh is neither politically nor economically that stable. Thus, one cannot rule out the reemergence of Islamist extremist forces in the country, as they breed and multiply in politically instable and economically vulnerable societies.[4]

The polity of Pakistan is also sharply polarized between the rich and powerful English-educated elite and the not-so-rich and powerful vernacular elite. Thanks to General Zia ul-Haq's Islamization and vernacularization programs, the English-educated elite's monopoly in government jobs, including the armed forces, has eroded; and Islamic ethos, including the prohibition on alcohol, has been pervasive throughout the country. The Islamization process has also influenced the education system. Under the rabid state-sponsored Islamization process, governments and regimes seem to be in competition with each other to prove their love for Islam. While the first two military rulers did not promote Islamism for legitimacy, Zia ul-Haq (1977–1988) assiduously promoted Islamism, and Musharraf (1999–2008) exploited Islamism to neutralize politicians in the northwestern subregion.[5]

The separation of Bangladesh made Pakistani rulers nervous about further disintegration of the country on ethno-national lines. Consequently, Pakistan's secular–socialist Prime Minister Zulfikar Ali Bhutto (1972–1977) started the rapid Islamization of the country, so much so that to appease and neutralize Islamist parties, in 1974 his government declared the tiny Ahmadiyya community (also known as the Qadiyani) as a non-Muslim minority. The Soviet invasion of Afghanistan in December 1979 came as a windfall for Islam-loving and hardcore Islamists in Pakistan.

The Aftermath of the Afghan "Jihad": New Polarizations and Conflicts in South Asia

Pakistan has been full of surprises since its inception. Although contrary to Jawaharlal Nehru's predictions, Pakistan did not disintegrate and merge with India six months after its emergence, but within 25 years of its existence, it lost its eastern wing (East Pakistan), which emerged as Bangladesh; and within another two decades, the country became one of the most ungovernable and dangerous places in the world. In view of its checkered history of unpleasant surprises for the country itself, its neighbors and others, one can take unpredictability as the main variable for Pakistan. The country went through 32 years of military rule and another 30 odd years of authoritarian, oligarchic democracy, a democratically elected government completed its full-term and was succeeded by another in May 2013 in its history. One may assume that Pakistan will functionally remain a democracy, albeit under the waning influence of the military and feudal aristocracy. Whether Pakistan remains an Islamic garrison state, a civilian illiberal democracy, or transforms itself into a liberal democracy in the coming years are important questions today. However, it appears that in the coming years the Pak-U.S. relationship will remain as awkward and unpredictable as it has been since the U.S.-led invasion of Afghanistan in 2001. Pakistan's identity crisis—"the mother of all conflicts"—is reflected in the state-sponsored Islamization process and the country's hovering between civilian and military rule.

After Zia, General Musharraf's cynical promotion of ultra-orthodox and radical Islamist coalition called the Muttahida Majlis e Amal (MMA) or the

United Council of Action in 2002 (two years after his military takeover of Pakistan) played the most regressive role by further emboldening radical Islamists, who are no longer willing to play the second fiddle in Pakistan's politics. It is noteworthy that the MMA was a coalition of Sunni and Shiite clerics. Interestingly, despite his promotion of Enlightened Moderation or liberal Islam, Musharraf conceded most to Islamist obscurantist forces, not out of conviction but sheer political opportunism.[6]

Since two former Prime Ministers Benazir Bhutto of Pakistan People's Party (PPP) and Nawaz Sharif of Pakistan Muslim League (PML) had been Musharraf's main political adversaries, he restricted their political activities by implicating them in corruption charges, making them incapable of running for office. Musharraf simply ensured the MMA victory in the provincial elections. The MMA formed government in the northwestern provinces of Khyber Pakhtunkhwa and captured second highest number of seats in Sind and Balochistan legislatures. It also captured 58 out of 342 seats in the National Assembly of Pakistan. MMA candidates gave inflammatory speeches through loudspeakers (others were not allowed loudspeakers) in favor of introducing Shariah at public rallies. MMA leaders put a 15-Point Program, which included the revival of fear of God, affection to Prophet Muhammad, and service to people to make Pakistan an Islamic welfare state to ensure justice to people and eradicate corruption; to ensure bread, clothes, shelter, education, jobs, and marriage expenses to all citizens. Last but not least, the MMA urged Pakistanis to fight Western imperialism and support all suppressed people in the world, especially Kashmiris, Palestinians, Afghans, and Chechens.[7]

Soon after forming the government in Khyber Pakhtunkhwa, MMA leaders publicly denounced democracy and General Musharraf for his support of the US-led War on Terror in Afghanistan. The American invasion of Iraq in 2003 further angered the MMA and other Islamists in Pakistan. Musharraf became their worst enemy as a quisling and agent of Imperialism. Within three years of MMA's forming the government in Khyber Pashtunkhwa in 2002, due to internal differences among leaders of the coalition, the MMA was out of power in 2005. Since the MMA was a coalition of Shias and Sunnis, Wahhabis and Barelvis (followers of Sufis Islam), extremist *Ahl-e-Hadis* and transnational Islamists belonging to the JI and promoters of Taliban and al Qaeda militants, its disintegration further intensified sectarian conflicts between Shias and Sunnis, Wahhabis/

Ahl-e-Hadis and *Barelvis*, JI and Wahhabis. Since then, bomb attacks on mosques and gunning down of innocent Shia and Sunni worshippers in different parts of Pakistan became the norm.[8]

Not long after, Islamists attempted on Musharraf's life and started vitriolic campaigns against his government, singling it out as pro-American and anti-Islamic and anti-Pakistan. In July 2007, some radical clerics and their students amassed weapons in the famous Red Mosque of Islamabad. Their vigilantism against prostitution, drinking and massage parlors in the neighborhood of the mosque (female students of a madrassa took leading role in attacks on massage parlors and beauty salons) in the heart of Pakistan's capital city was quite embarrassing for the government. Within days, Musharraf ordered military action against the Red Mosque radicals, which resulted in scores of deaths. This angered Islamists throughout the country and beyond. Even Ayman al Zawahiri issued an order to his followers to wage further attacks on Pakistan government. Not long after the Red Mosque episode, TTP started a reign of terror in parts of Waziristan and Swat. Many Western analysts and even Secretary Hillary Clinton raised alarms about the "impending Taliban takeover" of Islamabad.[9]

Thanks to the systematic and almost non-stop Islamization program Islamist fascists such as the JI and its ilk and umpteen number of Islam-loving and terror outfits committed to Islamize the polity gained enough power and influence in Pakistan to introduce the draconian Shariah law and start the systematic cleansing process by organizing selective and indiscriminate killing of Christians, Shiites, Ahmadiyyas, and other Muslims for their deviant beliefs and alleged anti-Pakistani activities. While the federal government formally declared the tiny Ahmadiyya community non-Muslim, Shiite Pakistanis have been facing the brunt of attacks by Sunni fanatics.

What is alarming is that contrary to the popular assumption and media reports, the organizers and perpetrators of the ongoing pogroms are not "crazy and deranged Muslims." As mullahs consider lesser Muslims as lesser Pakistanis, Sunni fanatics have no qualms about killing Shias, Ahmadiyyas, and other Muslims to cleanse the polity of Pakistan.[10] Islamism is so well entrenched in the country that the average Pakistani Muslim does not know if there is another Islamic or secular alternative to what he/she believes or practices in the name of Islam. Many mullahs believe polio vaccine as yet another Western conspiracy to sterilize Muslim children. The AFP reported from Waziristan in June 2012 that a warlord had imposed a ban on polio vaccination campaign among his people.[11] Parts of northwestern Pakistan have been very volatile due to the Pakistani Taliban-led insurgencies and terrorism since 2007.[12]

In hindsight, one can blame Pakistan for umpteen number of reasons for the prevalent chaos in and around the country, which includes promotion of Islamism, terrorism, insurgencies, and transnational conflicts, proxy wars, and last but not least, violations of human rights of minorities and women. Then again, one cannot only blame Pakistan for the prevalent bad governance, lack of democracy, and the preponderance of the military and Islamist militancy in the country. America not only supported (and promoted to a large extent) all the military dictators and undemocratic regimes in Pakistan since the 1950s, but it also was responsible for the promotion of Islamist parties and militant mujahedeen, even before the 1979 Soviet invasion of Afghanistan. In President Carter's National Security Adviser Zbigniew Brzezinski's own words:

> According to the official version of history, CIA aid to the Mujahedeen began during 1980, that is to say, after the Soviet army invaded Afghanistan, 24 Dec 1979. But the reality, secretly guarded until now, is completely otherwise: Indeed, it was July 3, 1979 that President Carter signed the first directive for secret aid to the opponents of the pro-Soviet regime in Kabul. And that very day, I wrote a note to the president in which I explained to him that in my opinion this aid was going to induce a Soviet military intervention.[13]

It is noteworthy that the day the Soviet Union invaded Afghanistan, Brzezinski wrote to Carter: "We now have the opportunity of giving to the USSR its Vietnam War."[14] He was also candid about having no regrets whatsoever for arming Islamist militants, who later emerged as the Taliban and terrorists, as he thought the collapse of the Soviet Union was more important for the U.S. than the rise of the Taliban.[15] One wonders as to why America since 1980 has been fighting its longest war in Afghanistan, especially in the wake of Soviet withdrawal and the end of the communist threat in the early 1990s. As one analyst observes,

> Afghanistan poses no military threat to the United States. They have no army, air force, or navy with which they could invade the United States. It takes a champion propagandist to make people believe that Afghans constitute a serious military threat to the United States.[16]

However, America's so-called AfPak doctrine has not paid rich dividends. Of late, President Karzai of Afghanistan—supposed to be a U.S. protégé—has become a bitter critic of America's military strategy in Afghanistan. After the U.S. air attacks which killed 10 Afghan civilians, mostly women and children in mid-February 2013, Karzai issued an air-raid ban decree asking the U.S. to stop all air attacks on Afghan territory.[17] This decree was followed by another stern warning by Karzai to the U.S. government. On February 24, Karzai banned American Special Forces from operating in Maidan Wardak province adjacent to Kabul which is seen as a key area in defending the capital from the Taliban, as there have been wide allegations of U.S. Special Forces torturing and killing local Afghans.[18] Despite Obama's keen interest in a negotiated peace with the Taliban, the Karzai government refused to talk with the Taliban at Doha (Qatar) in June 2013 as it was against recognizing the Taliban as custodians of the so-called Islamic Emirate of Afghanistan.[19]

Of late the Pakistan military—which claims to be the most patriotic element and behaves as the most well-organized political party of Pakistan—has been unhappy with America for several reasons. It feels humiliated and violated by America's unauthorized drone/aerial attacks on Pakistan that kill civilians and soldiers. The killing of bin Laden was the last straw. What is most worrisome about Pakistan is the unpredictability of its leaders. The way its politicians and generals forced East Pakistanis to opt out of Pakistan to create Bangladesh by terrorizing, killing, and humiliating Bengalis in the name of national integration of Pakistan in 1971 is an example in this regard. In view of the tradition of Pakistani leaders' thoughtless behavior, one believes they can go to any extent, including waging another war against India or even proliferating nuclear weapons, in the name of saving Pakistan or preserving the glory of Islam. Thus, Pakistan remains the most unpredictable and dangerous nation in the entire Muslim world.

The situation in Afghanistan is far from normal. One may attribute the spectacular rise in terrorist attacks on NATO-ISAF-Afghan troops and civilians in Afghanistan following the Abbottabad Operation (that killed bin Laden) to Pakistan's ISI. In one year, following the death of Osama bin Laden, 367 U.S. troops got killed in Afghanistan.[20] As per Obama–Karzai understanding, the bulk of U.S. and allied troops would leave Afghanistan in 2014, and only some U.S. forces will remain in a post-war Afghanistan as military advisers; but we do not know how many U.S. troops will stay there and for how long.[21] After the bungled peace talk between the Afghan government and Taliban at Doha in June 2013—which President Karzai unfairly imputed to America's faulty diplomacy—one is not sure if peace will ever be negotiated between the Taliban and Afghan government. One is not sure whether America and NATO will withdraw all their troops from Afghanistan or they will keep between 12,000 and 20,000 troops till the end of 2014. The Afghan situation in the event of total Western troop withdrawal looks quite bleak. Afghan soldiers are least likely to resist another Taliban takeover of Afghanistan without Western troops, logistics, air support, and intelligence.[22]

While Afghan military and police are least dependable, Pakistan is likely to emerge as the biggest beneficiary of Western troop withdrawal. Unless India stops playing its old game of destabilizing Pakistan's turbulent Balochistan and tribal areas in the northwest through Afghanistan, India and Pakistan would continue their proxy wars in Afghanistan, Balochistan, FATA, and Indian-occupied Kashmir. More Mumbai (2008) type attacks on Indian cities by Pakistan-based Islamist–narco-jihadist outfits in the coming years cannot be ruled out either.

However, due to the fragile security situation, it is evident that the struggle for power in Afghanistan will not end soon. Thus, the endgame or total U.S. troop withdrawal from the country will not take place by late 2014. American military bases, aircraft, Special Forces, and advisers will remain there at least until the U.S.–Afghan treaty expires in 2024.[23] The main contenders of power in Afghanistan—besides the American-sponsored government—are (a) the not-so-homogeneous Taliban fighters; (b) the Haqqani Group (Pashtun tribesmen under Jalauddin Haqqani and his son) on both sides of the Durand Line; (c) the Northern Alliance or the United Islamic Front for the Salvation of Afghanistan; (d) Pashtun mujahedeen under Gulbuddin Hekmatyar; (e) the Pashtun warlords, especially the group under Gul Agha Sherzai; and, last but not least, (f) the remnants of al Qaeda in the subregion. While the mainstream Taliban wants to capture Kabul and the rest of the country (although they have only around 30 percent of Afghan or two-thirds of the Pashtun support), the Haqqani Group strives for local Pashtun autonomy on both sides of the Durand Line (it does not recognize the Durand Line drawn in 1893) and fought against the Taliban in 1999 and 2000 challenging their attempt to impose centralized Afghan rule. Both the Taliban and Haqqani Group enjoy Pakistani patronage. America has been the main sponsor of the anti-Taliban Northern Alliance, a motley group of mainly Tajik and some Uzbek, Hazara, and Pashtun tribesmen. Interestingly, despite their mutual differences, all the above groups are in league with the Taliban against the Northern Alliance and the Karzai government. America's turning a blind eye to anti-Taliban warlords' promotion of narcotics in Afghanistan since the 1990s was mainly responsible for turning Afghanistan into the drug capital of the world. Later the Taliban also started promoting the production and trafficking of narcotics within and beyond the subregion.

Thanks to American and European shortsightedness and optimism about defeating the Taliban to restore democracy in the country, Afghanistan is far from normal today, and is unlikely to be any better after 2014 or by 2024. Thus, it is imperative that as America prepares to exit Afghanistan it should not be focusing on security only, overlooking the political elements of the transition. Some analysts rightly believe that: "To leave behind a stable government in 2014 Washington needs to push harder for electoral reforms, negotiations with the Taliban, and a regional settlement involving Pakistan."[24] As America is losing support even among its allies in Afghanistan (including the Karzai government), its continuing policy of containing the Taliban with drone attacks and expressing the desire to negotiate peace with them will not pay off any dividends at all. We may agree with Anatol Lieven, a renowned security analyst and expert on Afghan–Pakistan affairs, who believes that: "Instead of the current double strategy of 'shooting and talking' at the same time, it [the United States] should concentrate on 'talking instead of shooting.'"[25]

Unlike Pakistan, Afghanistan's exposure to Islamism was not by design but by default. The Soviet invasion (1979) and American and Pakistani joint-sponsorship of the jihad against Godless Communism ultimately paved the way for the rise of Islamist extremist forces in Afghanistan. Today, the fate of the Afghan Taliban depends on what happens to Pakistan's Afghan policy. If the Pakistani government decides to distance itself from Afghanistan by giving up its irrational demand for a strategic depth in Afghanistan, the Taliban would fizzle out in no time. Whatever cultural Islamization of the population has taken place since the beginning of the jihad in the 1980s can be neutralized through good governance and mass education. However, this would require India to alleviate Pakistan's fear of getting encircled by India from the south as well as the north. America can play a very important role by engaging Afghanistan, Pakistan, India, and China as an honest broker. This, however, is least likely to happen in the foreseeable future. Consequently, Afghanistan and Pakistan will remain the epicenter of the global jihad for an indefinite period.

Last but not least, Afghanistan's stability in the post-occupation period will depend on who controls Islamabad. The powerful Military–Islamist Complex in Pakistan (which appears to be a parallel to the American Military–Industrial Complex) in its quest for the strategic depth in Afghanistan is likely to install a Taliban government in Afghanistan. A Taliban leader has aptly described the Taliban reliance on Pakistan in the following manner: Some Taliban leaders consider Pakistan as important to them as the shoulder one needs to fire his rifle. A captured Taliban leader in 2008 quite philosophically told his American captors about the Taliban's post-occupation strategy in Afghanistan: "You may have the watches, but we have the time."[26] Some analysts suggest political reintegration of the Taliban and Hezb-e-Islami into a coalition government in Afghanistan in order to isolate the most radical groups.[27] Ahmed Rashid believes that the Obama administration by giving mixed signals to Pakistan and Afghanistan has miserably failed in convincing Pakistan to not support the Taliban and LeT fighters.[28]

The inability of more than 15,000 NATO, British, and U.S. marine troops in defeating a handful of Taliban fighters in Helmand is unbelievable. Helmand is considered the drug capital of the world and the Taliban profit enormously from the Helmand-based heroin trade. A handful of IED-armed Taliban fighters have remained a formidable adversary for the NATO and ISAF. In 2010 alone, Taliban fighters planted a staggering 14,661 IEDs to kill some 268 U.S. troops and injured another 3,360.[29] The transnational crime–drug–Islamist nexus in Afghanistan, Pakistan, India, and beyond is posing the biggest security threat to countries and regions beyond South Asia (including America), so is the surge in the number of Taliban fighters which is emerging as a new threat to the stability of Afghanistan and Pakistan. Based on his personal interaction with Mullah Wakil Ahmed Mutawakkil, the former Taliban foreign minister, Ahmed Rashid reveals that the New Taliban are more radical and enthusiastic to fight than the old ones.[30] It appears that neither military nor diplomatic victory for America is forthcoming in Afghanistan, while Pakistan is being alienated too.[31]

As Mullah Omar is shrouded with mystery so are the circumstances leading to the rise of the Taliban, their regional and international connections, and, last but not least, their relationship with al Qaeda. Thus, it is difficult to come to a definite conclusion if the Taliban is purely a proto-Wahhabi political movement, or an Islamist insurgent group not a terrorist outfit, or a transnational terrorist group backed by Iran, as General McChrystal imagined.[32] Then again, we find this unfounded allegation's rebuttal in Wikileaks documents.[33] The contradictory and inaccurate assessments of the Taliban by the U.S. top brasses, experts, and high civil officials reveal their lack of proficiency and understanding of the nature of the overall situation in the so-called AfPak subregion. We need to address the Taliban, al Qaeda, LeT, and the so-called jihad issues, said to have been brewing in the AfPak subregion and emanating from there with/or without Pakistan government's knowledge and connivance. We just cannot rely on government and media reports, sensational books, and irresponsible statements by garrulous people, say the likes of General McChrystal. Many post-9/11 writings, interviews, and eye-witness accounts on the Taliban, al Qaeda, and various facets of the global jihad smack of conspiracy theories and/or gimmicks and propagandas reflecting the proponents'/authors' prejudice and ignorance.

What is most enigmatic about the Taliban is that bands of devout, angry, and dedicated Pashtun madrassa students (having little exposure to military hardware such as tanks and artillery) are said to be the mainstay of this militia. We also find out in media about their fighting skill outmaneuvering Afghan army and sometimes NATO forces. Some Pakistani military officers, who had engaged Taliban fighters in northwestern Pakistan, told me that Taliban fighters seemed to be as well trained as American Marines. We have reasons to believe that the Taliban are not just a ragtag militia of madrassa students. Mere spontaneity, religious zeal, and fanaticism were not good enough to defeat the well-armed Northern Alliance fighters, as the Taliban did in 1996 to capture Kabul, and later most of Afghanistan. Last but not least, despite notes of optimism by NATO commanders, the war against the Taliban is far from over as nobody has yet defeated the Taliban decisively, and there seems to be no military solution to the problem. The ambivalence about what to do with the Taliban (since the overthrow of the Taliban regime in 2001) among American and Afghan policymakers is unbelievable. After failing to contain, let alone defeat them, the U.S.-backed Afghan regime started thinking aloud about a dialogue with the Taliban. Quite embarrassingly for the Karzai government, it had already talked with an imposter who claimed to be a Taliban representative in 2010.[34] It seems the Taliban has become so formidable and the Afghan government so nervous about its inability to defeat them that in July 2012 President Karzai asked the fugitive Mullah Omar to run for the Afghan presidency.[35]

We have reasons to agree with Ahmed Rashid that the end game in Afghanistan requires support from six neighbors: Iran, Pakistan, China, Turkmenistan, Uzbekistan, and Tajikistan, who have since long been interfering in Afghanistan. He has aptly pointed out how Pakistan's double game of helping the Taliban as well as Americans and its proxy war against India in Afghanistan has been the biggest obstacle to a durable peace in Afghanistan.[36] Most importantly, more than two decades after the end of the Afghan jihad in 1989, one wonders as to how the Taliban still manage to get young recruits who are equally good if not better than NATO and ISAF troops. Tom Friedman's observation is very pertinent in this regard. He said (to paraphrase):

> [A]mericans' training Afghans to fight is like someone training Brazilians to play soccer.... Who are training the Taliban? They even don't have maps and don't know how to use one.... America needs nation-building at home, spending another trillion dollars in Afghanistan won't work.... American involvement in Iraq and Afghanistan may be compared with an unemployed couple's adopting a child.[37]

As "Who are training the Taliban?" is an important question, so is "Who are the Taliban?" Contrary to the popular assumption, the Taliban are not Taliban in the literal sense of the expression, not any longer in the third decade of the post-Soviet Afghanistan. Most of them are very well-trained professional soldiers engaged in an insurgency against the American-sponsored Afghan government. We should not consider all Taliban as mere Islamist terrorists. Then there are Taliban soldiers in the payroll of drug lords, engaged in protecting poppy fields and the processing and trafficking of narcotics across the Afghan border. They may be classified as narco-terrorists or narco-jihadists as they have links with the Taliban ideologues that want to reestablish their lost caliphate in and around Afghanistan. Taliban are also fighting Pakistan's proxy war in Afghanistan against India, and, since the sharp deterioration of U.S.–Pakistan relations in late 2011, against America. Despite Taliban's close links with al Qaeda, we should not portray the militia merely as an offshoot of the latter. Taliban originated under the aegis of Pakistani/South Asian Wahhabism, which is quite different from its Saudi namesake, and have had totally different history, philosophy, and objectives.

Nevertheless, both Saudi and South Asian Wahhabis have profound influence on Afghan Taliban leaders and fighters. It is a unique hybrid Islamist outfit, a cross between al Qaeda and South Asian Wahhabi ideologies. Former MB and JI members, who have been disillusioned with the MB's and JI's aversion to violence, favor the Taliban. There are, however, differences between the Saudi and South Asian Wahhabis. While the Saudi Wahhabis belong to the Hanbali School (sect or *mazhab*) of Sunni Jurisprudence and have been traditionally pro-Western, South Asian Wahhabis have always been anti-Western and anti-imperialist, and its adherents either follow the more liberal Hanafi *mazhab* of Sunni Muslims or belong to the group called the *Ahl-e-Hadis* or People of the Hadis. They are very fanatical, puritanical, and some of them even espouse the cause of global caliphate through violence.

Contrary to the popular assumption, especially due to the Taliban rule (1996–2001), unlike Pakistanis, Afghans never promoted Islam as their identity. During the peak of the Indian Wahhabi movement in the 1820s–1850s in northwestern India (northwestern Pakistan today), Afghans avoided supporting the anti-Sikh and anti-British mujahedeen from North India and Bengal. Most Pashtuns were dead against Islamist Puritanism, reforms, and militancy throughout the 19th and 20th centuries. Pashtuns on both sides of the Afghan and British Indian borderline espoused secular/socialist Pashtun nationalism under Abdul Ghaffar Khan, the Frontier Gandhi (1890–1988), even after the accession of the Pashtun areas to Pakistan in 1947. One must not lose sight of the fact that many Afghans supported communist-oriented parties, who eventually came to power in 1978.

While the MB in Egypt had been either proscribed or marginalized politically till the end of Hosni Mubarak in 2011, the JI outfits in Pakistan and Bangladesh have been politically influential, and on several occasions, were parts of the government. As Muslim clerics in Pakistan—as custodians of Shariah law—had the privilege of registering their opinion in the

Constitution-making process in the 1950s, the JI played an important role in incorporating Islamic principles in the Constitution of the Islamic Republic. After General Zia ul-Haq staged a military coup and formally took over the administration of Pakistan, the country implemented Shariah in almost every sphere of life and administration in the country during his rule, 1977–1988. Zia was believed to be an ardent follower of the JI. Since he did not believe in democracy, political parties, secularism, and equal rights for women and minorities, the JI had its heydays in Pakistan. Even after Zia's death, Pakistan did not revert to what had existed in Pakistan in the realms of politics and composite culture of the people. The JI, in league with Zia, played an important role in the rapid Islamization of the country. As many radical Islamist militants in the Arab world, including top al Qaeda leaders, have had MB connections, similarly, alienated and more radical JI members have swelled the ranks of Islamist terror outfits in Pakistan and Bangladesh. Some JMB and HUJI men have had JI connections in the past. However, some JMB and HUJI members revealed after their arrests during 1999 and 2006 that they had left the JI as it had been opposed to violent jihad.

The "India Factor" and the Proxy War in Afghanistan

Having unresolved issues with India, both Pakistan and Bangladesh blame India for promoting and/or accentuating some of their internal and external problems, including ethno-national separatism, terrorism, and other destabilizing factors. India has similar allegations against the two. Kashmir since 1947, India's direct involvement in the creation of Bangladesh in 1971, and, of late, India's alleged promotion of the Pakistani Taliban TTP and Baloch separatists may be considered the main factors behind Pakistan's perennial Indophobia. It is noteworthy that India has not-so-good to very bad relationship with all its immediate neighbors. This may be considered the "India Factor," an important catalyst in the not-so-friendly relationship between India and its immediate neighbors, and is very relevant to the discourse of transnational security dynamics in South Asia. As Pakistani and Bangladeshi Indophobia are behind the Islamization of the polities, so are their perceptions of India as the bully impact transnational security in South Asia.[38] India's disillusion with Bangladesh began not long after the creation of the state. Bangladeshis fast turned anti-Indian due to the unfulfilled promises of the independence attained with Indian help, and thanks to the proliferation of anti-Indian conspiracy theories in the country.[39]

One is not sure if an acceptable resolution of the Kashmir problem can neutralize trans-border terrorism between India and Pakistan. The average Kashmiri Muslim under Indian occupation is not willing to accept nothing short of total independence or *azadi* as a solution to the Kashmir problem. Yoginder Sikand's recent first-hand experience in Kashmir is self-explanatory: "'Even if India were to pave the streets of Kashmir with gold, we would still refuse to identify ourselves as Indians,' insisted a Kashmiri Muslim friend of mine [who is no fervent Islamist or fiery Kashmiri nationalist]."[40] Not only Kashmiri Muslims but also Islamists from various parts of the world have been swelling the ranks of Kashmiri freedom fighters. While some Kashmiri militants espouse the cause of a transnational Islamic caliphate in South Asia, the Pakistan-based LeT, which came into being in 1987 to liberate Kashmir, is linked to drug-baron Dawood Ibrahim's D-Company.[41]

Analysts attribute the Mumbai massacre of 2008 and other terrorist attacks, Mumbai (2006); Jaipur (2008); New Delhi (2008); and Pune (2010), to the narco-Islamist terror nexus in the region. Narco-Islamists killed more than 500 Indians between 2005 and 2010 at the behest of the so-called Karachi Project run by Indian fugitive drug lord Dawood Ibrahim from Karachi. He is said to be in deadly alliance with the ISI and various jihadi groups based in Pakistan, India, and Bangladesh.[42] As analysts elucidate, the growing understanding between drug lords and jihadists within and beyond the Pak-Afghan subregion has jeopardized the ongoing military operations in Afghanistan and Pakistan's tribal areas. With a cautionary note to security practitioners and law-enforcers, they point out that Afghanistan produces around 90 percent of the world's opium supply, one-third of which is transported through Pakistan. The other routes are via Iran, Central Asia, and Russia. It also appears from the study that not only the Taliban and al Qaeda activists but also the least reliable northern warlords are engaged in drug trafficking across the Afghan borders, and that it is no longer a peripheral problem of law and order but a grave security threat in the entire region.[43]

The situation in Balochistan, the least developed, thinly populated, and largest Pakistani province in area, is least promising. Sections of Balochis have been fighting for independence. Alleged Indian interference through its numerous consulates in Afghanistan and Iran, in close proximity to the Pakistani border, is said to have aggravated the situation:

> Having visited the Indian mission in Zahedan, Iran, I can assure you they are not issuing visas as the main activity! Moreover, India has run operations from its mission in Mazar (through which it supported the Northern Alliance) and is likely doing so from the other consulates it has reopened in Jalalabad and Qandahar along the border. Indian officials have told me privately that they are pumping money into Baluchistan.... Even if by some act of miraculous diplomacy the territorial issues were to be resolved, Pakistan would remain an insecure state.... This suggests that without some means of compelling Pakistan to abandon its reliance upon militancy, it will become ever more interested in using it and the militants will likely continue to proliferate beyond Pakistan's control.[44]

The Baloch separatist movement has the potential to turn the region into another Kurdistan; safe havens for transnational insurgents there could destabilize the entire region. Indian non-interference in Balochistan is not the only solution to the problem, but Indian cooperation in this regard would substantially stabilize this strategically important province of Pakistan. Most Balochis, excepting a handful of rebels under Brahamdagh Bugti, despise Indian interference in Balochistan.[45] Many Pakistanis believe that TTP fighters killed by Pakistani troops in Waziristan and Swat in 2008 were uncircumcised, hence assumed to be non-Muslim infiltrators from India.[46] Indian leaders, media, and analysts are unwilling to accept that their country has anything to do with the TTP. "Circumcision no longer acid test to identify Indian spies," so goes the caption of an Indian daily.[47] A Pakistani government report reveals: "The arrested commanders of TTP have confessed that secret departments of India, including RAW, and Afghanistan have been providing them weapons and funds to fight against the Pakistan Army."[48]

What appeared to be the "emerging changes" in the U.S.'s Pakistan Policy—toward a better CBM between the two countries, after Pakistan's successful military operations against Islamist militants in the FATA and Swat Valley by May 2009—dissipated in the wake of the growing misunderstanding and mistrust between the two. The so-called unilateral

U.S. military action at Abbotabad that killed bin Laden in May 2011 further embittered the relationship. Meanwhile, what the U.S. Under-Secretary of State William Burns had told the Indian government in New Delhi on June 11, 2009 was significant. He publicly advised India to settle the Kashmir problem "in line with the aspirations of Kashmiris" and he stated this the day after his meeting with Kashmiri separatist leader Mirwaiz Umar Farooq. Quite embarrassing for India was Burns's advice to close or prune down its consulates in Afghanistan, which Pakistan insists have been "fomenting trouble" in the NWFP and Balochistan.[49] General McChrystal in his report to the Defense Secretary in August 2009 also pointed out how "increasing Indian influence in Afghanistan" was likely to "exacerbate regional tensions and encourage Pakistani countermeasures in Afghanistan or India."[50] The U.S. Defense Secretary Chuck Hagel in a speech at Oklahoma University in 2011 also suggested that India had been using Afghanistan as a second front against its old rival Pakistan.[51]

American ambivalence toward India and Pakistan is noteworthy. While the U.S. wants India to resolve the Kashmir dispute in accordance with the wish of the Kashmiri people, and urges India not to open a "second front" against Pakistan through Afghanistan, it has also been strengthening its civil and military ties with India. Despite the U.S. reservations about Pakistan's dubious role in Afghanistan, it cannot abandon its "major non-NATO ally," which a retired Indian general considers to be the "linchpin of its exit strategy" from Afghanistan.[52] While Parthasarathy sounds alarmingly pessimistic about the future of Indo-U.S. relations,[53] we find Ganguly more balanced in this regard. He highlights how America's coming closer to Pakistan is annoying India, which the U.S. can ill afford.[54] In the backdrop of the growing tension between Pakistan and America over the latter's unauthorized drone attacks to kill militants that mostly kill Pakistani civilians (and 24 Pakistani soldiers in late 2011) and the killing of bin Laden without the knowledge and permission of the Pakistani authorities, Pakistan and America are most likely to go in opposite directions.

Meanwhile America's retaliatory withholding of $800 million aid money to Pakistan (nearly one-third of its annual grant to the country) in June 2011 for the latter's alleged promotion of Taliban fighters through the ISI signaled a big departure from its so-called soft approach to Pakistan. The *Washington Post*'s publishing a letter in June 2011, allegedly written by a North Korean official to A.Q. Khan, the father of Pakistan's nuclear bomb in 2004, implicating two Pakistani retired generals as receivers of a $3 million bribe from North Korea for passing vital nuclear technology to the latter, has further embittered the Pak-U.S. relationship. Pakistan government's dispensing 33-year imprisonment to a Pakistani physician, Dr Afridi, for his alleged collaboration with the CIA in tracking bin Laden's den in 2011 led to further deterioration in the Pak-U.S. relationship. America cut down $33 million from its annual aid package to Pakistan in retaliation against the 33-year jail term for Dr Afridi. Meanwhile, accidental deaths of 24 Pakistani troops in a U.S. air raid (America insists it was a friendly fire) in 2011 resulted in Pakistan's closing down the NATO's supply route between Karachi and Afghanistan.

Consequently, the apparently pro-Pakistan shift in U.S. policy, which might have accelerated the Confidence Building Measures (CBM) between the two countries, has become irrelevant. American ambivalence about its ties with Pakistan is noteworthy. As we know, so long as America believes it needs to have its boots on the ground in Afghanistan, it needs Pakistani territory for the movement of heavy military hardware and fuel. America has so far enjoyed this privilege by giving a billion dollar a year in aid to Pakistan. Then again, as of late 2013, America did not stop its drone attacks that killed hundreds of innocent Pakistani civilians and violated Pakistan's sovereignty in the name of killing Islamist terrorists in northwestern Pakistan. "Of 746 people listed as killed in the drone strikes… [during 2006 and 2009], at least 147 of the dead are clearly stated to be civilian victims, 94 of those are said to be children,"[55] reveals one confidential report. Pakistani politician Imran Khan's ex-wife Jemima Khan rightly pointed out: "Can you imagine the uproar that would be caused anywhere else in the world if 94 children were reported murdered in just three years?"[56]

America does not like the growing Sino-Pakistani military and strategic collaboration, especially the Chinese help in the construction of the largest deep-sea port in the world at Gwadar in Balochistan. Pakistan's offering China a trade and energy corridor—the 2,000 km trade infrastructure corridor linking Gwadar with Kashgar in Xinjiang province—and a naval base at Gwadar are least palatable to the U.S. The prospect of importing oil and gas from the Middle East and Iran via roads, pipelines, or railway to China, and building of oil refineries at Gwadar to the benefit of China and Pakistan could remain unrealized. Some analysts believe that America will do anything to make the projects unfeasible, including its sponsorship of Baloch and Uyghur separatist groups to terrorize the entire region.[57] Selig Harrison gives credence to what seems to be an alarmist view about America's promotion of separatist violence in Balochistan (and Xinjiang):

> Most important, it [the US] should aid the 6 million Baluch insurgents fighting for independence from Pakistan in the face of growing ISI repression. Pakistan has given China a base at Gwadar in the heart of Baluch territory. So an independent Baluchistan would serve U.S. strategic interests in addition to the immediate goal of countering Islamist forces.[58]

The growing rift between Pakistan and America and the latter's avowed policy of withdrawing all troops from Afghanistan by 2014 are going to destabilize the entire region transcending Afghanistan and Pakistan. As one analyst predicts in the wake of America's (and the NATO's) total troops withdrawal from Afghanistan in 2014 the country will become the battlefield of the ongoing proxy war between archrival India and Pakistan, which promote different ethnic groups against each other. One cannot agree more with the estimate that: "...Afghanistan looks like a failure beside the dream of 2001, when NATO invaded. It will continue to be plagued by violence and insurgency.... Poppies will flourish and corruption will eat away at daily life."[59] One has no reason to agree with the alarmist view of Ashley Tellis, who believes that the complete troop withdrawal by NATO from Afghanistan would signal Pakistan's impending defeat in Afghanistan at the hands of the Afghan Taliban.[60] Last but not least, American ambivalent South Asia policy, which has been soft-on-India quite for sometime, is quite problematic. Its promotion of India as a bulwark against China and Pakistan in the long run might further aggravate the situation by turning Bangladesh into another battlefield for the proxy-war between India and Pakistan.

India's alleged hegemonic design in the region is quite discomforting for its smaller neighbors. We may agree with Kuldip Nayar that:

> India needs to reflect on why all the neighbouring countries have distanced themselves from it. No doubt its size deters them. But more than that, their feeling is that New Delhi is becoming increasingly conscious of itself as an emerging world power. It tends to throw its weight about in such a manner that the neighbours are having doubts about its bona fides.[61]

The Afghan Factor: Opium, Gun, and the Mad Mullah

An important catalyst for transnational security issues in South Asia is the "Afghan Factor" or whatever has happened to the country in security perspective since 1947. Islamist transnational insurgencies and narco-terrorism on both sides of Afghan border may be attributed to the phenomenon of failing state in Afghanistan. This landlocked conglomerate of diverse ethno-national entities experimented with monarchy, guided democracy, socialism, and Islamism in one generation since the 1970s. Pashtun nationalism on both sides of the Pak-Afghan border is another catalyst in the transnational security threat across the border. Numerically dominant and politically feeble/subjugated since late 2001, Afghan Pashtuns under the aegis of Taliban–al Qaeda and the narco-jihadist network are determined to turn the table to their favor. Their Pakistani counterparts share the same vision: a Taliban-led Islamic caliphate transcending Pakistan and Afghanistan and their unhindered control of the drug production and trafficking across the world.

The Afghan jihad of the 1980s impacted Muslims in far-flung lands from Chechnya to Dagestan and Bangladesh to southern Thailand and Philippines. The ongoing transnational violence across the Pak-Afghan boundary is a direct by-product of the large-scale possession of unaccountable weapons by thousands of unaccountable and unemployed Afghans. Intriguingly enough, what the Pakistani government through its military intelligence (ISI) and its Western and Arab allies had installed in Afghanistan in 1996 backfired. The surrogate Taliban regime to fight Pakistan's proxy wars against pro-Indian and pro-Iranian Tajik-Uzbek warlords collapsed soon after 9/11. Within months of its installation to power, the Taliban regime started distancing from its Pakistani patrons "as multiple rivalries along ethnic, sectarian, and party lines spilled over into active and very deadly conflict in and around Kabul."[62]

By early 2000s, the Taliban had become too powerful to be controlled by its former sponsors any longer. As clients of Afghan drug barons, anti-Iranian Arab regimes, Chechens, and other Islamist outfits, Pashtun Taliban in alliance with Chechens, Tajiks, Uzbeks, and possibly Uyghur separatists from Xinjiang are engaged in a war of attrition against the Karzai regime and its allies.[63] Analysts and top U.S. officials including Richard Holbrooke believed that 70 percent Pashtun insurgents were fighting merely for pay or strictly local aims and, therefore, could be alienated from the hard-core believers. However, a first-hand report from Afghanistan reveals a somewhat different situation. Taliban fighters in general assert that they are not fighting for jobs or money and are dead against signing any deal with the enemy foreign troops and Afghan government. One of them said: "If you're committed to jihad, you won't leave for a mountain of money." Another 18-year-old fighter declared, "I want to die in the jihad, not as a sick old man under a blanket at home." The same report reveals that the Taliban are fighting for (a) driving out the invaders; (b) establishing an Islamic Emirate under Mullah Omar; and (c) avenging the deaths of fellow Pashtuns killed by their enemies.[64] Some Taliban are also involved in manufacturing and marketing narcotics.[65] They are fast emerging as transnational narco-terrorists.[66] One may in this regard visualize what narco-terrorists in Columbia and, of late, in Mexico have been capable of doing. They can kill thousands, bleed countries, and destabilize regions for decades.

Besides Pashtuns, Uzbeks, Tajiks, Arabs, Chechens, and others also swell the ranks of the Taliban.[67] Interestingly, former military officers of the pro-Soviet Afghan government are running its military wing. So long as al Qaeda network is intact across the Pak-Afghan border and Afghan Taliban are in possession of one-third of the country, and the Pakistan-based Taliban movement or the TTP is not contained, peace will remain elusive throughout the region. The Afghan Taliban and the TTP are no longer ragtag bands of soldiers, but very well-trained, well-armed, and motivated battle-hardened fighters. As mentioned earlier, military experts liken their fighting skill with that of the U.S. Marines.[68] They are partially al Qaeda associates and partially producers and traffickers of opium. Hence the expression narco-jihadist to classify these organized criminals-cum-insurgents in the subregion. Then again, the U.S. officials believe that al Qaeda is on the brink of collapse across the Pak-Afghan border. They, however, seem to be right that al Qaeda might yet rally and that even its demise would not end the terrorist threat, which is increasingly driven by radicalized individuals as well as aggressive affiliates.

Although soon after they captured Kabul in 1996, the Taliban prohibited opium production and destroyed stacks of opium, yet later they did not totally prohibit its production and trafficking to a limited extent. Afghanistan under the Taliban produced around 100 tons of opium per year, but within six years of the U.S. and NATO occupation, the country produced more than 8,000 tons in 2007. Presently, there are no signs of any decisive victory for the U.S. and ISAF troops against the Taliban, let alone any signs of a concerted war against drugs and drug-traffickers in Afghanistan. What we hear from the U.S. administration since early 2011 is about the proposed dialogue between America and Afghan Taliban and the total withdrawal of Western troops from Afghanistan by 2014. Conversely, as credible evidences suggest, American civil and military authorities have had close ties with Afghan warlords and drug-lords, including the slain Ahmed Wali Karzai, half-brother of Hamid Karzai, who was on the payroll of the CIA for 10 years till his death in June 2011.[69] In this backdrop, it seems America has lost Afghanistan both militarily and diplomatically to the Taliban and drug mafia. One analyst has cynically raised the question if America really went to Afghanistan to jack up opium production or to get rid of the terrorists. He imputes Barnie Madoff and some other corrupt American businessmen unaccounted for sources of wealth to illicit drug money from Afghanistan.[70] Meanwhile as Tariq Ali puts it,

> [T]he number of Afghan civilians killed has exceeded many tens of times over the 2,746 who died in Manhattan. Unemployment is around 60 per cent and maternal, infant and child mortality levels are now among the highest in the world. Opium harvests have soared, and the "Neo-Taliban" is growing stronger year by year.[71]

In view of this, we cannot ignore the intense competition for the control of the $4 billion opium trade in Afghan market (a conservative estimate)—which the U.N. estimates to be worth $65 billion in the global market—as an important factor behind the transnational instability in the subregion. There are conflicting assumptions and speculations about the total worth of Afghan opium in the international market and the Taliban's share in it, some plausible and some very far-fetched. While some analysts believe the Taliban make around $50 billion or 25 to 50 percent of the total worth of Afghan opium in the world market annually, others think they do not make more than a $100 million per year. According to the

U.N. Under-Secretary General Antonio Maria, the Afghan opium (heroin) is worth about $65 billion, although he does not indicate how much the Taliban make out of it annually.[72]

Another source reveals that annually the Taliban and Afghan warlords make around $400 million from poppy. The same report reveals the helplessness of Afghan anti-narcotics officials in containing poppy cultivation and transnational drug trafficking. Pin pointing President Karzai's duplicity and his government's links with drug traffickers and warlords, the report reveals that drug has virtually become the alternative currency for Taliban, warlords, and drug mafias. According to one U.N. Office on Drugs and Crime (UNODC) official, "the value of the drugs multiplies by a factor of 10 every time they cross a border," and an average farmer makes 10 times more from opium than from wheat.[73]

As it is true that inadequate foreign troops will not be able to stop opium production, processing, and trafficking in territories under their control in the Helmand province of Afghanistan, which produces around 90 percent of opium in the world, it is also true that Afghan farmers do not prefer opium to other crops for money, as local warlords and drug mafia coerce them into growing opium at gunpoint. The media often wrongly portrays drug-barons' AK-47 totting gunmen as Taliban.[74] We have reasons to believe *Time* reporter McGirk that driving the Taliban out of certain pockets was the easy part, but "to keep them out, U.S. and Afghan officials must wean the region from its drug dependency" as thousands of hectares of poppy fields not only benefit drug czars and Taliban but also some 70,000 farmers of Marjah in Helmand. The reporter cites Grelchen Peters, an expert on Taliban drug ties with traffickers, who believes that: "Counternarcotics, just like counterinsurgency, is like playing whack a mole. You knock it out in one place, and it pops up somewhere else."[75] One U.S. report reveals that corrupt U.S. officials and contractors have been jeopardizing the U.S. war-efforts in Afghanistan by funneling more than $2 billion of U.S. taxpayer money to the Taliban through transportation contracts.[76] In this backdrop, one has reasons to be skeptic about the success of American war-efforts in Afghanistan and the end of the narco-jihad across the Pak-Afghan borders and beyond, in the near future.

However, the real problem is not petty corruption by U.S. officials and contractors, but the 65 to more than 100 billion dollar annual profits U.S. and NATO officials make through illicit drugs grown in Afghanistan.

What the CIA, Saudi intelligence, and Pakistan's ISI started promoting in post-Taliban Afghanistan in the Spring of 2002—massive poppy cultivation—soon turned Helmand and adjoining places to the "poppy capital" of the world. According to a British report, CIA in 2006 forced Hamid Karzai to sack Mohamed Daud as governor of Helmand. Daud was a key player in Britain's anti-drug campaign in Helmand.[77] Big banks and financial institutions in America and Europe are said to have a vested interest in maintaining and sustaining the drug trade.[78]

Despite the growing support among Afghans for U.S. military presence in Afghanistan (68 percent in late 2009)[79] people in general are skeptic about the prospect of peace in the country, and this skepticism makes sense.[80] In the wake of the proposed withdrawal of all Western troops by 2014, the Taliban are most likely to control Kabul eventually. Meanwhile, despite American willingness to talk to the Taliban leadership since 2009,[81] hard-core Taliban are less enthused to share power through any deal with America or Pakistan. They do not consider Pakistan an ally despite having safe havens in Balochistan, and have no qualms about killing more American troops or terrorizing Pakistan.[82] However, since influential Taliban leader Baradar's arrest in early 2010,[83] it is least likely that the U.S. and the Taliban are going to sign a peace-deal in the near future, unless the former takes Pakistan into confidence. Despite the bleak prospects of U.S.–Taliban talks, some analysts believe that patience and concessions on part of the U.S. would eventually pay off.

This might be conciliatory to some Taliban fighters who are primarily fighting for sustenance, not Islam; as, to quote one analyst, "the definition of Taliban...is young man without a job."[84] However, as discussed earlier, the core of the Taliban is motivated by the ideology of jihad and Pashtun nationalism. Afghan government's annual revenue of less than a billion dollars is considered too meager to rebuild the war-ravaged country, let alone defeat the insurgents militarily. On the other hand, while the Western allies are likely to raise not more than three billion dollars annually to meet the challenge, the Taliban-al Qaeda drug-barons earn scores of billion dollars globally.[85] In view of the continuing support for the Taliban in southeastern Afghanistan, and the Afghan government's declining mass support and inability to hold the ground without NATO troops, some analysts foresee neither a solution to the crisis nor a victory for America in Afghanistan.[86] In sum, the U.S. and its allies seem to have lost their war in Afghanistan both militarily and diplomatically. While America has been trying to extricate itself from Afghanistan by withdrawing all troops by 2014, its major allies, including Canada and France, have already withdrawn their troops from the country, which is fast turning into another unwinnable territory for the West. The upshot will be the preponderance of a pro-Pakistani regime and the continuation of the ethno-national conflicts between the Northern warlords and Pashtun Taliban and the proxy war between archrival India and Pakistan across the Pak-Afghan borders.

The TTP, LeT, and Mumbai Attacks (2008): State-Sponsored or Spontaneous Terrorism?

Since 2007, Pakistan is confronting the TTP or the Taliban Movement of Pakistan formed by an almost illiterate, a former waiter of a restaurant, Baitullah Mehsud (1974–2009) of the Mehsud tribe in northwestern Pakistan.[87]After the post-9/11 Pakistan army operations in the northwest, many Taliban fled to South Waziristan, home to the largest Tribal Agency (autonomous tribal territory) in Pakistan. Mehsud and Wazir tribesmen were the main followers of the Taliban. In 2002, Mullah Nazir of the Wazir tribe cofounded the TTP. Mullah Jalaluddin Haqqani, chief of the Haqqani Group of Taliban, patronized both the Afghan and the newly formed Pakistani Taliban group. In 2007, he unified various Islamist terror outfits under the TTP umbrella, which was already operational in 2002 in the wake of the Pakistani military operations against al Qaeda and its ilk in the FATA region of Pakistan.[88]

Baitullah's death in a U.S. drone attack in August 2009 jolted the TTP leadership and rival factions have emerged and are fighting each other. Yet another U.S. drone attack killed TTP's deputy leader Wali-ur-Rehman and four top leaders on May 29, 2013 in North Waziristan.[89] However, it is too early to write off the outfit. Its transnational links with al Qaeda can destabilize the region for quite some time. The TTP has been a shadowy umbrella organization manned by Pakistanis and foreigners: Pashtuns, Uzbeks, Tajiks, Chechens, Arabs, and Indians. Its transnational connections and avowed goal to establish an Islamist caliphate from Pakistan to Chechnya signal more terrorist attacks and insurgencies beyond Pakistan and Afghanistan. The Jordanian suicide bomber al-Balawi who killed seven CIA officials in Afghanistan in January 2010, a double agent working for both the Americans and al Qaeda, had been in league with the Taliban as well.[90] Both Afghan and Pakistani Taliban have al Qaeda connections. The TTP is not affiliated with the Afghan Taliban; and unlike the Afghan Taliban, it has no soft corner for Pakistan and have no links with its armed forces. It primarily attacks targets in Pakistan, NATO troops, and aims at enforcing Shariah code in Pakistan.[91] It has already claimed it had attacked Malala Yousufzai, a 14-year-old Pakistani girl, for advocating female literacy in October 2012.[92] It is said to have attempted to bomb the Times Square in May 2010.[93]

In view of the prevalent uncertainties in northwestern Pakistan, one may not only blame India and America for their alleged role in promoting militant groups to destabilize Pakistan, one may do some finger pointing at Pakistan too as it has been providing safe havens to various Islamist militant groups, including al Qaeda, Taliban, TTP, and LeT. By turning itself into the biting puppy of the army, the TTP has been targeting Pakistani civilians, military, and law enforcers since 2007. The Tehreek-e-Nafaz-e-Shariat-e-Mohammadi (TNSM) or the Movement for the Enforcement of Islamic Law, which wants the introduction of Shariah law in Pakistan, is another Islamist outfit which since 1992 has mainly been attacking Pakistani armed forces and politicians. It came into being in 1992 and was proscribed by General Musharraf in 2002. The TNSM is together with the TTP after the Pakistan army had attacked the latter's base at the Red Mosque of Islamabad in 2007. In late 2007, the TNSM was virtually running a parallel government in parts of Swat.[94] Pakistan had to compromise with the TNSM by signing a deal with it that the government would not introduce any law defying any principle of the code.[95]

Soon after becoming the prime minister for the third time in May, 2013, Nawaz Sharif showed interest in talking to the TTP to make Pakistan peaceful but the Army Chief General Kayani was not sure if the TTP could be engaged in peace talks. Some Pakistani analysts believe that "despite its murderous campaigns around the country," many Pakistanis considered the TTP movement an "understandable reaction to the American-led war in Afghanistan." Many members of the Prime Minister's party are said to have similar views.[96] American drone attack in early June that killed several Pakistanis days after Nawaz Sharif's condemnation of such unauthorized attacks (that violate Pakistan's sovereignty) seems to have further antagonized the bulk of Pakistanis toward the U.S. We know, about 90 percent of Pakistanis consider America as their main external enemy. In view of this, it appears that both due to ideological and geo-strategic reasons, successive governments and people in Pakistan favor Islamist militants that they might use against archrival India, and, of late, against American interests. Pakistani ambivalence toward Islamist militancy is understandable. While Pakistan has a soft corner for the LeT or the Soldier's of the Pure—which is primarily anti-Indian and is said to have capabilities to attack American mainland[97]—it despises the TTP for attacking Pakistani military and civilian targets.

The Elections of May 2013 did not signal the restoration of secularism and a departure from Islamist bigotry and prejudice against non-Muslims in Pakistan, well-entrenched since the beginning of the Zia regime. School textbook curricula in the country may be cited in this regard. In August 2013, the elected governments of Pakhtunkhwa and Sind provinces decided to undo curriculum reforms made during the previous governments in favor of teaching young children about Jihad, superiority of Islam, and the "virtues" of caliphate. Some textbooks portray the Hindus as "enemies" of Islam and Pakistan.[98]

The LeT, since its proscription by Pakistan in early 2002 is known as the Jamaat ud Dawa (JuD) (Party of the Calling), is the most active transnational terror outfit in South Asia. The liberation of Kashmir to the Islamists is not about liberating the territory from India's occupation but liberating a Muslim land from non-Muslim occupation. The LeT is a champion of a Wahhabi Islamic State in South Asia. It is no longer a purely Kashmiri jihadist outfit. Having its headquarters near Lahore, the LeT "still runs its training practically in the open," and this several thousand-strong organization in the past 20 years is estimated to have trained around 200,000 militants, hundreds from Europe and North America. Despite its ideological commitment to South Asian Wahhabism, nourished by the ultra-orthodox *Ahl-e-Hadis* (adherents of Hadis or traditions of the Prophet, not Muslim jurists) sect, the bulk of LeT gunmen are from rural Punjab and NWFP, overwhelmingly from the Hanafi sect of Sunni Islam, not adherents of the *Ahl-e-Hadis*.[99] It is noteworthy that the main leaders of the militant JMB also belong to the *Ahl-e-Hadis* sect of Sunni Islam. The JMB came to the limelight after exploding hundreds of bombs and resorting to suicide attacks for the first time in Bangladesh in 2005.

Since 9/11, the LeT seems to be the actual face of the elusive and shadowy al Qaeda. This Pakistan-based terrorist group seems to be the most well-organized and well-connected transnational terror outfit in the world. It has cells in Europe, throughout the Persian Gulf, India, Nepal, Bangladesh, Southeast Asia, and North America. On the one hand, we see LeT fingerprints in terror attacks in India, on the other hand, we see Lashkar men terrorizing Afghanistan, Iraq, Dhaka, and Copenhagen. We have reports about Chicago-based Pakistani-American David Headley's involvement in the 2008 Mumbai attacks and about another LeT plot to kill the officials of the Danish newspaper which published Prophet Muhammad's cartoon in 2005. The recent arrests of people in Dhaka (February 2010) reveal the latest LeT plot to attack the U.S. and British embassies in Bangladesh.[100] The reason why the LeT may be considered the most well-connected transnational terror outfit is its maintaining long relationship with al Qaeda affiliates in Afghanistan, such as the JI, Hizb-e-Islami, and Hizb-ut-Mujahideen, since early1990s.[101] It has very good coordination with another Pakistan-based Islamist group, the JeM or Soldiers of Muhammad. Having tentacles in Europe and North America, the JeM was responsible for the killing of American journalist Daniel Pearl in 2002. It was involved in a plot to bomb a New York synagogue and shoot stinger missile at U.S. military aircraft in the U.S. in 2009. In December 2001, it jointly attacked the Indian Parliament along with LeT gunmen. The LeT and JeM get money from rich donors from Saudi Arabia, Gulf countries, Europe, and Pakistan.[102] It is noteworthy that soon after becoming Pakistan's prime pinister for the third time in June 2013, Nawaz Sharif's government is alleged to have donated 95 million Pakistani rupees (more than a million U.S. dollars) to several JuD or LeT-run social welfare projects in Punjab.[103]

LeT's latest venture was the Mumbai massacre in November 2008. Some observers trace both Islamist and narco-terrorist fingerprints in the Mumbai attacks; they believe LeT has been in league with Dawood Ibrahim. A U.S. War College research paper has convincingly explained the LeT–D-Company involvement in the Mumbai massacre.[104] Having committed to bleed India, mainly for its occupation of Muslim Kashmir, the LeT had no problem in killing Indians, including Dawood Ibrahim's rivals in the name of jihad. One must not lose sight of Ibrahim's track record. He was instrumental in the indiscriminate bombing and killing of Hindus in Mumbai in 1993 to avenge the demolition of the Babri Mosque and killing of Muslims by Hindu fanatics in Mumbai and elsewhere in India. According to one Indian investigative report, the LeT–HUJI–Dawood–al Qaeda nexus came into being in 2003, allegedly with ISI support. Pakistani army personnel allegedly brought fugitives from India and other countries to Karachi via Bangladesh and Nepal where they were indoctrinated by videos of Babri Mosque and Gujarat rioting which led to the killing of Muslims by Hindu fanatics in India.[105]

Interestingly, while eight of the 10 gunmen randomly killed people in Mumbai, two of them allegedly executed Dawood's rivals, "Russian and Israeli members of the drug mafia," at Oberoi Hotel and Nariman House in "a typically gangland execution method."[106] This has been further substantiated by several TV documentaries. One comes across the cell phone conversation between a gunman at Nariman House and his mentor, presumably in Pakistan, recorded by Indian authorities. Their mentor ordered the two gunmen in charge of hostages: "Seat them upright and shoot at the back of their heads before you take care of yourselves. God bless you!"[107] The particular gangland execution method, as one comes across at Nariman House and Oberoi Hotel, is typical drug mafia way of eliminating rivals, not typical jihadist way of killing.

According to Maitra, British, Russian, Indian, Pakistani, and Israeli drug barons have been busy transporting Afghan drugs through Mumbai and Dubai, and clandestine Sikh separatists and Hindu militant Shiv Sena are also involved in drug trafficking. He considers Dawood Ibrahim the linchpin of the mafias.[108] Drug barons from the region and Europe, the so-called Dope, Inc., and terror groups, including the London-based Hizbut Tahrir and the Islamic Movement of Uzbekistan, are engaged in narco-terrorism and Islamism from Chechnya to Pakistan, India and beyond. Analysts believe in Osama bin Laden's personal involvement in drug trafficking to finance al Qaeda's transnational network.[109] Similar groups are active in Bangladesh and Southeast Asia. In short, the LeT story does not begin with attacks on India and Kashmir, nor ends with the Mumbai attacks in November 2008. Since its inception, it has engaged both Pakistani and Indian troops.[110] The emergence of the LeT and JeM as transnational terrorist organizations highlights how government-sponsored terrorism to bleed external enemies backfires. Unlike the Bangladeshi transnational Islamist terrorist groups, the Pakistani ones are mostly state sponsored. One is not sure, if Pakistanis who once promoted Islamist terrorists are now afraid to do anything about it, and that "It's a delicate dance with a Frankenstein of their own making."[111] However, from time to time Pakistan army finds its strategic assets very useful in bleeding archrival India. LeT fighters are said to have fought along with Pakistani troops against India during the Kargil War of 1999.

HUJI-B, JMB, and Transnational "Jihad" from Bangladesh

Within less than a decade after the end of the U.S.-led Afghan jihad, by 1999 Islamist terror networks made their presence felt in and around Bangladesh. What started as sporadic bombing that killed innocent people at public places in Bangladesh in 1999 under the aegis of the HUJI–B or the Movement for Islamic Jihad (a Pakistani prototype having links with al Qaeda), by 2004 this emerged as a serious threat to the stability of the region. The HUJI-B resorted to terrorizing people by indiscriminate bombing and grenade attacks. In 2004, it killed several Awami League (a political party that led the separatist movement in East Pakistan for independent Bangladesh) leaders at a public rally in Dhaka. This shadowy Islamist outfit is potentially much more powerful than similar Islamist groups in and around Bangladesh. Al Qaeda-sponsored HUJI-B seems to be a go-between other Indo-Pakistan-based Islamist outfits and their Southeast Asian counterparts from Myanmar to the Philippines. Muslim insurgents in southern Thailand are said to have received more arms and training from the HUJI-B than from the Jemaah Islamiyah of Indonesia.[112]

However, Islamism in Southeast Asia is altogether a different ball game. Despite the reported regrouping of some Islamist extremists in Indonesia, there is no imminent danger of their threatening the country and the region. The Crisis Group reveals that: "Fortunately for Indonesia, most of these would be terrorists have been singularly inept…. But the danger is not over."[113] Islamist terror groups in the Philippines and southern

Thailand have been mainly ethno-national separatist groups, least likely to play any significant role in regional/global perspective. The Thai and Filipino governments have contained (if not totally eliminated) these groups. Relative better governance and prosperity in Southeast Asia have successfully marginalized Islamist militants. Then again, the average Southeast Asian Muslim is angry with America for its foreign policy, especially due to its invasions/interventions in the Muslim world, and, last but not least, for its support for Israel.[114]

The HUJI-B came into being in 1992, not as a clandestine but as an open organization with a view to converting Bangladesh into an Islamic State. Mufti Abdul Hannan, the founder, a Bangladeshi Afghan veteran of the 1980s jihad against Soviet Union, arrested in 2006, confessed having bombed and killed scores of people in the country during 1999 and 2005. He also confessed having links with Arab, Pakistani, Burmese, and Bangladeshi Islamists and having supported Islamist militants outside Bangladesh, including the Rohingya Solidarity Organization (RSO) of Myanmar.[115] HUJI-B's sponsors included the ISI and Pakistani Islamist outfits such as the LeT and the JeM. It is believed to have trained Rohingya and Thai Islamist separatists, and is also implicated in the January 22, 2002 bombing of the American Center in Kolkata and the October 12, 2005 suicide bombing in Hyderabad, southern India. The outfit is said to have close ties with Kashmiri, Afghan, Islamist separatists in Assam, the proscribed Students' Islamic Movement of India (SIMI), and other Islamist groups in India.[116] The arrests of several Indian Islamist clerics in Bangladesh in July 2009, who had been illegally hiding and working in several madrassas, are very revealing. HUJI clerics and homegrown Islamist groups in Bangladesh had connections with D-Company's associates, Abdul Rouf Daud Merchant, Zahid Sheikh, and Arif, arrested in May 2009.

The HUJI-B has international donors as well as spontaneous local support from poor taxicab drivers, rickshaw-pullers, and garment workers. Another report reveals that at least 50 Indian gangsters having links with the D-Company, HUJI-B, and LeT frequently visit Bangladesh. Dawood's second-in-command, Chhota Shakeel, who operates from Pakistan and Dubai, has been sending large sums of money to finance the narco-jihadist terror network in and beyond Bangladesh. Pakistani Sunni extremist Sipah-e-Sahaba and Ahle Hadis JeM collaborate with HUJI-B and JMB.[117] Bangladeshi police since 2007 have arrested two Bangladesh-born British citizens, believed to have HUJI connections, with guns, explosives, and books on explosives and jihad.[118] Several Pakistani nationals, believed to have LeT connections, were arrested in early 2010. They were mainly involved in money laundering and plotting attacks on Indian and U.S. missions in Dhaka.[119]

Another terrorist outfit, the JMB, founded by Afghan veteran Sheikh Abdul Rahman, follows the footsteps of the HUJI-B. While the HUJI-B is an offshoot of al Qaeda, the JMB is homegrown. As some JMB activists had links with the JI in the past, many Bangladeshis, especially those having a soft corner for the Awami League (AL), love to portray the JMB as pro-BNP and pro-Jamaat. In view of the sharp polarization of the polity between the AL and BNP-Jamaat supporters, one should not give any credence to any unsubstantiated reports about JMB's alleged connections with the BNP-Jamaat alliance. Various JMB cadres in police custody admitted that they had snapped ties with the Jamaat for its stand against violence and terrorism.[120] In short, the JMB has very little transnational connections; it has links with some ultra-orthodox *Ahl-e-Hadis* sect members from India and northwestern and northern Bangladesh. It came to the limelight by organizing its jihad against Maoist insurgents and criminals in northwestern Bangladesh, in collaboration with some local BNP leaders and police. With a view to drawing attention to its demands for immediate introduction of the Shariah code, on August 17, 2005, the JMB blasted a few hundred bombs throughout the country. Soon after these synchronized bombings, which killed several innocent people, JMB suicide bombers randomly killed several judges, police officers, and civilians in Bangladesh. The JMB affirms the continuation of the 19th-century "jihad" waged in northwestern India and Bengal by the Indian Wahhabis.[121] After the execution of its top leaders and mass arrests of cadres since 2006, it is too early to assume that the JMB is unlikely to reemerge as a terror threat in the future.

Allegedly, sections of Bangladesh's armed forces have links with Islamists in Pakistan. Sometimes Bangladeshi journalists faced assassination attempts for exposing the military's alleged links with Islamabad. The most notorious case was that of CNN correspondent Tasneem Khalil. The military tortured him in solitary confinement and forced him to leave Bangladesh in 2007.[122] The BNP government and the military regime are said to have hurriedly executed the top leaders of the JMB after they had contacted the media to expose their links with the BNP and military intelligence.[123] Due to the prevalent terror–drug nexus, Islamist and secular terrorist groups are still posing security threats to the vast regions between Afghanistan and Myanmar. India has been experiencing the rapid escalation of Maoist insurgency in 20 of India's 28 states, which Prime Minister Manmohan Singh once considered as the gravest security threat to India.[124]

Thanks to the porous Indo-Bangladesh border, Maoist insurgents from West Bengal and southwestern Bangladesh during 2004 and 2007 literally established a reign of terror in the remote villages on both sides of the border.[125] Besides the Pakistan- and Indian-occupied Kashmir-based LeT, India periodically faces terrorist attacks from homegrown Islamist terror groups. The Indian Mujahideen (IM) may be mentioned in this regard. In February 2013, two bomb blasts in Hyderabad (South India) killed at least 16 people. While some reports point fingers at homegrown IM, others trace links to Pakistan-based LeT, which is said to have promoted the IM.[126] The Zee News of India points finger at Pakistan: "[T]he United Jehad Council (UJC) could be behind the blast. UJC, comprising of militant outfits like Jamiat-ul-Mujahideen (JuM), Jaish-e-Mohammed (JeM) and Al Badr, met on February 13 to plan revenge on India following the execution of Parliament attack accused Afzal Guru."[127]

Meanwhile, Bangladesh has already demonstrated its potential to reemerge as an exporter of foot soldiers for Islamic radicalism in the region.[128] Bangladeshi and Bangladesh-based Islamist militants have tentacles in India's West Bengal province and in northeastern India, Myanmar, Thailand, and beyond. They are linked with transnational smugglers, drug and human traffickers. Some Islamists also dream of creating an Islamist caliphate or greater Bangladesh in the subregion of Bangladesh and parts of Indian Northeast.[129] A report published in the *Time* confirms Bangladesh-based Islamist outfits' role in terror attacks in India. The HUJI of Bangladesh has had links with Indian Islamist extremists and was responsible for the 2007 bomb attacks in Hyderabad that killed 42 people.[130] Last but not least, what analysts and scholars hitherto considered totally apolitical and peaceful,[131] the transnational Islamic missionary Tablighi Jamaat (TJ) is now under surveillance for some *Tablighis'* alleged links to terrorist networks.[132] The vast network of this South Asia-based born-again Muslim evangelical movement—which holds international gatherings of millions of adherents near Lahore and Dhaka every year—could be infiltrated by Islamist terrorists to wreak havoc across the world. Despite the dearth of any credible evidence to link the organization with any terrorist network, its open-arm policy of letting any Muslim join the organization is worrisome. The TJ is an India-based Islamic organization having branches in Pakistan, Bangladesh, and in scores of countries across the world.

Can the Storm Be Averted?

No single country can contain transnational crime, terrorism, and insurgencies without active support from its neighbors. Due to lack of understanding and mutual trust among countries in South Asia, the region needs honest brokers to bring them closer to each other. One wonders if the U.S. and China are willing to play proactive roles in this regard. While the U.S. can play a vital role in bringing India and Pakistan closer: (a) by allaying Pakistan's fear of getting encircled by India and Afghanistan with tacit support from the U.S.; (b) by convincing Pakistan to withdraw support from all anti-Indian militant groups, including the LeT; and (c) by influencing India to be more accommodating to Bangladesh's grievances. Ideally, China can play a decisive role in bringing Myanmar and Bangladesh closer to each other. However, due to its unresolved border issues with India, its own geopolitical aspirations and exigencies, and above all, the growing Indo-American understanding, China has reasons to play the Pakistan and Myanmar cards to its advantage. Pakistan and Myanmar also need Chinese support and patronage to endure Indian pressure. Meanwhile, Pakistani and Bangladeshi leaders should stop the promotion of political Islam as it eventually leads to transnational Islamist extremism. Then again, political Islam has its own dynamism. Like elsewhere, both internal and external factors are responsible for the sustenance of Islamism in South Asia. America and India are the main external factors in this regard.

The first major step toward establishing transnational order in South Asia has to be taken in Afghanistan and adjoining northwestern Pakistan. Despite having more NATO troops in Helmand province, neither the Taliban are dislodged nor has the poppy cultivation come to an end.

In view of the growing drug–terror nexus, and some insurgents' (such as the Taliban's) direct links with drug cartels, abandoning war against drug cartels to contain terrorists/ insurgents will not give rich dividends. This is what happened in Latin America, and one is afraid, it is going to happen in Afghanistan. We need answers to the questions raised by one analyst: (a) whether allowing drug cartels to carry on their business is a good idea; (b) whether drugs, arms, and human trafficking are on the rise as the free flow of goods due to globalization has turned smuggling of consumer goods less profitable; and (c) whether drugs, arms, money laundering, and terrorism are different types of transnational threats or they represent the undifferentiated one. We do not know the right answer yet and are not sure "if the diagnosis must itself, as a matter of urgency, be diagnosed."[133]

Again, the signs of these countries getting engaged to resolve mutual differences are least promising. China has problems not only with India but with the U.S. as well. In view of this, Myanmar (despite its gradual opening up to the world, including the U.S. since early 2012) is least likely to cooperate with anybody without getting a nod from Beijing. Similarly, the prospect of engaging Iran in South Asian affairs is least likely in the foreseeable future. Iran's having stakes in both South and Central Asia makes the situation more complicated. Newer sanctions and threats of impending attacks on Iran for its alleged nuclear program will further aggravate the situation. As Pakistan is not prepared to accept Indian hegemony, Nepal and Bangladesh are also suspicious of the Indian design. So, while the prospect of getting international cooperation in resolving Pakistan's and Bangladesh's transnational security problems is uncertain, these countries can take certain bilateral measures with their immediate neighbors in resolving the long-drawn problems. As India's quest to become the new hegemon in South and Southeast Asia will be detrimental to transnational security cooperation in these regions, so is Pakistan's pursuit for the elusive strategic depth in Afghanistan against India. Drawing a parallel between the post-Soviet and post-U.S./NATO Afghanistan, Ayaz Amir believes that Afghanistan since the U.S./NATO occupation has become infinitely more complicated and dangerous for Pakistan. He has raised the following questions: "1) Are the Taliban based in Fata more loyal to Mullah Omar or to the state of Pakistan? 2) Is North Waziristan, in real terms, more a part of Pakistan or Afghanistan?"[134]

Not only Pakistan but also South Asia needs definitive answers to the questions for peaceful resolutions of transnational conflicts and proxy wars in the region.

Notes and References

1. Ramtanu Maitra, "Mumbai Massacre Calls for a Probe of British Role" (December 26, 2008). Available at: Countercurrents.org (accessed on December 8, 2013); Author's interviews with Afghan officials (one Pashtun and one Tajik) who worked for the Karzai Government (October 10, 2010).

2. Ehsan Ahrari, "The Dynamics of 'Narco-Jihad' in the Afghanistan-Pakistan Region," in *Narco-Jihad: Drug Trafficking and Security in Afghanistan and Pakistan* (December 2009), National Bureau of Asian Research (NBR) Report.

3. Mumtaz Ahmad, "Ahl-e-Hadith Movement in Bangladesh: History, Religion, Politics and Militancy," Iqbal International Institute for Research & Dialogue (May 2006). Available at: http://www.iqbalinstitute.com/blog/?page_id=75 (accessed on December 8, 2013); Taj Hashmi, "Islamism beyond the Islamic Heartland: A Case Study of Bangladesh," in Ishtiaq Ahmed (ed.), *The Politics of Religion in South and Southeast Asia* (London: Routledge, 2011).

4. Taj Hashmi, "Transnational Security Dynamics and Exigencies: Pakistan and Bangladesh," *Peace and Security Studies*, Vol. 4, No. 2 (December 2011); Taj Hashmi, "Islamism Beyond the Islamic Heartland: A Case Study of Bangladesh", in Ishtiaq Ahmed (ed.), *The Politics of Religion in South and Southeast Asia* (London: Routledge, 2011) and "Islamic Resurgence in Bangladesh: Genesis, Dynamics and Implications," in Situ P. Limaye, Robert G. Wirsing and Mohan Malik (eds), *Religious Radicalism and Security in South Asia* (Honolulu: Asia-Pacific Center for Security Studies, 2004).

5. Farzana Shaikh, *Making Sense of Pakistan* (New York: Columbia University Press, 2009), Chapters 5–6; Husain Haqqani, *Pakistan: Between Mosque and Military* (Washington, D.C.: Carnegie Endowment for International Peace, 2005), Chapters 5–7.

6. Ibid., Chapters 7–8.

7. Ibid.

8. Ibid.

9. Anatol Lieven, *Pakistan: A Hard Country* (New York: Public Affairs, 2011), Chapters 11–12.

10. Ibid.

11. "Pakistan to Talk with Militants on Anti-Polio Ban," *Daily Star*, Bangladesh (June 21, 2012).

12. Muhammad Zubair, "Army Operation in South Waziristan: The TTP and IDPs," *Daily Times* (June 19, 2012).

13. Zbigniew Brzezinski, "How Jimmy Carter and I Started the Mujahideen," Interview of Brzezinski with *Le Nouvel Observateur* (French newspaper) (January 15–21, 1998) (Translated by Bill Blum) *Counterpunch*. Available at: http://www.counterpunch.org/1998/01/15/how-jimmy-carter-and-i-started-the-mujahideen/ (accessed on July 13, 2012).

14. Ibid.

15. Ibid.

16. Jack Stevenson, "America's Afghanistan Odyssey: When Will Enough be Enough?" (December 13, 2012). Available at: http://www.juancole.com/2012/12/americas-afghanistan-odyssey-when-will-enough-be-enough-stevenson.html?utm_source=feedburner&utm_medium=feed&utm_campaign=Feed%3A+juancole%2Fymbn+%28Informed+Comment%29 (accessed on February 25, 2013).

17. "NATO Vows to Respect Karzai's Air-Raid Ban: Afghan President Set to Issue Decree to Prevent Local Forces from Calling for Foreign Raids in Residential Areas," Aljazeera News (February 17, 2013). Available at: http://www.aljazeera.com/news/asia/2013/02/2013217114747594869.html (accessed on February 25, 2013).

18. "Afghanistan Bars Elite U.S. Troops from a Key Province," *New York Times* (February 24, 2013); "Afghanistan Moves to Curb U.S. Forces," *Wall Street Journal* (February 24, 2013).

19. Amena Bakr, "Afghan Peace Bid Stumbles on Kabul-Taliban Protocol Row" (June 20, 2013). Available at: http://www.reuters.com/article/2013/06/20/us-afghanistan-taliban-talks-idUSBRE95J05T20130620 (accessed on June 20, 2013).

20. Amy Bingham, "Afghanistan War by the Number: Lives Lost, Billions Spent," ABC News (May 1, 2012). Available at: http://abcnews.go.com/Politics/OTUS/billions-dollars-thousands-lives-lost-afghanistan-war/story?id=1625; "NATO Soldier Killed by Assailant in Afghan Army Uniform," *New York Times* (May 11, 2012); "Afghanistan: Taliban Insurgents Attack Embassies and NATO Headquarters in Kabul," *Telegraph* (April 15, 2012).

21. CNN News, "In Afghanistan, Obama Pledges Cooperation, Vows to 'Finish the Job'" (May 1, 2012). Available at: http://articles.cnn.com/2012-05-01/politics/politics_afghanistan-obama_1_afghan-forces-afghan-government-afghan-laws?_s=PM:POLITICS (accessed on December 8, 2013).

22. "Afghanistan after 2014: Why Zero Is Not an Option," *The Economist* (July 20, 2013).

23. *The Telegraph* (19 August 2011); *Dawn* (July 17, 2012).

24. Stephen Hadley and John D. Podesta, "The Right Way out of Afghanistan: Leaving behind a State That Can Govern," *Foreign Affairs* (July/August 2012).

25. Anatol Liven, "Afghanistan: The Way to Peace," *The New York Review of Books* (2013).

26. *Guardian* (October 13, 2008).

27. Gilles Dorronsoro, "Afghanistan: The Impossible Transition," Carnegie Paper (June 2011). Available at: http://carnegieendowment.org/2011/06/15/afghanistan-impossible-transition/1ij (accessed on July 10, 2012).

28. Ahmed Rashid, *Pakistan on the Brink: The Future of America, Pakistan, and Afghanistan* (New York: Viking Penguin, 2012), pp. 90–97.

29. Ibid., pp. 100–112.

30. Ibid., p. 109.

31. Gilles Dorronsoro, "Afghanistan: The Impossible Transition," Carnegie Paper (June 2011). Available at: http://carnegieendowment.org/2011/06/15/afghanistan-impossible-transition/1ij (accessed on July 10, 2012).

32. "McChrystal: Evidence Is 'Clear' Iran Aids Taliban," *Washington Times* (May 30, 2010); VOA (May 29, 2010) (a radio broadcast).

33. "Wikileaks Gates: No Iranian Help to Taliban" (November 29, 2010). Available at: http://www.juancole.com/2010/11/wikileaks-gates-no-iranian-help-to-taliban.html (accessed on December 8, 2013).

34. "Taliban Leader in Secret Talks Was an Impostor," *New York Times* (November 22, 2010).

35. "Afghanistan's Karzai Urges Taliban Leader Omar to Run for President," *Los Angeles Times* (July 12, 2012).

36. Ahmed Rashid, *Pakistan on the Brink: The Future of America, Pakistan, and Afghanistan* (New York: Viking Penguin, 2012), p. 21.

37. CNN, Fareed Zakaria GPS (June 27, 2010).

38. U.S. State Department Classified Papers (released in 2009), *Prothom Alo* (August 16, 2009): Soon after the 1975 military takeover General Ziaur Rahman (later President of Bangladesh up to 1981) told the U.S. Ambassador Davis Boster: "Bangladesh has become pro-Pakistan, pro-Islam, and pro-Western."

39. Basant Chatterjee, *Inside Bangladesh Today: An Eye-Witness Account* (New Delhi: S. Chand & Co., 1973), pp. 68–70; Taj Hashmi, "Failure of the Welfare State: Political Islam and Islamization of Bangladesh," in Shahram Akberzadeh (ed.), *Islam and Political Legitimacy* (London: Routledge, 2003), pp. 106–114.

40. Yoginder Sikand, "Competing Nationalisms and Religions and the Kashmir Conflict" (August 9, 2010). Available at: Countercurrents.org (accessed on December 8, 2013).

41. *Dawn* (December 3, 2008); BBC News (December 4, 2008) (a radio broadcast).

42. Unnithan, Sandeep, "The Karachi Project," *India Today* (March 1, 2010).

43. Louis Shelley and Nazia Hussain, "Narco-Trafficking in Pakistan and Afghanistan Border Areas and Implications for Security," in NBR Report Narco-Jihad: Drug Trafficking and Security in Afghanistan and Pakistan (December 2009).

44. Christine Fair, "What's the Problem with Pakistan? Washington and the Generals," *Foreign Affairs* (March 31–April 1, 2009).

45. Shaukat Qadir, "Beyond Baitullah," *Daily Times*, Pakistan (August 22, 2009).

46. BBC News (June 6, 2009) (a radio broadcast); Interviews with Pakistani military officers.

47. *Times of India* (April 11, 2009).

48. *Dawn* (September 19, 2009).

49. Ibid.

50. "Commander's Initial Assessment," *Washington Post* (September 21, 2009).

51. BBC News (February 27, 2013). Available at: http://www.bbc.co.uk/news/world-asia-21601120 (accessed on March 5, 2013).

52. Ashok K. Mehta, "Crisis in Kashmir," *Wall Street Journal* (August 24, 2010).

53. G. Parthasarathy, "Does Mr. Obama Care about India?" *The Wall Street Journal* (April 12, 2010).

54. Sumit Ganguly, "India Is Annoyed by the U.S.," *Newsweek* (April 12, 2010).

55. The Bureau of Investigative Journalism, "Exclusive: Leaked Pakistani Report Confirms High Civilian Death Toll in CIA Drone Strikes" (July 22, 2013). Available at: http://www.thebureauinvestigates.com/2013/07/22/exclusive-leaked-pakistani-report-confirms-high-civilian (accessed on July 23, 2013).

56. Ibid.

57. William Engdahl, "Pakistan to Become the New 'Major Terror Ground' in Just Six Months" (August 9, 2013). Available at: http://rt.com/op-edge/pakistan-terrorism-separatism-economy-272/ (accessed on August 24, 2013).

58. Selig S. Harrison, "Free Baluchistan," *The National Interest* (2011). Available at: http://nationalinterest.org/commentary/free-baluchistan-4799 (accessed on August 24, 2013).

59. "Barack Obama and Afghanistan: A Gamble That May Not Pay Off," *The Economist* (June 25–July 1, 2011).

60. Ashley J. Tellis, "Pakistan's Impending Defeat in Afghanistan," Carnegie Endowment (June 22, 2012). Available at: http://carnegieendowment.org/2012/06/22/pakistan-s-impending-defeat-in-afghanistan/c6sn (accessed on June 29, 2012).

61. Kuldip Nayar, "Problems Galore in Bangladesh," *Dawn* (Pakistani daily) (September 18, 2009).

62. Rasul Bakhsh Rais, *Recovering the Frontier State: War, Ethnicity, and State in Afghanistan* (Karachi: Oxford University Press, 2008), p. 43.

63. Ahmed Rashid, *Descent into Chaos: The United States and the Failure of Nation Building in Pakistan, Afghanistan and Central Asia* (London: Penguin Books, 2008), Chapters 7, 12, 15–17.

64. *Newsweek* (February 22, 2010).

65. Ahmed Rashid, *Descent into Chaos: The United States and the Failure of Nation Building in Pakistan, Afghanistan and Central Asia*, pp. 317–332.

66. Raymond Whitaker, "Taliban Prepare to Unleash Their Deadliest Weapon: War on Terrorism: Drugs," *The Independent* (October 2, 2001); France 24, International News 24/7 (August 10, 2009).Vol. 4, 8 2011 pp.1–31

67. Anand Gopal, "Deep in the Land of the Taliban." Available at: www. TomDispathch.com, December 6, 2008 (accessed on December 8, 2013).

68. Author's interviews with Pakistani military officers at the APCSS.

69. "Barack Obama and Afghanistan: A Gamble That May Not Pay Off," *The Economist* (June 25–July 1, 2011); James Risen, "Reports Link Karzai's Brother to Afghan Heroin Trade," *New York Times* (October 4, 2008); "Brother of Afghan Leader said to Be Paid by CIA," *New York Times* (October 27, 2009); Peter Dale Scott, "Opium and the CIA: Can the US Triumph in the Drug-Addicted War in Afghanistan?" *Global Research* (April 9, 2010).

70. Ramtanu Maitra, "Get Rid of Opium, or Perish," *Executive Intelligence Review* (EIR), Vol. 36, No. 8 (February 27, 2009).

71. Tariq Ali, "Mirage of the Good War," *New Left Review,* Vol. 50 (March–April 2008).

72. CNN (October 25, 2009).

73. Paul Zabriskie, "The World's Toughest Job?" *Fortune* (a Special Report), Vol. 160 (October 12, 2009).

74. Maitra, "Get Rid of Opium, Or Perish."

75. Tim McGirk, "Afghanistan Fix," *Time* (March 22, 2010).

76. Karen DeYoung, "U.S. Trucking Funds Reach Taliban, Military-Led Investigation Concludes," *Washington Post* (July 24, 2011).

77. Andrew G. Marshall, "Afghan Heroin & the CIA" (April 1, 2008). Available at: http://www.geopoliticalmonitor.com/afghhan-heroin-the-cia-519 (accessed on January 11, 2013).

78. Ibid.; "Filthy Lucre: Afghan Drug Profits Too Juicy to Resist," RT TV (November 22, 2011). Available at: http://rt.com/news/afghan-drug-us-money-893/ (accessed on January 11, 2013); "UK Poppy-Growing Program Kept Hush-Hush," RT TV (September 10, 2011). Available at: http://rt.com/news/uk-afghanistan-poppies-shortage-243/ (accessed on January 11, 2013).

79. *Newsweek* (March 8, 2010).

80. Bobby Ghosh, "Taking It to the Taliban," *Time* (March 8, 2010).

81. Michael Ware, "Official: Pakistan Can Help Broker U.S.–Taliban Talks," CNN (July 11, 2009).

82. Ron Moreau, "America's New Nightmare: If You Thought the Longtime Head of the Taliban Was Bad, You Should Meet His No. 2" and Mullah Baradar's Interview, *Newsweek* (August 3, 2009).

83. BBC News (February 16, 2010).

84. Aryn Baker, "The Afghan Age Divide," *Time* (August 24, 2009).

85. Qantara, "Drugs Money Fills al-Qaeda Coffers." Available at: http://www. qantara.de.

86. Shahzad Chaudhry, "Why Obama May Fail in Afghanistan," *Daily Times* (Pakistani daily) (August 31, 2009).

87. My interview with LtG (ret.) Tahir Qazi, Pakistan's High Commissioner to Malaysia (June 12, 2009); Shaukat Qadir, "Beyond Baitullah," *Daily Times*, Pakistan (August 22, 2009).

88. Imtiaz Gul, *The Most Dangerous Place: Pakistan's Lawless Frontier* (New York: Viking, 2010), pp. 36–37.

89. "Pakistani Taliban Deputy Leader Reportedly Killed in US Drone Strike," *Guardian* (May 29, 2013).

90. CNN and BBC (January 5, 2010).

91. Hasan Abbas, "A Profile of Tehrik-i-Taliban Pakistan," *CTC Sentinel*, Vol. 1, No. 2 (January 2008). Available at: http://belfercenter.ksg.harvard.edu/files/CTC%20Sentinel%20-%20Profile%20of%20Tehrik-i-Taliban%20Pakistan.pdf (accessed on May 29, 2013).

92. "Taliban Says It Shot Pakistani Teen for Advocating Girls' Rights," *Washington Post* (October 10, 2012).

93. Mark Mazetti, "Evidence Mounts for Taliban Role in Bomb Plot," *New York Times* (May 5, 2010).

94. "Tehreek-e-Nafaz-e-Shariat-e-Mohammadi," South Asia Terrorism Portal (SATP). Available at http://www.satp.org/satporgtp/countries/pakistan/terroristoutfits/TNSM.htm (accessed on June 12, 2013).

95. BBC News, "Pakistan Agrees Sharia Law Deal" (February 16, 2009). Available at: http://news.bbc.co.uk/2/hi/south_asia/7891955.stm (accessed on June 12, 2013); Imtiaz Gul, *The Most Dangerous Place: Pakistan's Lawless Frontier* (New York: Viking, 2010), pp. xviii–xix.

96. "Dealing with Pakistan's Extremists: The Hawk and the Dove," *The Economist*, June 1, 2013.

97. Stephen Tankel, "Lashkar-e-Taiba Capable of Threatening U.S. Homeland," Testimony, House Homeland Security Committee, June 12, 2013. Available at http://carnegieendowment.org/2013/06/12/lashkar-e-taiba-capable-of-threatening-u.s.-homeland/g9z7 (accessed on June 12, 2013).

98. Zia ur Rehman, "KP Schools Will Teach Jihad Again"; Ali K. Chishti, "Textbooks and Tolerance," *Friday Times* (August 23–29, 2013).

99. Jeremy Kahn, "Terror Has a New Name: Lashkar-e-Taiba Is Getting Ready to Go Global," *Newsweek* (March 15, 2010).

100. Ibid.

101. Global Security. Available at: http://www.globalsecurity.org/military/world/para/hum/htm (accessed on March 10, 2010).

102. English Aljazeera. Available at: http://english.aljazeera.net/news/americas/2009/05/ 200952144536467973.html (accessed on March 10, 2010); *New York Times* (December 9, 2009).

103. *The Hindu* (June 18, 2013).

104. Ryan Clarke, "Lashkar-i-Taiba: The Fallacy of Subservient Proxies and the Future of Islamist Terrorism in India" (March 2010), The Letort Papers, U.S. Army War College, Carlisle, Pennsylvania, pp. 28–51.

105. Sandeep Unnithan, "The Karachi Project," *India Today* (March 1, 2010).

106. Myra MacDonald commented on "Russia Points Dawood Ibrahim in Mumbai Attacks," Reuters Blogs, comment posted on December 19, 2008. Available at: http://blogs.reuters.com/pakistan/2008/12/19 (accessed on December 8, 2013); Wayne Madson, Mumbai Attacks More Complicated than Corporate Press Reports." Available at: http://infowars.net/articles/december2008/031208Mumbai.htm (accessed on December 8, 2013); Ramtanu Maitra, "Afghan Opium and Terror in South Asia." Available at: Countercurrents.org (accessed on December 8, 2013); Mafiatoday.com, "Crime Boss Dawood Ibrahim May Be behind Mumbai Attacks." Available at: http://mafiatoday.com/other-mafia-orgs/crime-boss-dawood-ibrahim-may-be-behind-mumbai-attacks/ (accessed on December 8, 2013).

107. GPS Fareed Zakaria Show, CNN (November 15, 2009).

108. Ramtanu Maitra, "Mumbai Massacre Calls for a Probe of British Role" (December 26, 2008). Available at: Countercurrents.org (accessed on December 8, 2013).

109. Ibid.

110. *Dawn* (December 3, 2008).

111. Jeremy Kahn, "Terror Has a New Name: Lashkar-e-Taiba Is Getting Ready to Go Global," *Newsweek* (March 15, 2010).

112. B. Raman, "Bangladesh & Jihadi Terrorism—An Update," Paper No. 887 (January 7, 2004), South Asia Analysis Group (SAAG). Available at: http://www.southasiaanalysis.org/papers9/paper887.html (accessed on December 8, 2013); "Bangladesh-Myanmar-Thailand: The Jihadi Corridor," Paper No. 1102 (August 28, 2004). Available at: http://www.southasiaanalysis.org/papers12/paper1102.html (accessed on December 8, 2013).

113. International Crisis Group Asia Report No. 228, How Indonesian Extremists Regroup (July 16, 2012). Available at: http://www.crisisgroup.org/en/regions/asia/south-east-asia/indonesia/228-how-indonesian-extremists-regroup.aspx?utm_source=indonesiareport&utm_medium=execsum&utm_campaign=mremail (accessed on July 16, 2012).

114. My interviews with several Indonesian and Malaysian senior military officers and diplomats at my previous work place, APCSS, Honolulu, Hawaii (2007–2011).

115. BD News24 (November 22, 2006).

116. Bibhu Prasad Routray, "HUJI: Lengthening Shadow of Terror," *South Asia Intelligence Review* (*SAIR*), Vol. 5, No. 3 (2006). Available at: http://www.satp.org/satporgtp/sair/Archives/5_3.htm (accessed on February 24, 2014).

117. *Prothom Alo*, Bangladeshi Bengali daily, August 5, 2009.

118. *Daily Star*, Bangladesh (December 3–5, 2007 and April 17, 2010).

119. *Daily Star* (April 9, 2010).

120. Interviews with Bangladeshi Senior Police Officers, Dhaka (June 30, 2009).

121. International Crisis Group, The Threat from Jamaat-ul Mujahideen Bangladesh (March 1, 2010), Asia Report No. 187.

122 107 "Bangladesh: Tortured Journalist Describes Surviving Military Beatings," Human Rights Watch (February 15, 2008). Available at: http://www. hrw.org/en/news/2008/02/13/bangladesh-tortured-journalist-describes-surviving-military-bea (accessed on July 24, 2012).
123. Selig Harrison, "A New Hub of Terrorism? In Bangladesh, an Islamic Movement with Al-Qaeda Ties Is on the Rise," *Washington Post* (August 2, 2006).
124. "India Reiterates Maoist Threat," *Jane's Intelligence Weekly* (September 16, 2009).
125. V. Balachandran, "Insurgency, Terrorism, and Transnational Crime in South Asia," in Amit Pandya and Ellen Laipson (eds), *Transnational Trends: Middle Eastern and Asian Views* (Washington, D.C.: The Henry L. Stimson Center, 2008), p. 126.
126. "Indian Mujahideen Hand Becomes Clearer in Hyderabad Blasts," *Times of India* (February 23, 2013). Available at: http://timesofindia.indiatimes. com/india/Indian-Mujahideen-hand-becomes-clearer-in-Hyderabad-blasts/articleshow/18635772.cms (accessed on February 23, 2013).
127. "Hyderabad Blasts—'United Jehad Council May Be Behind Operation,'" Zee News (February 23, 2013). Available at: http://zeenews.india.com/state/news/index775.html (accessed on February 23, 2013).
128. Saleem Samad, "Are Jihadist from Bangladesh a Security Threat to Asian Region?" Paper Presented at Intelligence Summit, Virginia (February 17–20), Bangladesh Watchdog. Available at: http://by139w.bay139.mail.live.com/ (accessed on July 7, 2007).
129. Jaideep Saikia, "Terror Sans Frontiers: Islamic Militancy in North East India" (July 2003), Occasional Paper, Program in Arms Control, Disarmament, and International Security (ACDIS), University of Illinois at Urbana-Champaign.
130. "Hyderabad Bomb Blasts: Two Deadly Explosions Leave Terror Cloud over India," Time (February 21, 2013). Available at: http://world.time. com/2013/02/21/hyderabad-bomb-blasts-two-deadly-explosions-leave-terror-cloud-over-india/ (accessed on February 23, 2013).
131. Yoginder Sikand, *The Origins and Development of the Tablighi Jam'aat (1920–2000): A Cross-Country Comparative Study* (New Delhi: Orient Longman, 2002), passim.
132. Alex Alexiev, "Tablighi Jamaat: Jihad's Stealthy Legions," *Middle East Quarterly*, Vol. 12, No. 1 (2005); Farzana Shaikh, *Making Sense of Pakistan* (New York: Columbia University Press, 2009), pp. 155–157.
133. Phil Williams, "Cooperation among Criminal Organizations," in Mats Berdal and Monica Serrano (eds), *Transnational Organized Crime and International Security: Business as Usual?* (Boulder: Lynne Rienner, 2002), p. 203.
134. Ayaz Amir, "The Shadow over Pakistan," *The News* (Pakistani daily) (February 15, 2013).

7

Another Eye of the Storm: The Middle East and Northwest Africa

About ten days after 9/11, I went through the Pentagon…and one of the generals called me in. He said, "We've made the decision we're going to war with Iraq".… I said, "We're going to war with Iraq? Why?".… He said, "I guess they don't know what else to do.". So I said, "Well, did they find some information connecting Saddam to al-Qaeda?" He said, "No, no." He said, "There's nothing new that way. They just made the decision to go to war with Iraq." He said, "I guess it's like we don't know what to do about terrorists, but we've got a good military and we can take down governments." And he said, "I guess if the only tool you have is a hammer, every problem has to look like a nail."

General Wesley Clark (ret.), YouTube Video, March 2, 2007

The…Saudi backing for the Syrian rebels is part of a strategy to replace the Assad regime with a Sunni-dominated governance which might include Salafist elements. The presence of al-Qaida-linked paramilitaries in Syria may help to further the Saudi plan. Iran's efforts to prop up its Syrian ally reinforce the Riyadh-Tehran antagonism, as well as making the US even more determined to curb Iran's influence. Washington's strong support for its Saudi partner casts further doubt on the argument that its encouragement of the Syrian opposition has much to do with democracy.

Paul Rogers, "Syria, the Proxy War," *openDemocracy*, June 14, 2012

Overview

This chapter appraises the American obsession with the bogey of rogue Islamist states and state-sponsored terrorism in the Middle East and

Northwest Africa. This chapter appraises the role of America in intensifying world conflicts—directly or indirectly—through invasions or benign neglect of smaller countries. It aims at resolving the issues: (a) if America will eventually recover from its imperialist hangover; and (b) if the Muslim–West conflict is a derivative of American imperialism. This chapter supports the main theme of this study that global jihad is a hackneyed cliché and that neither Islam nor Muslims pose the greatest threat to world peace; rather whatever is inherently wrong with the West-sponsored New World Order is the biggest challenge to human civilization. There is no credibility of America's so-called "Global War on Terror," as terrorism has never been the most formidable threat to American or Western civilization and, more importantly, except for a handful of countries (not in North America and Western Europe) the world is fast entering the post-terrorist phase of modern history. It is not al Qaeda or the amorphous Islamic/Islamist global jihad that is threatening America's freedom and democracy, but it is the other way round. American and Western militarism, threats, and invasions of countries, especially Muslim-majority countries in the wake of the Vietnam War, are the biggest threat to human civilization. Ever since 9/11, the way America and its allies are on a warpath against undefined enemies, the world in the coming years is going to witness scores of full-blown total wars in different parts of the world—particularly in the Middle East, Northwest Africa, and South Asia.

Meanwhile, an ominous development is taking place in parts of the Muslim world and elsewhere. The so-called unipolar world is becoming history as American hegemony is on the decline and countries such as Russia and China are not likely to remain indifferent to this change for an indefinite period. Then again, America's Military–Industrial Complex and lobbies that profit immensely from wars and conflicts are not going to remain inert. Although the so-called global jihad and threats from rogue states, such as Iran and North Korea, are nothing but red herrings, America and its allies have been trying hard to prove something which is not provable to justify their "regime-change" operations in the Middle East and elsewhere. The real threat to American hegemony will not come from Islamist terror networks or anti-American autocracies in the Middle East and Africa but, in the long run, from emerging democracies in the Muslim world. Last but not least, since Osama bin Laden's death did not kill the hydra-headed, ever-transforming al Qaeda, this global terrorist movement still poses a big threat to American and Western interests. America's intrusive foreign policy in the Muslim world, especially its Israel policy, will remain the most important catalyst in the long run.

The "Regime Change" Perspectives and Ramifications

America has been obsessed with certain regimes in the Muslim world. The world has already witnessed the outcome of this obsession in the American-sponsored regime changes in Afghanistan, Iraq, Egypt, and Libya. Of late, America is obsessed with two regimes in the Middle East, the Islamist regime in Iran and the Baathist Alawite regime of Bashar al-Assad in Syria. Apparently, Iran's alleged nuclear program and violation of human rights have been the main justifications for the possible U.S.–Israeli invasion of the country to denuclearize and democratize it. America is obsessed with the Syrian regime for its genocidal war against its own people. If American selective regime-change operations in the Muslim world are pushing the world toward prolonged intrastate and interstate conflicts in the coming decades is the most important question today. This chapter aims at answering the following questions: (a) is the Muslim–West conflict a derivative of American imperialism? (b) are there better options for America than invading countries in the Muslim world in the name of democracy and human rights? This chapter is an appraisal of America's intrusive policies in the Muslim world in the wake of America-led invasions of Afghanistan and Iraq. It evaluates America's Syria and Iran obsessions in the light of its relations with Islamist parties such as the MB (and its offshoots) in the Arab world and JI in Pakistan and Bangladesh. It is time that we raise the following questions: (a) is American rendezvous with al Qaeda in Syria enigmatic or bare Machiavellian? (b) is America's Iran obsession all about appeasing the powerful Israel Lobby or protecting the oil-rich Sunni monarchies in the Gulf? As Engdahl's study reveals that: "The ultimate goal of the US is to take the resources of Africa and Middle East under military control to block economic growth in China and Russia, thus taking the whole of Eurasia under control," and that the Arab Spring was a plan "first announced by George W. Bush at a G8 meeting in 2003 and it was called 'The Greater Middle East Project.'"[1]

America has been at war with too many countries to mention here. Most of America's wars were needless and avoidable, and anything but defensive. This chapter is an appraisal of America's growing confrontational relationship with several Muslim-majority countries in the Middle East, Northwest Africa, and South Asia, and its short- and long-term ramifications. Is America on its way to invade seven countries in five years in the Muslim world, as a Pentagon official told retired General Wesley Clarke days after 9/11 at the Pentagon? According to Wesley Clarke, the said official told him:

> I just got this [classified note from Secretary Rumsfeld]...today.... This is a memo that describes how we're going to take out seven countries in five years, starting with Iraq, and then Syria, Lebanon, Libya, Somalia, Sudan, and, finishing off, Iran.... They just made the decision to go to war with Iraq.... I guess it's like we don't know what to do about terrorists, but we've got a good military and we can take down governments.... I guess if the only tool you have is a hammer, every problem has to look like a nail.[2]

In view of this, it seems America's obsession with regime change in the Muslim world has been the main plank of its foreign policy. One wonders if America is going to abandon its age-old regime-change policy in the developing world in the coming years or the world is destined to go through another Hundred-Year War.

The so-called Arab Spring heralded a new beginning in the Arab world. America's and Arab rulers' ambivalence and duplicities toward the Arab Spring have created problems for the entire Muslim world. While Arab monarchs and America have been selective in supporting the regime-change movements in the Arab world, they would love to see Syrian and Iranian regimes go the Mubarak-Qaddafi way. They are against similar changes in Saudi Arabia, Bahrain, and other monarchies in the Arab world. Iran also has serious reservations about any regime-change movement in Syria. American policymakers possibly know that democracy in the Muslim world is not going to benefit America and Arab monarchies. Yet, paradoxically, they favored regime-change movements in Egypt, Libya, and Syria.

Conservative Gulf monarchies were unhappy with America's support for regime change in Egypt. Israel is not pleased at the regime change in Egypt either, as it knows well that a democratic Egypt in the long run will not respect the peace treaty with Israel, signed by its dictator, the late Anwar Sadat in 1978. It is noteworthy that the MB declared that once elected to power, it would scrap the treaty. In view of the growing popularity of Islamism in Egypt, it is no longer a question of whether or not, but how soon the Islamists will be eventually calling the shots there. Most importantly, although the Arab Spring has overthrown only a handful of Arab regimes, the wind of change is blowing fast to weaken the already delegitimized Arab autocracies in Saudi Arabia, Kuwait, Bahrain, and the U.A.E. They will sustain as long as they have the oil money and American troops to support them. Having 25 percent youth unemployment, growing population pressure, and mass disapproval of America among Arab population, autocratic pro-American Arab regimes do not have good prospects in the coming years. One Brookings Institution opinion poll in October 2011 in five Arab countries—Egypt, Morocco, Jordan, Lebanon, and U.A.E.—revealed that more than 70 percent of Arabs support the Arab Spring and dislike America. Only around 35 percent of Arabs consider Iran a threat, while the bulk of them consider Turkey their role model.[3]

Meanwhile, the so-called Arab Spring has not brought rich dividends to the proponents of democracy in the Arab world. Tunisia seems to be the only beneficiary of the Arab Spring. The Islamist Ennahda Party-led coalition government with non-Islamist partners, including the centre-left Congress for the Republic and Ettakatol, gained substantial mass support by early 2012. Although the government will take time to create enough jobs for the 19 percent unemployed Tunisians, yet it has so far successfully resisted the Salafist demand for the imposition of Shariah law in the country. However, several Ennahda leaders have been engaged in a quiet dialogue with radical Islamist Salafists. One is not sure how long the Tunisian democracy will sustain.[4] Things are not that rosy in Libya and Egypt either. Egypt went through its parliamentary elections in January 2012, electing deputies who mostly belong to soft MB (47 percent) and hard-core Islamist Salafists (around 23 percent). However, soon the Egyptian military declared the elections null and void and dissolved the parliament. Meanwhile, Egypt had been thoroughly polarized between Islamists and non-Islamists. Most Egyptians want Shariah law and promise to liberate Egypt from "subservience to Israel and the West."[5] Although Egyptians have chosen their leader for the "first time in 5,000 years,"[6] the election of anti-American and anti-Israeli Islamists to power in this resource-poor populous country does not bode well for Western interests and peace in the region. Libya after the overthrow of Qaddafi is no haven for peace, progress, and prosperity. The killing of the American ambassador by Libyan, Arab, and African terrorist-cum-insurgents in Tripoli on the 11th anniversary of 9/11 in 2012 should be an eye-opener to all. And we know the state of anarchy and chaos in Iraq and Afghanistan, more than a decade after America and its allies liberated these countries from tyranny. Terrorist bombings killed more than 2,000 Iraqi civilians during April and June of 2013 while Americans are desperately trying to negotiate peace with the Taliban before their impending and undignified withdrawal from Afghanistan.

The regime-change movements, on the one hand, have weakened the strong hold of Arab autocracies and, on the other, have emboldened people in postrevolutionary Egypt and Tunisia. Arabs vying for democracy and human rights see Turkey as a role model. No longer considering Iran as an adversary, many Arabs are envious of Iranian men and women who have more freedom and better rights than they enjoy under Arab autocracies. Iran's persistent criticism of American hegemony and pro-American Israeli and Arab regimes has also been an important catalyst in this regard. In view of this, it seems Henry Kissinger was right in registering his skepticism about the success of revolutions in the Arab world. He thought the Arab Spring was counterproductive and criticized America's reengaging militarily in countries in the name of "humanitarian intervention."

The Arab Spring is widely presented as a regional, youth-led revolution on behalf of liberal democratic principles. Yet Libya is not ruled by such forces; it hardly continues as a state. Neither is Egypt, whose electoral majority (possibly permanent) is overwhelmingly Islamist. Nor do democrats seem to predominate in the Syrian opposition. The Arab League consensus on Syria is not shaped by countries previously distinguished by the practice or advocacy of democracy. Rather, it largely reflects the millennium-old conflict between Shiite and Sunni and an attempt to reclaim Sunni dominance from a Shiite minority.... The revolution will have to be judged by its destination, not its origin; its outcome, not its proclamations.[7]

Most importantly, the Arab Spring has indigenous roots although extraneous Western ideology of freedom and democracy has precipitated the movement. There is no reason to believe that the overthrow of the Morsi regime, which was a by-product of the Arab Spring and the turbulence in Syria, which has not yet succeeded in having its own Spring Moment, signals the onset of an Arab Winter. Bernard-Henri Levy rightly rejects the talk of an Arab Winter as a stupid slogan.[8] Far from being Islamist in orientation, for establishing God's sovereignty or Muslims' accountability to God, the Arab Spring is a post-Islamist phenomenon, which emphasizes rights instead of duties, plurality in place of a singular authoritative voice, historicity rather than fixed scripture, and the future instead of the past. Last but not least, it seems the adherents of post-Islamism are reverting to the Islamic modernism initiated by Sheikh Muhammad Abduh (1849–1905) in Egypt.[9]

The Post-Tahrir Turmoil in Egypt: The Coup and its Aftermath

Not long after Tunisian youths had come out on the street and successfully toppled autocratic President Ben Ali in January 2011, Egyptian youths started massive rallies at Cairo's Tahrir Square and later throughout the country for the overthrow of the corrupt autocratic regime of Hosni Mubarak. Finally after 18 days of protest, on February 11, they succeeded in forcing Mubarak to resign from the presidency. Things went awfully bad and uncertain in post-Tahrir Egypt. Within a year of the elections that installed Mohamed Morsi of the MB as Egypt's first democratically elected president, on July 3, 2013, the military overthrew the government and arrested Morsi and his followers. Soon the world witnessed a massacre of Morsi supporters by the military. More than 1,000 civilians got killed in less than a week following the military crackdown of August 14. It is evident that as Saudi Arabia and its allies were behind the coup, so was America, despite its apparent aversion to military takeovers anywhere in the world. Here, it seems, American geopolitics in the Arab world—that includes neutralizing the anti-American and anti-Israeli regimes and controlling the oil fields across the region—overpowered its commitment to democracy and human rights. The coup has disillusioned democratic forces in the Middle East about the prospect of having Arab democracies, and they are least likely to trust the West as the promoter of democracy and human rights across the region.

However, Morsi's fall was inevitable. Although he was elected to power, his regime turned out to be more authoritarian than Mubarak's.

One analyst believes that: "The Egyptian public did not elect the Muslim Brotherhood to reproduce an authoritarian regime, but rather to realize the aims and aspirations of a revolution that had broken many taboos."[10] On July 3, 2013—following three days of mass demonstration against shortage of electricity and growing inflation under President Morsi's year long government at the Tahrir Square and elsewhere in Egypt—General Abdel-Fattah al-Sisi, Egypt's deputy prime minister and defense chief, staged a pro-Saudi (and pro-American) military takeover of the country. Interestingly, while media and analysts across the world considered the removal of Morsi a military coup, America, on the other hand, considered the putsch a power change not coup. The Obama administration told the world that Egypt would shortly restore civilian governance and hold new democratic elections.[11] Some American analysts even portrayed the Egyptian coup a democratic military coup.[12]

The brutal military crackdown in Cairo on August 14 on pro-Morsi demonstrators "appears to have been a deliberate calculation of the military-appointed government to provoke violence from the Muslim Brotherhood…to demonize the Islamists in the eyes of Egypt's broader populace."[13] In view of the severity of the military crackdown—selective and indiscriminate killing and arrests of Brotherhood followers and leaders, including the arrests of Morsi and the party chief Mohamed Badie—the Islamist party has been going through the worst phase in its history. Egypt since the July coup and the military crackdown represents a polarized and fractured polity. Christians and Islamists have been the worst victims of sectarian and military violence, respectively. Within days Egyptian court ordered the release for Mubarak, the ousted dictator of Egypt. The country seems to be rolling back to the past. However, Morsi drove Egypt into a dead end—so dead that Egyptians took to the streets on June 30 and virtually begged the military to oust Morsi.[14] Following the July coup and the August massacre that killed thousands of Morsi supporters, Egypt has been thoroughly polarized on sectarian, religious, and ideological lines. It is least likely that Egypt will either become a Turkey or a Pakistan, but possibly another Somalia, Iraq, or Syria in the coming years. We need to understand that the overthrow of Mubarak in February 2011 was not purely a victory of the democratic forces. Mubarak's plans to have his son Gamal Mubarak succeed him as President did not go well with the power-hungry military.[15] The so-called Deep State favored Mubarak's removal, and after a year, it seems, the military regained its lost power. Nevertheless, it is too early to assume that the military has come to stay in the country for an indefinite period. We have no reason to believe that the mammoth mass upsurge that led to the overthrow of Hosni Mubarak was just a bubble. However, as the *Economist* observes, "the generals' killing spree is a reckless denial of the lessons from the Arab spring," that is the ordinary people yearn for dignity.[16]

The July coup was not purely an outcome of the clash between liberal democracy and Islamist dogmatism. American financial and moral support for the anti-Morsi putsch played an important role.[17] The coup also reflected the victory of the pro-Saudi Islamists against the Brotherhood.[18] Soon after Morsi's overthrow, Saudi Arabia, Kuwait, and the U.A.E. pledged $12 billion to the military regime.[19] While the military regime was engaged in mass killing of Morsi supporters, the U.S. response was quite muted. The Obama administration only halted the delivery of F-16s and Apache helicopters to Egypt but did not stop the $1.3 billion aid the U.S. gives mainly to the Egyptian military annually.[20] Although the $1.3 billion U.S. aid might look like a pittance for an economy of $256 billion, yet this aid is vital for Egypt to buy latest military hardware and spare parts for its arsenal from the U.S.[21]

Meanwhile, America's allies, clients, and partners in the region—Saudi Arabia, Israel, and Egyptian armed forces—played their respective roles in the removal of Morsi from power. Saudi Arabia has been promoting Islamist militancy in Iraq, Lebanon, Syria, and Libya through nihilistic sectarianism to counter and defeat Iranian/Shiite influence in the Arab world;[22] in Egypt, Saudi Arabia supported Hosni Mubarak, who was opposed to the Islamists. Saudi Arabia then favored the overthrow of Morsi's Brotherhood government. Had Morsi been more pro-Saudi, pro-U.S., and pro-Israel, Saudi Arabia, America, and their allies would have taken a different policy toward the Egyptian junta.

The removal of the Islamist Morsi seemed to have weakened anti-Assad rebels in Syria as well as the anti-Israeli Hamas in Gaza. It's noteworthy that Hamas's support for pro-Saudi Syrian rebels has alienated Iran from this Sunni Islamist outfit as well.[23] The Egyptian military regime's crackdown on the smuggling tunnels led to the sudden shortage of food and other necessary goods in Gaza. Iran took full advantage of the situation. Pro-Iranian militant Islamic Jihad extended generous help to the Palestinian groups in Gaza. Many Hamas militants swelled the ranks of the pro-Iranian Islamist outfit. The Islamic Jihad also became influential in Syria. Unlike Hamas, which went against the Syrian President Assad and left Syria, the Islamic Jihad stayed back in Syria to defend the Assad regime.[24]

Interestingly, while the anti-Brotherhood Egyptian military regime has been using Muslim clerics, including the Grand Mufti Ali Gomaa, who publicly justify the killing of Morsi supporters or divisive forces as a religious duty, many anti-Brotherhood Egyptians believe in the conspiracy theory that implicates Obama and America as the real patrons of Morsi and the Brotherhood.[25] It seems, in Egypt, both Islam and anti-Americanism have become integral parts of Muslim ideology. Meanwhile, both political Islam and anti-Americanism have become integral parts of the psyche of the Egyptian polity. The high rates of unemployment, illiteracy, and poverty also do not bode well for the country. While one-quarter of the Egyptians live below the poverty line—around 70 percent in the rural areas—illiteracy runs at more than 70 percent in the countryside.[26]

Egypt is going through turmoil and a class war, which is likely to escalate further into an all-out civil war and regional conflict to hard hit American, Israeli, and Western interests. As Chris Hedges argues, "What is happening in Egypt is a precursor to a wider global war between the world's elites and the world's poor, a war caused by diminishing resources, chronic unemployment and underemployment, overpopulation, declining crop yields caused by climate change, and rising food prices."[27] While radical Islam is the last refuge of many Muslim poor, their rituals and faith in the hereafter keep millions of them from despair, the bulk of Egyptians, who were instrumental in overthrowing both Mubarak and Morsi, are not adherents of dogmatic Islamism but followers of post-Islamism.

Although Arabs are not programmed to hate America, the bulk of them are worried about America's lack of support for genuine democracy and freedom in the Arab world. America should understand the difference between the mind-sets of the middle classes in oil-rich Arab monarchies and in relatively poor Egypt, Syria, Yemen, Tunisia, and Algeria. While the middle and upper classes in oil-rich pro-American Arab kingdoms, being recipients of state patronage, are mostly pro-American, the middle and lower classes in non-oil producing autocracies, being deprived of the state patronage, are predominantly anti-American, soft on Islamism and post-Islamism. This makes autocracy in oil-rich monarchies almost invincible than autocracy in non-oil producing Egypt, Yemen, and Syria.[28] America, which has been the longstanding patron of Egypt's generals, would have done better in real politic by cutting off its aid to its best-financed clients in Egypt. Americans should realize that most Egyptians hate their country for its patronage of their dictators. In sum, America in the name of buying influence is buying its way into trouble instead.[29]

America and the Assad Regime in Syria

It is unbelievable but true that America, Israel, Saudi Arabia, Qatar, al Qaeda, and other Western, Arab, and Islamist allies have been sponsoring and arming the Free Syrian Army and other militants with a view to staging another regime change in Syria. This time, very similar to what it did in Libya, America is not going to directly invade Syria in the manner it invaded Iraq to topple the Saddam Hussein regime. Thanks to the influence of the Israel Lobby, America has had a problematic relationship with Syria since the 1940s. America first intervened in Syria in March 1949 by toppling the democratically elected President Shure al-Quwatly, who had been elected for a five-year term in 1943. The CIA-sponsored coup d'état installed Colonel Husni al-Zaim, the America's Boy, to power. Unlike nationalist Quwatly, who did not toe the American line, al-Zaim was too compliant to fulfill American desire. He legitimized Israel by signing an armistice with it and allowed Arabian-American Oil Company (ARAMCO) to pipe Saudi oil through Syria to the Mediterranean coast. Between 1949 and 1955, America staged five military coups in Syria to complete the de-democratization process in the country.

Newly discovered documents reveal a joint Anglo-American ploy to overthrow the anti-Western Syrian regime in 1957. Interestingly, very similar to what America and its allies have been doing since 2011 to overthrow the Assad regime through the Free Syrian Army, President Eisenhower and Prime Minister Macmillan wanted a regime change in Syria in the name of the Free Syria Committee. The CIA and SIS (MI6) planned to stage fake border incidents between Syria and its pro-Western neighbors (Turkey and Jordan) as an excuse for an invasion by its neighbors. The plan was not only to topple the pro-Russian regime but also to eliminate some key figures in the Syrian government. Afterwards, with a brief union with Egypt as part of the United Arab Republic (1958–1961), Syria gradually distanced itself from the West and came under the avowedly anti-Western/anti-Israeli Arab Socialist Baath Party rule. America adopted a more hostile policy toward Syria after 9/11, and there were speculations about America-led regime change in Syria after the overthrow of Saddam Hussein in 2003. Bashar Assad's opposition to the U.S. invasion of Iraq, and his harboring Iraqi fugitives and opening Syrian border to encourage armed Syrian/Arab fighters to infiltrate into Iraq to fight Americans angered the Bush administration. In sum, America's Syria and Iran obsessions explain its rendezvous with al Qaeda.

In February 2012, American- and Israeli-armed and Saudi-financed Arab League mercenaries infiltrated into Syria in the guise of Free Syrian Army. Interestingly, they were fighting along with al Qaeda fighters against the Assad regime in Syria. Secretary Hillary Clinton later admitted that anti-Assad rebels and al Qaeda had fought together against Syrian army. By March 2012, the American- and Arab League-sponsored rebellion backfired. The U.N., America, and the Arab League agreed to a ceasefire and a negotiated peace in Syria under the mediation of former U.N. Secretary General Kofi Annan. However, because of American interest in breaking the Syria-Iran-Hezbollah nexus—and to diminish the growing Iranian influence in Iraq, Afghanistan, and Bahrain—a U.S.-backed war against Syria is very much on the cards.[30] As a former director of Mossad (Israeli intelligence agency) has written, the West needs to evict Iran from Syria to "cut off Iran's access to its proxies (Hezbollah in Lebanon and Hamas in Gaza)...and Israel and the West must prevent this at all costs."[31]

An understanding of the Syrian crisis requires an understanding of the Arab Spring. Tunisia, Egypt, Libya, Yemen, Syria, and Bahrain witnessed mass uprisings for democracy. However, as the Tunisian revolution was different from the Libyan, Egyptian, or Yemeni uprisings, so was the Syrian unrest very different from uprisings elsewhere in the Arab world. Unlike the Mubarak regime in Egypt, the Assad regime in Syria is neither at peace with Israel nor is friendly toward America. Syria also has a mutual defense pact with Iran and allows a Russian base on its territory. The Israel Lobby in America is trying to isolate and neutralize Syria, first through U.N.-sponsored sanctions and then through open invasion of the country to overthrow Bashar Assad à la Qaddafi. Syria, an adversary of Israel and a close ally of Iran and Hezbollah with 300,000 regular troops and 200,000 reservists, is an impediment to the Israeli design in Iran. Israel seems to believe that the road to Iran goes through Damascus. By early June 2013, Hezbollah had already demonstrated its solidarity with the Assad regime of Syria by attacking anti-Assad Sunni militias in Lebanon, which could eventually drag the country into another prolong civil war.[32] Hezbollah with more than 65,000 battle-hardened troops and thousands of Katyusha-122 rockets and hundreds of long-range scud missiles is a formidable adversary for the Syrian rebels.

America, Israel, and Saudi Arabia know it well that Syria must fall before they neutralize Iran. It is interesting that while America has turned a blind eye to Israeli threats to attack Iran to neutralize the latter's alleged nuclear program, on January 12, 2012, President Obama wrote a letter to the Iranian leadership. In the letter, he spelled out the position of the U.S., which Iranian officials read as a sign of American weakness. "The U.S. cannot afford to wage a war against Iran," they surmised. However, the reality is quite different. "What Washington is doing is exerting psychological pressure on Iran as a means of distancing it from Syria, so that the United States and its cohorts can go for the kill," observed one analyst.[33] King Abdullah of Saudi Arabia stated in 2011 that "nothing would weaken Iran more than losing Syria."[34] The so-called "Friends of Syria" that include America, Turkey, and Saudi Arabia decided in Istanbul, on April 1, 2012, to arm Syrian rebels. Arab nations pledged $100 million to pay the rebels.[35] As one analyst elaborates:

> [T]heir [the GCC member states'] interest is clearly in bringing down an ally of their arch-enemy Iran and not humanitarian.... The stakes are too high to make, and repeat big mistakes with terrible consequences.... More weapons in civilian hands would lead Syria to a mix of Lebanon in the 1970s, Algeria in the 1980s and Iraq since 2003.[36]

In February 2012, a Saudi TV station broadcast a Salafist religious leader giving his blessing for spilling the blood of foreign observers. Most people do not know that al Qaeda leader Ayman al-Zawahiri in a video recording—"Onwards, Lions of Syria"—appealed to Syrians and Muslims in Turkey, Iraq, Lebanon, and Jordan to help those who were fighting to topple the butcher, son of the butcher Bashar bin Hafiz.[37] One wonders, if the Salafists, al Qaeda, America, and its allies have discovered common friends and enemies in Syria. In the case of Libya, the American Oil Lobby achieved what they had wanted since long—to control the oil fields in Benghazi—through U.N.-sponsored sanctions against Libya to justify a full-fledged invasion of the country to topple the not-so-compliant Qaddafi regime. Nevertheless, as our experience tells us, America is not going to let Syria go its way. Not only the overpowering Israel Lobby is determined to overthrow the Assad regime, but also to paraphrase Michael Ledeen, "every ten years or so America also needs to invade some crappy little country." However, as the regime changes in the Arab world have so far strengthened the Islamists, Syria would not be an exception in this regard.

One analyst has succinctly explained the Western design to weaken the "axis of resistance" between Iran, Syria, and Hezbollah, eventually to attack Iran:

> The strategy was simple, clear, tried and tested. It had been used successfully not only against Libya, but also Kosovo (in 1999), and was rapidly underway in Syria. It was to run as follows: train proxies to launch armed provocations; label the state's response to these provocations as genocide; intimidate the UN Security Council into agreeing that "something must be done;" incinerate the army and any other resistance with fragmentation bombs and Hellfire missiles; and finally install a weak, compliant government to sign off new contracts and alliances drawn up in London, Paris and Washington, whilst the country tore itself apart.[38]

According to Samir Amin:

> The Muslim Brotherhood took advantage of the opportunity to appear as the "opposition." Thus, a coherent plan crystallized under the leadership of imperialism and its allies that sought not to "rid the Syrian people of a dictator," but to destroy the Syrian state, modelled on the United States' work in Iraq and Libya.[39]

He also believes that:

> Contemporary imperialism's strategy for the region (the "greater Middle East") does not aim at all at establishing some form of "democracy." It aims at destroying the countries and societies through the support of so-called Islamic regimes, which guarantee the continuation of a "lumen development" (to use the words of my late friend AG Frank), i.e. a process of continuous pauperization.[40]

He has aptly raised the question about autocratic Saudi Arabian and Qatari governments' support for democracy in Syria: "Isn't it a curiosity that we see now the emir of Qatar and the king of Saudi Arabia among the most vocal advocates of 'democracy?' What a farce!"[41]

America's sincere efforts to settle the Syrian–Israeli conflict could have enhanced America's position in the Middle East by cleaning up its "tarnished image as a neo-imperialistic crusader power" and stabilized the U.S.–Syria relationship.[42] Instead, George W. Bush during 2006 and 2007 exerted pressure on Syria to agree for a peace talk with Israel. The Israel Lobby was instrumental in America's adopting a confrontational policy toward Syria, although the country was not a serious military threat to nuclear-armed Israel. Then again, although Syria is not in a position to withstand an Israeli pressure, it can create problems for the latter through Hezbollah, Hamas, and Islamic Jihad. However, American belligerence toward Syria is unwarranted and counterproductive. Conversely, America should have remembered that Syria fought against Saddam Hussein along with America in the First Gulf War of 1991. Israeli unwillingness to return the Golan Heights to Syria has complicated the situation. Syria by default has come closer to Iran by distancing itself from America and Israel. Interestingly, Israel and Syria had some sort of understanding during the Clinton administration, which the Bush administration thwarted after the 9/11 attacks.[43] Since the road to Tehran goes through Damascus, an analyst has observed: "It appears that Syria has become a crucial fulcrum for the White House [to overthrow the Iranian regime], with the option of overt military intervention, on one side, and a continuation of diplomacy and covert action, on the other."[44]

Syria has all the potential to turn itself into another fractured country polarized on sectarian and ideological lines. Since early 2012, America- and Arab League-sponsored mercenaries (that include al Qaeda terrorists) and Assad loyalists are engaged in a bloody conflict. One may impute the indiscriminate killing of Syrians to government troops, foreign fighters, and Syrian rebels. However, not only the regime has substantial domestic support and powerful allies in Russia and China, it also has the support from neighboring Iraq, Jordan, and Hezbollah in Lebanon, and, last but not least, from Iran, another bête noir to the Western–Saudi–Israeli triumvirate. Interestingly, Prime Minister Nouri al Maliki of Iraq, who is very close to the Iranian President, does not want the removal of the Assad regime and allows Iranian convoys through Iraqi territories into Syria. As Fawaz Gerges reveals, of late the Tehran–Baghdad highway has virtually become the lifeline for Syria.[45] Thus, it appears that the Assad regime is not that vulnerable to Syrian rebels and foreign mercenaries.

Meanwhile, during and after the Houla Massacre in Syria in May–June 2012, which led to hundreds of civilian casualties, we heard contradictory statements as to who had been responsible for the killing. The Syrian government media and its counterpart circulated totally opposite stories about the massacre. We may consider the following BBC report a credible account on the killing: "They [presence of Syrian troops not far from Houla] do not prove conclusively that the Syrian regime was responsible for the deaths on 25–26 May." The same report describes the anti-Assad Shabiha militia, which was also around, "as armed paramilitary thugs... widely blamed for committing the bulk of the killings at Houla."[46] In sum, to a large extent, Syria is the battlefield for two proxy wars between the U.S. and Russia and between Iran and Saudi Arabia. The U.S.–Israel lobby is also interested in breaking Syria into pieces. They are using Kurdish separatists and other anti-Assad elements, including al Qaeda and Wahhabis, against the Syrian regime.[47] Iraq and Syria-based al Qaeda affiliate, the Jabhat al Nusra or the Front of Defence for the people of Greater Syria, which came into being in January 2012 is another important part of the anti-Assad Free Syrian Army. It believes in establishing a Sunni caliphate in the entire region.[48]

It is time that America and its allies understand what Kofi Annan emphatically stated after the failure of the U.N.-sponsored peace plan in Syria: "Syria is not Libya, it will not implode; it will explode beyond its borders." Contrary to the U.N. Secretary General Ban Ki Moon's stand on Syria—who one analyst believes frequently reflects Washington's interests—Saudi Arabia, Qatar, Turkey, and the CIA have been mainly responsible for the Syrian crisis.[49] Judy Bello's criticism of America for what she thinks is pouring gas on the fire in Syria—in view of her fact-finding report on Syria—seems quite pertinent. She singles out America as "incorrigible in its determination to control the wealth and peoples of the earth." She also blames the U.S. and Israel for their six-decade-long intervention in Syria and Palestine, for turning people into refugees and destitute even in their own countries—Palestinians and Kurds, for example—and she has raised the question if Egyptians and Jordanians are better off than Syrians under Assad. She has also raised issues such as American, Israeli, Saudi Arabian, and Islamist overenthusiasm about the prospect of overthrowing the Assad regime, through violence or through the U.N.-sponsored invasion of Syria. She pointed out that Syria under Assad was not a Shiite–Alawite minority rule but a joint Shiite–Sunni–Christian–Kurdish rule. The summary of her findings is as follows:

1. Many of the "facts" presented in media about the situation in Syria are undocumented and the truth is difficult to ascertain, a "continual stream of reports of atrocities in Syria has over time been shown to be untrue or distorted." "The London Observatory, a significant source of information on the Syrian crisis from day 1, has no one on the ground in Syria, and has rather shady credentials."

2. "However, even a year ago, about 1/3 of the casualties were members of the police and military, though this fact was not reported in [W]estern news outlets. Suicide bombings of government buildings have killed scores and injured hundreds in Damascus and Aleppo. The question as to who perpetrated the recent massacres in Hula and Hama remains unanswered. Investigations have not been completed."

3. "The Free Syrian Army is not a single organization, but rather an assortment of militias composed of conscripts who have defected from the Syrian Army, Islamic fighters from within Syria and Islamic fighters from neighboring states along with members of al Qaeda and militiamen from other Middle East wars in Libya, Lebanon and Iraq looking for a new war."

4. "Muslim Brotherhood fighters have assassinated Christian, Alawite, and Druze, and leaders of these communities."

5. "US Ambassador Robert Ford was meeting with and advising members of the Syrian Opposition from the day he set foot on the ground in Syria, which was only shortly before protests began there. The US has been demanding that the Syrian President step down from day one of the protests. The US has been training and arming a military insurgency in Syria that initially took cover behind peaceful protesters, and now has driven them from the streets. The US admits to having CIA agents on the ground in Turkey assisting Syrian militants."[50]

As Paul Rogers puts it, Syria (very much like post-Cold War Afghanistan) since the open rebellion against Bashar Assad in 2011 has become a battlefield of a long-drawn proxy war between Saudi Arabia and Iran, and between the U.S.–Israeli duumvirate and Iran. The old Cold War adversaries, Russia and America, have had their interests in Syria as well, both vying for compliant regimes in the country. The upshot has been the Syrian civil war. In view of the presence of hard-core Islamist fighters in the anti-Assad coalition, I think Rogers has aptly explained the Syrian conundrum:

> The implication is that Saudi backing for the Syrian rebels is part of a strategy to replace the Assad regime with Sunni-dominated governance, which might include Salafist elements. The presence of al-Qaeda-linked paramilitaries in Syria may help to further the Saudi plan. Iran's efforts to prop up its Syrian ally reinforce the Riyadh–Tehran antagonism, as well as making the U.S. even more determined to curb Iran's influence. Washington's strong support for its Saudi partner casts further doubt on the argument that its encouragement of the Syrian opposition has much to do with democracy.[51]

In June 2013, while the Obama administration favored giving arms to the Syrian rebels, a Pew Poll revealed that around 70 percent of Americans were against the move. Obama's justification for giving arms to Syrian rebels was Assad's alleged use of chemical weapons against them. Interestingly, as the U.N. was not convinced of Obama's unsubstantiated claim about Assad using chemical weapons, the Russian President Putin ridiculed the Western idea of arming "those [Syrian rebels] who kill their enemies and eat their organs flouts Europe's humanitarian values."[52] A Free Syrian Army representative claimed on June 22, 2013 that it had already received a shipment of arms from allies, which he said would soon change the course of the war.[53]

The post-Assad Syria under America- and Arab League-backed regime would not be a stable country. Russia and China—along with Iran and Hezbollah—are not going to give up their interests in Syria. They have different interests in Syria. Russia is not going to accept a pro-Western regime in Syria. It has more than 100,000 advisers in Syria. As already discussed, Russians would go to any extent to defend their strategic interests in Syria. America's apparent benefits would backfire as hard-core Islamists would call the shots in Syria, which would go through a violent civil war that could kill as many as four million people out of its

20 million population. Turkey would not gain anything either. Turkey is not likely to intervene further as it depends on Russia; more than 80 percent of its natural gas comes from Russia. Israel is likely to be a major loser, as any pro-American post-Assad regimes would not have any control over Hezbollah. And Islamists would not be that friendly toward Israel in the long run.[54] As the *Economist* has put it:

> [T]hose who wish Syrian well now need to focus not just on how to bring about Mr. Assad's swift fall from power, but also on how to spare the post-Assad Syria from murder and chaos and how to prevent violence from spreading across a combustible region.[55]

America is least likely to pay heed to its analysts who believe that Syria has all the potential to become "another Iraq," to the detriment of America:

> Washington should stay focused on four key objectives: preventing outside groups from benefiting from the power vacuum; denying weapons to extremists; providing humanitarian aid to those in need; and supporting efforts to build opposition unity. Through material, technical, communications and other nonlethal assistance, the United States should work with allies and neighboring countries to ensure that those who are organizing the courageous internal resistance against the regime and leading the revolution will have a key role in the transition to a new Syria.[56]

By late August 2013, there was a dramatic turn of events in Syria. On August 21st, several hundred Syrian rebels and more than 400 women and children died in a chemical attack in Damascus. Soon America blamed the Assad regime for the illegal use of chemical weapons to kill people, and declared punitive actions against Syria was in the offing for crossing the "red line." President Obama in 2012 declared that any use of chemical weapon by Assad would tantamount to crossing the red line, which would justify U.S. punitive actions against his regime. Within days, the entire U.S. administration said there was "very little doubt" that the Syrian regime had used deadly chemical weapons against civilians.[57] Soon the entire U.S. administration and sections of Western media started vitriolic anti-Assad campaign and favored bombing Syria, "even if it is illegal" for crossing the red line. Washington declared that it was going to attack Syria "more briefly but grievously," as punishment for Assad's alleged use of weapons of mass destruction (WMD), and that the U.S. had no intention of overthrowing his regime.[58]

America and its handful of allies refused to give any credence to reports that pointed fingers at Syrian rebels, not at the Assad regime for the gas attack. Prince Bandar bin Sultan, a former Saudi ambassador to the U.S. (referred to as *habib* or friend by pro-al Qaeda rebels in Syria), is said to have been the main provider of arms to Syrian rebels.[59] Months before the controversy about Assad's alleged use of Sarin gas to kill Syrian rebels in May 2013, Carla del Ponte, a member of the U.N. Independent International Commission of Inquiry on Syria, told Swiss TV: "Testimony from victims strongly suggests it was the rebels, not the Syrian government, that used Sarin nerve gas during a recent incident in the revolution-wracked nation."[60] Interestingly, the Obama administration did not wait to hear from the U.N. weapon inspectors (who had inspected the site of gas attack in Damascus) and within days of the gas attack, mobilized its navy and air force to punish Assad. Many analysts believe Assad did not use chemical weapons against the rebels, as the act would unnecessarily provoke the West to intervene into Syria, while he was "winning" the war.[61]

While it seemed the Obama administration was adamant to punish Assad for his alleged use of chemical weapons, some dramatic development took place on September 9, 2013. Almost to the surprise of the whole world, Obama accepted a Russian proposal to withhold a military strike on Syria on President Putin's assurance that Assad would allow international observers to take control of Syria's chemical weapons. The Assad regime seemed to have accepted the proposal and an armed conflict was averted.[62] Obama's eleventh hour decision to not seek Congressional approval on the issue of invading Syria, and his acceptance of Russian President Putin's "peace formula" instead saved Syria from a possible US air assault. It is worth mentioning that within three days, Assad asserted that unless America stopped arming Syrian rebels and ceased hostility toward his regime, he would not surrender his chemical weapons.[63] Interestingly, President Putin, who is said to have eclipsed Mr Obama as the world leader by stopping the latter from launching his cruise missiles to Syrian targets,[64] also rejected the idea that Assad had gassed Syrian rebels, and told America to "stop using the language of force and return to the path of civilized diplomatic and political settlement."[65] After three days of marathon meetings in Geneva, U.S. Secretary of State John Kerry and Russian Foreign Minister Sergei Lavrov agreed in mid-September on the plan that: (a) the Syrian government had one week to hand over an inventory of its chemical weapons arsenal to the U.N.; (b) all such weapons would be destroyed by mid-2014; (c) if Syria refused to cooperate with the U.N., then in accordance with Chapter 7 of the U.N. Charter, the world body would be entitled to make armed intervention into the country; and (d) Syria would also become a party to the Organization for the Prohibition of Chemical Weapons (OPCW), which outlaws their production and use. On Syrian compliance to the terms of the agreement, the Obama administration agreed to relent on threat of force on Syria. Then again, U.S. officials made it clear to their Russian counterparts in Geneva that "military strikes against Mr. Assad's chemical weapons infrastructure remained a possibility," and that "such strikes would be under the auspices of an international coalition, not the U.N."[66]

One may wonder why America is so ambivalent about Syria and other countries in the region. On the one hand, it projects itself as a champion of freedom and democracy and, on the other, it fails to hide its real motive. Knowing it fully well that it has nothing to gain by toppling the Assad regime, and that "a victory by either side would be equally undesirable for the United States,"[67] Washington can ill afford to ignore the long-term geopolitical interests of its regional allies in the region, especially Israel, Saudi Arabia, and other Gulf states. Zionist Israel and the autocratic Arab kingdoms have a common enemy in Iran. While for Israel, the ideologically committed Islamist regime of Iran is a potential threat to its existence; the oil-rich Sunni Arab monarchies fear Iran for two reasons: (a) its promotion of militant Shiism and Khomeinism in the Muslim world, which is avowedly anti-Sunni and anti-monarchical in spirit; and (b) Iran's long-term pipeline diplomacy to connect Europe, South Asia, and China to sell its oil and natural gas. The Gulf monarchies do not want a pro-Iranian regime in Damascus to allow the Iranian pipeline to go through Syria and Turkey to Europe to sell its oil and LNG. This explains why Qatar, which has the third largest LNG reserve in the world after Iran and Russia, by August 2013, had spent $3 billion to arm Syrian rebels to overthrow the Assad regime.[68]

Other sources reveal that Britain and the U.S. were planning an intervention in Syria to topple the Assad regime in 2007, long before the anti-Assad movement started in 2011. "Massacres of civilians [in Syria] are being exploited for narrow geopolitical competition to control Mideast oil, gas pipelines," observes one analyst.[69] In May 2007, the Bush administration authorized CIA operations against Iran, while anti-Syria operation had been in full swing with active cooperation from Saudi Arabia, which had been mobilizing Sunni extremists having links with al Qaeda and exiled Syrian MB leaders to weaken the Assad regime. They wanted Assad to become more conciliatory and open to negotiations with Israel, and to weaken Iran and Hezbollah.[70] Former French Foreign Minister Roland Dumas told French Television on June 18, 2013 that two years before the eruption of the crisis in Syria in 2011, the British government had prepared for war in Syria to topple the Assad regime to contain the growing Iranian influence in the country, and it was "primarily in relation to pipeline geopolitics."[71] Assad's refusal to allow Qatar to build an LNG pipeline through Syria to supply gas to Europe through Turkey to the detriment of Russia angered Qatar and its allies.

In the long run, if the Assad regime were to emerge victorious, growing Iranian and Hezbollah influence would pose a direct threat to the U.S. allies in the region, Sunni Arab states and Israel. A rebel victory "would also be extremely dangerous for the United States" and its allies in Europe and the Middle East, as some rebels are affiliated with extremist groups such as al Qaeda. If the rebels win, they would almost certainly try to form a government hostile to the U.S. and Israel.[72]

As secular opponents of the Assad regime fear the preponderance of al Qaeda elements in post-Assad Syria, Islamist rebels think America would come after them, after overthrowing the Assad regime.[73] Brzezinski has aptly described America's over-involvement in the Syrian crisis inept. He wonders as to why America is fighting al Qaeda in Afghanistan, Yemen, and elsewhere, and supporting it in Syria.[74] Washington seems to have failed to understand that Syria is not another Iraq or Libya. It is home to a Russian naval base in the Mediterranean. So, there is hardly any reason to be perpetually complacent about Russia's role in the Syrian crisis; it might go beyond vetoing an American proposal to invade Syria at the Security Council in the long run. A popular Russian tabloid *Komsomolskaya Pravda* has warned Washington that: "If optimists in the Pentagon believe that Russia will limit itself to warnings and expressions of anger, like it did over Iraq and Yugoslavia, they may well be mistaken." Meanwhile, Russia's Deputy Prime Minster felt that the West is playing with the Islamic world like a monkey with a grenade.[75] Although a Russo-American military conflict over Syria is not on the cards, yet Russia's overtly anti-American policy in the Middle East—precipitated by the American intervention in Syria—is likely to further destabilize the region. Moscow is likely to increase weapon supplies to Damascus, forge closer ties with Iran, and make an already difficult relationship with America even more strained. America should pay heed to the following and refrain from intensifying the Syrian crisis just to punish Iran: (a) the Red Cross considered the Syrian conflict a civil war between pro- and anti-Assad groups, not a genocide initiated by the Syrian government;[76] and (b) a Syria-based anti-Assad opposition group, "Building the Syrian State," led by Louay Hussein blamed both the government and opposition for their cynical zero-sum games in Syria: while the Assad regime wanted either the authority or anarchy, the opposition demanded "Burn the Country Until Assad Falls."[77]

The post-Assad Syria is not going to be a stable country. It could become a fractured country of rival sects, religions and ethnic communities, or even worse, five different political entities run by five major sects/ethnic groups. "For most of the past 5,000 years, Syria was not a sovereign state." In the event of Assad's forced exit, Syria is likely to disintegrate into at least five warring states: Alawites in the mountains by the sea (constitute 12 percent of the population), the Druze in the southern mountains, Maronite Christians in the Mount Lebanon, Kurds in the north, and Sunni majority (60 percent of the population) elsewhere in the country. It can be a replica of post-Saddam Iraq and even worse, a failed state. The conflict is likely to overflow into Lebanon, Turkey, and Iraq among Kurds and others. Syrian Kurds might also strive for autonomy. The spillover effect of the Syrian sectarian conflicts would further destabilize Iraq. Since Hezbollah in Lebanon depends on Syrian support, a Sunni Islamist regime could be lukewarm to hostile to the Shiite militia. One is not sure if the post-Assad Syria could still be friends with Iran and Hezbollah. However, Iran is likely to control Iraq for decades, and through Iraq is likely to keep an eye on Syria and influence Syrians. However, interestingly, after two years of civil war, support for Assad was said to have sharply increased, by May 2013 around 70 percent of Syrians preferred the Assad regime to an Islamist takeover of their country.[78]

Meanwhile, thanks to American and Arab League sponsorship, al Qaeda and militant supporters of the MB are likely to go for an Islamist takeover in Syria. An Islamist Syrian regime would be anything but pro-U.S. and friendly to Israel. The departure of Assad—who maintains the balance by restraining/controlling the Hezbollah—would be a headache for Israel. Syrian chemical and biological weapons could also threaten Israel, as Hezbollah's 30/40,000 missiles are capable of carrying chemical weapons to Israel.[79] Al Qaeda operative and Osama bin Laden's Libyan accomplice Abdelhakim Belhadj, who fought against Qaddafi along with pro-U.S./ pro-NATO fighters, has hundreds of Islamist mercenaries in Syria fighting against Assad.[80] Things in neighboring Iraq are far from normal. Terrorist bomb attacks are killing Iraqi civilians and soldiers on a regular basis. Secular political parties are giving way to Islamists and the pro-Iranian al Maliki government.[81]

Iran, Another Unbeatable Adversary

Ever since the Islamic Revolution of Iran in 1976, America and its allies have not abandoned their regime-change efforts in the country. After the failure of the "mass movement" for democracy in the wake of the so-called rigged parliamentary elections in mid-2009 in Iran, America was back to square one. It simply underestimated the "raw power of nationalism" in Iran, that is, the average Iranian was not willing to accept America as a friend.[82] Since then America has been vigorously projecting Iran as an imminent nuclear threat to Israel and other countries in the region. In March 2012, Obama told Netanyahu to wait and see if crippling sanctions against Iran worked. In March 2012, Obama also threatened Iran at an AIPAC meeting in Washington: "Iran's leaders should know that I do not have a policy of containment.... I have a policy to prevent Iran from obtaining a nuclear weapon.... I will not hesitate to use force when it is necessary to defend the United States and its interests."[83] While Israel had been publicly threatening to bomb Iran's "nuclear facilities" in early 2012, Obama offered to give Israel advanced weaponry—including bunker-busting bombs and refueling planes—in exchange for Israel's agreement not to attack Iran "until 2013, after U.S. elections."[84] Meanwhile, Israel is allegedly fabricating a smoking gun to justify its attack on Iran, and its spies disguised as Iranian soldiers have already been working inside Iran.[85]Several incidents of Iranian nuclear scientists being assassinated by unknown assailants for several years may be mentioned in this regard. Iranian and foreign experts are pointing fingers at Israel for these assassinatio.is.[86]

As we know, Western nations—directly or indirectly—controlled Iran up to the Islamic Revolution of 1979. Although the nationalization of the Anglo-Iranian Oil Company by the government in 1951 signaled the end of British hegemony in Iran, the short-lived freedom of Iran was over with the CIA-sponsored military coup in 1953 that toppled the elected nationalist government of Prime Minister Mossadegh. Interestingly, Iran's Shiite clerics under the leadership of Ayatollah Kashani (CIA is said to have bribed the Ayatollah) actively supported the anti-Mossadegh coup. The coup was followed by a period of 25 years of tyranny under the Shah, while American and British oil companies owned 80 percent of the oil revenue. Afterwards Iran was practically an American protectorate up to the 1979 Islamic Revolution. Since then—thanks to Iran's avowedly anti-American and anti-Israeli stand—we have hardly heard anything positive about the country. George W. Bush in 2002 abruptly named Iran, together with Iraq and North Korea, among his Axis of Evil. Iranians least expected this from America while relations between the two countries had remarkably improved in the previous five years. In 1998, President Khatami extended an olive branch to America stressing the need for "dialogue among civilizations." Former senior policymakers, such as Brzezinski and Scowcroft, also favored a rapprochement with Iran.[87]

The Western support for aggressors, such as Saddam Hussein (who invaded Iran in 1980 and got tacit Western support till the end of the Iraq–Iran War in 1988), and internal dissidents, such as the Marxist–Islamist Mujahedeen-e-Khalq (MeK), have failed to overthrow the ayatollahs. Pulitzer Prize winning investigative reporter Seymour Hersh has documented evidences of American troops training Iranian terrorist MeK guerrillas in Nevada desert (during 2005 and 2008).[88] Interestingly, America is backing the MeK, which it formally declared as a terrorist group in 1997. Soon after the Iranian Revolution in 1979, MeK fighters stormed the U.S. Embassy in Tehran and took diplomats and staff hostage for 444 days. MeK fighters had fought for Saddam Hussein and were captured by the U.S. troops in 2003. In 2004, considering them protected persons not Prisoners of War (POWs), Defense Secretary Rumsfeld decided to release them. In 2007, President Bush set aside part of the $400 million, allocated for overthrowing the Iranian regime, for the MeK.[89]

In the above backdrop, it is evident that the U.S. hawks and neocons are adamant to fight the Islamic regime of Iran, which they portray as a "fundamentalist autocracy" and a "totalitarian one-party state" modeled on fascism and communism. By 2002–2003, the joke making the rounds in Washington was: "Everybody wants to go to Baghdad; real men want to go to Tehran."[90] As Samir Amin points out, America and Israel, "under the pretext of its [Iran's] nuclear development," would like to destroy the country as it "does constitute an obstacle to the deployment of the U.S. military control over the region. This country must, therefore, be destroyed."[91]Although it is time that Americans realize Iranians hate America more intensely than they hate the ayatollahs, we notice American analysts and policymakers debating what would be the best time to attack Iran. Rejecting skeptics of military action against Iran, hawkish American analysts and policymakers believe that a military strike to destroy Iran's nuclear program could only spare the world from a nuclear-armed Iran.[92] Some even consider Obama foolish for not considering tiny Iran a serious threat to America.[93]

However, it is least likely that America will attack Iran in the near future. Israeli human rights activist Uri Avnery believes that:

> The United States will not attack [Iran]. Not this year, nor in years to come. For a reason far more important than electoral considerations or military limitations. The United States will not attack, because an attack would spell a national disaster for itself and a sweeping disaster for the whole world.[94]

Avnery believes that Israel is also not likely to attack Iran as the latter is closing down the Strait of Hormuz in the wake of an attack as that would spell disaster for the entire world.[95] To close the discussion on American and Israeli hawks' Iran Obsession,[96] we may argue that Iran is not a threat to anybody in the region, let alone America or any NATO power in the foreseeable future. We have reasons to believe that Iran has no reason to build nuclear weapons (unless it is forced to do so). We may agree with Robert Fisk that Iran has already "won almost all its recent wars without firing a shot" as America and NATO destroyed "Iran's nemesis in Iraq" by defeating Saddam Hussein and killing thousands of Sunni militants. Fisk believes that arming Arab states in the Gulf is counterproductive as armies in these countries "could scarcely operate soup kitchens" let alone fight Iran.[97] Last but not least, unlike Iraq, Iran would not be another cakewalk for America. There are people in the Pentagon who believe that Iran could "spell disaster for the United States and its military" in the Persian Gulf.[98] However, America's "Iran Obsession" is so intense that some influential Americans, 10 years after 9/11, formally implicated the Iranian government and its top leaders in the attacks on September 11, 2011.[99]

Meanwhile, in April 2012, Saudi Arabia and Bahrain decided to form a union called the Arabian Gulf Union, in opposition to the Iranian efforts to form a union with Iraq.[100] Meanwhile, America has been arming conservative Gulf monarchies, Saudi Arabia, Bahrain, U.A.E., Kuwait, and Qatar. America's double standard in missile proliferation in the Gulf is noteworthy. A State Department official said in early 2012 that the U.S. was "working hard to prevent missile proliferation [in the Gulf]." Vijay Prashad has aptly inferred, "such hypocrisy could be disheartening" as it essentially means that "the Good Guys (the monarchs) can have missiles, but the Bad Guys (the Iranians) cannot."[101] One may agree with Kenneth Waltz that in view of Israel's nuclear capability, a nuclear-armed Iran would bring stability in the entire region.[102]

One is not sure if the U.S. policymakers pay heed to the Russian interests in Iran and the entire South Caucasus region, and what Russia is likely to do in the event of an U.S.–Israeli invasion of Iran. Iran is vital for controlling (what Brzezinski wrote in his 1998 book, *The Grand Chessboard*) "about three-quarters of the known energy resources in the world." Russia is least likely to allow any foreign power control Iran and the oil and gas fields in the region. Russian troops and a missile division have already been stationed in and around Iran, including Armenia and the Caspian Sea. Russian aircraft carrier Kuznetsov frequently visits the Syrian port Tartous following the conflict in that country in late 2011. It is noteworthy that in April 2012, General Leonid Ivashov, President of the Academy of Geopolitical Science, wrote that "a war against Iran would be a war against Russia," and he also sought closer ties with China and India for stable Iran and Syria. American use of Azerbaijan airfields against Iran could provoke Russia to interfere, signaling a major war in Southern Caucasus and beyond.[103] Meanwhile, Russia is quite apprehensive of NATO's missile defense facilities in Eastern Europe. While the then President Medvedev warned the NATO in 2011 that

Russia would retaliate militarily if Russia and America could not come to an agreement on the missile defense system, the Russian Chief of General Staff Nikolai Makarov went even further. On May 3, 2012 he told senior U.S. and NATO officials at an international conference that Russia would not hesitate in using destructive force preemptively against NATO if the situation worsens further.[104]

As Russia considers both Syria and Iran vital for its strategic interests in the Middle East, any U.S.–NATO and/or Israeli attack on these countries could drag Russia into the conflict zones. Some analysts believe that America "is more seriously preparing for military action against Iran than is widely realized." After the failure of the third round of talks between Iran and the P5+1 Group (Five U.N. Security Council Members plus Germany) in June 2012 over Iran's nuclear program, America was considering an attack on Iran in early 2013.

It does not want Israel to do the job as U.S. hawks believe "it is much better that the U.S. 'does the job properly' than lets Israel, with its much smaller forces, take the lead." The Pentagon has already earmarked what types of aircraft, bombs, and missiles it should use, and from which bases—Fairford in Gloucestershire, England, and Diego Garcia to be precise—in the invasion of Iran. The U.S. would like to use B-2s (Stealth Bombers) and F-22s, F-15E and F-16 strike aircraft and air-to-surface standoff missiles (JASSMS).[105] However, as Paul Rogers observes, "[N]othing has been learned [by America] from the experience of two long and bloody wars, and that is the real cause for worry."[106]

As discussed earlier, America needs a major war every 10 years or so for reasons known to those who understand the dynamics of the American Military–Industrial Complex. We also know that a U.S. retired General Wesley Clark has also reiterated this by revealing the Pentagon's confidential list of seven Muslim-majority countries that the U.S. had been planning to invade since September 2001. The list includes Iraq, Syria, and Iran. American politicians, media, and think tanks have been untiringly demonizing Iran since the Islamic Revolution to justify the invasion. Meanwhile, the U.S. administration wholeheartedly supported Saddam Hussein's eight-year-long war against Iran (1980–1988) to bleed and weaken both the belligerents for its long-term strategic interests in the entire region. Of late, we notice an alarming growth in the anti-Iranian campaigns in prestigious American dailies, magazines, and think-tank reports (along with the vitriol of politicians). Quoting the Associated Press, the *Washington Post* and many other print and electronic media in America in late June and early July 2012 circulated a story about Iran's alleged terror plan (said to have been unearthed by Kenyan officials who had arrested two Iranian agents) to attack the U.S., Britain, Israel, or Saudi Arabian interests in Kenya.[107] We even find the prestigious *Time* magazine and *Foreign Policy* publishing sensational items on Iran's testing of long-range missiles, capable of hitting Israel (with no mention of Israel's capability to nuke countries in the region, including Iran).[108] It is least likely that a country such as Iran, which is under constant threat of attacks by Israel and/or America for its alleged nuclear program, would sponsor terrorist attacks on America or Israel to provoke retaliatory attacks by them.

Nevertheless, America and its allies are determined to invade Syria to preempt Iran's nuclear ambition. Western media, besides politicians and think tanks, has also justified the invasion. Days after the election of moderate cleric Hassan Rouhani as the new President of Iran, the *Economist* in its cover story demonized him and his country:

> The smiling Mr Rohani's public pronouncements encourage optimism, for he sounds like a different sort of president from the comedy-villain, Mahmoud Ahmadinejad, who precedes him. Yet even if his election bodes well for Iranians, it does not necessarily hold equal promise for the rest of the world. Iran's regional assertiveness and its nuclear capacity mean that it is a more dangerous place than it ever was before.[109]

Portraying the rounds of Western negotiations with Iran not to go nuclear, as nonsense, the *Economist* suggested that: "The growing risk of a nuclear Iran is one reason why the West should intervene decisively in Syria not just by arming the rebels, but also by establishing a no-fly zone." Meanwhile, as of June 2013, inflation in Iran was running at over 30 percent, the economy was shrinking, and inequality growing, with high unemployment figures, while around 40 percent of Iranians were living below the poverty line. In May 2013, Western sanctions restricted Iran's oil exports to just 700,000 barrels a day, one-third of what they used to be.[110]

Meanwhile, as an Iranian insider Hossein Mousavian believes, if attacked by Israel or the U.S., the already nervous and estranged Iran would definitely go for the nuclear option by withdrawing from the NPT.[111] Now, in view of the growing nuclear build up in Pakistan and Iran's potential to become a nuclear power, how the U.S. is likely to react to these developments is anybody's guess. Since America is fast moving toward "The Golden Age of Special Operations," drone operations or wars by remote on a massive scale by abandoning the "boots-on-the-ground" policy[112]will be the new way of fighting America's new wars in the coming years, and mostly in the Muslim world. However, America has not abandoned the idea of using freedom fighters including Islamist terrorists, anarchists, and mercenaries to fight, weaken, and topple noncompliant regimes. So far it has been successful only in Libya; America had to use its own armed forces to topple regimes in Iraq and Afghanistan. It seems America and its allies want to topple the Syrian regime first before they take on Iran, which they believe, is going to be nuclear-armed by the end of 2013. Meanwhile, the subregions of the Gulf, Afghanistan, and Pakistan have been sharply polarized between pro-Sunni and pro-Shiite forces. Not long after the beginning of the Arab Spring, Saudi Arabia, the main patron of the Sunni regimes in the Gulf, substantially raised its defense budget to $46 billion, which is the highest in the Muslim world.[113]

The War in Mali and AFRICOM's Agenda

As discussed earlier, although Mali did not appear in Donald Rumsfeld's list of seven countries America was going to invade in five years following 9/11, as revealed in General (retired) Wesley Clarke's 2007 statement, of late the U.S.'s AFRICOM has taken interest in Mali and some northwestern African countries. Interestingly, America has been pursuing its hegemonic policy in northwest Africa through its NATO allies such as France and Britain. As discussed in Chapter 5, in January 2013, France invaded Mali and afterwards some other NATO and African Union (AU) pursued Islamist rebels and terrorists in the adjoining subregion. It is noteworthy that the sparsely populated Mali, with a 12 million population (more than 90 percent are Muslims) in a landmass three and a half times the size of Germany, a landlocked largely Saharan Desert country in West Africa or *Maghrib*, with subsistence agriculture, illiteracy, and poverty, suddenly became the center of a new Global War on Terror. As discussed earlier, France, the 63rd in the Global Terrorism Index out of 158 countries in December 2012, justified the invasion of Mali to protect itself from Islamist terrorists in West Africa. We may agree with Frederick William Engdahl, a famous American historian and analyst of world affairs, that:

> Mali at first glance seems a most unlikely place for the NATO powers, led by a…. French government of Socialist President Francois Hollande (and quietly backed to the hilt by the Obama Administration), to launch what is being called by some a new Thirty Years' War against Terrorism.[114]

He has discussed in detail the U.S. blueprint to control the oil-rich nations in the world in his seminal book published soon after the American-led second invasion of Iraq in 2003.[115]

We know, in January 2013, the American-backed Anglo-French invasion of Mali led to a swift victory for the invaders (discussed in Chapter 5). We also know that President Hollande justified the French invasion to overpower a tiny group of jihadists of Tuareg tribesmen (who virtually posed no threat to France) in the name of protecting France from Mali-based terrorists under Asnar al-Din, affiliated with al Qaeda. The French Foreign Minister Le Drian believed that his country was engaged in a real war in Mali.[116] Despite the claim by America, Britain, France, and its NATO allies, their agenda in Mali was "anything but humanitarian." Le Drian carelessly admitted, "The goal is the total reconquest of Mali." Mali is rich in mineral resources, gold, uranium, and oil. The West condoned the military coup in Mali to overthrow the elected President Amadou Toure as he had initiated a systematic mapping of Mali's vast mineral resources. In view of this, we may agree with Engdahl that, "The truth about what is really going on in Mali and with AFRICOM and NATO countries…is a little bit like a geopolitical 'Victoria's Secret'—what you think you see is definitely not what you will get." The AFRICOM's and NATO's New Thirty Year's War in Africa is based on phony theories about the so-called influence of the al Qaeda in the Islamic Maghrib (AQIM) in West Africa. AQIM is little more than a well-armed criminal band linked with Latin American drug lords, engaged in drugs, arms, and human trafficking in Africa and Europe, posing no security threat to Europe and America.[117]

In sum, one cannot have the last word about the future of Mali in the coming years. Everything will depend on which way the Islamist and separatist rebels, insurgents, and terrorists in Mali, Libya, and elsewhere in Northwest Africa go and, most importantly, if France decides to take its troops out of Mali. It is too early to assume that Mali is secure as the terrorist threat is not over. An elected government alone cannot restore peace in the country. The Tuareg insurgents in the North are not likely to give up their struggle for autonomy, if not complete freedom from Mali. As of August 2013, there were 200,000 Malian refugees living in neighboring countries and more than 200,000 were internally displaced. We may agree with one African expert that the Islamists have been defeated, not neutralized yet. They are hiding in Northern Niger, Southern Tunisia, in the South of Libya, "which is completely out of control at the moment," and Islamist terrorists are extremely flexible and unpredictable. Last but not least, conceding autonomy to northern Mali would not neutralize terrorism and insurgency in the country as other subregions would also ask for more autonomy and freedom, which might lead to total disintegration of the country.[118]

Conclusions

We know about the American, French, Saudi, Qatari, and Algerian sponsorship of al Qaeda in Syria, Libya, and, among other countries, Mali.[119] Thus, we may agree with the view that France reportedly armed and financed the Tuareg Rebellion in Mali to justify its invasion of the country, and that, the U.S. is fully backing France as AFRICOM's "cat's paw." The growing al Qaeda influence in the Islamic Maghreb and elsewhere in Africa and the Arabian Peninsula might eventually lead to full-fledged NATO military interventions in countries across the vast regions.[120] Last but not least, as early as 2007, Dr J. Peter Pham, a U.S. State Department advisor, commented on AFRICOM's strategic objectives of

protecting access to hydrocarbons and other strategic resources which Africa has in abundance, a task which includes ensuring against the vulnerability of those natural riches and ensuring that no other interested third parties, such as China, India, Japan, or Russia, obtain monopolies or preferential treatment.[121]

It seems, the U.S. and NATO are working on the Balkanization of Africa for the reconquest of the continent. John Pilger believes that:

> A full-scale invasion of Africa is under way. The United States is deploying troops in 35 African countries, beginning with Libya, Sudan, Algeria, and Niger.... The invasion has almost nothing to do with "Islamism," and almost everything to do with the acquisition of resources—notably minerals—and an accelerating rivalry with China. Unlike China, the U.S. and its allies are prepared to use a degree of violence demonstrated in Iraq, Afghanistan, Pakistan, Yemen, and Palestine.[122]

America's long-term military ambition in Africa is no longer a matter of speculation. In February 2013, it formally established its drone base in the Niger.[123]

Millions have already fallen victim to the U.S.-sponsored violence, from Hiroshima to Vietnam, Rwanda–Burundi to Iraq, Afghanistan, and Pakistan. And many more are likely to follow them in the coming decades, mostly from the Muslim world. America is least likely to spare the Muslim world from further regime-change operations in the name of "freedom, democracy, and counterterrorism." There is no reason to assume that America is likely to shake off the overpowering influence of the Israel Lobby and the Military–Industrial Complex in the coming decades. If America becomes free from the powerful lobbies that profit from wars and withdraws troops from overseas bases in Africa, Middle East, and the Asia–Pacific regions, then several other belligerent nations from the Muslim world and beyond are likely to settle old scores in the coming decades. If not addressed, the conflicts would proliferate to engulf many more countries, including China, Russia, Japan, India, Pakistan, and Iran. One must always keep in mind that the apparently insignificant event, such as the Sarajevo incident, led to World War I and Hitler's invasion of Poland to World War II. Unfortunately, we have already crossed the threshold of many more similar events, including 9/11 and the unlawful invasions of Iraq and Afghanistan. How America behaves with Iran and Syria will be an important catalyst in this regard.

However, how Israel behaves with its immediate neighbors, with Iran, and, most importantly, with the millions of besieged Palestinians—both in Israel and the territories it occupied in 1967—will be the most important catalyst of global war or peace in the coming years. Israel, since Benyamin

Netanyahu became the prime minister for the second time in 2009, has been vigorously denying the Palestinians any right to live as citizens of the elusive Palestinian State. Since Netanyahu does not believe in the so-called "Two-State Solution" to the Arab–Israeli dispute, his government has been building Jewish settlements in the territories Israel occupied from Arabs in 1967. Consequently, even if the hawkish Israeli leadership and America try to negotiate peace between Israel and Hamas, it would not work. Palestinians are fast becoming Islamist radicals, and the election victory of Islamist Mohamed Morsi in Egypt has further emboldened Palestinians and other Islamists in the Arab world and beyond.[124]

The concepts and implications of global jihad and the Hundred-Year War, as I have explained in this work, do not only reflect global Muslims' disenchantment with America and the West in general, they also reflect the growing inner contradictions and in-fighting among Muslims on ethno-national, sectarian, tribal, class, and ideological lines. As the Muslim world primarily represents the postcolonial world, most Muslim-majority countries are fractured states[125] or artificial entities created by colonial rulers, where people belonging to different histories, ethnic, linguistic, sectarian, and other identities and aspirations were lumped together as colonial subjects of countries such as Mali, Nigeria, Niger, Sudan, Iraq, Syria, Jordan, Israel, Lebanon, Afghanistan, and, among others, Pakistan, Indonesia, and Malaysia. Scholars and world leaders mostly fail to notice the ethnic, linguistic, tribal, and sectarian fault lines that often flare up in the garb of Islamic jihads which are primarily separatist movements, often aimed at uniting diverse population representing particular ethnic, linguistic, tribal, or sectarian identity. Lack of liberal and democratic traditions among Muslims in general has legitimized Islam as their main or only identity. We may cite the following examples where ethno-national separatists use Islam as their main identity to highlight their differences with others: the Kurdish separatism in Turkey, Iraq, Syria; the Palestinian Islamist movements, especially Hamas; the Tuareg tribesmen's jihad or separatist movement (in northern Mali); the Kanuri tribesmen's transnational independence movement under Boko Haram (in Nigeria, Niger, Chad, and Cameron).

It is important that we understand global jihad not only in terms of its anti-Western, anti-Zionist, or anti-Indian rhetoric and activities, but it is also important that we appraise the phenomenon as the main factor behind the state of chaos and disorder in most Muslim communities of the world. Jihad or what Muslims and non-Muslims misconstrue as the holy war has killed more Muslims than non-Muslims or enemies of Islam since the early 1980s. The different schools of the Sunni and Shiite Muslims have their own versions of jihad, and they mostly kill fellow Muslims as the main enemies of Islam. It would be an oversimplification that Muslims in general hate Americans, hence they justify waging their jihad against them. They do not hate the American democracy and way of life; they simply hate America's foreign policy, which has been detrimental to the growth of democracy and freedom in the Muslim world.

In view of the turbulent situation in Tunisia, Egypt, Iraq, Syria, Mali, Algeria, Libya, Nigeria, and the prevalent uncertainties about the future of Morocco, Jordan, Iran, and Turkey among other Muslim-majority countries in the Afro-Asian continents, we may only expect further destabilization of these regions in the coming decades. Irrespective of what happens to the Assad regime in Syria and to Iran if and when the latter becomes a nuclear power, one thing is apparent: The youth bulge and the swelling number of educated unemployed/underemployed youths (as high as 40 percent in Saudi Arabia) will not be the harbingers of peace and stability in the Muslim world. Civil wars on class, sectarian, and tribal lines are on the cards. America/West, Israel, and Arab autocrats are likely to be the main targets of attacks by the growing number of disenchanted underclasses of Muslims. Now, the two most bugging questions are: (a) can America defend its interests in the Muslim world? (b) can Muslim autocracies sustain themselves in the coming decades?

Despite the prevalent alarmist Western views about the power of global jihad or terrorism, we know, as of December 2012, neither America nor any of its European allies are prime targets of terrorism. So, there is no reason to assume that the pro-American regimes in the Arab world are likely to be overtaken by the Islamist militants in the near future. The oil-rich kingdoms have nothing to fear from the jihadists. So long as, they have oil and American troops on their soil, pro-Western Arab autocracies have not much to fear from the jihadists, at least not in the near future. However, their long-term immunity from the radical Sunni and Shiite revolutions cannot be guaranteed. Jordan is one of the most vulnerable Arab monarchies. It has two million Palestinians and more than a quarter million Iraqi refugees out of a population of less than seven million. So far,

King Abdullah II has maintained a semblance of order through political skill and modest reform but he is likely to face "renewed challenges given his nation's grim economic prospects, continuing government corruption and fast-growing population," observes one analyst.[126]

The situation in Bahrain is very fragile. Thanks to the direct Saudi military intervention in March 2011, the restive Shiite majority failed to overthrow the Sunni ruler. The American Fifth Fleet, which is stationed in this tiny kingdom, has also been a factor in the sustenance of the Sunni autocracy in Bahrain. It is noteworthy that the U.S. criticized the Saudi action [in Bahrain] without explicitly condemning the kingdom.[127] As one senior analyst, Leigh Nolan of the Brookings Doha Center points out, "most Saudi elites have been co-opted by the regime," while, "the opposition is divided, and King Abdullah remains popular." But, as Nolan argues, "oil does not render the Al-Saud regime immune to popular discontent." She sounds quite alarmist: "The ruling family may stave off discontent for a while, but if it fails, the collapse of the existing order will be sudden, traumatic and violent. The regime may hang on, but the cost will be great."[128]

Despite America's strong presence in the Arab world, in addition to its bases in Saudi Arabia, Qatar, and Bahrain, the CIA operating a secret airbase for unmanned drones in Saudi Arabia,[129] all is not well for the region or for the U.S. One American analyst gives a doomsday scenario about the success of global jihad in the Arab world:

America might not be so lucky in the next wave of the Arab Spring. Political uprisings or even revolution in Oman and Jordan would be damaging but probably not disastrous for U.S. interests. Saudi Arabia would be a very different matter. If the Saudi regime fell or faced significant internal conflict, Bahrain, which hosts the U.S. Fifth Fleet, would soon follow. It would be increasingly difficult for the United Arab Emirates, Qatar, Oman and even Kuwait to remain stable. Put bluntly, the collapse of the Saudi regime would unhinge U.S. security strategy as it exists today, potentially threatening the flow of oil that underpins global economic stability ... the United States would no longer have the ability to sustain major military operations in the region or determine the outcome of conflict. Hope is not a strategy, as the old saying goes.[130]

It is noteworthy that long before the rise of Saddam Hussein to power, America had started meddling in Iraq's internal affairs, since the 1950s. Saddam Hussein was on CIA's payroll up to the early 1960s, and later he was in the best of terms with Reagan and Bush Sr. Later in 1990, the U.S. Ambassador—sort of—duped him into invading Kuwait in 1990. During the Iraq–Iran War (1980–1988), America provided intelligence and logistics to Saddam Hussein against Iran. The whole world watched Donald Rumsfeld meeting Saddam Hussein in Baghdad during the War. However, soon after the end of the Iraq–Iran War in a stalemate, America clipped the wings of Saddam Hussein after he had become "menacingly powerful" to the detriment of its allies in the Middle East. The American Ambassador to Iraq April Glaspie on purpose misled Saddam Hussein, and, sort of, gave him the green signal. The Iraqi invasion of Kuwait in August 1990 led to the American-led invasion of Iraq, the Operation Desert Storm, in early 1991, which Saddam Hussein classified as the "Mother of All Battles." What the U.S. ambassador is said to have told Saddam Hussein, it appears, was only to encourage him to invade Kuwait: "But we have no opinion on the Arab–Arab conflicts, like your border disagreement with Kuwait." [131]

In view of the hawkish policy of the Obama administration toward Syria and Iran, it appears that General Wesley Clark is right that the U.S. really loves to use the hammer (its military) to fix whatever it thinks has gone wrong anywhere in the world. It also loves to invade countries because its military is great to take down governments.[132] Immanuel Wallerstein has elucidated the "lose–lose situation for the dominant forces in the world" (the U.S. and Western Europe) in relation to their aggressive policies in the Middle East. He thinks, "it is a lose–lose for the [W]est, while not being at the same time a 'win' for people in the Middle East."[133] Last but not least, several fault lines and open hostilities in the Middle East and northwest Africa, between Arabs and Israelis, Sunnis and Shiites, secular and conservative Muslims, democratic and dynastic forces, pro-Arab and pro-Iranian forces, pro-Western and anti-Western forces, the vast region is likely to emerge as another "eye of the storm" in the long-drawn Hundred-Year War, that we believe started with the first Arab–Israeli War in 1948.

Notes and References

1. F. William Engdahl, "Arab Spring Is about Controlling Eurasia," *Russia Today News* (November 1, 2011). Available at: http://rt.com/news/arab-engdahl-us-africa-273/ (accessed on February 18, 2013).

2. "General Wesley Clark: Wars Were Planned—Seven Countries in Five Years," YouTube Video (October 3, 2007). Available at: http://www. youtube.com/watch?v=9RC1Mepk_Sw&feature=player_embedded (uploaded on September 11, 2011 and accessed on February 18, 2013).

3. Shibly Telhami, "The 2011 Arab Public Opinion Poll," Brookings Institution (November 2011). Available at: http://www.brookings.edu/ reports/2011/1121_arab_public_opinion_telhami.aspx (accessed on May 10, 2012).

4. "Tunisia's Islamists Have Survived a Shaky First 100 Days in Power," *The Economist* (April 7, 2012).

5. "Egypt's Presidential Race: Battle of the Beards," *The Economist* (April 7, 2012).

6. Headline in London's *Daily Telegraph* (May 23, 2012).

7. Henry A. Kissinger, "A New Doctrine of Intervention?" *Washington Post* (March 30, 2012).

8. "Epiphanies," Bernard-Henri Levy's Interview by Eric Pape, *Foreign Policy* (January/February 2013), p. 21.

9. Asef Bayat, "Post-Islamism at Large," in *Post-Islamism: The Changing Faces of Political Islam* (New York: Oxford University Press, 2013), Chapter 1, pp. 3–30.

10. Azmi Ashour, "Islamist Clash with Society," *Al-Ahram* (August 25, 2013).

11. Bradley Klapper, "Obama Administration Officials: No Coup in Egypt," *Huffington Post* (July 25, 2013). Available at: http://www.huffingtonpost. com/2013/07/25/obama-egypt_n_3653775.html?view=print&comm_ ref=false (accessed on July 26, 2013).

12. Joshua Keating, "Was Egypt a 'Democratic Coup?'" *Foreign Policy* (July 17, 2013). Available at: http://8.foreignpolicy.com/posts/2013/07/17/ democratic_coups_revisited (accessed on July 26, 2013).

13. Rick Gladstone, "Attacks on Protesters in Cairo Were Calculated to Provoke, Some Say," *New York Times* (August 16, 2013).

14. Thomas Friedman, "Egypt's Three Revolutions," *New York Times* (July 24, 2013).

15. Larbi Sadiki, "Like Father, Like Son: Dynastic Republicanism in the Middle East," Carnegie Endowment for International Peace. Available at: http:// carnegieendowment.org/files/dynastic_republicanism.pdf (accessed on August 25, 2013); Gregory Aftandilian, "Presidential Succession Scenarios in Egypt and their Impact on U.S.-Egypt Strategic Relations," External Research Associate Program Monograph, Strategic Studies Institute (September 2011). Available at: http://www.strategicstudiesinstitute.army.mil/pubs/display. cfm?pubID=1084 (accessed on August 25, 2013); Walter Russell Mead, "Our Failed Grand Strategy," *Wall Street Journal* (August 24–25, 2013).

16. "The Battle for Egypt," *The Economist* (August 17, 2013).

17. "Exclusive: US Bankrolled Anti-Morsi Activists: Documents Reveal Us Money Trail to Egyptian Groups That Pressed for President's Removal,"

Aljazeera English (July 10, 2013). Available at: http://www.aljazeera.com/indepth/features/2013/07/2013710113522489801.html (accessed on July 27, 2013).

18. James M. Dorsey, "The Struggle for Egypt: Saudi Arabia's Regional Role," *RSIS Commentary #130*, Nanyang Technological University, Singapore (July 16, 2013).

19. "Egypt after the Coup: The Struggle to Restore Calm," *The Economist* (July 20, 2013).

20. "White House Response Muted to New Mass Killing of Egyptian Protesters," *New York Times* (July 29, 2013).

21. Eric Schmitt, "Cairo Military Firmly Hooked to U.S. Lifeline," *New York Times* (August 21, 2013).

22. Finian Cunningham, "Saudi Rulers Pour Money into Arming Militants in Region," Press TV (Ireland) (August 10, 2013). Available at: http://www.presstv.ir/detail/2013/08/10/318030/saudi-rulers-sponsor-militants-in-region/ (accessed on August 20, 2013).

23. "Pressure Rises on Hamas as Patrons' Support Fades: Islamists' Sudden Ouster in Egypt Ruptures Lifeline for Gaza's Militant Rulers," *New York Times* (August 24, 2013); Lihi Ben Shitrit, Mahmoud Jaraba, "Hamas in the Post-Morsi Period," *Sada*, Carnegie Endowment for International Peace. Available at: http://carnegieendowment.org/sada/2013/08/01/hamas-in-post-morsi-period/gh2c (accessed on August 1, 2013).

24. "In Gaza, Iran Finds an Ally More—Agreeable Than Hamas," *New York Times* (August 1, 2013).

25. "Egypt Military Cites Religion to Quell Ranks: Seeking to Justify Attacks on Civilians," *New York Times* (August 26, 2013).

26. "Poverty Rate Rises in Egypt, Widening Gap between Rich and Poor: CAPMAS," *Ahram Online* (November 29, 2012). Available at: http://english.ahram.org.eg/NewsContent/3/12/59433/Business/Economy/Poverty-rate-rises-in-Egypt,-widening-gap-between-.aspx (accessed on August 26, 2013); Chris Hedges, "Murdering the Wretched of the Earth," (August 14, 2013). Available at: http://www.truthdig.com/report/item/murdering_the_wretched_of_the_earth_20130814/ (accessed on August 26, 2013).

27. Chris Hedges, "Murdering the Wretched of the Earth," *Truthdig*, August 14, 2013, Available at: www.truthdig.com/report/item/murdering_the_wretched_of_the_earth_20130814 (accessed on March 29, 2014).

28. Amaney A. Jamal, "Can Washington Win over the Arab Street? The Sources of Middle Eastern Anti-Americanism;" "It's Not Who We Are, It's What We Do," *Foreign Affairs* (September–October 2013), p. 152.

29. Ross Douthat, "Let Our Client Go," *New York Times* (August 18, 2013).

30. Chris Marsden, "Pentagon Plans US-Backed War Against Syria" (February 10, 2012). Available at: (www.WSWS.org) (accessed on February 12, 2012);

Ben Schreiner, "War: Marching towards Syria: Eyes Cast on Iran" (March 7, 2012). Available at: www.globalresearch.ca (accessed on March 10, 2012); Finian Cunningham, "Syria: The Western Deception Over Regime Change Unravels: NATO Prepares for All Out War," *Global Research* (8 March 2012). Available at: www.globalresearch.ca (accessed on March 10, 2012); Michel Chossudovsky, "Syria: NATO's Next 'Humanitarian' War?" *Global Research* (February 11, 2012). Available at: www.globalresearch.ca (accessed on February 15, 2012).

31. Efraim Halevy, "Iran's Achilles' Heel," *New York Times* (February 7, 2012).

32. "Syrian Rebels, Hezbollah I Deadly Fight in Lebanon," Reuters (June 2, 2013); "War Next Door Challenges Hezbollah Role in Lebanon," *Wall Street Journal* (June 5, 2013).

33. Mahdi Darius Nazemroaya, "Obama's Secret Letter to Tehran: Is the War against Iran on Hold? 'The Road to Tehran Goes through Damascus,'" *Global Research* (January 20, 2012).

34. John Hannah, "Responding to Syria: The King's Statement, the President's Hesitation," *Foreign Policy* (August 9, 2011).

35. Mariano Aguirre, "Syria's Crisis: Weapons vs Negotiations," *openDemocracy* (April 7, 2012). Available at: http://www.opendemocracy.net/mariano-aguirre/syrias-crisis-weapons-vs-negotiations (accessed on April 8, 2012).

36. Ibid.; Finian Cunningham, "Syria—The Western Deception Over Regime Change Unravels: NATO Prepares for All Out War," *Global Research* (March 8, 2012). Available at: www.globalresearch.ca (accessed on March 15, 2012).

37. *Daily Star*, Bangladesh (February 12, 2012).

38. Dan Glazebrook, "The West's Greatest Fear," Al-Ahram Weekly Online (May 3–9, 2012). Available at: http://weekly.ahram.org.eg/2012/1096/op8.htm (accessed on December 8, 2013).

39. Samir Amin, "The Arab Revolutions: A Year After," *Interface* (May 2012).

40. Ibid.

41. Ibid.

42. Moshe Ma'oz, "Damascus vs Washington: Between the 'Axis of Evil' and 'Pax Americana,'" in Bruce Cumings, Ervand Abrahamian, and Moshe Ma'oz (eds), *Inventing the Axis of Evil: The Truth about North Korea, Iran and Syria* (New York: The New Press, 2004), pp. 157–158 and 208–209.

43. John J. Mearsheimer and Stephen M. Walt, "Taking Aim at Syria," in *The Israel Lobby and U.S. Foreign Policy* (New York: Farrar, Straus and Giroux, 2007), Chapter 9, pp. 263–279.

44. Evan Taylor, "Militarizing the Conflict in Syria," *Z Magazine*, Vol. 25, No. 4 (April 2012).

45. Fareed Zakaria, GPS Show, CNN (June 3, 2012).

46. BBC News Middle East (May 31, 2012). Available at: http://www.bbc.co.uk/news/world-middle-east-18274542 (accessed on June 22, 2012).

47. Michel Chossudovsky, "Hidden US-Israeli Military Agenda: 'Break Syria into Pieces,'" *Global Research* (June 16, 2012). Available at: http://www.globalresearch.ca/index.php?context=va&aid=31454 (accessed on December 8, 2013); Scott Taylor, "Syria Strategy Looks like Bloody Repeat," *Global Research* (June 18, 2012). Available at: http://www.globalresearch.ca/index.php?context=va&aid=31476 (accessed on June 22, 2012).

48. Agence France-Presse (AFP), "Qaeda in Iraq Confirms Syria's Nusra Is Part of Network" (April 9, 2013); "Inside Jabhat al Nusra—The Most Extreme Wing of Syria's Struggle," *Daily Telegraph* (December 2, 2012).

49. Phyllis Bennis, "Syria: No to Intervention, No to Illusions," Mondoweiss (June 30, 2012). Available at: http://mondoweiss.net/2012/06/syria-no-to-intervention-no-to-illusions.html (accessed on July 3, 2012).

50. Judy Bello, "Who Is Driving the Syrian Uprising? Hands off Syria!" *Counterpunch* (June 30–July 02, 2012). Available at: http://www.counterpunch.org/2012/06/29/hands-off-syria/print (accessed on July 2, 2012).

51. Paul Rogers, "Syria, The Proxy War," *openDemocracy* (June 14, 2012). Available at: http://www.opendemocracy.net/paul-rogers/syria-proxy-war (accessed on June 19, 2012).

52. *Guardian* (June 16, 2013); RT News (June 22, 2013).

53. Al Jazeera English. Available at: http://www.aljazeera.com/news/middleeast/2013/06/201362113326945851.html (accessed on June 22, 2013).

54. George Friedman, "Consequences of the Fall of the Syrian Regime," Stratfor (July 24, 2012). Available at: http://www.stratfor.com/weekly/consequences-fall-syrian-regime?ut...gweekly&utm_content=readmore& elq=f1368d7a587748358f420156494daec7 (accessed on July 25, 2012); F. William Engdahl, "Putin's Geopolitical Chess Game with Washington in Syria and Eurasia," *Global Research* (July 23, 2012). Available at: www.globalresearch.ca/PrintArticle.php?articleId=32019 (accessed on July 25, 2012).

55. "Towards the End Game," *The Economist* (July 19, 2012).

56. Katherine Wilkens, "Avoiding the Iraq Experience in Syria," *National Interest*. Available at: http://carnegieendowment.org/2012/08/02/avoiding-iraq-experience-in-syria/d5c1 (accessed on August 2, 2012).

57. Kimberly Dozier, "Syria Chemical Attack: 'Very Little Doubt' Assad Regime Used Weapons, U.S. Official Says," *Huffington Post* (August 25, 2013). Available at: http://www.huffingtonpost.com/2013/08/25/syria-chemical-attack-us_n_3812796.html (accessed on August 28, 2013).

58. Thom Shanker, C.J. Chivers, and Michael R. Gordon, "Obama Weighing 'Limited' Strikes on Syrian Forces," *New York Times* (August 28, 2013); Ian Hurd, "Bomb Syria. Even if It Is Illegal," *New York Times* (August 28, 2013); "Syria: A Step Too Far," *The Economist* (August 24, 2013); Michael Weiss, "How to Oust Assad: And Why the United States Should Try,"

Foreign Affairs (August 28, 2013). Available at: http://www.foreignaffairs.
com/articles/139874/michael-weiss/how-to-oust-assad?cid=nlc-this_
week_on_foreign_affairs-082913-how_to_oust_assad_4-082913&sp_
mid=42434740&sp_rid=dGFqX2hhc2htaUBob3RtYWlsLmNvbQS2
(accessed on August 30, 2013); "Hit Him Hard," *The Economist* (August
31, 2013).

59. Dale Gavlak and Yahya Ababneh, "Syrians in Ghouta Claim Saudi-Supplied
Rebels behind Chemical Attack" (August 31, 2013). Available at: http://
original.antiwar.com/Dale-Gavlak/2013/08/30/syrians-in-ghouta-claim-
saudi-supplied-rebels-behind-chemical-attack/ (accessed on December 8,
2013).

60. Shaun Waterman, "Syrian Rebels Used Sarin Nerve Gas, Not Assad's Regime:
U.N. Official," *Washington Times* (May 6, 2013). Available at: http://www.
washingtontimes.com/news/2013/may/6/syrian-rebels-used-sarin-nerve-
gas-not-assads-regi/#ixzz2dJ1NugCW (accessed on December 8, 2013).

61. "Arab League Rejects Attack against Syria," *New York Times* (August 28, 2013);
Tim Stanley, "Syria: Why Would Assad Invite a Western Intervention by
Using WMDs in a War He Was Winning?" *The Telegraph* (August 27, 2013).
Available at: http://blogs.telegraph.co.uk/news/timstanley/100232698/
syria-why-would-assad-invite-a-western-intervention-by-using-wmds-in-a-
war-he-was-winning/ (accessed on December 8, 2013); Peter Osborne, "The
Rush to Judgment on Syria Is a Catastrophic and Deadly Error," *Telegraph*
(August 29, 2013).

62. *New York Times*, "Obama Embraces Russian Proposal on Syria Weapons,"
New York Times (September 10, 2013).

63. CNN News (September 12, 2013).

64. *New York Times*, "As Obama Pauses Action, Putin Takes Center Stage," *New
York Times* (September 12, 2013).

65. Vladimir V. Putin, "A Plea for Caution from Russia," *New York Times*
(September 12, 2013).

66. Peter Baker and Michael Gordon, "U.S.-Russia Talks on Syria's Arms
Make Progress," *New York Times* (September 14, 2013); Jay Solomon and
Carol Lee, "U.S. Holds Fire As Syria Talks Move Forward," *The Wall Street
Journal* (2013); Michael Gordon, "Deal Reached to Destroy Syria's Chemical
Arsenal," *New York Times* (September 15, 2013).

67. Edward N. Luttwak, "In Syria, America Loses if Either Side Wins," *New
York Times* (August 24, 2013).

68. Michael Snyder, commented on "Is the United States Going to Go to War With
Syria over a Natural Gas Pipeline?" The Economic Collapse Blog (comment
posted on September 3, 2013). Available at: http://theeconomiccollapseblog.
com/archives/is-the-united-states-going-to-go-to-war-with-syria-over-a-
natural-gas-pipeline (accessed on September 13, 2013).

69. Nafeez Ahmed, "Syria Intervention Plan Fueled by Oil Interests, Not
Chemical Weapon Concern," *The Guardian* (August 30, 2013). Available

at: http://www.theguardian.com/environment/earth-insight/2013/aug/30/
syria-chemical-attack-war-intervention-oil-gas-energy-pipelines (accessed
on September 12, 2013).

70. Ibid.
71. Roland Dumas, "The British Prepared for War in Syria 2 Years before the
Eruption of the Crisis in 2011" (June 18, 2013). Available at: http://www.
youtube.com/watch?v=jeyRwFHR8WY (accessed on September 14, 2013).
72. Edward N. Luttwak, "In Syria, America Loses if Either Side Wins," *New York Times* (August 24, 2013).
73. David D. Kirkpatrick, "Looming Airstrikes in Syria Test for Egypt's Leaders
and Opposition," *New York Times* (August 29, 2013); Michael R. Gordon,
"Aim of a U.S. Attack on Syria: Sharpening a Blurred 'Red Line,'" *New York Times* (August 30, 2013).
74. Fareed Zakaria, GPS Show, CNN (September 1, 2013).
75. Steven Rosenberg, "Syria Crisis: Gauging Russia's Reaction to Strike Scenario,"
BBC News, Moscow (August 28, 2013). Available at: http://www.bbc.co.uk/
news/world-europe-23865053 (accessed on December 8, 2013).
76. "Red Cross Classifies Syrian Conflict as Civil War," *Foreign Policy* (July
16, 2012). Available at: https://bay165.mail.live.com/default.aspx?id=6
4855#n=641914279&fid=1&fav=1&mid=a6708d60-cf43-11e1-9e09-
00215ad7e1ca&fv=1 (accessed on July 16, 2012).
77. Louay Hussein, "Saving the Syrian Homeland," *Monthly Review*, Vol. 64, No.
3 (2012). Available at: http://mrzine.monthlyreview.org/2012/syria130712.
html (accessed on July 17, 2012).
78. "NATO Data: Assad Winning the War for Syrians' Hearts and Minds,"
Special to WorldTribune.com (May 31, 2013). Available at: http://www.
worldtribune.com/author/admin/ (accessed on June 2, 2013).
79. Karl Vick, "Five Ways Life after Assad Could Get Much, Much Worse,"
Time (August 6, 2012).
80. "Profile: Libyan Rebel Commander Abdel Hakim Belhadj," BBC News,
Africa (July 4, 2012). Available at: http://www.bbc.co.uk/news/world-
africa-14786753 (accessed on December 8, 2013); Ruth Sherlock, "Leading
Libyan Islamist Met Free Syrian Army Opposition Group," *Telegraph*
(November 27, 2011).
81. "Iraq's Secular Opposition: The Rise and Decline of Al-Iraqiya," International
Crisis Group—New Report, Baghdad/Brussels (July 31, 2012).
82. Fareed Zakaria, "The Wall Isn't Falling: Historical Parallels Don't Work in
Iran," *Newsweek* (July 13, 2009).
83. *The Telegraph* (March 4, 2012).
84. *New York Post* (March 8, 2012).
85. Julie Levesque, "Fabricating a 'Smoking Gun' to Attack Iran? Israeli Spies
Disguised as Iranian Soldiers on Mission inside Iran," *Global Research*
(March 27, 2012). Available at: www.globalresearch.ca (accessed on April
15, 2012).

86. "Target Iran: Assassinations, Cyber attacks, Sabotage—Has the War against Tehran Already Begun?" *Newsweek* (December 20, 2010); Christopher Dickey et al., "Someone Is Killing Iran's Nuclear Scientist: But a Computer Worm May Be the Scarier Threat"; Ronen Bergman, "Killing the Killers: Israeli Hit Teams Have a History of Eliminating Weapons Scientists," *Newsweek* (December 20, 2010).

87. Bruce Cumings, Ervand Abrahamian, and Moshe Ma'oz, *Inventing the Axis of Evil: The Truth About North Korea, Iran and Syria* (New York: The New Press, 2004), pp. 94–95.

88. Seymour Hersh, "Training Terrorists in Nevada: Seymour Hersh on U.S. Aid to Iranian Group Tied to Scientist Killings" (April 10, 2012). Available at: http://www.democracynow.org/2012/4/10/training_terrorists_in_nevada_seymour_hersh (accessed on December 8, 2013); Seymor M. Hersh, "Our Men in Iran?" *The New Yorker* (April 6, 2012). Available at: http://www.newyorker.com/online/blogs/newsdesk/2012/04/mek.html (accessed February on 24, 2014).

89. Jonathan R. While, *Terrorism & Homeland Security* (Belmont, California: Wadsworth, 2012), pp. 358–359.

90. Bruce Cumings, Ervand Abrahamian, and Moshe Ma'oz, *Inventing the Axis of Evil: The Truth about North Korea, Iran and Syria* (New York: The New Press, 2004), pp. 100–101.

91. Samir Amin, "The Arab Revolutions: A Year After," *Interface* (May 2012).

92. Matthew Kroenig, "Time to Attack Iran—Why a Strike Is the Least Bad Option," *Foreign Affairs* (January–February 2012).

93. Carl Rove and Ed Gillespie, "How to Beat Obama: The President Is Far More Vulnerable Than He Thinks On Foreign Policy," *Foreign Policy* (March–April 2012).

94. Uri Avnery, "Israel Will Not Attack Iran," *Outlook* (March 13, 2012). Available at: http://outlookindia.com (accessed on March 31, 2012).

95. Ibid.

96. S.P. Seth, "US's Iranian Obsession," *Daily Times* (December 14 and 15, 2011).

97. Robert Fisk, "We've Been Here Before—And It Suits Israel That We Never Forget 'Nuclear Iran,'" *The Independent* (January 25, 2012).

98. Mahdi Darius Nazemroya, "The Geo-Politics of the Strait of Hormuz: Could the U.S. Navy be defeated by Iran in the Persian Gulf?" *Global Research* (January 8, 2012).

99. United States District Court, Southern District of New York, Case 1:03-cv-09848-GBD Document 294, Filed 12/22/11, Civil Action No. 03 MDL 1570 (GBD), IN RE Terrorist Attacks on September 11, 2011. Available at: http://information.iran911case.com/Havlish_Findings_of_Fact_and_Conclusions_of_Law_Signed_12-22-11.pdf (accessed on June 22, 2012).

100. "Bahrain, Saudi Arabia to Form 'Arabian Gulf Union' Next Month," *Ya Libnan* (April 26, 2012). Available at: http://www.yalibnan.com/2012/04/26/

bahrain-saudi-arabia-to-form-gulf-arab-union-next-month/ (accessed on April 29, 2012).

101. Vijay Prashad, "Washington Bets on the Gulf Royals" (April 26, 2012). Available at: *Counterpunch*.org (accessed on April 28, 2012).

102. Kenneth N. Waltz, "Why Iran Should Get the Bomb: Nuclear Balancing Would Mean Stability," *Foreign Affairs* (July–August 2012).

103. Clara Weiss, "Russia Prepares for a US–Israeli Military Strike against Iran." Available at: World Socialist website; Michael Chossudovsky, "The Iran War Theater's 'Northern Front': Azerbaijan and the US Sponsored War on Iran," *Global Research* (April 9, 2007).

104. "Russia's Military Threatens Pre-Emptive Strike if NATO Goes Ahead with Missile Plan," Associated Press (May 3, 2012). Available at: http://www. foxnews.com/world/2012/05/03/russian-military-ups-ante-on-missile-defense/ (accessed on May 10, 2012).

105. Paul Rogers, "America's War on Iran: The Plan Revealed," *openDemocracy* (June 30, 2012). Available at: http://www.opendemocracy.net (accessed on July 2, 2012).

106. Ibid.

107. Stephen Manual, "Two Iranian Agents in Kenya Planned Attack on US, Israeli Targets," *All Voices* (July 2, 2012). Available at: http://www.allvoices.com/ contributed-news/12508330-two-iranian-agents-in-kenya-planned-attack-against-us-israeli-targets (accessed in February 2014); "Iranian Charged in Kenya with Planning an Attack Says Israeli Agents Interrogated Him," *Washington Post* (June 27, 2012); "Kenya: Iranians Held in Bomb Plot: Target Israeli?"Associated Press (July 2, 2012). Available at: http://www.sfgate.com/ world/article/Kenya-Iranians-held-in-bomb-plot-target-Israeli-3680359. php (accessed on July 3, 2012).

108. "Iran Tests Long-Range Missile," Foreign Policy, *Morning Brief*. Available at: www.foreignpolicy.com (accessed on July 3, 2012).

109. "Persian Power: Can Iran Be Stopped?" *The Economist* (June 22, 2013), p. 11.

110. Ibid.

111. Carnegie Endowment for International Peace, "Insider's Account of Iran's Nuclear Negotiations," Video Q&A (May 29, 2012). Available at: http:// carnegieendowment.org/2012/05/29/insider-s-account-of-iran-s-nuclear-negotiations/bOFT (accessed on June 6, 2012).

112. Paul Rogers, "America's New Wars, and Militarized Diplomacy," *openDemocracy* (May 31, 2012). Available at: http://www.opendemocracy. net (accessed on June 2, 2012).

113. *The Economist* (April 7, 2012).

114. F. William Engdahl, "The War in Mali and AFRICOM's Agenda: Target China," *Global Research* (February 10, 2013). Available at: http://www. globalresearch.ca/the-war-in-mali-and-africoms-african-agenda-target-china/5322517 (accessed on February 11, 2013).

115. F. William Engdahl, *A Century of War: Anglo-American Oil Politics and the New World Order* (London: Pluto Press, 2004).
116. "France Action in Mali Is Real War, Says Le Drian," BBC News, Africa (February 6, 2013). Available at: http://www.bbc.co.uk/news/world-africa-21348335 (accessed on February 19, 2013).
117. F. William Engdahl, "The War in Mali and AFRICOM's Agenda: Target China," *Global Research* (February 10, 2013). Available at: http://www.globalresearch.ca/the-war-in-mali-and-africoms-african-agenda-target-china/5322517 (accessed on February 11, 2013).
118. "Mali's Uncertain Future," *Qantara.de*. Available at: http://en.qantara.de/content/interview-with-mali-expert-marie-rodet-malis-uncertain-future (accessed on August 18, 2013).
119. Ernst Wolff and Alice Lantier, "France Launches War in Northern Mali," *Countercurrents* (January 14, 2013); Nicola Nasser, "Qatar, Sponsor of Islamist Political Movements, Major Ally of America," *Global Research* (January 23, 2013). Available at: http://www.globalresearch.ca/qatar-sponsor-of-islamist-political-movements-major-ally-of-america (accessed on January 24, 2013); Tony Cartalucci, "The Geopolitical Recording of Africa: US Covert Support to Al Qaeda in Northern Mali, France 'Comes to the Rescue,'" *Global Research* (January 15, 2013). Available at: http://www.globalresearch.ca/geopolitical-reordering-and-dirty-tricks-us-covert-support-to-al-qaeda-in-northern-mali-france-comes-to-th (accessed on January 17, 2013).
120. F. William Engdahl, "The War in Mali and AFRICOM's Agenda: Target China," *Global Research* (February 10, 2013). Available at: http://www.globalresearch.ca/the-war-in-mali-and-africoms-african-agenda-target-china/5322517 (accessed on February 11, 2013).
121. Julie Lévesque, "America's Secret War in Africa," Alexander's Oil and Gas Connections (October 13, 2012). Available at: http://www.gasandoil.com/oilaround/geostrategy/792e35e7d5243c33fe1dbc279dd55a21 (accessed on February 19, 2013).
122. John Pilger, "The Real Invasion of Africa and Other Not-Made-for-Hollywood Holy Wars," *Truthout* (February 1, 2013). Available at: http://www.truth-out.org/author/itemlist/user/44655 (accessed on February 19, 2013).
123. Eric Schmitt and Scott Sayare, "New Drone Base in Niger Builds U.S. Presence in Africa," *New York Times* (February 22, 2013).
124. Peter Beinart, "Israel's Fatal Game: Bombing Hamas Won't Stop the Violence—Why Washington and Jerusalem Desperately Need a New Strategy," *Newsweek* (November 26 and December 3, 2012).
125. Evelyn Farkas, *Fractured States and U.S. Foreign Policy: Iraq, Ethiopia and Bosnia in the 1990s* (London: Palgrave-Macmillan, 2003); David McDowall, *A Modern History of the Kurds* (London: I.B. Tauris, 2010); Robert G. Wirsing

and Ehsan Ahrari (eds), *Fixing Fractured States: The Challenge of Ethnic Separatism in the Asia-Pacific* (London: Palgrave-Macmillan, 2010).

126. Steven Metz, "Strategic Horizons: American Defense and Arab Monarchies," *World Politics Review*. Available at: http://www.worldpoliticsreview.com/articles/print/12714 (accessed on February 13, 2013).

127. David Sanger and Eric Schmitt, "U.S.-Saudi Tensions Intensify with Mideast Turmoil," *New York Times*, March 14, 2011.

128. Steven Metz, "Strategic Horizons: American Defense and Arab Monarchies," *World Politics Review*. Available at: http://www.worldpoliticsreview.com/articles/print/12714 (accessed on February 13, 2013).

129. "CIA Operating Drone Base in Saudi Arabia, US Media Reveals," BBC News, Middle East (February 6, 2013). Available at: http://www.bbc.co.uk/news/world-middle-east-21350437?print=true (accessed on February 13, 2013).

130. Metz, "Strategic Horizons: A U.S. Strategic Pivot to Nowhere," Column in *World Politics Review* (October 9, 2013). Available at: http://www.worldpoliticsreview.com/articles/13286/strategic-horizons-a-u-s-strategic-pivot-to-nowhere (accessed on February 24, 2014).

131. *New York Times* (September 23, 1990).

132. General Wesley Clark's Interview with Amy Goodman, *Democracy Now* (March 2, 2007).

133. Immanuel Wallerstein, "Syria: No Win for the West," Commentary No. 353 (May 15, 2013). Available at: http://www.iwallerstein.com/syria-win-west/ (accessed on June 3, 2013).

8

Conclusion

Playing a dominant role in world politics does not make for an easy
life. Even very powerful states encounter problems they cannot solve
and situations they would prefer to avoid. But as Macbeth remarks after
seeing the witches, "Present fears are less than horrible imaginings." What
really scares American foreign policy commentators is not any immediate
frustration or danger but the prospect of longer-term decline.

Robert O. Keohane (Foreign Affairs, July/August 2012)

Are we creating a sustainable government? Are we getting the politics right?
Will there be an Afghan Army and civil service to take over when we leave,
or will we just switch off the lights when we go?

A Western Ambassador in Kabul to Ahmed Rashid (November 2010)

Overview

"Global jihad" is a myth. We cannot study the phenomenon, which only
exists in the imagination of Islamist fanatics, misinformed people, and,
most importantly, in the vocabulary of Islamophobes. Then why use the
expression, as I have done? My global jihad is as unsound and hyperbolic
as the so-called War on Terror. The prefix global only widens the scope of
the holy war, either to glorify or demonize it. In sum, as it is too simplistic
to demonize all mujahedeen as terrorists, it is equally wrong to glorify all
of them as freedom fighters. There is a fine line between them. It is time
that we refrain from implicating countries or religions as impending threats
to freedom and democracy, as it is time for de-accelerating the vehicle of

War on Terror for the sake of global peace and order. And nothing short of shunning America's imperialist hangover or pursuit of emerging as the only superpower in the world (while there has been a steady decline in its hegemony), can usher in the New World Order, promised by the Senior Bush in 1991.

Although violent Islamists and their admirers consider terrorism a strategy in winning their jihad, the moment the so-called jihad turns violent, poses threat to human life, property, and dignity, we can classify it as terrorism. Both global jihad and state-sponsored proxy wars and violent attacks on civilians fall in the same category. We know terrorism, which is a weapon of the weak, sometimes helps terrorists/freedom fighters achieve their goals and sometimes it simply fails to attain anything and fizzles out. The fate of the global jihadists will not be that different from that of the scores of terrorist outfits, who in the past have failed to attain their goals without majority support and logistics to overpower state machinery. Nevertheless, global jihad is a menace for America. The 9/11 alone cost America at least $3 trillion, while others estimate the cumulative loss to $15 trillion, as of 2011. However, as the world has already entered the post-terrorist phase of history and Islamist militancy is losing ground to fundamental rights and freedom-oriented post-Islamism, democracy and ethno-national identities are going to mold Muslim politics across the Muslim world.

Then again, terrorism never wins. The LTTE or the Tamil Tigers of Sri Lanka, once known to be the most efficient terror outfit in the world, finally lost its asymmetrical war to the Sri Lankan government and has fizzled out since 2009. The LTTE survived 26 years, terrorized millions, and killed thousands of people with impunity. The group introduced "suicide vest," which al Qaeda and several other terrorist groups replicated and have been using in Iraq, Afghanistan, Pakistan, and elsewhere. One may, again, compare al Qaeda and its ilk with some of the most successful terrorists or freedom fighters working for the National Liberation Front (FLN), who waged a 10-year long violent struggle against the French colonial rulers to liberate Algeria in 1962. In view of their resilience, al Qaeda, Hezbollah, the LeT, and several other Islamist militant groups in the world, it is too early to write them off. As I have discussed in the text, al Qaeda has morphed into a global terrorist franchise and movement from what it was prior to 9/11.

Islamist rebellions and insurgencies are all about the rebels' interests, identity, and ideology, not in any particular order. Islamism is a new ideology and identity for marginalized Muslims. Unlike people's interests, there is nothing permanent about their ideologies and identities. Islamist insurgencies are not pre-political violence or leaderless jihads at the grassroots. In premodern communities, people do not always act to safeguard their economic interests, but their social standing, social claims, and social assets.[1] Class-consciousness in precapitalist societies is primarily noneconomic.[2] Dalrymple explains how religion was the main factor behind the Great Indian Revolt (1857–1858) in British India: "The religious nature of the Uprising was becoming immediately apparent. British men and women who had converted to Islam were invariably spared, yet all Indian converts to Christianity…were sought out and hunted down."[3]

Secular aspect of religion may play an important role in mobilizing mass support for a rebellion. Islamist resurgence, insurgency, and violence may be attributed to some secular *casus belli*. One may pose the question in the Gramscian style: "But why call this unity of faith 'religion' and not 'ideology' or even frankly 'politics?'"[4] Partha Chatterjee's observations are quite pertinent that religion for victims and underdogs is more than mere faith; it provides them with a code of ethics, including political ethics. He also believes that premodern people are not integrated into the organized state, which is something distant in their consciousness with which they have certain norms of reciprocity, nothing more than that.[5] Religion as the code of ethics means different things to different categories of people. Sometimes it is for restoring their faith in movements with religion-as-aim, while it becomes the frame of revolt in movements with religion-as-reason. The religion-as-aim type movement drags the followers into a holy war, jihad or Crusade, against the enemy of the faith. The enemy of a particular class or category of people is easily converted into the enemy of the faithful when the people concerned suffer religious persecution at the hands of the exploiting classes adhering to a different faith.[6]

It is noteworthy that masses are not only prone to fight for rights under religious flags, but also for secular programs/problems under secular leadership. One may cite the examples of Catholic French peasants' support for the dechristianization movement in the 1790s. Another example may be cited from colonial Bengal in the 1940s. Devout Muslims

302 GLOBAL JIHAD AND AMERICA

participated in communist-led movements against their class enemies.[7] As I indicated at the very outset, all Islamists do not act in accordance with the teachings of Islam and all of them do not want to restore an Islamic global system under Shariah law. The Islamists who I earmark as anarchic–nihilists do not want to restore anything but want to destroy everything un-Islamic. They are not that different from psychopaths or serial killers, they love to kill for the sake of killing.

Although some scholars exclude violence from the scope of politics, as it is more warlike, we believe transnational Islamist insurgents are politically motivated, their banditry being social banditry in the Hobsbawmian sense of the expression.[8] Again, sometimes liberation theologians organize rebellions in the name of social justice and religion.[9] Outsiders, itinerant mullahs, teachers, religious and secular college students work together with tribal and faction chiefs to mobilize mass support for insurgency. Tribesmen rather than factious peasants and urban poor have been the most committed rebels and social bandits throughout the Muslim world. Relative homogeneity of tribes and vertical relationship between tribal chiefs and ordinary tribesmen seem to be the main factors in this regard. Understanding the tribal factor is very pertinent to our understanding of Islamist militancy in Afghanistan, northwestern Pakistan, Iraq, Libya, and elsewhere in the Muslim world. We have several examples of small but highly effective people's militias in the Muslim world. Hezbollah, the Taliban, LeT, and the Mahdi Militia of Iraq are among such groups who are formidable adversaries to America and its allies. America has reasons to worry about difficult non-state actors, such as the Taliban and Hezbollah, as it has not yet been able to defeat them decisively.

The symbolic use of religion by rebels does not make the rebellions religious. We must understand that: (a) all movements/rebellions are primarily based on local issues; (b) local rebels, insurgents, and terrorists forge ties with groups and individuals having similar views beyond their own localities; and (c) grassroots-based subalterns (underdogs) rebel whenever they see others doing so. Thanks to the Globalization process, mobilization for terrorism or insurgencies has become easier as distant lands and people have come closer to each other. Consequently, some Muslims in southern Philippines espouse bin Laden's anarchic–nihilism and some Somali Americans champion the cause of Somalia-based Harakat ash-Shabāb al-Mujāhīdīn (mujahideen youth movement) in America.

People at the grassroots cannot mobilize themselves to bring about a desired situation by their own efforts without outside (elite) leadership or ideology.[10] Hence, the significance of the external mobilizing factors—individuals or ideologies—a Mao or Khomeini, a Bin Laden or Mullah Omar, Marxism–Leninism, Millennial Shiism or al Qaeda. There is nothing spontaneous, pre-political, or leaderless about jihad.[11]

Then again, Islamist terrorists are not the only adversaries of modern civilization. There are others who promote anti-Western Islamo-supremacist (fascistic/chauvinistic) and anarchist ideas to the detriment of peace and order within and beyond the Muslim world. Last but not least, narco-jihad has emerged as one of the major threats to durable peace in and around Afghanistan. I have discussed Western duplicities and connivance in the promotion of illicit drugs in Afghanistan. I have singled out America and its allies for the destabilization of the vast Arab world, Syria, Iran, Afghanistan, and Pakistan, and also for the growth of intra and interstate conflicts on sectarian, tribal, and ethno-national lines in parts of Africa, South Asia, and beyond.

America and its allies—at least since the end of World War II—have been ignorant, opportunistic, myopic, and Machiavellian with regard to diplomacy and war. British conservative politician and author Rory Stewart (who served in post-occupation Iraq and Afghanistan) thinks that: "The West always lacked the knowledge, power, or legitimacy to transform Afghanistan fundamentally."[12] Seth G. Jones of the Rand Corporation believes that: "The West [in Afghanistan] was trying to do something it couldn't do, and it was trying to do something it didn't need to do." He is emphatic in asserting that the West has been trying to do the impossible in Afghanistan, and that there has never been any right way of fixing the problem in Afghanistan, such as "tackling the warlords" or "fixing Pakistan." We cannot agree with him more when he says that "Afghanistan did not pose an existential threat to international security."[13] However, the situation is very different in both post-occupation Afghanistan and Iraq. Ironically, for America and its allies, they have been in the best of terms with Western sanction-stricken pariah nation of Iran, which is likely to emerge as the possessor of the Shiite Bomb by 2016.

Significantly, what American policymakers do not admit publicly is that: (a) due to the American invasions and the unbridled corruption by U.S. contractors, most Iraqis and Afghans are much worse off than they were under Saddam Hussein and the Taliban, respectively; (b) the U.S. and NATO troops are responsible for turning Afghanistan into the drug capital of the world; (c) thanks to the American invasions/interventions, Islamist extremists from Pakistan, Afghanistan, and Iran are now linked to their Iraqi, Syrian, and Egyptian counterparts to the detriment of U.S. and Israeli interests. Thanks to America's failure to engage the people in Iraq and Afghanistan, criminals and terrorists thrive in these places. Ironically, the Taliban are no longer a threat (as they were in 2001) but are going to be in the government after 2014. The post-9/11 world has taught us at least two things: (a) we have to learn how to live with jihadism and the asymmetric wars of attrition between state- and non-state actors and (b) we cannot rule out the possibilities of further mega attacks à la 9/11 in America and elsewhere in the West. Meanwhile, America's intrusive policies, support for autocrats, ambivalence, lack of understanding of people's war, and above all, American government's unceremonious surrender to the Military–Industrial Complex and the Israel Lobby have dragged the whole world into another Hundred-Year War.

America's unwillingness to learn anything from its past military misadventures is amazing. As reflected in his book, *No More Vietnams*, Nixon realized quite late that America should not allow its foreign policy to be paralyzed by fear of another Vietnam. I have already cited Senator Fullbright who wrote in the 1960s that there was something like voodoo about the U.S. foreign policy. Its military doctrine is not that different either. Interestingly, top U.S. generals since World War II relied on military hardware as answers to their enemies' military capabilities. They had no respect for their enemies' guerrilla tactics and reliance on people's support. They do not believe in David Galula's theory that counterinsurgency is 80 percent political and 20 percent military, and it is all about winning the hearts and minds of the insurgents. We rather come across U.S. generals Westmoreland's "firepower" and Petraeus's "money is ammunition" doctrines to defeat insurgents and guerrillas. Westmoreland's "firepower" doctrine failed abysmally in Vietnam, Americans lost 58,000 troops and killed around 600,000 Vietnamese troops and 3.2 million civilians and lost the war in 1975. Petraeus's doctrine was very expensive. America neutralized Iraqi insurgents by bribing them right and left. Meanwhile, more than a million Iraqis and several hundred thousand Afghans have died because of American invasions, directly and indirectly. In two months alone (April–June 2013), more than 2,000 Iraqi civilians fell victim to terrorism. Only Eisenhower and Reagan seem to be pragmatic U.S. presidents since the Korean War. They were against committing large number of U.S. troops in overseas for an extended period.

Paradoxically, as senior American security analyst Richard Betts observes: "When the United States became more secure… it has spent far more than any other country… it has sent forces into combat more frequently than it did in the era of much bigger threats to national security." He rightly believes that America is the "most militarily active state in the world" and that keeping America on path to a permanent war would be catastrophic to all concerned.[14] He advises America not to do "faulty threat assessments, forgetfulness about history, and shortsighted policymaking." He believes that Obama's Iran policy "to prevent," not "contain" her from acquiring nuclear weapons will not work, and that: "There is simply no real evidence that war with Iran would yield any more safety than handling the problem with good old deterrence." With regard to China, he thinks America should determine "whether to treat Beijing as a threat to be contained or a power to be accommodated."[15]

America should discard the ideas of considering itself as an empire of liberty, which goes back to the days of Thomas Jefferson, and the post-1945 hangover that it is "the leader of the free world." It should rather pay heed to what Eisenhower realized at the far end of his presidency in January 1961 about the destructive role of America's Military–Industrial Complex, which he singled out as the main contributor to all wars America had fought in the 20th century. We need a transparent, soft, and smart America in relation to the rest of the world. American duplicities are least desirable. As China and Russia, among others, are emerging as America's adversaries in the coming years, the Muslim–West conflict should not become part of the growing conflict of interests between America and its yesteryears' adversaries, Russia and China. America should avoid promoting Islamist parties, such as the MB in Egypt, and stop creating new enemies in the Muslim world. The way Egyptians received Hillary Clinton in Cairo in July 2012 was anything but flattering for America. Tomato and shoe-throwing Egyptians told the Secretary of State: (a) "Egypt is not another Pakistan" and (b) "the Muslim Brotherhood is not a democratic force."

While Iraq has remained turbulent and number one in the list of most terror-infested countries in the world, Afghanistan is going to be the next major battlefield of the proxy war between India and Pakistan (and their promoters), and we do not know which way nuclear-armed fractured Pakistan will go in the coming years. What will happen to its sophisticated nuclear warheads has remained the tricky question. One is not sure whether its Islamized military will eventually take over the country, which might lead to nuclear proliferation and even reckless (suicidal) use of nuclear weapons against India. In the backdrop of Pakistan army's reckless and unpredictable behavior since the 1950s—military takeovers, the separation of East Pakistan (creation of Bangladesh) in 1971, irreversible Islamization of Pakistan, the Kargil misadventure, promotion of Islamist terror within and outside the country, especially in India and Afghanistan, political instability in Pakistan—one has every reason to anticipate further unpleasant surprises from the Pakistan army, including dragging the entire region into a nuclear war. Things are fast turning unpredictable and volatile in neighboring Bangladesh. The country is sharply polarized between Islam-loving and pro-India people. A long-lasting civil war in the country is not totally off the card. Meanwhile, India being the fourth most terror-infested country in the world (since late 2012) is likely to go through more encounters with homegrown and Pakistan-sponsored Islamist terrorists. Thanks to its hegemonic behavior and occupation of Muslim-majority Kashmir, the country is destined to face more frequent attacks from Islamist militants in the future.

Revolutionary changes in the Muslim world or the "falling of dominos" might pose greater threat to Western and Israeli hegemony than sporadic terrorist attacks or insurgencies in a handful of countries or subregions in the long run. Conservative analyst Pat Buchanan has registered his concern at the rapid evaporation of American influence in the Middle East. He argues, "As the British elbowed aside the Ottoman Turks and the Americans shouldered aside the British after Suez (1956), now it is America that appears to be the receding power in the Middle East and Turkey the rising power."[16] One may find Buchanan's views quite alarmist and Kishore Mahbubani's thesis about the impending decline of America and the rise of the Asia–Pacific not so convincing. Nevertheless, in view of Iran and Turkey's growing influence in the region (thanks to European obduracy if not Islamophobia, Turkey does not consider EU membership that tempting any longer), all is not well in American diplomacy in the Muslim world. Turkey is a country to be watched. As the anti-Erdogan demonstrations in June 2013 made it obvious, many Turks are very unhappy with his government's support for pro-American/pro-Saudi Syrian rebels. It is a question of time when Turkey will come out of the U.S.–Saudi orbit and join the fast emerging bandwagon of Muslim solidarity. Very similar to Egypt, it will also distance itself from Israel. If the Syrian regime loses control of the Kurdish minority—very similar to what happened after the overthrow of Saddam Hussein in Iraq—Syrian Kurds might also join the Kurdish nationalists across the region, transcending Syria, Turkey, Iraq, and Iran.

Since terrorism or global jihad still poses a big threat to American/ Western interests, unless there is an attempt in the West to understand the Muslim anger and frustration with the West, there is no way of resolving the conflict. Overzealous Muslims believe in the existence of a united and powerful *Ummah*. Their wishful thinking makes them believe that they can subdue Washington, London, Jerusalem, and New Delhi, and "reconquer" their lost empires from Spain to Sicily and Palestine to the Philippines. Shiite Muslims also believe in their version of the Kingdom of God, which the 12th Imam (believed to have disappeared in 941) will establish after his return to dominate the world. Thus, there is no room for any complacency about Islamo-supremacist anarchist/nihilist extremism. Not only America and the West but also other countries are still vulnerable to non-state terrorist attacks. There are several fault lines in the Muslim world: between Sunni majority and Shiite minority; Kurdish minorities in Turkey, Iraq, Syria, and Iran, who in collaboration with European imperialists after World War I divided and grabbed Kurdistan among themselves; Pashtuns and non-Pashtuns in Afghanistan; Shia–Sunni, Baluchi, non-Baluchi, Punjabi-non-Punjabi, and Islamist and liberal Muslims in Pakistan; Wahhabi, non-Wahhabi in the Arab world. The perennial tribal, sectarian, ethno-linguistic, and class differences are also there. The Arab–Israeli and Kashmiri–Indian fault lines provide enough fissile materials to keep the Middle East and South Asia burning for decades.

This study demonstrates that the bulk of terrorists are terrorists by default. They are under foreign occupation or despotic rule, and they resort to violence to improve their lot. Some Islamist extremists adopt terrorism by choice. Some Islamist terrorists represent socio-politically and economically deprived, angry, and isolated individuals, who use Islamist

308 GLOBAL JIHAD AND AMERICA

extremism as an anarchist or nihilist ideology, not aiming at establishing any alternative order. The leaders and followers of these anarchist/nihilist cults—with rare exceptions—are not Islamic scholars or clerics but technocrats, mostly engineers and medical doctors (techno-clerics). Osama bin Laden, Ayman al-Zawahiri, Anwar Awlaki, Khalid Sheikh Muhammad, Ramzi Yousef, and other terrorist masterminds were educated as engineers or technocrats, not as Islamic scholars. While the Quran promotes universal love, condemns violence, forbids suicide, and even allows non-Muslims to wage their jihad to protect their lives, property, honor, and places of worship, Islamist anarchists promote the doctrine of hate, total war against everybody, and an Islamo-supremacist ideology.

As I have argued in this work, the cry wolf syndrome in the West and parts of the Muslim world strengthens warmongers, terrorists, and fanatics. I believe as Islamophobia in the West is counterproductive, so is the so-called Westophobia among Muslims. Surprisingly, even second/third generation members of the Muslim diasporas in the West promote hate against Western culture and espouse the cause of the ill-defined global jihad or anarchy. The growing hatred for America and the West among Muslims does not bode well for peace. As Islamist fanatics are responsible for the surge in anti-America/anti-West feelings among Muslims, so are American/Western invasions and interventions in the Muslim world responsible for this. Muslims' siege mentality and feelings of humiliation and subjection because of America, West, and Israel have been widening the gulf between the Muslim and Western worlds. I have argued that it is not global jihad but the problematic globalization process has been the main destabilizing factor, responsible for alienating people from the so-called New World Order by widening the gulf between the rich and powerful North and the poor and disempowered South. Muslims represent the South. I have also argued that Muslim alienation from the West can benefit Russia, China, and other rising powers who will eventually challenge American/Western hegemony in the coming decades. The Syrian and Iranian crises and the average Pakistani and Egyptian (and Muslim) alienation from America and Israel are going to play important roles in boosting the hands of the Russo-Chinese duumvirate and its allies.

I have argued that Muslims throughout the world suffer from tremendous identity crisis, vainglory, and victimhood. They believe that due to Western, Jewish, and Hindu "conspiracies," Muslims have been marginalized and are at the receiving end of civilization. I have traced this to the Muslim world's colonial past. As descendants of clients of British, French, or Dutch colonial patrons/masters, Muslims in general grow with hatred for everything Western. And one really cannot blame them for this mind-set either. Due to their lack of exposure to modern ideas, science, and technology—both by design and default—Muslims in general are not fit for rational thinking. They are the typical "no-where-men," suffering from tremendous identity crisis and sense of direction. Thus, there is no reason to believe that the so-called democratized Islamist outfits such as the MB and JI (which are proto-fascist parties of disenchanted lower middle-class Muslims) are going to usher in liberal democracy in the Muslim world. In short, the Muslim world and bulk of Muslims everywhere are not that different from what Europeans were in the medieval and early modern periods. They were more Protestants or Catholics than Christians, Europeans or even human beings. Thus, lynching of Jews and Protestants, witches, and black Africans or indigenous Americans and Australians was as common as anything. This study has shown that not only Muslims' lack of exposure to modern ideas, democracy, and secularism has retarded their advancement, but also European colonial policies were responsible for their retardation.

America's divisive policies and promotion of Muslim autocracies are also responsible for the lack of democracy and civility in many parts of the Muslim world, including Saudi Arabia, Syria, Iraq, Iran, and Pakistan. America's post-World War II policy toward the Muslim world has not been about strengthening democracy, secularism, and good governance. It was all about serving America's short-term geopolitical interests. Its state department hardly has any long-term vision and program, at least not in the Third World. Thanks to its reliance on inept experts, neither the state department nor the CIA had any clues about the Islamist takeover of Iran months before the 1979 Revolution. Thus, not surprisingly, after Khomeini's triumphant return to Tehran in February 1979, CIA came up with a hackneyed appraisal of the ayatollah (to paraphrase): "This mullah has no political ambition." Ironically, America has been promoting Saudi Wahhabis, MB, and other Islamist parties considering them lesser evils than communism and other radical anti-Western ideologies. America's promotion of autocratic regimes in Saudi Arabia and elsewhere in the Muslim world smacks of its same old apathy and ignorance about countries beyond North America and West Europe. America's turning a blind eye to the Saudi-backed persecution and killing of freedom-loving majority Shiites in Bahrain by the minority Sunni monarchy only reflects its short-term security and energy policies. Bahrain is home to America's Fifth Fleet in the Middle East and is a source of cheap oil. Consequently, there is nothing surprising about marginalized Muslims' support for radical Islamists or whoever promises good governance and challenges Western hegemony.

Last but not least, there is no inevitability in Islamist takeover of the Muslim world. America can (and should) play a proactive role by rehashing its Muslim policy. Preemptive invasions and unauthorized drone attacks in Muslim-majority countries and selective support for regime change in the Middle East are not going to help America win over the Muslim mind. It is time that America and its allies understand that neither Syria nor Iran is Libya, they will not implode; if pushed to the extreme they would explode beyond their borders. Since Russia and China have stakes in Syria and Iran, America should not risk a war with Russia. A full-blown conflict between Iran and Arab League countries would also be disastrous. America took about 50 years to understand that Israel was the main problem between Arabs and Jews, one hopes American does not take another 50 years to understand the real solution to the problem. American support for regime change in Egypt, Libya, Syria, and Iran, and its opposition to spontaneous regime change movements in countries such as Bahrain and other pro-Western countries in the Muslim world are problematic. One is not sure if America will be able to preserve the reactionary Arab monarchies, especially the Islamist regime of Saudi Arabia, for an indefinite period only with its military bases across the region. America must remember, what is good for the goose is good for the gander.

America's tacit and not-so-tacit support for Anglo-French-German interventions in Mali and neighboring countries in northwest Africa since early 2012 does not bode well for peace between the Muslim and Western worlds. The way America is intensifying its drone attacks in Africa, Middle East, and South Asia, one is not sure if the so-called sequestration, the automatic spending reductions of defense expenditure by 8 percent to the tune of $500 billion in the next 10 years (effective from March 1, 2013), is going to wreck the U.S. military at all. As one analyst appraises:

[A] military's effectiveness is measured against its potential opponents, and the United States has enjoyed a large gap for decades. However, if a military is not growing in capabilities and other militaries or groups are, then its relative power is decreasing. This means that after sequestration is implemented or the continuing resolution is maintained, the U.S. military will remain dominant for years to come, but not as dominant as it has been relative to other forces.[17]

Islamist militants have no reason to respond positively to the U.S. defense cut, as despite this sequestration, America will remain the most powerful nation on earth. As we do not foresee total withdrawal of American troops from the Arab world in the near future, democracy- and freedom-loving Arabs are least likely to achieve their goal in the near future, let alone getting any help from America in their struggle for democracy and human rights in countries such as Saudi Arabia, Bahrain, or Egypt. They know that not only Muslim autocrats but also most elected governments in the Muslim world, from Algeria to Afghanistan and Pakistan, are friends with Washington. Thus, we do not foresee anything but sustained conflicts, not long-term understanding, between the Muslim and Western worlds in the coming decades.

Notes and References

1. Karl Polanyi, "Primitive, Archaic and Modern Economics," in George Dalton (ed.), *Essays of Karl Polanyi* (Boston, 1971), p. 7.
2. Eric Hobsbawm, "Class Consciousness in History," in Istvan Meszaros (ed.), *Aspects of History and Class Consciousness* (London, 1971), pp. 8–9.
3. William Dalrymple, *The Last Mughal—The Fall of a Dynasty: Delhi, 1857* (New York: Alfred A. Knopf, 2007), pp. 143, 251–252.
4. Antonio Gramsci, *Selections from the Prison Notebooks of Antonio Gramsci* (edited and translated by Quintin Hore and Geoffrey Smith) (London: 1971), p. 326.
5. Partha Chatterjee, "Bengal Politics and Muslim Masses 1920–1947," *Journal of Commonwealth and Comparative Politics*, Vol. 20 (March 1982): 32–33.
6. Janos M. Bak et al., *Religion and Rural Revolt* (Manchester: Macmillan Press, 1984), pp. 2–5.
7. Taj Hashmi, *Pakistan as a Peasant Utopia* (Boulder: Westview Press, 1992), Chapter 7.

8. Eric Hobsbawm, *Bandits* (London: The New Press, 2000) (revised edition), *passim*.

9. Ranajit Guha, *Elementary Aspects of Peasant Insurgency in Colonial India* (New Delhi: Oxford University Press, 1983), pp. 34–35; A. Gramsci, *Selections from the Prison Notebooks of Antonio Gramsci*, p. 326.

10. Charles Tilly, *From Mobilization to Revolution* (Random House, 1978), pp. 7–10.

11. Marc Sageman, Introduction to *Leaderless Jihad: Terror Networks in the Twenty-first Century* (University of Pennsylvania Press, 2008).

12. Rory Stewart, "Mistakes Were Made," *Foreign Policy* (March/April 2013).

13. Rory Stewart, "Trying to Do the Impossible," *Foreign Policy* (March/April 2013).

14. Richard K. Betts, "From Cold War to Hot Peace: The Habit of American Force," *Political Science Quarterly*, Vol. 127, No. 3 (2012).

15. Richard K. Betts, "The Lost Logic of Deterrence: What the Strategy That Won the Cold War Can—and Can't—Do Now," *Foreign Affairs* (March/April 2013).

16. Patrick J. Buchanan, "A Middle East without America?" *The American Conservative* (February 17, 2011). Available at: http://www.amconmag.com/blog/2011/02/17/a-middle-east-without-america (accessed on February 21, 2011).

17. "U.S.: What the Sequester Will Do to the Military," *Stratfor Global Intelligence Report* (March 1, 2013). Available at: http://www.stratfor.com/sample/analysis/us-what-sequester-will-do-military (accessed on March 2, 2013).

Index

About the Author

Taj Hashmi was born in 1948 in Assam, India. He has an M.A. and a B.A. (Hons) in Islamic History and Culture from Dhaka University and a PhD in Modern South Asian History from the University of Western Australia.

Hashmi is currently Professor of Security Studies at the Austin Peay State University at Clarksville, Tennessee. Prior to this, he taught Islamic and Modern South Asian History and Cultural Anthropology at various universities in Bangladesh, Australia, Singapore, and Canada, including the Curtin University (1987–1988), Dhaka University (1972–1981), National University of Singapore (1989–1998), and the University of British Columbia (2003–2004). Hashmi has also worked for four years as a professor of Security Studies at the US Department of Defense, College of Security Studies at the Asia-Pacific Center for Security Studies in Honolulu, Hawaii.

Hashmi is fluent in several South Asian and Islamic languages. He is a regular commentator on current affairs and global conflicts in the print and electronic media. He is a fellow of the Royal Asiatic Society of Great Britain and Ireland (since 1997). He was a visiting fellow at the Centre of International Studies, Oxford University, and a fellow at the National Centre for South Asian Studies, Monash University, Australia. Hashmi is on the editorial board of two international journals, the *Contemporary South Asia* and the *Journal of South Asian Studies*. He is a regular reviewer of manuscripts for several publishers, including SAGE and Routledge.

Hashmi has authored scores of academic and popular essays and articles on various aspects of history, society, religion, politics, culture, and security issues in South Asia, Middle East, the Asia-Pacific, and North America. His major publications are:

- *Women and Islam in Bangladesh: Beyond Subjection and Tyranny* (2000).
- *Pakistan as a Peasant Utopia: The Communalization of Class Politics in East Bengal, 1920–1947* (1992).

- *Colonial Bengal* (in Bengali) (1985).
- *Islam, Muslims and the Modern State* (coedited) (1994 and 1996).

His *Women and Islam in Bangladesh* was a bestseller in Asian Studies and was awarded the Justice Ibrahim Gold Medal (Bangladesh) in 2001.